Current Trends in Nigerian Pidgin English

Contributions to the Sociology of Language

Edited by
Ofelia García
Francis M. Hult

Founding editor
Joshua A. Fishman

Volume 117

Current Trends in Nigerian Pidgin English

A Sociolinguistic Perspective

Edited by
Akinmade T. Akande and Oladipo Salami

DE GRUYTER
MOUTON

ISBN 978-1-5015-2150-8
e-ISBN (PDF) 978-1-5015-1354-1
e-ISBN (EPUB) 978-1-5015-1358-9
ISSN 1861-0676

Library of Congress Control Number: 2021939863

Bibliographic information published by the Deutsche Nationalbibliothek
The Deutsche Nationalbibliothek lists this publication in the Deutsche Nationalbibliografie;
detailed bibliographic data are available on the Internet at http://dnb.dnb.de.

© 2023 Walter de Gruyter Inc., Boston/Berlin
This volume is text- and page-identical with the hardback published in 2021.
Cover image: sculpies/shutterstock
Typesetting: Integra Software Services Pvt. Ltd.
Printing and binding: CPI books GmbH, Leck

www.degruyter.com

Foreword

Nigerian Pidgin (NP) has in recent times received considerable attention from linguistic scholars and other interested stakeholders. I was particularly glad to learn that corporate members of Unicode (including Adobe, Apple, Facebook, Google, IBM, Microsoft, Netflix and SAP SE) launched a dedicated NP keyboard on October 28, 2020 (Roy Okonkwo: personal communication). The keyboard uses NP standardised orthography. This development is a milestone in the promotion of NP given that the choice of standard orthography has been one of the major contending issues for the language. Other challenging issues include the status of NP (i.e. whether it is a pidgin, a creole, or still in the process of creolising); its structure (i.e. whether it enjoys an independent structure from English); and the lack of official recognition for it by language policy makers in Nigeria.

The publication of *Current Trends in Nigerian Pidgin English: A Sociolinguistic Perspective* is, therefore, timely because it provides authoritative answers to many of the seemingly intractable issues listed above. The highly reputable editors, Akinmade Timothy Akande and Oladipo Salami, are leading researchers of NP in particular, and varieties of English, in general. The volume provides readers with current updates on NP research and convincing insights on its functional domains, morphology and syntax. It consists of twelve well researched papers that offer new perspectives and fresh data on the various theoretical and applied issues addressed.

The contributors to this volume consist of some of the best known names in Pidgin and Creole linguistics. Expectedly, they have put in a splendid effort to ensure that their research is current, painstaking and scientific. *Current Trends in Nigerian Pidgin English: A Sociolinguistic Perspective* is an invaluable companion for students and researchers of Pidgin and Creole linguistics.

Herbert Igboanusi
University of Ibadan

Contents

Foreword —— V

List of abbreviations —— IX

Notes on contributors —— XI

Akinmade T. Akande
Introduction —— 1

Nicholas Faraclas
Chapter 1
Naija: A language of the future —— 9

Christian Mair
Chapter 2
Nigerian Pidgin: Changes in prestige and function in non-Anglophone diasporic contexts —— 39

Francis O. Egbokhare
Chapter 3
The accidental lingua franca: The paradox of the ascendancy of Nigerian Pidgin in Nigeria —— 67

Idom Inyabri and Eyo Mensah
Chapter 4
Nigerian Pidgin, identity and national re-invention in Naija stand-up comedy —— 115

Mirka Honkanen
Chapter 5
Nigerian Pidgin in authenticating immigrant identities —— 147

Eyo Mensah, Eunice Ukaegbu and Benjamin Nyong
Chapter 6
Towards a working orthography of Nigerian Pidgin —— 177

Akinmade T. Akande and Saheed O. Okesola
Chapter 7
Morpho-syntactic features of Nigerian Pidgin on Radio programmes rendered in Naija —— 201

Macaulay Mowarin
Chapter 8
Emphasis, focalization and topicalization in Nigerian Pidgin —— 221

Adesoji Babalola
Chapter 9
Metalanguage of football commentary in Nigerian Pidgin —— 249

Oluwabunmi O. Oyebode
Chapter 10
A social semiotic investigation of Nigerian Pidgin in select Nigerian church posters —— 275

Joseph Babasola Osoba
Chapter 11
Nigerian Pidgin as national language: Prospects and challenges —— 299

Oladipo Salami and Akinmade T. Akande
Chapter 12
Non-state actors, language practices, language policy and Nigerian Pidgin promotion —— 321

Index —— 341

List of abbreviations

UNDP	United Nations Development Program
HDI	Human Development Index
NBS	National Bureau of Statistics
WPR	World Population Review
AAELC	Varieties of Afro-Atlantic English lexifier Creole
ELF	English as a Lingua Franca
CMC	Computer-mediated Communication
NP	Nigerian Pidgin
MC	Master of Ceremony
NTA	Nigerian Television Authority
ABC	Anambra Broadcasting Corporation
NCAT	Net Corpora Administration Tool
WAPE	West African Pidgin English
PE	Pidgin English
TMA	Tense, Mood and Aspect
AAL	African American Language
NPL	Nigerian Pidgin Language
ANP	Anglo Nigerian Pidgin
CE	Contact English
REWA	Restricted English in West Africa
GP	Ghanaian Pidgin
CP	Cameroonian Pidgin
SFL	Systemic Functional Linguistics
UNILAG	University of Lagos
UNIBEN	University of Benin
BBC	British Broadcasting Corporation
NPF-PCRRU	Nigeria Police Force's Public Complaint Rapid Response Unit
ELIT	Ethnolinguistic Identity theory
LPP	Language Planning and Policy
NPE	National Policy on Education
SNSs	Social Network Sites

Notes on contributors

Akinmade Timothy Akande is a Professor of English Language in the Department of English, Obafemi Awolowo University, Nigeria. He obtained his PhD in English Language from the School of English, University of Leeds in the United Kingdom in 2008 where he was awarded Overseas Research Student Award: UniversitiesUK, United Kingdom, Tetley and Lupton Scholarship Award: University of Leeds and Bonamy Dobree Scholarship Award: University of Leeds, Leeds. He is also the recipient of Language Learning Grants: Modern Language Centre, Ontario, Canada, 2006; The Alexander von Humboldt Fellowship Award, 2011 and African Humanities Program Fellowship Award, 2013. He has over fifty publications in books and reputable journals across the globe.
Email Address: akinmakande@yahoo.com OR atakande@oauife.edu.ng

Adesoji Babalola currently teaches in the Department of English, Obafemi Awolowo University. He is an upcoming and promising sociolinguist and has five publications in reputable journals across the country. His areas of interest include applied English Linguistics, sociolinguistics and creoles and pidgins.
Email Address: sojibabs4cool@yahoo.com

Francis Egbokhare is a renowned Professor of Linguistics at the University of Ibadan, in Nigeria. He has published in the areas of grammar, phonology, language documentation, language and development and Nigerian Pidgin. Among his works are *Beyond Chance, Sentiments and Prejudice: Engaging The Challenges Of Nigerian Pidgin Development*, plenary paper at the World Congress on Pidgins and Creoles, Accra, Ghana in 2010; *The Story of a Language: Nigerian Pidgin in Spatiotemporal Social and Linguistic Context*, Lucko, P. Peter, L. Wolf, H. (eds.), *Studies in African Varieties of English*; *The Nigerian Linguistic Ecology and Changing Profiles of Nigerian Pidgin,* H. Igboanusi (ed.), *Language Attitude and Language Conflicts in West Africa*. Francis is currently involved in NAIJASYNCOR, a collaborative project on Nigerian Pidgin funded by French Research Financing Agency, ANR.
Email Address: foegbokhare@yahoo.com

Nicholas Faraclas is a full tenured Professor in Linguistics at the University of Puerto Rico, Rio Piedras. He received his PhD in Linguistics from the University of California at Berkeley in 1989, where he was awarded a National Science Foundation Fellowship and two Fulbright Fellowships. He has published more than 25 books and 80 scientific articles and chapters, and presented at more than 100 professional conferences in more than 40 countries in Africa, Asia, the Pacific, South America, the Caribbean, Europe, and North America. Having supervised more than 40 PhD and MA theses, he has also developed and taught more than 50 different courses in a considerable number of distinct areas of theoretical, descriptive, socio-, and applied linguistics at universities in North and South America, Africa, the Pacific, Europe, and the Caribbean. Over the past three decades, he has been conducting research on colonial era creole languages, as well as promoting community based popular education and literacy activities for both adults and children in the Caribbean, Latin America, Africa, and the Pacific.
Email Address: nickfaraclas@yahoo.com

Mirka Honkanen completed her undergraduate degree at the University of Turku, Finland, and graduate studies in Freiburg, Germany. In her PhD, she investigated Nigerian immigrants' multilingual communication on a Nigerian web forum. Currently, she is working on a postdoctoral project at the University of Freiburg on the topic of morphological productivity in World Englishes.
Email Address: mirka.honkanen@anglistik.uni-freiburg.de

Idom T. Inyabri is a Senior Lecturer at the Department of English and Literary Studies, University of Calabar, Nigeria. He obtained B.A from the University of Calabar. His M.A. and Ph. D. were gotten from the University of Ibadan and Calabar respectively. Dr Inyabri is a Fellow of the African Humanities Program (AHP) / American Council for Learned Societies (ACLS). He teaches African Poetry (Oral and Written) and Theory and Criticism. His research interest is in Ecocriticism and Popular Culture. His current publication, entitled "The Discourse of Tattoo Consumption among Female Youth in Nigeria" (co-authored with Eyo and Eyamba Mensah) is Published by *Communicatio* . . . 44:3.

Christian Mair has held a Distinguished Professorship ("Chair") in English Linguistics at the University of Freiburg in Germany since 1990. As the compiler of three widely used digital reference corpora of Modern English (F-LOB, Frown, ICE-Jamaica), he is familiar with all stages of the corpus-linguistic work-flow. His research over the past three decades has focussed on the corpus-based description of modern English grammar and on variability and change in Standard Englishes world-wide. It has resulted in the publication of several monographs (among them *Infinitival clauses in English: a study of syntax in discourse*, 1990, and *Twentieth-century English: history, variation, and standardization*, 2006) and more than 100 contributions to scholarly journals and edited works. Mair's current research focusses on the role of global English in a multilingual world, on multilingual and nonstandard language practices in computer-mediated communication, and on the sociolinguistics of diaspora and migration. Throughout his career, he has cultivated an additional interest in English-German contrastive linguistics, which has resulted in a number of student textbooks aimed at the German-speaking undergraduate market. From 2011 to 2014 he served as President of ISLE, the International Society for the Linguistics of English.
Email Address: christian.mair@anglistik.uni-freiburg.de

Eyo O. Mensah is an Associate Professor of Structural and Anthropological Linguistics at the University of Calabar, Nigeria. He is a CAS Leventis Postdoctoral Research Associate (SOAS, University of London, UK), AHP/ACLS Postdoctoral Fellow and Firebird Anthropological Research Fellow. He is the pioneer President of the Nigerian Name Society (NNS). Some of his latest publications have appeared in *Anthropological Linguistics* (2017), *Communicatio: South African Journal for Communication Theory and Research* (2018), *Journal of Cognitive Science* (2019), *Journal of Asian and African Studies* (2019), and *Journal of Black Studies* (2019) He is a member of the Linguistic Association of Nigeria (LAN), and West African Linguistic Society (WALS). He sits in the Editorial Boards of *Sociolinguistic Studies* and *English Language Teaching*. He is also a member of the Governing Council of the University of Calabar, Nigeria.
Email Address: eyomensah2004@yahoo.com

Macaulay Mowarin is a Professor of English language in the Department of English and Literary Studies, Delta State University, Abraka. Nigeria. His areas of research interest include syntax, contact linguistics, pidgins and creoles and language endangerment. He is currently, the editor of Abraka Humanities Review. (A journal in the faculty of Arts, Delta state University, Abraka.) He has articles and chapter contributions in peer,-reviewed journals and books.
Email Address: mamowarin@yahoo.co.uk

Benjamin Nyong is a Graduate Research Assistant in the Department of Languages and Linguistics, Arthur Jarvis University, Akpabuyo, Cross River State, Nigeria. He is interested in Phonology, Sociolinguistics and Efik Language teaching. He is a member of the Linguistic Association of Nigeria.

Saheed Omotayo Okesola teaches in the Department of English, Obafemi Awolowo University, Ile-Ife. He was a recipient Fulbright Foreign Language Teaching Grant at the University of California, Los Angeles, USA and a fellow of African Humanities Program of the American Council of Learned Society (ACLS). Okesola has published in reputable journal in his areas of research interest – Sociolinguistics, multilingual studies, applied linguistics and cyber linguistics.
Email Address: soraheem@oauife.edu.ng

Joseph Babasola Osoba is an Associate Professor of English Linguistics at the Alex Ekwueme Federal University, Ndufu-Alike, Ikwo, Abakaliki, Ebonyi State, Nigeria. He was a former Senior Lecturer at the University of Lagos, Akoka, Yaba, Lagos State. His teaching and research interests include sociolinguistics, pidgin linguistics, psycholinguistics, applied linguistics, critical linguistics, discourse analysis, and phonetics and phonology. He has published extensively in the narrow field of Nigerian Pidgin with special focus on Ajegunle variety.
Email Address: jbosoba@gmail.com

Oluwabunmi Opeyemi Oyebode is a Senior Lecturer in the Department of English, Obafemi Awolowo University, Ile-Ife, Nigeria. She was a Fulbright Fellow at the University of Texas at Austin, USA in the 2007/2008 academic session and a Guest Researcher at the University of Southern Denmark, Odense, Denmark where she worked with that erudite scholar on Visual Communication and Multimodality, Prof. Theo van Leeuwen in 2015/2016 academic session. Her areas of interest include (Multimodal) Discourse Analysis, Applied Linguistics and Media Communication. She has published articles in reputable local and international outlets, including *Journal of Pan African Studies*, *Discourse Studies* and *Discourse & Society*.

She has also co-authored two books on Multimodality in order to contextualise the theoretical approach in Nigeria. She has continued to intensify efforts to acquaint herself with latest developments in the area of Multimodality by interrogating verbal and non-verbal modes as frames in the Nigerian political, religious and health discourse respectively. The major arguments in her research are that all semiotic resources deployed for representation are socially and culturally motivated for meanings; and that like language, visuals are strategically used as rhetorical discourse constructs in texts to project certain ideological stances within the Nigerian social milieu that resonate with the target audience. Thus, her academic engagement shows the propensity of the critical dimension in multimodal discourse in analyzing visual texts.
Email Address: oabim2@yahoo.co.uk

Oladipo Salami is a Professor in the Department of English, Obafemi Awolowo University, Ile-Ife, Nigeria. He holds a DPhil degree in Linguistics from the University of Sussex, Brighton, United Kingdom. His area of specialization is Sociolinguistics but has teaching, research experience and interests in phonetics/phonology; language variation and change; ethnography of speaking; bilingualism and bilingual education; discourse analysis; psycholinguistics (language disorders); language policy and planning and the sociology of language and religion. He has published in *Language in Society*; *Anthropological Linguistics*; *Journal of Asian and African Studies*; *SKASE: Journal of Theoretical Linguistics*; *LinguistikOnline*; *International Journal of Language, Culture and Society*; *Language Policy*; *Current Issues in Language Planning* and *Journal of Language, Identity and Education*. His works have appeared as chapters in books, including **Faith and Language Practices in Digital Spaces** (Multilingual Matters, 2017); **Explorations in the Sociology of Language and Religion: Change, Conflict and Accommodation** (PalgraveMacmillan, 2010); **Explorations in the Sociology of Language and Religion** (John Benjamins, 2006); and **Forms and Functions of English and Indigenous Languages in Nigeria** (Group Publishers, 2004). He is a member of both the Network of the Study of the Sociology of Language and Religion and Research Network on Language and Literacy in Africa and the Diaspora.
Email Address: diposalami@yahoo.com

Eunice Ukaegbu is a lecturer and a doctoral candidate in the Department of Linguistics and Nigerian Languages, University of Calabar, Calabar. Her research interests include phonology, language development and orthography design.

Akinmade T. Akande
Introduction

Nigerian Pidgin (NP) is an important language which evolved from the contact between Nigerians, especially those in the Niger Delta region, and the European traders who visited the region to transact business with the locals (Elugbe & Omamor, 1991). NP enabled these foreigners who could not speak any of the indigenous languages to communicate with the Niger Delta natives who did not understand the language(s) of their European traders. It need be pointed out here that while Mufwene (2020) is right to a large extent in claiming that the linguistic repertoires of African repatriated Caribbean plantation labourers (most of whom worked as interpreters) influenced West African English lexifier Creoles greatly, the emergence of Creoles and Pidgins (including Naija) cannot be traced to a single source (see Faraclas, 2021).

As we shall see, NP has expanded to cover more domains than it initially served. NP used to be seen and considered as the language of the socially disadvantaged, the less-privileged and that of the uneducated (Agheyisi, 1971; Kattanek, 2011). As remarked by Akande, Adedeji & Robbin (2019: 92), NP's linguistic makeup is that of a combination of English which supplies its lexicon and Nigeria's indigenous languages which control its syntax. A little wonder Adegbija (2001) refers to it as an indo-exogenous language: English is its superstrate while indigenous languages are its substrates. NP has one major advantage over either English or indigenous languages and this is the fact that "it has neither the elitist connotations of English nor the ethnic connotations of the indigenous languages" (Deuber, 2005: 51). Akande (2016) further underscores the neutrality of NP by stating that NP can be found in every part of the country and its usage is not dependent on any educational background as it can be spoken by both the literate and illiterate.

NP used to be perceived by some linguists and non-linguists, like every other creole language across the globe, as a highly stigmatized language. The prejudice most elite used to have against NP as a language of informal communication has abated during the twenty first century. Akande (2008) observes that undergraduates, graduates and even lecturers in many Nigerian universities communicate informally in NP. Faraclas (personal interaction) noted that "Naija is now being used on billboards along major highways in the New York City area to advertise products, the BBC now has a 'Pidgin Service', there are now university level courses where Naija is taught as a foreign language." In addition, there are now many programmes in NP in the electronic media in Nigeria as demonstrated by Akande & Okesola, (2021). This bias against NP and against pidgins and creoles across the globe is clearly evident in the derogatory names "broken English", "adulterated English", "bad English", "substandard English", "Nigger French" inconbuistaelije (cook house lingo) and Isikula (cookie language) often used to refer to it (Holm, 1988; Akande, 2008).

Huber (1999) draws attention to the prejudice of most Ghanaians against Ghanaian Pidgin just as Ayafor & Green (2017) state that there is a widespread bias against Cameroonian Pidgin by most educated Anglophone Cameroonians. Although NP has the highest prevalence as it is the most widely spoken language in Nigeria, it is socio-economically inferior to English. Given its socio-economic inferiority compared to English, it is highly stigmatized. The stigmatization it attracted then was reflected in the words of Kouwenberg and Singler (2008: 3) when they claim that:

> Popular attitudes against pidgins and creoles were reflected in academic settings as well. Thus, up until this period linguists' willingness to apply the concept of linguistic relativism – whereby every language is understood to be complete and valid – may have been extended to Hopi and Hausa, but it generally stopped short of being extended to pidgins and creoles.

In the same vein, Akande (2008) reported that many of his respondents, all of whom are university graduates and lecturers, were of the view that NP is often used by people who could not speak English very well because of their low level of education. The paradox however was that when these same respondents were prompted during spontaneous interviews with them, they were speaking NP freely. This general attitude suggests that sometimes people, even scholars, do consider NP as a variant or a dialect of English. As a matter of fact, Mafeni (1971: 99) noted that the majority of Nigerians "consider it [NP] a debased form of English and not a language in its own right." However, as argued by Akande (2010), NP is a distinct language with its own grammar and it is not linguistically (albeit socially) inferior to English.

Today, the sociolinguistic profile of NP has shown that the negative attitudes and the stigmatization it was characterized by are gradually fading. NP is now a language of informal communication in Nigeria and it is also the lingua franca of Nigerians in the diaspora especially in Europe and has crept into multifarious domains which were hitherto forbidden for it. It is now spoken freely by different professionals such as lawyers, doctors, bankers, accountants and engineers; and it is being used in the print and electronic media to cast news, for jingles and political adverts (Osoba, 2014). It is the default language of hip-hop music (Akande, 2012) and popular culture generally just as it is the prominent language of standup comedy in Nigeria (Akande, Adedeji & Robbin, 2019). The covert prestige that NP has and is still gaining cannot be complete without mentioning its important role in the fight against the COVID-19 pandemic. Given the multilingual nature of Nigeria, NP has become a major language that is being used to sensitize the citizenry, create awareness and instruct Nigerians on how to win the vicious war against the ongoing pandemic. NP seems to be the best linguistic choice since it is understood by the majority of Nigerians irrespective of their educational, ethnic and religious backgrounds and, as such, the language is perceived to have the capacity to make the war more effective as messages and instructions related to the pandemic rendered in it can reach out to almost all Nigerians.

As noted above, NP has the highest numerical strength in terms of its number of speakers. It has been estimated that speakers of NP in Nigeria are well over 110 million (Faraclas, 2021). However, these speakers have varying degrees of competence as there are those who speak it as a native language and sometimes the only language in their repertoire especially in Warri, Benin, Sapele and other riverine areas (Marchese & Schnukal, 1982; Faraclas, 1996) while we also have those who use it as a second language in places like Lagos (Deuber, 2005). Apart from its enviable numerical strength, its geographical spread is such that no other language in Nigeria can compete with. There is no region, zone or state in Nigeria where speakers of NP do not abound. Given its numerical strength and geographical spread, NP has become the unofficial lingua franca in several domains in Nigeria. Jowitt (2019: 11) seems to be emphasizing this when he says NP "has become creolized in some parts of the South (notably in the coastal area of Delta State), but its principal function is as a lingua franca, especially where numerous first languages are spoken and therefore also in the cities."

The book

This book foregrounds diverse contributions to the sociolinguistics of Nigerian Pidgin. Its major aim is to serve as a compendium which touches different major aspects of NP as it has been observed that most of the earlier works in this area have focused only on one aspect or the other. It thus offers a broad survey of the form and functions of NP in different domains. One major strong point of this volume is the fact that it directs attention to different fertile areas of NP by focusing, *inter alia*, on its social functions, its morphology and syntax. The book contains twelve chapters and each chapter is devoted to a particular aspect of the language.

In Chapter One, Nicholas Faraclas provides a comprehensive assessment of the number of people who speak NP in Nigeria. He observes that with about 110 million speakers of NP in Nigeria, the language is not just the biggest language in Nigeria, it is certainly one of the most widely spoken languages in the world. He notes that in spite of the fact that NP has never been officially recognized, standardized or upheld as a model to be learned for social or economic mobility, its speakers have continued to increase faster in number on account of the rapid population growth in Nigeria. He further argues that, based on the present number of NP speakers, the language is one of the important languages in the world and its status will continue rise as its speakers may increase to about 300 million by 2050.

Chapter Two focuses on the changes in prestige and functions of NP in non-Anglophone diasporic contexts such as Germany, Italy, Belgium and Switzerland. In the chapter, Christian Mair, by using Germany as a demonstration case, explores the role of Nigerian English and NP in immigrants' evolving multilingual repertoires. He points out that, given the fact that Nigerian immigrants are not usually competent in German on arrival, they often have to engage in the process of linguistic accommodation which often involves the adaptation of English in order to be able to communicate with the local population. According to him, Pidgin serves not just as an in-group code and a means of expressing 'Naija' identity, it also gains a new function by serving as a lingua franca among West African immigrant community generally. By relying on language-biographical interviews with Nigerians living in Germany and contributions to the global Nigerian web-forum, Nairaland, by users who can be located in Germany on the basis of their user profiles, it is shown that NP, as a lingua franca, has the capacity to bridge ethnic, political and religious boundaries just as it can neutralize the Anglophone and Francophone postcolonial spheres.

Francis Egbokhare argues in Chapter Three that Nigeria's linguistic milieu is characterized by complexities, continuities and discontinuities occasioned by the existence of over 500 languages in the country. For him, the heavy multilingual nature of the country has created complex problems for integration and communication. Basing his argument on the premises that certain fundamental socio-political forces in the country account for its (Nigeria's) linguistic realities and that the competing ideologies are replicated as linguistic choices and behaviour, the author examines the crucial roles NP plays in Nigeria's linguistic landscape from different perspectives. Examining the ideological currents, the social transformations and the political events that have shaped the fortunes of NP over time, the author describes the epochs and milieus defining the pidginization of the Nigerian linguistic spaces and the role of cultural transitions, especially popular culture, social media, the dynamics of economic structure, urban settlement patterns, interactional flows, forces of disintegration and political events that are responsible for converting pidgin from a marginal stigmatized language to a cool lingua franca.

Idom Inyabri and Eyo Mensah, in Chapter Four, investigate the remote and immediate impulses that gave birth to stand-up comedy in Nigeria and explore the role that it plays in the Nigerian public space. The authors identify and interrogate the performative forms that make *Naija* stand-up comedy NP oral genre, which the youth explore as a resource for agency, subjectivity and socio-political engagements. The theoretical framework of postcolonialism is used to analyse selected performances of Naija stand-up comedies as ideological and performative means of installing a new notion of identity and nationhood through NP.

Similarly, Mirka Honkanen, in Chapter Five, focuses on the nexus between migration, authenticity, and computer-mediated communication in the Nigerian context, and examines the role of NP in the construction of 'authentic Nigerianness', particularly among people of Nigerian heritage abroad. By analyzing interactions between Nigerians residing in Nigeria and in the global diaspora on Nairaland, a web forum, she provides an overview of NP vocabulary related to the themes of authenticity and migration, examines diasporic Nigerians' attitudes toward Pidgin based on metalanguage on the forum and, finally, presents and analyses examples of Pidgin often used strategically to claim Nigerian identities.

The major argument in Chapter Six is that NP lacks a unified orthographic system and has hindered its capacity to function as a medium of literacy in Nigeria. In the chapter, Eyo Mensah, Eunice Ukaegbu and Benjamin Nyong examine the issues and approaches in designing the best possible orthography to suit contemporary demands of NP. The authors make a case for the adoption of a unified phonetic-based system that avoids dialectal differences, variation in pronunciation and redundant letters but accurately maps each sound in the language with a corresponding symbol. The chapter concludes that a phonetic-based orthography is more suitable as it will make NP easier to read and write than any other spelling system.

Akinmade T. Akande and Saheed O. Okesola are concerned with morpho-syntactic features of NP on Radio programmes rendered in Naija in Chapter Seven. They observe that the major rationale for using NP in the media is to reach out to a wider audience and to ensure that people of different linguistic and cultural backgrounds are enabled to participate or make their contributions. By focusing on the analysis of morpho-syntactic features used in ten randomly selected recorded episodes of *Wetin dey shele*, a Radio programme being anchored by MC Reo, they observe that such morphological features as duplication, acronymy and clipping and syntactic features such as lack of inflectional marker, the use of *am* and *una* as pronouns, the use of the complementizer *say* and the use of *wey* as a relativizer are prominent in the data. The chapter concludes that morphological and syntactic features being used on Radio programmes delivered in NP are not radically different from those NP features observed in other domains. The reason adduced to this is that the grammar of NP is universal irrespective of the domain or variety being studied.

In Chapter Eight, Macaulay Mowarin addresses the syntactic processes of topicalisation, focus construction and emphatic marker in NP. He adopts Chomsky's Checking and Phase theories of Minimalist Program as the theoretical framework for the analysis of the processes. By making use of tape recorded utterances from NP speakers in Warri, Sapele and Abraka areas where NP is a pidgincreole, the study finds out, *inter alia*, that focus construction is derived through cleft and that for cases of dislocation to the left periphery of topicalizers, there are special instances of co-indexation of topicalized DP. The chapter concludes that emphasis, topic constructions and topicalisation are not haphazard but structural in NP.

Chapter Nine deals with the metalanguage of football commentary in NP. Adesoji Babalola draws data from five hours of NP commentary of the two semi-finals and the final of the 2018 FiFa World Cup that was aired on Digital Satellite Television (DSTV). Using Halliday´s systemic functional linguistics as the theoretical framework for the analysis, the study shows that coinages, neologism and linguistic creativity constitute the essential features of NP commentary. It is further revealed that most of the existing superstrate and substrate linguistic forms are undergoing morphological remodification with new semantic orientations in the code. The study concludes that while the metalanguage of NP football commentary thrives on peculiar lexical, phrasal, clausal and metaphoric features, NP is gradually developing its linguistic resources through internal processes and creativity to further project its independent linguistic status from its lexifier (English).

In Chapter Ten, Oluwabunmi O. Oyebode examines NP as a semiotic resource strategically deployed to interrogate religious and ideological issues that resonate with average Nigerians in some Nigerian church posters. Data comprised purposively selected church programme posters uploaded online by Nigerian netizens to critique different strategies Nigerian churches adopt to woo the masses to their programmes. Using van Leeuwen's (2005) approach to social semiotics which provides a descriptive framework for analysing semiotic resources as the actions and artefacts we use to communicate, the study reveals that church special programme posters' designers appropriate NP specifically to invoke different layers of meaning such as projection of 'delegitimated Others', revolution against oppression, construction of emotive appeal and depiction of interpersonal relation/close affinity with the Christian God. The study concludes that the utilisation of NP as a semiotic mode in religious context unravels specific social structures and practices that reflect the belief system of the posters' designers about Christianity.

Joseph Babasola Osoba's contribution, Chapter Eleven, highlights and examines the planning and policy implications of the status, corpus and acquisition of NP, using a meta-analytical approach based on ethnographic and sociolinguistic principles, theories and methodologies. Osoba proposes that, since the positive impact of this language in political and economic life is seen and felt by all Nigerians today, it should be officially recognized as Nigeria's second and national (official) language. He argues that the recognition of NP as an official language may go a long in solving our socio-political problems of developing and sustaining a fledgling democratic structure, forging unity amongst diverse ethnic groups and resolving our national language question. He argues that NP is a potential official national language not only for its political neutrality but also its inherent value as a language of political communication and economic success.

In the last chapter, Chapter Twelve, Oladipo Salami and Akinmade T. Akande examine the roles of non-state and pseudo-state actors in the management of NP in the country. In order to do this, they investigate language use activities involving NP in the domains of education, the electronic and print media and argue that these domains form essential parts of language policy. They conclude that the motivations for the language policy options taken by the non-state actors they studied varied. They observe that NPE is gradually disrupting the social space occupied by the English language and indigenous languages in Nigeria. For them, the disruption is occasioned by the speakers' right to make use of the language of their choice in specific domains in the social space.

References

Adegbija, Efurosibina. 2001. *Multilingualism: A case study of Nigeria*. New York: Africa World Press.
Agheyisi, Rebbeca. 1971. *West African Pidgin English: Simplification and simplicity*. Stanford: Stanford University PhD dissertation.
Akande, Akinmade T. 2008. *The verb in Standard Nigerian English and Nigerian Pidgin English: A sociolinguistic approach*. Leeds: University of Leeds PhD dissertation.
Akande, Akinmade T. 2010. Is Nigerian Pidgin English English? *Dialectologia et Geolinguistica* 18, 3–22.
Akande, Akinmade T. 2012. *Globalization and English in Africa: Evidence from Nigerian hip-hop*. New York: Nova Science.
Akande, Akinmade T. 2016. Multilingual practices in Nigerian army barracks. *African Identities* 14(1), 38–58.

Akande, Akinmade T., Kofoworola Adedeji & Anjola Robbin. 2019. Language, vulgarity and social critique: The case of Nigerian Pidgin in stand-up comedy. *Lagos Notes and Records* 25(1), 89–109.

Akande, Akinmade T. & Saheed O. Okesola. 2021. Morpho-syntactic Features of Nigerian Pidgin on Radio Programmes Rendered in Naija. In Akinmade T. Akande & Oladipo Salami (eds.), *Current trends in Nigerian Pidgin English: A sociolinguistic perspective*, 201–220. Berlin/Boston: De Gruyter Mouton.

Ayafor, Miriam & Melanie Green. 2017. *Cameroon Pidgin English: A comprehensive grammar*. Amsterdam: John Benjamin.

Caron, Bernard. 2019. Clefts in Naija: A Nigerian Pidgincreole. Paper presented at the *International Naija Symposium* (ms.).University of Ibadan, 27–29 June.

Deuber, Dagmar. 2005. *Nigerian Pidginin Lagos: Language ontact, variation and change in an African urban setting*. London: Battlebridge.

Elugbe, Ben & Augusta Omamor. 1991. *Nigerian Pidgin: Background and prospects*. Ibadan: Heinemann Educational Books.

Faraclas, Nicholas. 1996. *Nigerian Pidgin*. London: Routledge.

Faraclas, Nicholas. 2021. Naija: A language of the future. In Akinmade T. Akande & Oladipo Salami (eds.), *Current trends in Nigerian Pidgin English: A sociolinguistic perspective*, 9–38. Berlin/Boston: De Gruyter Mouton.

Jowitt, David. 2019. *Nigerian English*. Berlin/Boston: De Gruyter Mouton.

Kattanek, Sita Maria. 2011. The Nigerian coming-of-age novel as a globalization device: A reading of Chris Abani's *GraceLand*. *Rupkatha Journal on Interdisciplinary Studies in Humanities* 3(3), 426–433.

Kouwenbery, Silvia & John Victor Singler. 2008. Introduction. In Silvia Kouwenbery & John Victor Singler (eds.), *The handbook of Pidgin and creole studies*, 3–16. Oxford: Wiley Blackwell.

Holm, John. 1988. *Pidgins and creoles*. Cambridge: Cambridge University Press.

Huber, Magnus. 1999. *Ghanaian Pidgin English in its West African context: A sociohistorical and structural analysis*. Amsterdam: Benjamins.

Mafeni, Bernard. 1971. Nigerian Pidgin. In John Spencer (ed.), *The English Language in West Africa*, 95–112. London: Longman.

Mufwene, Salikoko S. 2020. Creoles and pidgins: Why the latter are no the ancestors of the former. In Evangelia Adamou & Yaron Matras (eds.), *The Routledge handbook of language contact*, 300–324. London: Routledge.

Marchese, Lynell & Anna Schnukal. 1982. Nigerian Pidgin English of Warri. *Journal of the Linguistic Association of Nigeria* 1. 213–219.

Osoba, Joseph Babasola. 2014. The use of Nigerian Pidgin in media adverts. *International Journal of English Linguistics* 4(2), 26–37.

van Leeuwen, Theo. 2005. *Introducing social semiotics*. London/New York: Routledge.

Nicholas Faraclas
Chapter 1
Naija: A language of the future

Introduction

Varying estimates have been put forward of the number of speakers of Naija (aka Nigerian Pidgin) (BBC 2016; Ethnologue, 2019; Faraclas, 1991, 2008, 2013, 2021; etc.) but up until the present, there have been few attempts to make an educated guess as to the number of people who actually speak it. In this chapter, we begin by using official census data regarding degree of urbanization, proximity to the coast, extent of local plurilingualism, and levels of formal education of the populations of the 36 states and Federal Capital Territory of Nigeria to make a preliminary comprehensive assessment of the number of people who speak Naija in Nigeria today, and we obtain some unexpected results. Our estimates reveal that, even by the most conservative measures, with well over 110 million speakers, Naija is already one of the biggest and most widely spoken languages in the world, whether or not we consider it to be part of a bigger language that includes other very closely related and mutually intelligible varieties of Afro-Atlantic English lexifier Creole*, such as Cameroonian Pidgin, Sierra Leone Krio, etc., in West Africa, and Jamaican, Trinidadian, Guyanese and other closely related and mutually intelligible varieties of Afro-Atlantic English lexifier Creole spoken outside of West Africa. In this work, we utilize a functional definition of the category "creole", which means that since Naija and most of the English lexifier varieties related to it are used in all walks of life (rather than being restricted to limited contexts, such as markets, etc.), and since most are already spoken by significant numbers of people, even whole communities, as one of their first and/or home languages, the term "pidgin" no longer applies to these varieties, and "creole" is the more appropriate term.

Next, we examine how and why the rapid growth of Naija has taken place, and we obtain some equally unexpected results. Even though Naija has never enjoyed official recognition, has never been standardized, has never been forced on any militarily or culturally conquered or colonized population, and has never been upheld as a model or norm to be learned for social or economic mobility,

---
Note: In this chapter, we will adopt the practice of capitalizing the term "Creole" when used as a noun referring to a particular variety or particular set of varieties, and not capitalizing the term "creole" when used otherwise.

https://doi.org/10.1515/9781501513541-002

the number of people who speak it has increased faster than might reasonably be expected based on rapid population growth in Nigeria alone. These facts oblige us to revisit and critically question some of the dominant discourses of linguistics as a science, as well as to challenge some of the underlying assumptions routinely made by linguists in their work.

Finally, we turn our attention to the future, and we find that, just as Nigeria has become one of the most rapidly growing countries in the world in terms of its population, Naija has also become one of the world's most rapidly growing languages, and the same can be said for the varieties of English lexifier Creole most closely related to Naija spoken elsewhere along the coast of West Africa and beyond. We conclude that while Naija is one of the most important languages on the planet at present, it will become an even more important world language in the future, as the number of its speakers is set to double or treble to some 200 to 300 million by 2050.

1 Some conceptual and methodological challenges

The calculation of the number of speakers of Naija in Nigeria poses more than a few conceptual challenges. The legacies of colonialism and neo-colonialism have led those in positions of symbolic and political power in Nigeria and elsewhere (not to mention many speakers of Naija themselves) to exclude Naija and the rest of the Afro-Atlantic English lexifier Creoles spoken along the coast of West Africa from the class of linguistic varieties which qualify as "languages". This prejudice, which once extended to any linguistic variety spoken mainly by Africans and other colonized peoples, has gradually been overcome among linguists as well as among an increasing number of non-linguists, so that now there are some 500 sets of varieties that are generally recognized as distinct languages spoken in Nigeria. In the case of creole languages, however, these prejudices are still prevalent, even among linguists who consistently ignore or trivialize these languages by underestimating their numbers of speakers, their geographic spread and their importance in daily life (Faraclas, 2012, 2021).

Since it has been classified under the ideologically problematic and contradictory categories of "pidgin" and "creole" (Faraclas, 2021), Naija has no official recognition, and thus there has never been a serious attempt by governmental or non-governmental agencies to count its speakers. Although its phonology, morphosyntax, semantics and pragmatics are in many ways typologically similar to the hundreds of other languages spoken along the coast of West Africa, the great majority of the lexicon of Naija can be traced back to English, and for this reason we refer to Naija as an English lexifier creole. Because English is also one of the official languages of Nigeria, and especially because English is the predominant language used as language of instruction and testing in formal education throughout the country, many, if not most of its speakers consider Naija to be some form of "incorrect" or "broken" English. In fact, more Nigerians refer to this variety as "Broken" than as "Naija", so that the idea of counting the number of people who speak it has not been taken very seriously. In any case, in this chapter, we make no claims about how speakers of Naija and other varieties of Afro-Atlantic English lexifier Creole perceive the relationships among different varieties in their own linguistic repertoires or in the repertoires of others.

As a creole language, Naija has not undergone much in the way of standardization by linguists, policy makers or educational authorities. Translanguaging and other forms of code alternation have been demonstrated to be the norm rather than the exception in human interactions (Canagarajah, 2012) rendering the concept "language" itself highly problematic (Makoni & Pennycook, 2006). That said, the pervasive and creative weaving together of Naija, English and other Nigerian languages in everyday spoken and written interactions among Nigerians make it much more difficult for them to pretend to draw the arbitrary language boundaries that they have been taught in school to draw between standardized "languages" such as English, Hausa, Yoruba and Igbo. This also complicates the process of estimating the numbers of people who speak Naija.

One thing that makes any kind of demographic analysis in Nigeria particularly challenging is the fact that the national population is growing very quickly. Nigeria's population doubled from 100 million to 200 million over the past three decades (between 1992 and 2019) (World Population Review, 2020) and is set to more than double again in the next three decades. By 2050, Nigerians will number some 411 million, which means that Nigeria will have a greater population than that projected for the United States (398 million), with only India (1,730 million) and China (1,460 million) having a greater number of inhabitants (UNDESA, 2015; Faraclas, 2021). One consequence of this rapid growth is that from 40% to 50% of the population of Nigeria is at present 14 years of age and younger (National Bureau of Statistics, 2018: 4). This amplifies the effects of any age-indexed changes, one of which is the rate of growth in the number of speakers of Naija, which has for decades been a language used more commonly among young people, especially those in the formal education system, than among other age groups. When these young people grow older, they then typically go on to use Naija throughout adulthood more than their parents did. Another challenge which complicates tracking demographic variables in Nigeria are the extremely high rates of population mobility and urbanization in the country, both of which are also associated with increased rates in the use and spread of Naija. From independence in 1960 to the present, the proportion of Nigeria's population living in urban areas has increased from less than 15% to over 50% (National Bureau of Statistics, 2018: 12).

Dramatically divergent estimates have been made as to how many people speak Naija in Nigeria. The most Eurocentrically underestimated figures are those of the US fundamentalist missionary linguists who publish Ethnologue (2019), who put the number of speakers of Naija at 30 million, a figure that absolutely no-one with any experience on the ground in Nigeria could reasonably agree with. A more realistic assessment was made by the BBC in 2016, in the runup to the 2017 launch of their broadcast news service in Naija and related varieties of Afro-Atlantic English lexifier Creole, such as Gambian Aku, Sierra Leone Krio, varieties of Liberian "Pidgin", Ghanaian "Pidgin", Cameroonian "Pidgin", Equatorial Guinean Pichi, etc.: "Pidgin [Naija] . . . is said to be a second language to . . . up to 75 million people in Nigeria alone – about half the population" (BBC, 2016). The BBC figure, however, could also be considered to be low, given the fact that in the very same year of 2016, the National Population Commission of Nigeria calculated the total population of the country to be 193,392,517 (National Bureau of Statistics of Nigeria, 2018: 7–8), half of which would be closer to 85 million speakers of Naija, rather than 75 million. Meanwhile the national population as of 1 January 2020 has been conservatively estimated to be 203,527,455 (World Population Review, 2020), half of which would be some 100 million Naija speakers.

Using the assumption that the proportion of the population of Nigeria who speak Naija has steadily risen from at least 40% before the mid-1990s to at least 50% thereafter, while at the same time taking into account the country's spectacular demographic growth using more accurate census figures than those used by the BBC, in a series of publications Faraclas has estimated that by 1985 there were at least 40 to 50 million speakers (1991: 507; 1996: 1), by 2000 there were at least 70 million speakers (2008: 340), by 2005 there were at least 75 million speakers (2013: 1), and that by 2020 there were at least 100 million speakers of Naija in Nigeria (2021).

Because the numbers arrived at by both the BBC and Faraclas utilize the very blunt instrument of the estimated proportion of the population that speaks Naija times the estimated national population, they do not take into account factors which almost certainly have an impact on the extent to which Naija is spoken in any given region or community in Nigeria such as: 1) extent of urbanization (the higher the level of urbanization, the greater the proportion of Naija speakers); 2) proximity to the coast (the closer to the coast, the greater the proportion of Naija speakers); 3) degree of local plurilingualism (the greater the linguistic diversity, the greater the proportion of Naija speakers) and 4) the average number of years of formal education (the higher the average number of years spent by young people in the formal education system, the greater the proportion of Naija speakers). In this chapter, we attempt to begin to remedy this situation by using these four factors to more accurately estimate the number of Naija speakers in Nigeria.

2 Toward an accurate estimate of the number of speakers of Naija

In order to make an accurate estimate of the numbers of Nigerians who speak Naija, we need an accurate estimate not only of the national population in 2020, but also of the distribution of that population throughout the country. Nigeria is presently divided into 36 states plus a Federal Capital Territory, as shown in Figure 1.

As listed in the first six columns of Table 1, the National Population Commission of Nigeria (National Bureau of Statistics, 2018: 7–8) has compiled state-by-state census-based figures for all 36 states and the Federal Capital Territory for each year from 2012 to 2016. In order to estimate the growth in population for each state by 2020, we calculated the average annual population increase of each from 2012 to 2016 and multiplied it by a factor of 3 for the three years 2017–2019, as shown in column 7 of Table 1. We then added that estimated 3-year growth figure to the total for 2016 to obtain the estimated population at the beginning of 2020, listed in column 8 of Table 1. In the final row of Table 1, the projected total population of Nigeria on January 1, 2020 is calculated to be some 211,570,000, which is some 8 million more than the estimate cited above of 203,527,455 (World Population Review, 2020). For the purposes of this study, we will adopt the more conservative World Population Review (WPR) figure and adjust our totals accordingly in the tables that follow.

2.1 Factor 1: Extent of urbanization (UB)

One key factor that has favored the growth and spread of Naija is urbanization, which is occurring in Nigeria at exponential rates, as observed by Eze Duruiheoma, the Chairman of the National Population Commission of Nigeria in 2018:

Figure 1: Map showing the 36 states plus the Federal Capital Territory of Nigeria (source: Researchgate.net).

> Nigeria remains the most populous [nation] in Africa, the seventh globally with an estimated population of over 198 million. The recent World Population Prospects predicts that by 2050, Nigeria will become the third most populated country in the world. Over the last 50 years, Nigeria's urban population has grown at an average annual growth rate of more than 6.5 per cent . . . . [The proportion of urban dwellers] grew substantially from 17.3 in 1967 to 49.4 per cent in 2017. (UNCPD 2018)

Constant movement of peoples and extensive contact among languages and cultures has been the norm rather than the exception throughout Nigerian history, arguably from prehistoric times (Faraclas, 1995, 2008, 2012). The rapid growth of cities in Nigeria over the past few decades has been accompanied by an ever greater degree of population mobility, which in turn has led to a steady increase in the extent to which any particular Nigerian comes into contact with speakers of languages other than those that are already included in her or his existing linguistic repertoire. As is generally the case for the other contact languages that emerged in the colonial era, these conditions have proved to be optimal for

Table 1: State-by-state population in Nigeria 2012–2016 (source: National Population Commission, National Bureau of Statistics 2018: 7–8) with estimated growth in population to 2020, based on the average annual population increase from 2012 to 2016.

STATE	2012	2013	2014	2015	2016	+2017–2020	2020 (millions)
ABIA	3,345,769	3,437,336	3,531,408	3,628,055	3,727,347	.10 × 3 = .30	3.73 + .30 = 4.03
ADAMAWA	3,783,127	3,894,444	4,009,037	4,127,001	4,248,436	.12 × 3 = .36	4.25 + .36 = 4.61
AKWA IBOM	4,785,078	4,950,568	5,121,781	5,298,916	5,482,177	.18 × 3 = .54	5.48 + .54 = 6.02
ANAMBRA	4,942,106	5,082,440	5,226,760	5,375,177	5,527,809	.15 × 3 = .45	5.53 + .45 = 5.98
BAUCHI	5,706,046	5,903,388	6,107,554	6,318,781	6,537,314	.21 × 3 = .63	6.54 + .63 = 7.17
BAYELSA	2,028,468	2,088,154	2,149,597	2,212,849	2,277,961	.06 × 3 = .18	2.28 + .18 = 2.46
BENUE	5,092,533	5,247,624	5,407,438	5,572,118	5,741,815	.17 × 3 = .51	5.74 + .51 = 6.25
BORNO	5,115,017	5,291,918	5,474,937	5,664,285	5,860,183	.20 × 3 = .60	5.86 + .60 = 6.46
CROSS R.	3,442,816	3,544,120	3,648,404	3,755,757	3,866,269	.11 × 3 = .33	3.87 + .33 = 4.20
DELTA	4,982,928	5,144,961	5,312,262	5,485,004	5,663,362	.17 × 3 = .51	5.66 + .51 = 6.17
EBONYI	2,575,190	2,648,315	2,723,515	2,800,851	2,880,383	.08 × 3 = .24	2.88 + .24 = 3.12
EDO	3,801,987	3,906,039	4,012,938	4,122,764	4,235,595	.11 × 3 = .33	4.24 + .33 = 4.57
EKITI	2,889,357	2,980,330	3,074,167	3,170,959	3,270,798	.10 × 3 = .30	3.27 + .30 = 3.57
ENUGU	3,912,311	4,031,459	4,154,235	4,280,750	4,411,119	.13 × 3 = .39	4.41 + .39 = 4.80
GOMBE	2,865,649	2,958,833	3,055,047	3,154,389	3,256,962	.10 × 3 = .30	3.26 + .30 = 3.56

(continued)

Table 1 (continued)

STATE	2012	2013	2014	2015	2016	+2017–2020	2020 (millions)
IMO	4,758,912	4,913,660	5,073,440	5,238,416	5,408,756	.16 × 3 = .48	5.41 + .48 = 5.89
JIGAWA	5,189,835	5,342,543	5,499,746	5,661,573	5,828,163	.16 × 3 = .48	5.83 + .48 = 6.31
KADUNA	7,319,192	7,542,095	7,771,785	8,008,472	8,252,366	.24 × 3 = .72	8.25 + .72 = 8.97
KANO	11,459,817	11,844,300	12,241,682	12,652,397	13,076,892	.41×3 = 1.22	13.08 + 1.22 = 14.3
KATSINA	6,945,757	7,157,287	7,375,259	7,599,869	7,831,319	.23 × 3 = .69	7.83 + .69 = 8.52
KEBBI	3,922,250	4,045,745	4,173,127	4,304,520	4,440,050	.13 × 3 = .39	4.44 + .39 = 4.83
KOGI	3,967,630	4,088,462	4,212,974	4,341,279	4,473,490	.13 × 3 = .39	4.47 + .39 = 4.86
KWARA	2,831,842	2,918,084	3,006,953	3,098,528	3,192,893	.10 × 3 = .30	3.19 + .30 = 3.49
LAGOS	11,042,686	11,401,767	11,772,524	12,155,337	12,550,598	.40×3 = 1.20	12.55 + 1.2 = 13.75
NASSARAWA	2,238,051	2,306,209	2,376,444	2,448,817	2,523,395	.07 × 3 = .21	2.52 + .21 = 2.73
NIGER	4,849,730	5,017,456	5,190,982	5,370,510	5,556,247	.18 × 3 = .54	5.56 + .54 = 6.10
OGUN	4,572,499	4,725,908	4,884,465	5,048,342	5,217,716	.16 × 3 = .48	5.22 + .48 = 5.70
ONDO	4,143,422	4,269,608	4,399,637	4,533,626	4,671,695	.14 × 3 = .42	4.67 + .42 = 5.09
OSUN	4,140,228	4,274,858	4,413,866	4,557,394	4,705,589	.14 × 3 = .42	4.71 + .42 = 5.13
OYO	6,843,840	7,080,532	7,325,409	7,578,755	7,840,864	.26 × 3 = .78	7.84 + .78 = 8.62
PLATEAU	3,770,432	3,873,621	3,979,633	4,088,547	4,200,442	.11 × 3 = .33	4.20 + .33 = 4.53

RIVERS	6,375,176	6,595,659	6,823,767	7,059,764	7,303,924	.24 × 3 = .72	7.30 + .72 = 8.02
SOKOTO	4,432,908	4,567,910	4,707,024	4,850,374	4,998,090	.14 × 3 = .42	5.00 + .42 = 5.42
TARABA	2,730,940	2,811,296	2,894,018	2,979,173	3,066,834	.08 × 3 = .24	3.07 + .24 = 3.31
YOBE	2,863,785	2,965,792	3,071,433	3,180,836	3,294,137	.11 × 3 = .33	3.29 + .33 = 3.62
ZAMFARA	3,972,914	4,102,103	4,235,493	4,373,221	4,515,427	.14 × 3 = .42	4.52 + .42 = 4.94
FCT ABUJA	2,456,945	2,696,403	2,959,199	3,247,608	3,564,126	.30 × 3 = .90	3.56 + .90 = 4.46
NIGERIA	170,157,060	175,690,143	181,403,148	187,301,926	193,392,517	6.06×3 yrs. = 18.18	193.39 + 18.18 = 211.57

the growth and spread of Naija. In many areas of the country, typically urban institutions such as large markets, major motor parks/transport hubs, universities, military installations, police headquarters, prisons, hospitals, secondary schools, etc. have all historically served, not only as key points from which Naija has spread through the general population, but also as key venues in which Naija has been acquired by children as one of their first and/or home languages.

In attempting to estimate the proportion of the population of each of the 36 states and National Capital Territory of Nigeria that speaks Naija, it is necessary to consider the extent to which each has undergone processes of urbanization. The largest cities in Nigeria are listed in Table 2 (columns 1 and 4) along with the state or territory in which they are found (columns 2 and 5) and their respective population in 2006 (columns 3 and 6) (Federal Republic of Nigeria 2006 Population Census).

An additional, and perhaps more accurate indicator of urbanization is the agglomeration of cities and towns into metropolitan areas. Table 3 lists the largest metropolitan areas in Nigeria (columns 1 and 4) together with the states in

Table 2: Largest cities in Nigeria 2006 listed along with the state in which they are located and their population as of 2006 (source: Federal Republic of Nigeria 2006 Population Census).

City	State	Population 2006	City	State	Population 2006
Lagos	Lagos	8,048,430	**Makurdi**	Benue	249,000
Kano	Kano	2,828,861	**Badagry**	Lagos	241,093
Ibadan	Oyo	2,559,853	**Ilesa**	Osun	233,900
Benin City	Edo	1,147,188	**Gombe**	Gombe	230,900
Port Harcourt	Rivers	1,005,904	**Obafemi Owode**	Ogun	228,851
Jos	Plateau	821,618	**Owo**	Ondo	218,886
Ilorin	Kwara	777,667	**Jimeta**	Adamawa	218,400
Abuja	FCT	776,298	**Suleja**	Niger	216,578
Kaduna	Kaduna	760,084	**Potiskum**	Yobe	205,876
Enugu	Enugu	722,664	**Kukawa**	Borno	203,864
Zaria	Kaduna	695,089	**Gusau**	Zamfara	201,200
Warri	Delta	557,398	**Iwo**	Osun	191,377
Ikorodu	Lagos	535,619	**Bida**	Niger	188,181
Maiduguri	Borno	543,016	**Ugep**	Cross River	187,000

Table 2 (continued)

City	State	Population 2006	City	State	Population 2006
Aba	Abia	534,265	Ijebu Ode	Ogun	186,700
Ife	Osun	509,035	Epe	Lagos	181,409
Bauchi	Bauchi	493,810	Ise Ekiti	Ekiti	167,100
Akure	Ondo	484,798	Gboko	Benue	166,400
Abeokuta	Ogun	451,607	Ilawe Ekiti	Ekiti	160,700
Oyo	Oyo	428,798	Ikare	Ondo	160,600
Uyo	Akwa Ibom	427,873	Osogbo	Osun	156,694
Sokoto	Sokoto	427,760	Okpoko	Anambra	152,900
Osogbo	Osun	421,000	Garki	Jigawa	152,233
Owerri	Imo	401,873	Sapele	Delta	151,000
Yola	Adamawa	392,854	Ila	Osun	150,700
Calabar	Cross River	371,022	Shaki	Oyo	150,300
Umuahia	Abia	359,230	Ijero	Ekiti	147,300
Ondo City	Ondo	358,430	Ikot Ekpene	Akwa Ibom	143,077
Minna	Niger	348,788	Jalingo	Taraba	139,845
Lafia	Nasarawa	330,712	Otukpo	Benue	136,800
Okene	Kogi	320,260	Okigwe	Imo	132,237
Katsina	Katsina	318,459	Kisi	Oyo	130,800
Ikeja	Lagos	313,196	Buguma	Rivers	124,200
Nsukka	Enugu	309,633	Funtua	Katsina	122,500
Ado Ekiti	Ekiti	308,621	Abakaliki	Ebonyi	151,723
Awka	Anambra	301,657	Asaba	Delta	149,603
Ogbomosho	Oyo	299,535	Gbongan	Osun	117,300
Iseyin	Oyo	286,700	Igboho	Oyo	115,000
Mubi	Adamawa	280,009	Gashua	Yobe	109,600
Onitsha	Anambra	261,604	Bama	Borno	102,800
Sagamu	Ogun	253,412	Uromi	Edo	101,400

which they are located (columns 2 and 5) and the estimated number of inhabitants of each (columns 3 and 6) in 2016.

Table 3: Largest metropolitan areas in Nigeria 2016 listed along with the state in which they are located and their estimated population as of 2016 (source: Demographia, 2016).

Metro Areas	State	Population 2016	Metro Areas	State	Population 2016
Lagos	Lagos	12,830,000	Jos	Plateau	790,000
Onitsha	Anambra	7,425,000	Maiduguri	Borno	765,000
Kano	Kano	3,680,000	Owerri	Imo	750,000
Ibadan	Oyo	2,910,000	Ikorodu	Lagos	740,000
Uyo	Akwa Ibom	1,990,000	Zaria	Kaduna	735,000
Port Harcourt	Rivers	1,865,000	Enugu	Enugu	715,000
Nsukka	Enugu	1,735,000	Warri	Delta	695,000
Abuja	FCT	1,580,000	Osogbo	Osun	680,000
Benin City	Edo	1,355,000	Akure	Ondo	585,000
Aba	Abia	1,215,000	Sokoto	Sokoto	580,000
Kaduna	Kaduna	1,100,000	Abeokuta	Ogun	520,000
Ilorin	Kwara	890,000	Bauchi	Bauchi	520,000

On the basis of the information in Tables 2 and 3, for the purposes of the present study each of the 36 states and the Federal Capital Territory was assigned an urbanization score from 0 (lowest) to 3 (highest) to be used in estimating the numbers of speakers of Naija there. These urbanization scores (UB) are listed in Table 5, column 5.

2.2 Factor 2: Proximity to the coast (NS)

Some of the precursors to Naija and the other varieties of West African Afro-Atlantic English lexifier Creole emerged along the coast of West Africa by the 16th century and gradually spread inland. The Atlantic coast, which forms the southern border of Nigeria, was the first part of the country to be integrated into the Afro-Atlantic linguistic and cultural colonial era contact zone (Gilroy, 1993), which is minimally defined to include West Africa and the Caribbean (including the Guianas and the Caribbean coast of Central and South America), and maximally defined to include West Africa, the Caribbean, the northern regions of Brazil, points on the Gulf of Mexico (such as Veracruz, Campeche, and Louisiana), areas along the Atlantic coast of North America (such as the Sea Islands and other parts of the southeastern United States) as well as other major concentrations of Afro-Atlantic diasporic populations such as London, Toronto, New York, Paris, Amsterdam, Lisbon, etc.

The contact phenomena which eventually gave rise to Naija can be traced back to the emergence from the 15th century onward of Afro-Portuguese linguistic and cultural repertoires along the west coast of Africa, including along the coast of present day Nigeria (Holm, 1989: 426). This contact can be said to have begun with the *lançados*, that is, an appreciable number of mainly male renegade Portuguese sailors/traders/outcasts, who found refuge in West African villages and eventually assimilated into local societies, adopting African languages and cultures and marrying African wives. These *lançados* and their descendants often played the role of intermediary between African and European traders by integrating Afro-Portuguese lifeways and varieties into their West African linguistic and cultural repertoires. One key Afro-Portuguese contact zone on the Nigerian coast in the 15th century was centered in the city of Benin, whose rulers incorporated Portuguese mercenaries into their armies and Portuguese merchants into their trade networks. By the 16th century English pirates began raiding and trading along the coast, and evidence of the use of West African Afro-English contact varieties, perhaps Afro-Portuguese varieties that had been relexified to English, date from then (Dillard, 1972: 76 in Holm, 1989: 410). By the 17th and 18th centuries, the English had become firmly entrenched in the area, and had engaged the peoples of what is today the entire coast of southern Nigeria from Lagos to Bonny to Calabar in the transatlantic trade in the enslaved. English influence was consolidated over West Africa during the 19th and 20th centuries when Nigeria became a British colony, a status which ended with its independence in 1960. During the early years of the colonial period, speakers of Caribbean English lexifier Creole-influenced Sierra Leone Krio were often employed by the British in West Africa as missionaries, administrative assistants, teachers and other functionaries, and they contributed to the vitality and structure of the English lexifier Creole which had already established itself along the Nigerian coast since the 16th century.

Up until Nigerian independence in 1960, Naija was generally considered to be a variety exclusively used in the south, but the spread of Naija to inland regions, such as the *sabon garuruwa* ('strangers' quarters') of Kano, Zaria, and other northern cities had already begun under British colonial rule, and perhaps even before. That said, among the several generations of Nigerians who have lived and died since independence day, the increase in this northward spread has been rapid and significant. In the post-independence neo-colonial order of the 20th and 21st centuries, the people and resources of Nigeria continue to be plundered at ever increasing rates by the big corporations of the former colonial metropoles, enabled by the multilateral institutions that serve their interests. The disruption of traditional societies and economies that have resulted from these higher levels of exploitation have driven ever greater numbers of Nigerians from the northern inland regions of the country southward toward the coast, as well as from the countryside to the cities of both the north and the south, resulting in ever more pervasive plurilingualism and language contact, all factors which are correlated with greater use and spread of Naija (Faraclas, 2005).

Among all of the regions of Nigeria, it is the southern area along and near the coast where Naija is most widely spoken, where the greatest proportion of the population use Naija most frequently in day-to-day life, and where the greatest number of communities whose children acquire Naija as one of their first and/or home languages can be found. To factor in the extent to which the use of Naija is related to distance from the Atlantic coast for the purposes of the present study, each of the 36 states and the Federal Capital Territory was assigned a north/south score from 0 (northernmost or furthest from the coast) to 3 (southernmost or closest to the coast) to be used in estimating the numbers of speakers of Naija there. These north/south scores (NS) are listed in Table 5, column 6.

2.3 Factor 3: Level of plurilingualism (PL)

Naija and the other varieties of West African Afro-Atlantic English lexifier Creole first emerged and later spread primarily in plurilingual contact situations, which for centuries have been the norm rather than the exception in West Africa (Faraclas, 1995). That said, in a number of areas of Nigeria, varieties of Hausa, Yoruba, Igbo and other larger languages are the ancestral languages of the great majority of the population. In areas of the country bordering on the "heartlands" of these bigger languages, people who have other ancestral languages have used these larger languages for centuries as regional "market" varieties, especially when they find themselves in daily contact with people with whom their linguistic repertoire does not otherwise overlap. Up until independence, Naija was in many cases used less than might otherwise be the case in areas where these larger languages are spoken by the great majority as one of their first languages, and slightly less than might otherwise be the case in areas where these bigger languages are spoken by the great majority as second "market" languages. Since independence in 1960, however, Naija has often come to co-exist with languages such as Hausa, Yoruba and Igbo as "market" languages used in contact situations. More recently, Naija has been making significant inroads as well into the heartlands of even some of the largest ancestral languages of the country, but it is still the case that the more plurilingual the area, the faster the spread of Naija tends to be.

To factor in the extent to which the use of Naija is related to the degree of local plurilingualism, linguistic maps were used to assign each of the 36 states and the Federal Capital Territory a plurilingualism (PL) score from 0 (least plurilingual) to 2 (most plurilingual) to be used in estimating the numbers of speakers of Naija there. Given the fact that the extent of urbanization (UB, column 5 of Table 5) and proximity to the coast (NS, column 6 of Table 5) seem to play a more important role in the use and spread of Naija than does local plurilingualism, a maximum of only 2 points is allotted to PL, while a maximum of 3 points are allotted to UB and NS. These plurilingualism scores (PL) are listed in Table 5, column 7.

2.4 Factor 4: Average years of formal education (ED)

An additional factor that has proved to be correlated with higher numbers of speakers of Naija and other West African Afro-Atlantic English lexifier Creoles is the number of years spent in the formal education system. In general, the more years Nigerians remain in the formal education system, the more likely it is that they speak Naija. Columns 1 and 4 of Table 4 list the 2018 United Nations Development Program (UNDP) Human Development Index (HDI) rankings for the 36 states and National Capital Territory of Nigeria (columns 2 and 5). This ranking is to some degree correlated to the UNDP Education Index (columns 3 and 6) which is based on mean years of formal schooling and expected years of formal schooling for the population of each state.

Since average years of formal schooling is highly correlated with extent of urbanization (UB, column 5 of Table 5) and to a lesser extent, proximity to the coast (NS, column 6 of Table 5), factors which have already been considered above, the UNDP Education Index values based on a scale of minimum 0 (lowest average years of formal schooling) and maximum 1 point (highest average years of formal schooling) were used in column 8 of Table 5 to include this factor (ED) in our calculations.

Table 4: Human Development Index (HDI) Ranking and Education Index for the 36 states and National Capital Territory of Nigeria in 2018 (source: UNDP 2018).

HDI Rank	State	Education Index (ED)	HDI Rank	State	Education Index (ED)
1	Lagos	1.007	19	Plateau	0.766
2	Federal Capital Territory	0.815	20	Benue	0.806
3	Bayelsa	0.926	21	Taraba	0.755
4	Akwa Ibom	0.905	22	Kogi	0.857
5	Ekiti	0.894	23	Oyo	0.683
6	Delta	0.906	24	Ebonyi	0.763
7	Cross River	0.857	25	Adamawa	0.661
8	Ogun	0.780	26	Kaduna	0.642
9	Rivers	0.922	27	Gombe	0.492
10	Abia	0.881	28	Niger	0.560
10	Enugu	0.894	29	Kebbi	0.396
12	Edo	0.849	30	Jigawa	0.431
13	Imo	0.916	31	Kano	0.496
14	Osun	0.855	32	Zamfara	0.424
15	Kwara	0.697	33	Borno	0.587
	AVERAGE NIGERIA	0.797	34	Yobe	0.330
16	Nasarawa	0.786	35	Bauchi	0.415
17	Ondo	0.871	36	Katsina	0.440
18	Anambra	0.921	37	Sokoto	0.334

2.5 Aggregate numbers based on UB, NS, PL and ED

To calculate the estimated proportion of the population of the 36 states and the Federal Capital Territory which speaks Naija, the points assigned to each state for the factors UB (extent of urbanization, column 5 of Table 5, maximum 3 points), NS (proximity to the coast, column 6 of Table 5, maximum 3 points), PL (degree of plurilingualism, column 7 of Table 5, maximum 2 points), and ED

Table 5: Estimated numbers of Naija speakers in the 36 states and the Federal Capital Territory of Nigeria in 2020 (in millions), calculated by multiplying an aggregate score (AG) based on levels of urbanization (UB), proximity to the coast (NS), extent of local plurilingualism (PL) and levels of formal education (ED) by estimated population figures for 2020 (see Table 1) (sources: National Population Commission, National Bureau of Statistics – NBS – 2018: 7–8 and World Population Review – WPR – 2020).

STATE	2016	+2016–2019	Est. population 2020 (millions)	UB	NS	PL	ED	AG	Est. Naija speakers 2020 (millions)
ABIA	3.73	.10 × 3 = .30	3.73 + .30 = 4.03	3	3	0	.9	6.9	4.03 × .69 = 2.78
ADAMAWA	4.25	.12 × 3 = .36	4.25 + .36 = 4.61	1	2	2	.7	5.7	4.61 × .57 = 2.63
AKWA IBOM	5.48	.18 × 3 = .54	5.48 + .54 = 6.02	3	3	1	.9	7.9	6.02 × .79 = 4.76
ANAMBRA	5.53	.15 × 3 = .45	5.53 + .45 = 5.98	3	3	0	.9	6.9	5.98 × .69 = 4.13
BAUCHI	6.54	.21 × 3 = .63	6.54 + .63 = 7.17	1	1	1	.4	3.4	7.17 × .34 = 2.44
BAYELSA	2.28	.06 × 3 = .18	2.28 + .18 = 2.46	1	3	2	.9	6.9	2.46 × .69 = 1.70
BENUE	5.74	.17 × 3 = .51	5.74 + .51 = 6.25	1	2	2	.8	5.8	6.25 × .58 = 3.63
BORNO	5.86	.20 × 3 = .60	5.86 + .60 = 6.46	2	0	1	.6	3.6	6.46 × .36 = 2.33
CROSS RIVER	3.87	.11 × 3 = .33	3.87 + .33 = 4.20	2	3	1	.9	6.9	4.20 × .69 = 2.90
DELTA	5.66	.17 × 3 = .51	5.66 + .51 = 6.17	2	3	2	.9	7.9	6.17 × .79 = 4.87
EBONYI	2.88	.08 × 3 = .24	2.88 + .24 = 3.12	0	3	0	.8	3.8	3.12 × .38 = 1.19
EDO	4.24	.11 × 3 = .33	4.24 + .33 = 4.57	3	3	1	.8	7.8	4.57 × .78 = 3.56
EKITI	3.27	.10 × 3 = .30	3.27 + .30 = 3.57	1	3	0	.9	4.9	3.57 × .49 = 1.75
ENUGU	4.41	.13 × 3 = .39	4.41 + .39 = 4.80	3	3	0	.9	6.9	4.80 × .69 = 3.31

(continued)

Table 5 (continued)

STATE	2016	+2016–2019	Est. population 2020 (millions)	UB	NS	PL	ED	AG	Est. Naija speakers 2020 (millions)
GOMBE	3.26	.10 × 3 = .30	3.26 + .30 = 3.56	0	1	1	.5	2.5	3.56 × .25 = 0.89
IMO	5.41	.16 × 3 = .48	5.41 + .48 = 5.89	2	3	0	.9	5.9	5.89 × .59 = 3.48
JIGAWA	5.83	.16 × 3 = .48	5.83 + .48 = 6.31	0	0	0	.4	0.4	6.31 × .04 = 0.25
KADUNA	8.25	.24 × 3 = .72	8.25 + .72 = 8.97	3	1	2	.6	6.6	8.97 × .66 = 5.92
KANO	13.08	.41 × 3 = 1.23	13.08 + 1.23 = 14.31	3	0	1	.5	4.5	14.31 × .45 = 6.44
KATSINA	7.83	.23 × 3 = .69	7.83 + .69 = 8.52	1	0	0	.4	1.4	8.52 × .14 = 1.19
KEBBI	4.44	.13 × 3 = .39	4.44 + .39 = 4.83	0	0	1	.4	1.4	4.83 × .14 = 0.68
KOGI	4.47	.13 × 3 = .39	4.47 + .39 = 4.86	1	2	2	.9	5.9	4.86 × .59 = 2.87
KWARA	3.19	.10 × 3 = .30	3.19 + .30 = 3.49	2	2	1	.7	5.7	3.49 × .57 = 1.99
LAGOS	12.55	.40 × 3 = 1.20	12.55 + 1.20 = 13.75	3	3	2	1.	9	13.75 × .90 = 12.38
NASSARAWA	2.52	.07 × 3 = .21	2.52 + .21 = 2.73	1	2	2	.8	5.8	2.73 × .58 = 1.58
NIGER	5.56	.18 × 3 = .54	5.56 + .54 = 6.10	1	2	2	.6	5.6	6.10 × .56 = 3.41
OGUN	5.22	.16 × 3 = .48	5.22 + .48 = 5.70	2	3	0	.8	5.8	5.70 × .58 = 3.31
ONDO	4.67	.14 × 3 = .42	4.67 + .42 = 5.09	2	3	0	.9	5.9	5.09 × .59 = 3.00
OSUN	4.71	.14 × 3 = .42	4.71 + .42 = 5.13	2	3	0	.9	5.9	5.13 × .59 = 3.03

OYO	7.84	.26 × 3 = .78	7.84 + .78 = 8.62	3	3	0	.7	6.7	8.62 × .67 = 5.78
PLATEAU	4.20	.11 × 3 = .33	4.20 + .33 = 4.53	2	2	2	.8	6.8	4.53 × .68 = 3.08
RIVERS	7.30	.24 × 3 = .72	7.30 + .72 = 8.02	3	3	2	.9	8.9	8.02 × .89 = 7.14
SOKOTO	5.00	.14 × 3 = .42	5.00 + .42 = 5.42	1	0	0	.3	1.3	5.42 × .13 = 0.70
TARABA	3.07	.08 × 3 = .24	3.07 + .24 = 3.31	0	2	2	.8	4.8	3.31 × .48 = 1.59
YOBE	3.29	.11 × 3 = .33	3.29 + .33 = 3.62	0	0	1	.3	1.3	3.62 × .13 = 0.47
ZAMFARA	4.52	.14 × 3 = .42	4.52 + .42 = 4.94	0	0	0	.4	0.4	4.94 × .04 = 0.20
FCT ABUJA	3.56	.30 × 3 = .90	3.56 + .90 = 4.46	3	2	2	.8	7.8	4.46 × .78 = 3.48
NIGERIA	193.39	6.06 × 3 = 18.18	193.39 + 18.18 = 211.57						**NBS: 114.84** /211.57 (54.3%) **WPR: 110.52** /203.53 (54.3%)

(average years of formal schooling, column 8 of Table 5, maximum 1 point) were added together and the aggregate sum (AG) was listed in column 9 of Table 5. This aggregate score was then divided by 10 to yield a percentage that represents the estimated proportion of the population of each state that speaks Naija. A maximum aggregate score of 9 points was possible, which corresponds to a maximum proportion of 90%, with the assumption that at least 10% of the population of any state in Nigeria does not speak Naija, as well as to ensure that our calculations might err on the conservative side. In column 10 of Table 5, this percentage was then multiplied by the estimated 2020 population of each of the 36 states and the Federal Capital Territory as listed column 4, Table 5 (based on columns 2 and 3, which summarize the information in Table 1) to yield the estimated number of Naija speakers per state.

In the last row of column 10 of Table 5, two estimated figures for the number of speakers of Naija in Nigeria in 2020 are listed, that of the National Bureau of Statistics (NBS) and that of the World Population Review (WPR). The first figure of 114,840,000 Naija speakers was obtained by utilizing the less conservative NBS census-based estimate of the entire population of Nigeria in 2020 of 211,570,000, calculated using the 2016 census and the average annual population increase for 2012–2016 in Table 1 (National Population Commission, National Bureau of Statistics 2018: 7–8). This indicates that 54.3% of the national population speak Naija. The second, more conservative WPR-based estimate of the number of Naija speakers in Nigeria at some 110,520,000 was obtained by taking the same percentage (54.3%) and multiplying it by the World Population Review (2020) estimate of the national population in 2020 at some 203,520,000. In the rest of the present work, we will use the latter more conservative number of 110,520,000 speakers of Naija in Nigeria in our calculations.

2.6 Naija in the Nigerian diaspora

The conservative estimate of 110,520,000 speakers of Naija in Nigeria cannot be considered apart from the Naija speakers in the Nigerian diaspora, which has spread in significant numbers to every corner of the world, making Naija not just one of the world's biggest languages in terms of numbers of speakers, but also one of the world's biggest languages in terms of the global spread of those speakers. The numbers of diasporic persons of recent Nigerian descent have been estimated to be from 2 to 15 million people (Nigerian Diaspora, 2020). We will adopt the conservative figure of 4 million Nigerians in diaspora for the purposes of the present study, and the equally conservative proportion of Naija speakers found in the general population of Nigeria (54.3%, as calculated in

Table 5) to estimate the number of diasporic Nigerians who speak Naija to be some 2,000,000 speakers. This is undoubtedly an underestimate, since Nigerians from extensively urbanized areas (UB), from areas of the country close to the coast (NS) and who have higher than average levels of formal education (ED) are much more heavily represented in the diaspora than they are in the general population of Nigeria, making them much more likely than others to speak Naija (Nigerian Diaspora, 2020).

2.7 How many people speak Naija? 112 million speakers as a conservative estimate

Based on all of the calculations in the previous sections of this work, a conservative final figure that emerges for the total number of Naija speakers worldwide in 2020 is some 112,000,000, or more than 1% of the world's population. Table 6 is an example of the "league tables" compiled by linguists of the world's largest languages in 2019 (Ethnologue, 2019). Although our estimate puts the number of Naija speakers at 112 million, which should rank it as the 14th largest language among the 6,000 to 7,000 languages spoken in the world today (in the 99th percentile, between Japanese and Kiswahili), it is nowhere to be found among the world's most widely spoken languages on virtually any such tables compiled by linguists. Instead, many tables do not include Naija as a language at all (Parkvall, 2007) and Ethnologue ranks Naija in 50th place with some 30 million speakers (Ethnologue, 2019).

Table 6: Rankings of the world's 15 biggest languages in 2019 including first language (L1) and second language (L2) speakers, with Naija (14th place with 112,000,000 speakers) absent (source: Ethnologue 2019).

Rank 2019	Language	Speakers (L1 and L2)
1	English	1,132,000,000
2	Mandarin	1,117,000,000
3	Hindi	615,000,000
4	Spanish	534,000,000
5	French	280,000,000
6	Standard Arabic	274,000,000
7	Bengali	265,000,000

Table 6 (continued)

Rank 2019	Language	Speakers (L1 and L2)
8	Russian	258,000,000
9	Portuguese	234,000,000
10	Indonesian (Malay)	199,000,000
11	Urdu	170,000,000
12	Standard German	132,000,000
13	Japanese	128,000,000
14	Kiswahili	98,000,000
15	Marathi	95,000,000

When we consider the numbers of people who speak Naija, it is important to also consider the populations who speak closely related, mutually intelligible English lexifier Creoles on the west coast of Africa as well as in the greater Afro-Atlantic. All of these varieties taken together could easily be considered to be dialects of a larger language, which we could call Afro-Atlantic English lexifier Creole (Faraclas, 2021). Outside of Nigeria, the numbers of first language, second language and diasporic speakers of these West African varieties could conservatively be estimated to include: 1) some 250,000 Gambian/Aku Afro-Atlantic English lexifier Creole speakers (Holm, 1989:426–432); 2) some 4,500,000 Sierra Leone Krio Afro-Atlantic English lexifier Creole speakers (Awadajin Finney, 2013); 3) some 2,000,000 speakers of several Liberian Afro-Atlantic English lexifier Creoles (Holm, 1989: 421–425); 4) some 6,500,000 Ghanaian Pidgin English lexifier Creole speakers (Huber, 2013); 5) some 8,500,000 Cameroonian Pidgin English lexifier Creole speakers (Holm, 1989:426–432); and 6) some 250,000 Equatorial Guinean Pichi English lexifier Creole speakers (Yakpo, 2013). As indicated in Table 7, when these numbers are added to the 112,000,000 obtained above for Naija, the total reaches some 134,000,000 speakers, surpassing German to take 12th place in the rankings of the world's languages with the greatest number of speakers (see Table 6).

Considering the population figures for the Afro-Atlantic English lexifier Creole (AAELC) speaking countries and territories of the island Caribbean and the Guianas in Table 8, along with the numbers of speakers of varieties of AAELC spoken elsewhere, such as the numerous varieties spoken along the Caribbean coast of Central America such as Limonese, the Gullah varieties spoken along the coast of the southeastern United States, and the Afro-Seminole varieties spoken in the United States and Mexico, etc., we arrive at a conservative estimate of some

Table 7: Varieties of Afro-Atlantic English lexifier Creole (AAELC) spoken in West Africa and the estimated numbers of their first language (L1), second language (L2) and diasporic speakers (sources: World Population Review 2020 and others noted in column 2).

COUNTRY	Variety of Afro-Atlantic English lexifier Creole	Est. L1, L2 and Diaspora Speakers
Gambia	Aku AAELC (Holm 1989: 426–432)	250,000
Sierra Leone	Krio AAELC (Awadajin Finney 2013)	4,500,000
Liberia	Liberian AAELCs (Holm 1989: 421–425)	2,000,000
Ghana	Ghanaian Pidgin AAELC (Huber 2013)	6,500,000
Nigeria	Naija AAELC (present study)	112,000,000
Cameroon	Cameroonian Pidgin AAELC (Holm 1989: 426–432)	8,500,000
Equatorial Guinea	Pichi AAELC (Yakpo 2013)	250,000
TOTAL		**134,000,000**

4,000,000 first language, second language and diasporic speakers of non-West African AAELCs. When these speakers are added to the 134,000,000 West African speakers of Afro-Atlantic English lexifier Creole, we arrive at a global total of some 138,000,000 million speakers. Given the global spread of all of these varieties and their diasporas, Afro-Atlantic English lexifier Creole is by far one of the most widely spoken languages in the world today.

Table 8: Populations of the countries and territories where varieties of Afro-Atlantic English lexifier Creole are spoken in the island Caribbean and the Guianas (source: World Population Review 2020).

AAELC speaking country	Est. population 2019	AELC speaking country	Est. population 2019
Anguilla	15,000	Saba and St. Eustatius	5,000
Antigua and Barbuda	98,000	Saint Kitts and Nevis	53,000
Barbados	287,000	Saint Lucia	183,000

Table 8 (continued)

AAELC speaking country	Est. population 2019	AELC speaking country	Est. population 2019
British Virgin Islands	30,000	Saint Martin	38,000
Dominica	72,000	St. Vincent and the Grenadines	111,000
Grenada	112,000	Suriname	585,000
Guyana	785,000	Trinidad And Tobago	1,395,000
Jamaica	2,949,000	Turks And Caicos Islands	38,000
Montserrat	5,000	United States Virgin Islands	105,000

3 How can we explain the rapid growth of Naija? Failure of current Eurocentric models

According to the dominant linguistic discourses on language acquisition, development, planning, and policy, Naija should be an "unviable", dead or dying language. Instead, the use of Naija is spreading faster than would normally be predicted by rapid natural increase among its speakers, even if it were considered by the "experts" to be a "viable" language. The massive growth of Naija questions many of the colonial assumptions that saturate modern linguistics as well as unsettling and upending the inventory of Eurocentric understandings, processes and structures that are unquestioningly and arrogantly promoted as linguistic "universals" in the "professional" literature. For example, the erroneous presupposition that monolingualism, monoculturalism and mono-identification are the norm rather than the exception in most human societies and during most of human history, makes much of linguistic theory on language acquisition utterly useless to most of humanity. Most Nigerians and other West Africans cannot pretend to be living in monolingual, monocultural and mono-identified societies, with a single "target" language and clear dividing lines between a single "L1" and perhaps a single "L2" as the peoples of much of Europe and the US have been taught to pretend to do by centuries of hegemonic standardization and discursive domination. Rather than replace or extinguish other Nigerian languages, Naija has become an indispensable variety in a plurilingual repertoire of varieties that is deftly used by most Nigerians in their daily lives to weave complex spoken and written texts in their own images and interests.

Dominant discourse on historical linguistics, creolization, language spread and language endangerment read like patriarchal social Darwinian dogma, with linguistic input from mothers trivialized and erased in favor of "universals" of language acquisition, with features in a pool competing like genes for selection in a "survival of the fittest" zero-sum game, with the "competitive" languages of the conquerors and colonizers exterminating and erasing the "unviable" languages of the conquered and colonized, and with Afro-Atlantic colonial era creole varieties being reduced to the status of dialects of their European lexifier languages (for further discussion on each of these points, see Faraclas & Delgado, 2021 and Faraclas, 2012, 2021).

Naija and many of the other Afro-Atlantic English lexifier Creoles and the subaltern cultures associated with them such as Nollywood cinema and Jamaican music leave the underlying fabric of dominant discourses on language development and spread in tatters. This is because, while they lack any official support or recognition, and they have rarely, if ever, been imposed on others by conquest or colonization, they are literally taking the world by storm. Naija and Nollywood are not spreading via artificial and predictable processes of top-down domination in the image and interests of ruling classes, which is the only possibility allowed for in the currently dominant discourses on language development and policy which serve those interests, but instead via organic unpredictable processes of bottom-up conviviality and cosmopolitanism in the image and interest of real communities of people who are presently facing unprecedented attacks on their livelihoods under the neo-colonial world order of corporate globalization.

In the dominant discourse on language development, the more a language is accorded some type of official recognition, the more viable it should be. Throughout its history, Naija has never been given any official status whatsoever by the colonial order that preceded independence or by the neocolonial order that followed. Even though it is the most widely spoken language in terms of sheer numbers and geographic spread in Nigeria, Naija remains to this day unrecognized as either an official or a national language. There is no policy or plan in place to promote Naija as a language or to challenge negative attitudes toward Naija and its speakers. In spite of all of this, however, Naija has become the most vibrant and rapidly growing language in the country. To demonstrate this paradoxical relationship between policy and reality, we need only point out that the few areas where Naija is given some modest formal recognition is in the arts, in advertisements and in public service announcements, where resonating in a maximally effective manner with the maximum number of Nigerians takes precedence over pretense and prejudice inherited from the colonial masters. Unfortunately, the same could be said for nearly all of the other varieties of Afro-Atlantic English lexifier Creole on both sides of the Atlantic.

Standardization is another factor singled out as crucial to the viability of a language in the dominant discourse on language development. But, as is the case for nearly all varieties of Afro-Atlantic English lexifier Creole, there has never been a serious attempt to standardize Naija. There is no official or even generally agreed upon orthography or set of grammar rules for Naija, no comprehensive dictionary compiled, no non-technical grammar available, no word banks of technical terms developed, etc. Because Naija has not undergone much in the way of standardization, when Nigerians speak and write Naija, they have much more control over the language than do speakers of standardized languages. This control over the awesome powers of language is arguably something that Naija shares with most of the rest of the ancestral languages of Nigeria, only a few of which have undergone extensive standardization, and it could be said that it is this power over non-standardized language that has contributed in a significant way to the successful spread of Naija. The license to claim sovereignty over the expressive, creative and signifying powers of language that is still very much alive in West Africa, but which has largely been extinguished in Europe and the US, makes Nigerians feel free, at home and in control when speaking Naija. Once again, Naija challenges the largely unquestioned assumption among linguists that standardization plays a positive and useful role in the spread of language. While, from the Eurocentric point of view that saturates modern linguistics, standardization may be necessary for the top-down imposition of languages of conquerors or colonizers on their subjects, from a non-Eurocentric point of view, standardization may actually be a hindrance to the vitality of bottom-up community based and community controlled language use and spread (Ursulin Mopsus, 2015).

According to dominant discourse on language development, the use of a language in formal education is another key factor which should contribute to its viability. Naija and the other varieties of Afro-Atlantic English lexifier Creole, however, have almost never been promoted as languages of formal education at any level. To the contrary, the classroom has traditionally been the venue for the most systematic, relentless, and violent attack on Naija (and other colonial era creole varieties), which seems to have as its goal its complete erasure from the face of the earth. Teachers try their best (but often fail) to avoid speaking Naija at school and reserve particularly perverse and psychologically damaging punishments for students who do so. Naija is never validated as a language by appearing on chalkboards, whiteboards, classroom walls, on electronic screens or in any of students' reading materials. Despite all of this and contrary to all of the predictions of the "experts", Naija not only continues to survive, but also to thrive. Ironically, outside of the classroom, institutions of formal education, especially universities and secondary schools, have always been significant and strategic epicenters for the use and spread of Naija and some other varieties of Afro-Atlantic English lexifier Creoles in West Africa, such as Ghanaian Pidgin. As far as informal education is concerned, Naija plays a major role in equipping the younger generations to face the challenges of the future. For example, the ritualized insult tradition of "wording" routinely utilizes Naija to strengthen young people's abilities to take control over language and use it to their advantage, while at the same time preparing them to cope with verbal abuse from others (Faraclas et al., 2005).

4 Naija: Language of the future

The neocolonial onslaught propelled by corporate globalization that is currently extinguishing traditional communal sovereignty over land and thus destroying traditional food, housing, employment and social security across Africa, Asia, Latin America and the Pacific, is bringing about dramatic increases in urbanization, movement toward coastal areas, and plurilingualism across the globe (Faraclas, 2005). As we have demonstrated above, it is precisely these factors that have always favored the use and spread of Naija and other colonial era creole languages. It is therefore reasonable to expect that the proportion of the population of Nigeria that speaks Naija will rise significantly from its present level of some 55% (see Table 5) to between 65% and 75% over the next few decades, which for the relatively young population of Nigeria (40% of which is 14 years of age or under) represent the span of one to two generations. This proportional increase to 65% to 75%, coupled with the rapid growth predicted for the national population, means that by 2050, when the number of people in Nigeria is expected to double from some 203 million today to some 411 million, it would not be unreasonable to project that the number of Naija speakers in Nigeria will nearly treble from some 110 million today to some 287 million (70% of the population).

Massive emigration is yet another result of corporate globalization, and it can be expected that the number of speakers of Naija in the diaspora will increase from at least the current estimate of some 2 million to at least 6 million by 2050. Given that Nigerians who emigrate are more likely than others to come from highly urbanized areas near the coast and that Naija has become an important part of the repertoires used among diasporic Nigerians of different linguistic backgrounds, by 2050 there could be some 293 million speakers of Naija in Nigeria and across the globe. This nearly unrivalled increase in speaker numbers in comparison with that of some of the other languages that are currently ranked higher on the "league tables" but which are actually losing speakers, (such as Russian with 258 million and German with 132 million), will almost certainly push Naija even higher up in the rankings of the largest languages in the world (Table 6).

Finally, if we consider the equally high rates of projected growth in other West African nations, both in population numbers as well as in the proportion of the population that speaks non-Nigerian varieties of Afro-Atlantic English lexifier Creole, the present estimate of some 22 million first language, second language and diasporic speakers of these other varieties (Table 7) could reasonably be expected to double to some 44 million by 2050, bringing the total number of speakers of all West African varieties of Afro-Atlantic English lexifier Creole to some 337 million. Adding in an expected increase in the numbers of speakers of Caribbean and other non-West African varieties of Afro-Atlantic English lexifier Creole (Table 8) from some 4 million to some 6 million first language, second language and diasporic speakers by 2050, we arrive at a grand total of some 343 million speakers of all varieties of Afro-Atlantic English lexifier Creole, with a significant and vibrant presence in virtually every single corner of the world. In terms of global rankings, this could put Afro-Atlantic English lexifier Creole on par with Arabic and French by 2050, with only Mandarin, English, Hindi, and Spanish spoken by greater numbers of people (Table 6).

Of course, these estimates of the numbers of Naija speakers in 2050 may prove in the end to be either understated or exaggerated, given the myriad unforeseen factors that could intervene to either quicken or slow down its rate of growth. What is certain is that Naija is already one of the world's most important languages, both in terms of the sheer numbers of its speakers, as well as in terms of the geographic distribution of those speakers, and that this importance will no doubt increase in the future.

References

BBC. 2016. Pidgin – West Africa lingua franca. https://www.bbc.com/news/world-africa-38000387 (posted 16 November 2016, accessed 4 March 2020).

Canagarajah, Suresh. 2012. *Translingual practice: Global Englishes and cosmopolitan relations*. London: Routledge.

Demographia. 2016. World Urban Areas. Archived as PDF April 2016. https://en.wikipedia.org/wiki/List_of_Nigerian_cities_by_population (accessed 1 January 2020).

Dillard, Joey Lee. 1976. *American talk*. New York: Random House.

Ethnologue 2019. SIL International. https://www.ethnologue.com/guides/ethnologue200 (accessed 11 March 2020).

Faraclas, Nicholas. 1991. Laying the groundwork for the linguistic study of Nigerian Pidgin: The pronoun system. In Jenny Cheshire (ed.), *English around the World: Sociolinguistic perspectives*, 509–516. Cambridge: Cambridge University Press.

Faraclas, Nicholas. 1995. They came before the Egyptians: The linguistic prehistory of the Afro-Asiatic languages. In Silvia Federici (ed.), *Enduring Western civilization*, 175–196. London: Praeger.

Faraclas, Nicholas. 1996. *Nigerian Pidgin*. London: Routledge.

Faraclas, Nicholas. 2005. Globalization and the future of pidgin and creole languages. *Journal of Language and Politics* 4(2), 135–164.

Faraclas, Nicholas. 2008. Nigerian Pidgin. In Bernd Kortmann, Edgar W. Schneider, Kate Burridge & Rajend Mesthrie (eds.), *Varieties of English*, 340–367. Volume 3. The Hague: Mouton.

Faraclas, Nicholas. 2012. (ed.) *The question of agency in the emergence of creole languages*. Amsterdam: Benjamins.

Faraclas, Nicholas. 2013. Nigerian Pidgin. In Susanne Maria Michaelis, Philippe Maurer, Martin Haspelmath & Magnus Huber (eds.), *The survey of pidgin and creole languages. Volume 1: English-based and Dutch-based languages*. Oxford: Oxford University Press. https://apics-online.info/surveys/17 (accessed 11 March 2020).

Faraclas, Nicholas. 2021. Identity Politics. In Umberto Ansaldo & Miriam Meyerhooff. (eds.), *Routledge handbook of Pidgin and creole languages*. New York: Routledge/Francis & Taylor.

Faraclas, Nicholas, Lourdes Gonzalez, Magdalena Medina & Wendell Villanueva Reyes. 2005. Ritualized Insults and the African Diaspora: "Sounding" in African American Vernacular English and "Wording" in Nigerian Pidgin. In Susanne Mühleisen & Bettina Migge. (eds.), *Politeness, face, and the social construction of personhood in Caribbean creoles*, 45–70. Amsterdam: Benjamins.

Faraclas, Nicholas & Sally Delgado (eds.). 2021. *Creoles, Revisited: Language Contact, Language Change and Post-colonial Linguistics*. New York: Routledge/Francis & Taylor.

Federal Republic of Nigeria 2006 Population Census. Archived as PDF 5 March 2012. https://en.wikipedia.org/wiki/List_of_Nigerian_cities_by_population (accessed 1 January 2020).

Finney, Malcolm Awadajin. 2013. Krio. In Susanne Maria Michaelis, Philippe Maurer, Martin Haspelmath & Magnus Huber (eds.), *The survey of pidgin and creole languages. Volume 1: English-based and Dutch-based languages*. Oxford: Oxford University Press. https://apics-online.info/surveys/15 (accessed 11 March 2020).

Gilroy, Paul. 1993. *The Black Atlantic*. Cambridge, MA: Harvard University Press.

Holm, John. 1989. *Pidgins and creoles*. Volume 2: *Reference Survey*. Cambridge, UK: Cambridge University Press.
Huber, Magnus. 2013. Ghanaian Pidgin. In Susanne Maria Michaelis, Philippe Maurer, Martin Haspelmath & Magnus Huber (eds.), *The survey of pidgin and creole languages. Volume 1: English-based and Dutch-based Languages*. Oxford: Oxford University Press. https://apics-online.info/surveys/15 (accessed 11 March 2020).
Makoni, Sinfree & Alastair Pennycook (eds.) 2006. *Disinventing and reconstituting languages*. New York: Bristol, UK: Multilingual Matters.
National Bureau of Statistics of Nigeria. 2018. 2017 Demographic Statistics Bulletin. National Bureau of Statistics: Abuja.
Nigerian Diaspora. 2020. The Nigerian Diaspora – #NotShithole. https://www.nigeriandiaspora.com (accessed 1 January 2020).
Parkvall, Mikael. 2007. Världens 100 största språk 2007 [The World's 100 Largest Languages in 2007]. In *Nationalencyklopedin*. Malmo, Sweden: NE Nationalencyklopedin AB.
UNCPD (United Nations Commission on Population and Development). 2018. *Nigeria's country report to the 51st session on Sustainable cities, human mobility and international migration*. New York, 9–13 April 2018. https://en.wikipedia.org/wiki/Demographics_of_Nigeria (accessed 1 January 2020).
UNDESA (United Nations Department of Economic and Social Affairs). 2015.
UNDP. 2018. *National Human Development Report 2018: Achieving Human Development in North Eastern Nigeria*. Abuja: UNDP.
Ursulin Mosus, Diana. 2015. *The attitudes toward Caribbean creole of propertied European descended communities in the Caribbean*. Puerto Rico: University of Puerto Rico PhD dissertation, Rio Piedras campus.
World Population Review. 2020. https://worldpopulationreview.com/countries/ (accessed 11 March 2020).
Yakpo, Kofi. 2013. Pichi. In Susanne Maria Michaelis, Philippe Maurer, Martin Haspelmath & Magnus Huber (eds.), *The survey of pidgin and creole languages*. Volume 1: *English-based and Dutch-based Languages*. Oxford: Oxford University Press. https://apics-online.info/surveys/19 (accessed 11 March 2020).

Christian Mair
Chapter 2
Nigerian Pidgin: Changes in prestige and function in non-Anglophone diasporic contexts

Introduction

Since the end of the Cold War, new currents of migration and the digital revolution have changed the languagescape of Europe and the world, creating new transnational and multilingual spaces. One instance of this development is provided by the spread of Nigerian and other West African varieties of English and their associated English-lexifier pidgins/creoles to areas which have had little or no exposure to them before. Using the case of Germany, this chapter will explore how West African Englishes and pidgins/creoles develop in migration and how new contexts of use change speakers' attitudes towards this part of their linguistic heritage. Studies of linguistic adaptation in migration are necessarily interdisciplinary. The present study will therefore draw on ethnography/cultural anthropology, the sociolinguistics of globalisation and World Englishes studies.[1]

As far as the **ethnographic/anthropological** context is concerned, it has benefited from Appadurai's (1996) model of cultural globalisation. This model proposes five transnational *-scapes* to account for the growing mobility of technological, financial and cultural resources in our contemporary world. Two of them, the *technoscape* and the *financescape*, refer to the technological and economic 'hard-wiring' of globalisation. They provide the essential background to the present study, but will play a minor role in the argument itself. The other three – *ethnoscape*, *mediascape*, and *ideoscape* – are central to an understanding of contemporary West African immigration to Europe. *Ethnoscapes* are shaped by the physical migration of people, with migration being understood in the widest sense, from tourism via longer-term foreign experience such as study abroad

---

[1] This research is funded by *Deutsche Forschungsgemeinschaft* (DFG) through grant MA 1652/12-1 "West African Englishes on the Move: New Forms of English as a Lingua Franca (ELF) in Germany." The author gratefully acknowledges this support. He would also like to thank project team member Dr. Samson Ajagbe for his help with data collection, transcription and the analysis of examples.

or various types of circular migration all the way to permanent resettlement. Although these forms involve rather different degrees of cultural immersion, they all bring about a considerable mobilisation of linguistic and cultural resources. Note, however, that while physical migration of speakers always entails a mobilisation of their cultural resources, it is also very common in the modern world for cultural resources to be mobilised without any major physical movement of their bearers. The two notions of *mediascape* and *ideoscape* serve to capture such movements of cultural and semiotic resources rather than people. Taking the example of Nigerian Pidgin, there are large numbers of people in the world who have gained some familiarity with it not primarily through interaction with its speakers, but in the global mediascape, through channels as diverse as the Nigerian movie industry ('Nollywood'), the music of the late Fela Anikolapo Kuti or the literary works of Chinua Achebe, Wole Soyinka, Ken Saro-Wiwa, Chimamanda Ngozi Adichie, and others.

To complement Appadurai's five *-scapes*, Mair (2018, 2020) has proposed the notion of *languagescape* to account for the specifically linguistic dimensions of cultural globalisation. The present chapter will apply this concept to a – hitherto understudied – empirical test case, namely the West African contribution to the growing multilingualism in contemporary Germany. It will do so using a qualitative ethnographic-linguistic approach in which the starting point of the analysis will be the point of view of the immigrants themselves, as articulated in social-media communication and informant interviews. The study will show:

(i) that the presence of a growing Anglophone immigrant community from West Africa is changing the ethnoscape, mediascape and languagescape of contemporary Germany in small but perceptible ways, and
(ii) that there are rather greater processes of cultural and linguistic accommodation required from the new immigrants themselves.

With regard to the **socio(linguistic)** context, the present research situates itself in the frame of the sociolinguistics of globalisation (Coupland, ed. 2010, Blommaert 2010), which Blommaert defines as a "sociolinguistics of mobile resources and not of immobile languages" (2010: 180). Ties between dialects/varieties, territories and communities are weakened in migration, and nowhere is this more obvious than in the global 'English Language Complex' (McArthur 2003, Mesthrie and Bhatt 2008), where new national standard varieties have long ceased to be the only natural end-point of linguistic emancipation from colonialism (Mair 2013, 2016, 2017).

The relatively rich literature on Nigerian English (e.g. Gut 2004, Alo and Mesthrie 2004, Jowitt 2019) and Nigerian Pidgin (e.g. Elugbe 2004, Faraclas 2004) mostly deals with these languages in their postcolonial African context.

This means that questions which are central to the present study are rarely asked. How, for example, does Nigerian English evolve in the German context, where this well-established second language variety is in frequent contact with German English as a Lingua Franca (ELF) varieties and other native and non-native varieties of English? As regards Pidgin, the data obtained will show that it continues to thrive in the German diaspora. In the medium and long term, this will raise issues of authenticity. For example, what level of fluency is required for German-based second- and third-generation Nigerian immigrants to be considered authentic users? To what extent is Nigerian Pidgin used for in-group communication, and to what extent does it also serve in communication with speakers of English-lexifier pidgins and creoles from Ghana or Cameroon? How does this use across different groups affect the pidgins/creoles? Given rapidly rising immigrant numbers in the recent past, these questions are not just theoretical exercises in contact linguistics, but have practical relevance for tens of thousands of African immigrants and large numbers of Germans interacting with them in institutional and informal contexts.

Before moving on to a survey of recent demographic trends, a few more words are required on the data used. The social-media data have been obtained from the Nairaland web-forum (https://www.nairaland.com/), a globally dispersed community of practice comprising more than 2.3 million members contributing on a wide range of topics.[2] A large part of Nairaland's forum archive has been developed for geographically sensitive corpus-linguistic searches (see Mair 2017: 12–21 and Honkanen 2020 for technical details). In this format, the data have already been used successfully for several studies exploring Nigerians' multilingual language practices on the Web, among them Heyd and Mair's (2014) investigation of "digital ethnolinguistic repertoires" and the important role of Pidgin in them and Honkanen's 2020: 47–69 study of how first- and second-generation Nigerian immigrants in the US use Pidgin alongside other varieties of standard and nonstandard English in their digital communication. The present study will break new ground by focussing on forum members who, on the basis of their user profiles, can be located in Germany, a non-Anglophone environment. The second source of data is interviews with Nigerian immigrants from a wide range of social backgrounds based in and around Freiburg, a mid-sized city situated in the Southwest of Germany. The interviews are conducted in the frame of the research project mentioned in footnote 1 above, which aims to explore the use of West African varieties of English in lingua franca communication in

---

[2] The forum statistics of 2 October 2019 refer to 2,340,040 members and 5,184,771 topics or threads.

Germany, with a view to exploring language contact and linguistic accommodation in migration (see Mair 2018: 62–70 for further details and a discussion of representative extracts from the material). This perspective complements previous research on African immigrants' language use in Germany (Meierkord and Fonkeu 2013, Meierkord, Fonkeu and Zumhasch 2015), which has generally focused on in-group communication.

1 West African immigration to Germany: Current demographic trends

Germany has a considerable history of immigration from Africa (Mazón and Steingröver, eds. 2005) and a sizable number of immigrants today. The internal composition of this group, however, is more fragmented and complex than in the cases of classic post-colonial immigration from Africa found in France and the United Kingdom, the crucial linguistic difference being that – with the exception of Namibia (irrelevant to the present study) – German plays no significant role as a second-language in any of the major African countries of origin and that, as a result, immigrants usually have limited or no fluency in German on arrival. The 'New African Diaspora' (cf. Koser, ed. 2003 and Okpewho and Nzegwu, eds. 2009 for global and Tsagué Assopgoum 2011 for European trends) in Germany is diverse with regard to practically any major social parameter. It comprises well-established academics and professionals as well as refugees with uncertain legal status and economic prospects. It includes people from all postcolonial African language spheres (Anglophone, Francophone, Lusophone) and a wide spectrum of religious beliefs.

A good starting point to study trends in this rapidly changing demographic landscape are census records, in particular the *Ausländerzentralregister* (central register of foreign residents). Figure 1 is based on it and shows steep increases between 2011 and 2019 for Nigeria, Ghana, Cameroon and The Gambia, the four West African countries accounting for most of the immigration from this region. Beyond that, however, there are also significant differences. While there is broad gender parity in immigration from Ghana and Cameroon, males dominate in the case of Nigeria and even more so The Gambia. Note that these figures considerably under-report the size of the relevant communities. Obviously, they do not cover illegal immigrants, but neither do they include first- and second-generation immigrants who have German citizenship.

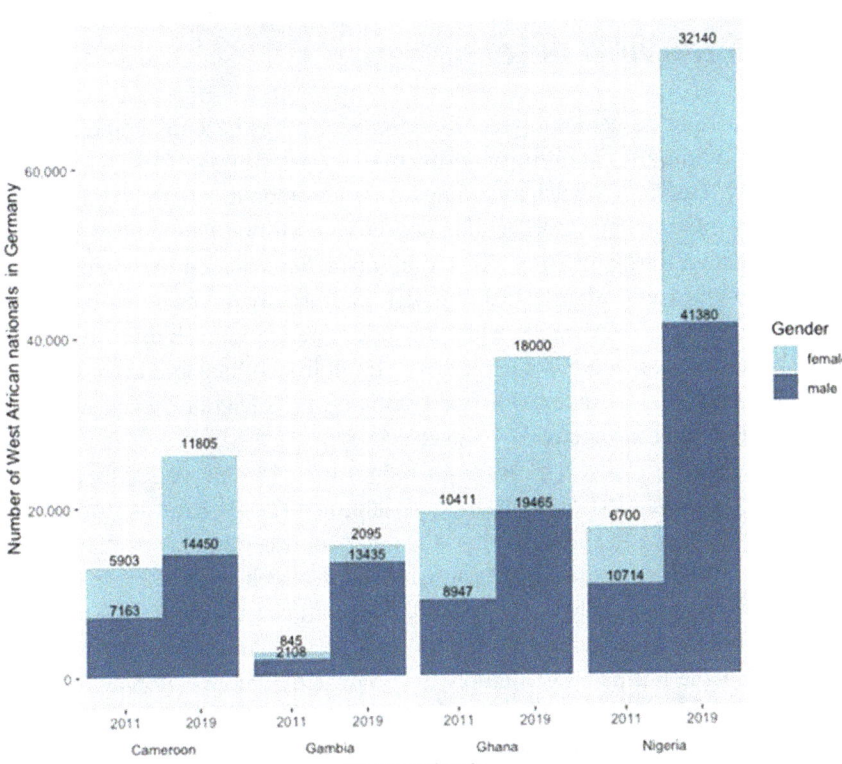

Figure 1: Foreign nationals from four West African countries in Germany – 2011 and 2019.

To illustrate the forms, functions and prestige of (Nigerian) Pidgin in Germany, section 3 will analyse a discussion from the Nairaland forum which lasted about two weeks in January/February 2008 and to which members based in Germany actively contributed. This will be complemented by extracts from the interview transcripts, which occasionally show Pidgin being used even in this relatively formal context but, more importantly, provide rich ethnographic evidence on how speakers themselves assess this part of their multilingual repertoires in the German context. This will be followed by a summary discussion of continuity and discontinuity in the ways in which Pidgin serves its speakers in the different multilingual ecologies of Nigeria and continental Europe.

2 Nigerian Pidgin in Germany: Evidence from computer-mediated communication (CMC) and interview data

Contrary to what its name implies, Nigerian Pidgin has become a creole – and hence the dominant community vernacular – for millions of its speakers in present-day Nigeria. A longish monolingual conversation in Pidgin is thus an unremarkable thing in itself, and yet this not the way we find Pidgin used either in the CMC data of the Nairaland corpus or in interactions among Nigerians in Germany. In both cases, Pidgin is just one part (and usually not even the dominant one) of multilingual repertoires which include Nigerian English and African indigenous languages, and in some cases also input from other varieties of English. Nigerians based in Germany will add German, and sometimes even elements from other European languages, to this mix.

The following analysis of Nigerian Pidgin used in CMC concerns a previously unexplored aspect of the Nairaland data, namely the contributions made by participants based in Germany and the neighbouring German-speaking countries of Central Europe. The database consists of a web-scraped sample of ca. 843 million words of text from the Nairaland forum covering a nine-year period from March 2005 to February 2014. As use of German is an exceedingly rare phenomenon in the Nairaland community, the unwieldy amount of material is an asset in this case. In preparing the data as an offline 'shadow' corpus of the forum,[3] the 3,000 most prolific members were identified automatically on the basis of the number of posts they had contributed to the forum during this period.[4] A considerable number of users provided information about their current place of residence in their profiles. This information was verified for plausibility by brief checks against the content of their posts. Key contributors who did not give relevant information in their profiles were 'located' on the basis of a more thorough reading of their contributions – a strategy which, obviously, did not

---

[3] Offline storage was chosen not only to enhance searchability, but also to safeguard the material in case all or parts of the forum archive might be taken off the Web. This has not happened in the case of www.nairaland.com, but in others. For example www.cameroon-info.net, now a news site without audience participation, used to be a lively forum community providing rich data for the study of Cameroonian English-lexifier Pidgin and Camfranglais, the country's urban slang fusing French and English. An offline shadow corpus of ca. 22 million words covering the years from 2000 to 2008 is still available for research.
[4] Note that this criterion, while simple to manage, is not the only relevant indicator of core membership in the community. Another one, duration and regularity of online presence, could be taken into account, too.

work in all cases. In the end, it was possible to trace about one third of the text produced by the top 3,000 contributors to specific geographical locations at country and sometimes also at city level. This geographically located content produced by some of the most active members of the forum will be referred to as the Nairaland core. The annotation of the original online data may be laborious, but certainly provides extra value. After all, online language use is partly determined by offline geographical location.

What the Nairaland core reveals is three prominent geographical foci of forum activity – Nigeria, the UK, and the US (in that order) – but also the truly global spread of the Nairaland community. Table 1 lists all countries which contributed more than 1,000 posts to the Nairaland core; continental European countries appear in bold print:

Table 1: Number of posts per country contributed to the Nairaland core.

Country	Number of posts
Nigeria	1,163,643
United Kingdom	441,420
United States	427,108
Canada	38,654
Australia	24,787
Sierra Leone	13,297
Slovenia	**11,732**
Malaysia	9,527
South Africa	9,210
Japan	9,058
Jamaica	8,942
Italy	**8,229**
Ghana	7,373
Germany	**6,695**
France	**5,499**
Netherlands	**5,371**

Table 1 (continued)

Country	Number of posts
Egypt	4,403
Cote d'Ivoire	4,344
Spain	**3,290**
United Arab Emirates	3,146
Belgium	**2,623**
India	2,486
Norway	**2,216**
China	2,094
Benin	1,959
Ireland	1,883
Liberia	1,628
Guatemala	1,532
Gambia	1,476
Cuba	1,427
British Virgin Islands	1,251
Macau	1,215
Kenya	1,177
Finland	**1,066**

The top ten contributing cities are: Lagos (404,540), London (215,854), Abuja (85,943), Port Harcourt (61,127), New York City (53,417), Columbus OH (21,916), Chicago (20,530), Enugu (19,484), Washington DC (15,711) and Toronto (14,459).

In order to identify data showing Pidgin and German used alongside each other or even in code-switching, searches were undertaken for the highly frequent Pidgin grammatical markers *na* and *wetin* co-occurring with the German first-person personal pronoun *ich* within a span of 15 words on either side.[5]

---

[5] Other frequent German grammatical morphemes, such as the definite articles *der* or *die*, were used, too. Unlike *ich*, however, they did not identify relevant data with great precision because of homography with standard (*die*) or various kinds of nonstandard (*der*) spellings in English or Pidgin.

Using this procedure, it turned out to be quite easy to identify a few hundred instances of intra-utterance and even intra-sentential code-switching between German and Pidgin in the Nairaland forum. Extracts (1) and (2) are typical examples:

(1) u want learn deutsch abi wetin?
Guten tag!wo bist du?ich warte auf dich. (brutal, 09-07-2009, 11:10 a.m.)
[*You want to learn German, or what? Hello! Where are you? I'm waiting for you.*]

(2) Schatz na only u go fit suck my pinky tongue,shcatz ich liebe dich (jenibayo, 24-01-2010, 6:30 p.m.)
[*Darling, it's only you that will be able to suck my pink tongue, darling I love you*]

Given that the database for the CMC study comprises more than 800 million words, code-switching between Pidgin and German remains an extremely rare phenomenon on the forum overall. On the other hand, if one follows the activities of forum members based in Germany and the other German-speaking countries in Europe, many of them do incorporate some German into their online language repertoire, so that the phenomenon merits sociolinguistic study.

It is probably not an accident that the more extreme examples of linguistic playfulness illustrated above are from the Dating, Meet-up and Romance sections of the forum. In order to ensure that the bawdy humour typical for these sections does not deflect attention from the sociolinguistic analysis of multilingualism on the forum, the following analysis of language shift and code-switching in the full discourse context will be based on a thread with a more serious topic, namely challenges faced by expatriate Nigerians in the work-place.

The thread "For Those Of You Working In Foreign Countries" (https://www.nairaland.com/108313/those-working-foreign-countries) was started by female forum member Blackcat in the Career section of the forum on 25 January 2008 and remained active until 6 February of the same year. It collected 35 contributions from eight different members, among them core users debosky (rank 14), romeo (rank 550) and oziomatv (rank 1,377).[6] In line with forum guidelines, Blackcat launches the topic in (very standard) English, also appropriate to the serious topic of professional advancement:

---

[6] The highest-ranking contributor with a proven knowledge of German is 'Freiburger' (rank 287). His profile makes clear that he is not based in Freiburg in Germany, but in the city of the same name in Switzerland (also known as *Fribourg*), the capital of the eponymous German-French bilingual canton.

(3) How is the working environment like? How do you relate to your colleagues and how do they relate to you?
I work in Europe. I was the only black girl working in the company I work for until recently when another black girl from Brazil was employed. Although in my team I still work alone with whites and an Asian girl, sometimes it's really a competition especially with my American colleague to prove to our boss who is better. Let's compare notes, what are your offices like? (25-01-2008, 8:14 p.m.)

This well-formulated introduction proves a non-starter. After failing to elicit a single response for three days, Blackcat adds a challenge in Pidgin:

(4) Na wao nairalanders so all una wey de abroad wetin una de do there wey no body fit answer abit [abi?] na only drug barons, dish /toilet cleaners full here? (28-01-2008, 6:40 p.m.)[7]
[*Oh-oh, Nairalanders! So what are all of you that are staying abroad doing there not answering? Is it that you are only drug barons, dishwashers and toilet cleaners here?*]

In spite of its potentially insulting content, the switch to Pidgin is intended and received as an appeal to the in-group solidarity of the Nairaland community. Participant Dreloaded responds a mere nine minutes later – in English that is of a more informal kind than the first post:

(5) where in aEurope do you work and what kind of company is it that you're the only black person?
I work as a Biochemist in a Medical Diagnostics Company. We have some black people here, ironically out of us most of the black americans work in the Administrative field while most of the the researchers/scientists/chemist are AfricansNot much competition here. Everyone is doing what they can to survive basically. Although you ahve a few blacks trying to "outwhite" each other, kinda pathetic. (6:49 p.m.)

By 8:03 p.m. debosky has joined the conversation, as the first male participant. Blackcat has specified her place of residence from the very general 'Europe' to

---

[7] All forum posts are given in the original spelling. Layout has occasionally been changed to save space. Visual elements, such as emoticons and photos, have been removed unless they are necessary to make sense of the text.

'Hitlers [sic!] homeland', provoking the follow-up inquiry whether she is talking about Germany or Austria.[8] She, in turn, has consulted Dreloaded's user profile and admits to being confused by the "JYork" given as her place of residence. This is the point in the conversation when the discourse marker *sha* – common in Pidgin, but not restricted to it – is used, bringing in a distinctly Nigerian linguistic element again (though not a switch to fully fledged Pidgin yet):

(6) I sympathize with you sha. Anyway I live in New York aka Jew York.

The particle *sha* highlights the preceding noun phrase, marking it as discourse-relevant topic (Faraclas, 1996: 69, 121, 183): Here it establishes a contrast between 'you' and the speaker ('I') in the following sentence. It is worth recalling at this point that this productive online conversation was 'kick-started' by a mock insult delivered in Pidgin. About half way through the conversation, Blackcat repeats a similar insult in English:

(7) @D-reloaded could it be that most nairalanders are doing dubious businesses?: Hmmm I guess one shouldn't believe all the bullshit they write up in here about been [being?] successful and all that (30-01-2008, 10:13 a.m.)

Formulated in English, the insult cannot be argued away as mere banter and quickly earns Blackcat a reprimand from one-off contributor Tats:

(8) When people don't respond, it is not necessarily that they are doing dubious business. Well, since you did not specify professionals, cleaners and so on can still respond to your post as they also work in companies and have colleagues too.

UK is very multicultural and anyway, for us here, you are likely to find some blacks in our companies at different levels (from managers to cleaners). There are blacks in both my company and client company and many of them are Nigerians. We are 5 in my team (two British, a Portuguese and a Swiss) and all of us get along very well and they do respect me a lot and same for the other Nigerians. (10:28 a.m.)

Since this example shows that the choice of Pidgin instead of English serves as a conversational cue establishing a relaxed and friendly atmosphere, it is worth pointing out that Dreloaded's post also happens to contain one of the rather few

---

[8] The answer is provided at 4:06 p.m. on 3 Feb 2008: "Ich arbeite in Wien [*I work in Vienna*]."

examples of local Nigerian English usage in this conversation: the use of plural forms for what are non-count collective or abstract nouns in International English. Examples mentioned in Alo & Mesthrie (2004: 821) include *advice, aircraft, behaviour, blame, deadwood, equipment, information, personnel* and *underwear.* Blackcat uses *businesses,* which is correct in International Standard English as a plural for the count sense of the word ('an enterprise' or 'a shop'), but not for the abstract sense of 'commercial activity' intended here. Note that Tats uses the internationally correct singular form *business.* Accent variation in World Englishes, variation between British and American English and instances of disputed grammatical usage tend to arouse considerable comment elsewhere on Nairaland. Unlike a shift into Pidgin, however, the use of local Nigerian English variants does not seem to influence the conversational atmosphere.

The first use of German occurs when freelancer (F) joins the conversation, pointing out (in English) that he is based in Germany, too. Blackcat (B) responds partly in German:

(9)   F: I work in Germany and i happen to also be the only black in the company. Some colleagues are a bit funny as they feel too important, but, i must say that there are some nices ones too that are not bothered about the colour. I'm used to it anyway, after having already spent 2 years for a Masters degree in the country. (2:42 p.m.)

B: Wie geht es dir? Wie lange haben sie in Deutschland gewohnt?
[*How are you? How long have you lived in Germany?*]
I guess the biggest problem is that people relate to us based on what they see and not what we have upstairs.

In the Nairaland data such shifts into unexpected languages generally serve two functions. If Blackcat doubted that freelancer was based in Germany, a quick switch into German would be a way to test the claim. Here the shift more likely serves as a polite gesture to establish common ground between two Nairalanders based in the same foreign-language zone. In terms of discourse function, there is a clear division between English and German. The German bit is mostly about politeness and relational work, whereas the serious content of the message is delivered in English. This shows that German is clearly the weaker element than English in Blackcat's repertoire – an impression which is confirmed by Blackcat's shaky use of German address pronouns. She starts off using *dir*, the dative of the informal second-person singular pronoun *du*, but then switches to the polite and distant *Sie* (here misspelled in lower-case) in the second.

German remains part of the multilingual fabric of this forum conversation from this point onwards, and it is interesting to study both the production itself and the language-ideological debate on German. Posting from New York, Dreloaded draws on a wide-spread stereotype and suggests that "German is such an ugly language," to which Blackcat replies that "I completely agree with you but hey I live there."[9] On 2 February (from 10:19 p.m.) freelancer and Blackcat have the following exclusively German exchange:

(10) F: Hallo, ich bin in Deutschland für 3 Jahre. Hat meine Diplom hier und jetzt arbeiten. Ich habe zu leben, in der Ost-, aber nun in den Norden. Wie lange sind Sie schon hier?
[*Hi, I've been in Germany for three years. Have done my diploma here and work now. I have to live, in the East but now to the North* [I had to live in the East but have now moved to the North?]. *How long have you been here?*]

B: Ich bin gerade zwei jahre hier. Nairaland Ich glaube hat viele prolete hier nicht so viel gute mensch sind hier. Was denken Sie?
[*I've been here just two years. Nairaland, I think, has got a lot of proles here not so many good people are here. What do you think?*]

Blackcat uses German here, presumably to insult other Nairalanders with impunity – which is quite a different rhetorical gesture than her mock insult in Pidgin that got the conversation going. Note that both speakers' German is far from perfect. There are portions (*Wie lange sind Sie schon hier? Was denken Sie?*) that are fully correct and idiomatic. Others, however, contain numerous errors and/or instances of structural simplification.[10] The one that will turn out to be important further on in the

---

9 As rather soon after this, Pidgin will become the dominant language in the conversation, a note is order on the use of *there* in "hey I live there." Like all participants in social-media communication, Blackcat has two ways of 'locating' herself: **here** [in Germany], addressing people out **there** in cyberspace; or interacting with people **here** on Nairaland, and telling them about life out **there** in Germany. At this point in the conversation, she has mentally transferred herself into Nairaland, thus establishing the type of close relationship to the other contributors that will prepare the coming shift to Pidgin.

10 The present chapter is not the place to explore this aspect further – except to point out that some of the errors are due to interference from L2 English on L3 German, as in "ich bin in Deutschland für 3 Jahre." The sentence "Ich bin für drei Jahre in Deutschland" happens to be formally correct, but does not fit the present context. It can be paraphrased as 'I am/will be in Germany for a total duration of three years,' whereas what freelancer actually wants to say is that he 'has already been in Germany for three years.' This is also the meaning inferred by Blackcat, who responds – correctly – with "Ich bin gerade zwei [J]ahre hier" (see Mair 2018: 65–70, for further discussion of similar cases).

present conversation is *prolete* 'prole', a form which neither corresponds to the correct singular (*Prolet*) nor to the plural (*Proleten*) required in the context of the utterance.

At this stage, a conversation which started as a serious discussion of workplace racism and general prejudice against Nigerians and Africans in the West is on the brink of turning into entertainment and banter – a development which is helped by the appearance of forum regulars oziomatv and romeo. Like many contributors' pseudonyms, oziomatv is a name with a message. *Ozioma* means gospel in Igbo, and the final two letters (*tv*) in the poster's pseudonym refer to the city of Treviso in Italy, where he lives. Undermining the aspiration expressed in the name, he describes himself as "a 419er"[11] and asks for permission to post, which Blackcat, accepting the joke, grants. Meanwhile romeo, who has consulted machine translation software and found out that Blackcat has insulted Nairalanders as 'liars' and 'proles' in German, uses the same software to defend the community's honour, writing: "Sie sind ein grösserer Lügner von allen und außer Ihnen sind ein Buschmädchen" [riddled with errors, but intended to convey: 'you are the biggest liar of them all and a bush-girl in addition!']. Romeo also gains the upper hand in terms of contents, because he reminds members that, in addition to being a German insult, *prolete* is the trademark of a sports fashion company (https://www.proletesports.com/). After some more banter, Blackcat manages to establish her definition of the term:

(11) B: It is dialect deutsch. The translation sites can't help you with this one. romeo stop chasing Blackcat oh go and look for juliet (I have seen someone with that nickname already) hmmm a word is enough for the wise oh (04-02-2008, 10:17 p.m.)

O: So two of una dey play love with dutch language but use english to deceive members in the forum sey una dey quarel, eehh, ok. I no go put mouth for una case again. (05-02-2008, 10:16 a.m.) [*So the two of you are flirting in German, but use English to deceive members in the forum that you are quarreling. OK, I'm not going to say anything about your case again.*]

R: I know about a fabric called prolete for making sport wears and i am truely using online transaltion for german But you have not answered my questions I have Juliet and thanks for offering yourself though (05-02-2008, 7:14 p.m.)

---

11 The Nigerian name for a person practising a common type of online fraud (see Chiluwa 2009).

In sum, the interactional-sociolinguistic analysis of this forum conversation has revealed three linguistic points of reference:
- a stylistically informal and fairly neutral International Standard English which is appropriate to a web forum such as Nairaland with its global reach,
- Pidgin, which is mostly deployed consciously and skillfully as a conversational cue,
- German, also used consciously as a conversational cue and present as learner varieties of different levels of fluency and even in the computer-generated form.

It seems that in CMC performances of this kind, Nigerians are more ready to 'play' with Pidgin and foreign languages such as German than with 'their own' Standard Nigerian English. To what extent online and offline language use are similar in this regard will be the subject of the second part of this section.

At the time of this writing, the funded phase of the "West African Englishes on the Move" project is entering its third month. This means that data collection is still in progress. The material available so far comprises seven individual interviews and two focus-group interviews amounting to about ten hours of recorded speech. The number of individuals represented is 15 (of whom 10 are male and 5 female). The time of residence in Germany varies between three and twelve years. The group is diverse in terms of immigration history, comprising individuals who have been through the asylum process, with many of the attendant hardships, as well as people who have entered Germany as spouses/dependent family members or on educational visas. For two research partners Pidgin is a native language and used for communication within the family; all others have at least some fluency in it. Attitudes are broadly positive, with Pidgin being considered a welcome linguistic bond uniting Nigerians in the diasporic situation. These are two typical expressions of this sentiment (FG 4, 4:29–4:59):[12]

---

[12] To save space, all transcriptions from the spoken data are given as plain text. Speakers are identified as "I" (= interviewer) and "RP" (research partner(s), numbered as RP 1, 2 etc. in group discussions). Prosodic and other annotation has been removed. The default unit of transcription is the tone group (one tone group per line). Exceptions are successive tone groups which constitute integrated syntactic constructions or logical propositions, in which case brief pauses are indicated by "(.)". Line-numbering follows the original transcription; translations and glosses are not counted. Passages that are the subject of discussion are printed in bold. References are to the number of the text in the project archive, "FG" referring to focus-group discussions and "I" referring to interviews with individuals. Passages within the interviews/focus-group discussions are identified by the time-stamps of the beginning and the end of the passage quoted ("minutes:seconds").

(12) I: May I ask you about your Pidgin English (.) Naija
 RP 3: Ah if na dat one I dey house o [*ah if it's that, I'm ready*]
 I dey Kampe [*I'm good to go*; Kampe = 'strong', 'solid']
 I: But you're not teaching– you're not teaching it to your children
 RP 3: Dat one na street language [*that is street language*]
 RP 1: We don't speak it with the children
 We speak it when we meet our African brothers and sisters outside (.) when we go out

Even one of the native speakers of Pidgin, for whom it would obviously be a language also used around the house, emphasises its mixed and hybrid nature, using a Yoruba word meaning 'blend' (I 5, 5:20–5:50):

(13) RP: The Warri Pidgin English we call it **parapo**
 I: When you speak Pidgin you mix it with your local language
 RP: You get the point
 Most of the Pidgin English we Warri guys speak
 If you go into details they mix it with Urhobo
 I: Okay
 RP: Which kine slang dis guy dey speak na [*what kind of language is this guy speaking?*]
 De guy dey yan **parapo** [*the guy is speaking 'mixed'*]
 Free dat guy [*leave him alone*]
 I: Okay

As far as **use** of Pidgin is concerned, our recorded material is unremarkable. The default language of all interviews, whether carried out by the out-group interviewer (Mair) or the in-group interviewer (Ajagbe), is English. In individual interviews carried out by Ajagbe, Pidgin is used in accordance with the rules of 'in-group' linguistic etiquette, but – in view of the relatively formal situation – probably somewhat more sparingly than in free conversation. In interviews with Mair, Pidgin is hardly used at all, except for purposes of demonstration, when it is the topic of the conversation. The following example of the use of Pidgin is taken from a focus-group discussion in which participants were given twenty minutes' time by themselves about half way through the interview. The outgroup interviewer announces that he has to leave the room for some time and suggests that the participants might either continue their discussion of problems encountered in everyday life in Germany or have a look at a copy of *Lagos: A city at work* (Tejuoso 2007), a lavishly illustrated documentation of contemporary life in Nigeria's metropolis. Given that all three female research partners are Yoruba, the interviewer's departure triggers a shift from English to Yoruba (FG 4, 50: 27–53:04):

(14) I: I'll be back in fifteen minutes and will just leave this running and
              uhm (.) I felt it's a weird book in one way but also interesting
      RP 1:   [reads from p. 9 of the book]: The idea of the Lagos project –
      I: So if you don't want to talk about Germany or if you only want
              to talk about Germany for five minutes
   5   you talk about the book for the rest of
      RP 1:   Okay
      RP 2:   Ijalá [poetry]
      RP 1:   Uhm Eré ọdẹ [Hunter's play]
      RP 2:   Ṣe awon ara ibí n gba ohún wa sí lẹ ni [are we being recorded
              by these people?]
   10 RP 1:   Kí lẹ sọ [what did you say?]
              ẹhn won gba lẹ [yes, we are being recorded]
      RP 3:   wọn gba lẹ [we are being recorded]
      RP 1:   wọn gba lẹ, emí gan gba lẹ [we are being recorded, I am also
              recording it]
      RP 2:   tọ [all right or 'I get it']
   15   Ẹhẹn (.) okay [I see, okay]
      RP 1:   Ki ní a fẹ sọ bayí [what can we say now?]
              The only challenge I have in this country is that I cannot work
              with my Certificate
      RP 3:   Exactly
      RP 2:   Same thing with me
   20 RP 1:   Yea
              I think they – **dem dey feel say our if we dey work say we go
              dey collect moni pass dem**
              [I think they feel that if we are working, we will be earning more
              than them]
      RP 2:   We can compare here with the English-speaking **pass dem**
              [more than them]
   25 RP 1:   That's the way I think (.) that's the way I feel
      RP 2:   Because for them not to recognize our this thing certificate (.)
              mi no really understand [. . . I don't really understand]

Disregarding an isolated *okay* (line 6), the shift back into English occurs between lines 16 and 17. It coincides with a return to the major topic of discussion, life in Germany. Seconds later, there is a shift from English to Pidgin (line 21).

As the outgroup interviewer is absent, mixing English with Pidgin seems unremarkable, a mere reflection of the informal atmosphere of the conversation at this point. Given that the conversation takes place in Germany, and in a semi-formal setting, however, the shift into Pidgin deserves a more detailed analysis in terms of speaker *stance* (Jaffe, ed. 2009).

Stance has been defined as a "public act by a social actor, achieved dialogically through overt communicative means (language, gesture, and other symbolic forms) through which social actors simultaneously evaluate objects, position subjects (themselves and others), and align with other subjects, with respect to any salient dimensions of the sociocultural field" (Du Bois 2007: 163). Inevitably, migration causes heightened linguistic and meta-communicative awareness, intensified here by the fact that languages and communication are the overarching topic of the interview itself. Therefore, let us revisit the short extract turn-by-turn, from the perspective of stance-taking.

After the interviewer has left, the three research partners shift to Yoruba, an unproblematical choice in a situation in which they are 'talking among among themselves'. By taking up one of the previously suggested topics for discussion, the interviewer, while absent physically, is admitted to the conversation at least metaphorically, which is appropriately represented by a shift to English, the default language of the interview. The subsequent switch to Pidgin, however, shows the speaker taking a more complex 'in between' stance. While the English sentence states a fact (that professional qualifications obtained in Nigeria are generally not recognised in Germany), the continuation in Pidgin proposes a subjective and potentially controversial explanation, namely that this is largely motivated by Germans' self-interested desire to keep African immigrants away from high-paying employment. In this particular 'us versus them' constellation, Pidgin becomes a natural choice as a linguistic symbol for the in-group ('us'). If the speaker had switched back to Yoruba, that would have been a return to the 'among ourselves' stance of lines 7 to 16. The stance established by the use of Pidgin, by contrast, leads to situation in which the (absent) interviewer can still feel included in the sense that he will understand what is being said, but also realises that he is cast as part of 'dem' rather than 'us'. In the German context, Pidgin is used to establish a clear-cut line of demarcation between 'dem' and 'us'. In this light, the switching point (*I think* **they- dem** *dey feel*) is significant; in the context of lingua-franca communication English is used to bridge gaps between groups, and potential referents of *they* are more difficult to specify than for Pidgin *dem*.

What is shown by an individual instance of English-Pidgin code-switching in the micro-context of this conversation will ultimately determine the status of the languages in the wider sociocultural field. In the German context, English loses some of the social prestige which it enjoys in Nigeria as a sign of wealth, status and education, but retains or even expands its utilitarian value as a lingua franca. Pidgin, on the other hand, may lose much of its utilitarian value, but will gain in covert prestige – as a powerful way of asserting group identity in an unfamiliar, unsettling, confusing and sometimes hostile environment.

Even if the focus of the present study is on the functional division of labour between English and Pidgin, it should be emphasised that interviewees' multilingual repertoires are more complex, as is shown by the following extract, which shows Yoruba in contact with English, Pidgin, and even German:

(15) RP 2: Oshodi tí yáto ní isin yí [*Oshodi has changed now*]
  RP 3: O ti dí **small London** ní isin yí [*it has become a small London now*]
  RP 2: Ẹ o le gbo ohun ti a n wí (.) a fí ti ẹ bá lowa eyan ti o bá yín tumọ ẹ [*you can't understand what we are saying except you look for someone to translate it for you*] [. . .]
  RP 1: **So** ẹ wo **I beg** [so *that's it,*[13] *please*]
5 RP 2: **At times** ti n bá kán ro [*at times when I think about it*]
  Aná (.) mo ṣí ṣo myth fun NAME laná [*yesterday, I was telling NAME yesterday*]
  RP 3: **In fact** ti n ba kán [*in fact when I sometimes*]
  Mó fi owó atí ọmọ dí yin lẹnu [*can I interrupt you for a moment?*]
  RP 2: Mó ni ki ni koko gán [*what is it exactly?*]
10 Iwe wo lẹ ni kín máká [*why should I be studying?*]
  Believe me I can't further

Line 4 is interesting in that it integrates elements from English (the connector/discourse particle *so*), Yoruba, and Pidgin (*I beg*, archaic in English and hence irrelevant here, but conventionalised in several grammatical and discursive functions in Pidgin, for example the polite imperative (Faraclas 1997: 23)). Other switches also feature sentence adverbs (*in fact*) and fixed expressions (*at times*), but two involve productive syntactic phrases (*small London*) and even clauses. Note, in particular, that the expression *I can't further* represents a level of localised Nigerian English which would be almost certain to cause comprehension problems in a German ELF environment.

The following two brief switches into German feature a discourse particle (*ach so* 'I see' [literally: interjection expressing surprise, followed by adverb *so*])

---

13 Literally: Take a look.

and the noun *Landratsamt*, the official name of the local-government administrative head office. As the bolded passages show, this passage also features pervasive code-switching between Yoruba and English.

(16)   RP 3:   **No** (.) bi wọn ti ẹ ṣe tu wá **multitalented** ti ẹ tu ni [*no, as she's even multitalented I mean*]
             RP 1:   **Ach so**
             RP 3:   Wọn ṣe **beadi** (.) wọn we gele [*she makes beads, she does headties*]
             RP 1:   Wọn lé [*she can't*]
5   RP 3:   Wọn **make-up** [*she does make-up*]
             RP 1:   Wọn ṣe **make-up** ní ibí ba yi [*she does make-up here*]
             RP 3:   Wọn ṣe irún [*she makes hairdo*]
                     wọn le **anything** [*she can do anything*]
             RP 1:   Yea (.) it's true
10   Ṣe iru awa ba yi iru emi ba yi ti o jẹ pe mi o
                     [*it's people like us people like me that*]
                     leyin pe mo lọ **school** [*apart from going to school*]
             RP 2:   Mo kan má n ro ni nipe ki gan ní [*I used to think about it that what is it really*]
             RP 3:   O yẹ ki iru NAME le ṣiṣẹ ni **Landratsamt** because iṣẹ ijọba ni wọn ṣe
                     [*people like NAME should be able to work in Landratsamt because she has worked in the civil service government work*]

As this part of the group discussion took place in the absence of the interviewer, the choice of languages is not different from what could have been observed in Nigeria – with the exception, of course, of the two brief switches into German.

    As has been pointed out, migration promotes a heightened sense of linguistic awareness. Among other things, this is shown by the following attempt to make sense of of the sociolinguistic variability of German through the lens of Pidgin. In several interviewees' experience, Pidgin is a street language and, as a mixed language, is a natural choice for informal lingua-franca communication across ethnic and linguistic boundaries. Our research partners are aware that the German they learn in the classroom is sometimes rather different from what they encounter in naturalistic settings. Relevant dimensions of variability are the widespread standard-dialect continua and various forms of simplified learner varieties spoken by other immigrants. A wide gap between the standard and a particular regional dialect will often lead to situations in which the Nigerian learner of German will be understood when asking a question, but may not be able to interpret the answer because of a strong regional accent and numerous lexical and grammatical deviations from Standard German. This explains why one research partner comes to the following conclusion (FG 4, 50:20):

(17) ORP 3: I think the the German has Pidgin also [. . .] street street Deutsch

Needless to add, the relation between Pidgin and (Nigerian) English is not the best template to understand the dynamics of German standard-dialect continua. On the other hand, the category *street Deutsch*, based on the interviewee's personal experience with German, may work better to come to terms with the various simplified varieties of German used in communication between native speakers and foreign learners or among foreigners themselves.

It seems worth mentioning a specifically 'diasporic' function of Pidgin in the German environment which – given its wide currency – it could not perform in Nigeria itself, namely that of a secret code (FG 4, 48:22–49:02):

(18) I: Is it useful in Germany Pidgin
      RP 2: Yeah it's useful
             For example I have a colleague at work
             She works in the kitchen in the Speisesaal[14]
   5   You know I'm Pflege [*nursing*, i.e. 'I'm part of the nursing team']
             She works in you know so any time we want to gossip we don't speak English so that the other people will not understand
             Because some patients understand English
             And some of the Pflege too they understand English
  10   So when we start speaking even if we (.) even ask us what language are you speaking
             They pick some English words but they cannot put them together (.) don't understand what we are saying (.) so at times it's useful

---

14 'Dining hall'; the speaker uses a spelling pronunciation of the initial cluster (/sp/) instead of the correct /ʃp/.

When asked, most of our research partners confirmed that they were aware of Pidgin being used in other West African countries (FG 1, 56:05–57:15):

(19) I: [. . .] say if you meet people from Ghana or The Gambia
       Would you speak English or Pidgin to them (.) or from Cameroon
   RP 1: It depends
   RP 2: When you know they are not from Nigeria you preferably speak
5   English
       But there are some who mixed up with Nigerians
       And they really speak Pidgin too
   RP 3: Most especially the Cameroonians
   RP 1: Some of them they don't speak English (.) they learnt only Pidgin
10 I: Cameroonians
   RP 1: Yea most of the Cameroonians I've seen so far
   RP 3: Because Pidgin is really easy (.) English –
   RP 1: Like English is difficult for them
       We say German is difficult
15   English is also difficult
       Pidgin is very much comfortable for them to express themselves
   I: Is it the same kind of Pidgin
       When a Cameroonian speaks Pidgin do you understand them
   RP 2: Yes (.) they learn from Nigeria
20 RP 1: It's easy but quite different
       [*several seconds of overlapping talk not transcribed*]
   RP 2: Yea in Nigeria if you go to Warri
       They speak Pidgin there and their Pidgin is real Pidgin
       Konk Pidgin [*authentic Pidgin*]
       That's where the Pidgin was created

In the course of the project's research, we hope to explore the possible role of West African Pidgin (Englishes) as in-group lingua francas among African immigrants. This is not merely a linguistic issue, but also bears on the question of how an extremely heterogeneous group of recent immigrants and sojourners – different in language and ethnic identity, in nationality, in education, social class and religion and, not least, in Anglophone or Francophone (post-)colonial allegiances – can reach out across all these boundaries in their new environment, build communities and create a sense of belonging.

3 Conclusion

The present chapter has studied a specific example of a world-wide trend that Mufwene has identified as the central (socio)linguistic consequence of globalisation:

> To be sure, higher living standards and regional wars have increasingly contributed to population movements and contacts, especially through the free relocation of individuals or families, through tourism, deportations, and refugeeism. [. . .] these migrations have borne on the vitality of languages – both those of the indigenous populations and those [of] the migrants – in various ways, constantly changing the 'linguascape' (or the spatial distribution of languages) of the world. (Mufwene 2010: 35f.)

For Nigerians settling in Germany, the traditional African languages they bring with them will lose much of their status as community languages and may survive as family languages for some time in favourable circumstances. English, as the global lingua franca, is a useful asset for immigrants in Germany.

It is beyond the scope of this chapter to explore the extent to which the promise of English is fulfilled for the Nigerian migrants interviewed, but a few comments on this topic are necessary. Obviously, Anglophone African immigrants have advantages over Francophone ones and immigrants from Syria or Afghanistan, many of whom do not speak English fluently. The promise of English referred to above, however, goes beyond mere success in basic lingua-franca communication. After all, English is widely seen as key to upward social mobility, economic success and participation in the attendant consumer lifestyle – both in immigrants' countries of origin and in Germany. This part of the promise of English tends to be fulfilled for those migrants destined for the academic and professional domains. For all others, including those with academic and professional qualifications obtained in Nigeria, however, immediate entry into their preferred fields of employment is blocked – either because qualifications obtained abroad are not recognised or because advanced competence in German is required for employment. In those domains of work which tend to be open – from the restaurant kitchen briefly referred to above to the care for the elderly (which employs several of our research partners) – fluency in English is not as much of an asset.

Within this wider context of multilingual communication, the focus of the present chapter has been on Pidgin. Using CMC and interview data, it has looked at the role that Pidgin plays in the multilingual repertoires of Nigerian immigrants to Germany. In this diasporic context, Pidgin retains a high symbolic value as an expression of immigrants' social and cultural identity, as has emerged both from the CMC and the interview data. In addition, Pidgin has utilitarian potential as a lingua franca used alongside English, but in different communicative contexts and within a more restricted group of people, namely the speakers of the various English-lexifier pidgins and creoles spoken along the West African coast, from The Gambia and Ghana in the West to Cameroon and Equatorial Guinea in the East. The data analysed so far are insufficient to explore this potential in depth, but they make clear in which direction further research must proceed.

Nigerian immigrants to Germany are faced with two challenges, (i) finding their place in their new country of residence and (ii) defining their place in a very heterogeneous 'Afro-German' community. As for the first challenge, a high degree of fluency in German is essential for full participation (at least in the long-term) and fluency in English, essential in the short term, will retain some value also in the long term. With regard to the second challenge, several research partners have pointed out that they feel a sense of general solidarity with all black people they encounter, which, for example, manifests itself in the fact that they tend to acknowledge black strangers they meet in the street with a brief greeting. More lasting bonds tend to be established along ethnolinguistic (e.g. 'Igbo', 'Yoruba'), national (e.g. 'Nigerian', 'Ghanaian'), religious (e.g. 'Christian', 'Muslim') or ex-colonial ('Anglophone', 'Francophone') allegiances. In contemporary West Africa, these various allegiances cut across each other in complex ways. It is definitely an advantage of Pidgin that it has the potential to reach out across many of these boundaries.

From a German 'host-country' perspective, the English Nigerians bring with them is an "interim lingua franca" (Wilson 2021: 221). Eventual fluency in German is key to full participation in German society, but English will open many doors in the transitional period that is needed for competence in German to build up. German institutions should recognise immigrants' competence in English as an asset which can be built on rather than an obstacle to integration. Anglophone immigrants, by contrast, need to be aware that the relative comfort of being able to communicate with some Germans in English is not a long-term substitute for understanding what is going on in German social life at large.

In spite of a strong media tradition of complaint about the growing number of English borrowings ('Anglizismen') and mixing of English and German ('Denglish'), contemporary Germany has been described as an environment increasingly friendly to English (Hilgendorf 2007, 2010). Fluency in English among the country's political, economic and educational elites is high, as it is among large segments of the general population, particularly in urban regions. The use of ELF has been increasing not only in international contexts, but also within the country itself, which Mair (2019: 20) takes as justification to claim that English is the only language apart from Standard German to carry open prestige on the national level. Referring specifically to Berlin, Fuller has argued that it has become a "multilingual city which has German as the everyday language for public interactions, but caters to speakers of prestigious international languages, especially English" (2015: 156). Fuller's observation is correct, but what still needs to be confirmed is whether this new openness to English is restricted to Standard English spoken in prestigious accents such as British R.P. and General American, or whether it extends to all Englishes – even if, as is the case with Nigerian English – they come with unfamiliar second-language accents and some unfamiliar words and expressions. While Nigerians in Germany have every reason to maintain a strong investment in English, to what extent they are interested in maintaining the salient features of a specifically Nigerian variety remains an open question. American and British norms of usage generally prevail in Germany, and will no doubt exert some pressure on Anglophone immigrants coming from other backgrounds.

References

Alo, Moses. & Rajend Mesthrie. 2004. Nigerian English: Morphology and syntax. In Bernd Kortmann & Edgar W. Schneider (with Kate Burridge, Rajend Mesthrie, Clive Upton) (eds.), *A handbook of varieties of English*, vol 2, 813–827. Berlin: Mouton de Gruyter.

Appadurai, Arjun. 1996. *Modernity at large: Cultural dimensions of globalization*. Minneapolis: University of Minnesota Press.

Blommaert, Jan. 2010. *The sociolinguistics of globalization*. Cambridge: Cambridge University Press.

Chiluwa, Innocent. 2009. The discourse of digital deceptions and '419' emails. *Discourse Studies* 11, 635–660.

Du Bois, John W. 2007. The stance triangle. In Robert Englebretson (ed.), *Stancetaking in discourse: Subjectivity, evaluation, interaction*, 137–182. Amsterdam: Benjamins.

Elugbe, Ben. 2004. Nigerian Pidgin English: Phonology. In Bernd Kortmann & Edgar W. Schneider (with Kate Burridge, Rajend Mesthrie, Clive Upton) (eds.), *A handbook of varieties of English*, vol. 1, 831–841. Berlin: Mouton de Gruyter.

Faraclas, Nicholas. 1996. *Nigerian Pidgin*. London: Routledge.

Faraclas, Nicholas. 2004. Nigerian Pidgin English: Morphology and syntax. In Bernd Kortmann & Edgar W. Schneider (with Kate Burridge, Rajend Mesthrie, Clive Upton) (eds.), *A handbook of varieties of English*, vol 2, 828–853. Berlin: Mouton de Gruyter.

Fuller, Janet M. 2015. Language choices and ideologies in the bilingual classroom. In Jasone Cenoz & Durk Gorter (eds.), *Multilingual education: Between language learning and translanguaging*, 137–158. Cambridge: Cambridge University Press.

Gut, Ulrike. 2004. Nigerian English: Phonology. In Bernd Kortmann & Edgar W. Schneider (with Kate Burridge, Rajend Mesthrie, Clive Upton) (eds.), *A handbook of varieties of English*, vol 1., 813–830. Berlin: Mouton de Gruyter.

Heyd, Theresa & Christian Mair. 2014. From vernacular to digital ethnolinguistic repertoire: The case of Nigerian Pidgin. In Veronique Lacoste, Jacob Leimgruber & Thiemo Breyer (eds.), *Indexing authenticity: Sociolinguistic perspectives*, 244–268. Berlin: De Gruyter.

Hilgendorf, Suzanne K. 2007. English in Germany: Contact, spread, and attitudes. *World Englishes* 26, 131–148.

Hilgendorf, Suzanne K. 2010. English and the global market: The language's impact in the German business domain. In Helen Kelly-Holmes & Gerlinde Mautner (eds.), *Language and the market*, 68–80. London: Palgrave-Macmillan.

Honkanen, Mirka. 2020. *World Englishes on the web: The Nigerian diaspora in the United States* (Varieties of English Around the World). Amsterdam: Benjamins.

Jaffe, Alexandra (ed.). 2009. *Stance: Sociolinguistic perspectives*. Oxford: Oxford University Press.

Jowitt, David. 2019. *Nigerian English*. Berlin: De Gruyter Mouton.

Koser, Khalid (ed.). 2003. *New African diasporas*. London: Routledge.

Mair, Christian. 2013. The World System of Englishes: Accounting for the transnational importance of mobile and mediated vernaculars. *English World-Wide* 34, 253–278.

Mair, Christian. 2016. Beyond and between the Three Circles: World Englishes research in the age of globalisation. In Elena Seoane & Cristina Suárez-Gómez (eds.), *World Englishes: New theoretical and methodological considerations*, 17–36. Amsterdam: Benjamins.

Mair, Christian. 2017. Crisis of the 'Outer Circle'? – Globalisation, the weak nation state, and the need for new taxonomies in World Englishes research. In Markku Filppula, Juhani Klemola, Anna Mauranen & Svetlana Vechinnikova (eds.), *Changing English: Global and local perspectives*, 5–24. Berlin: Mouton de Gruyter.

Mair, Christian. 2018. Stabilising domains of English-language use in Germany: Global English in a non-colonial languagescape. In Sandra C. Deshors (ed.), *Modeling World Englishes*, 45–75. Amsterdam: Benjamins.

Mair, Christian. 2019. English in the German-speaking world: An inevitable presence. In Raymond Hickey (ed.), *English in the German-speaking world*, 13–30. Cambridge: Cambridge University Press.

Mair, Christian. 2020. World Englishes in cyberspace. In Daniel Schreier, Marianne Hundt & Edgar Schneider (eds.), *The Cambridge handbook of World Englishes*, 360–383. Cambridge: Cambridge University Press.

Mazón, Patricia & Reinhild Steingröver (eds.). 2005. *Not so plain as black and white: Afro-German culture and history 1890-2000*. Rochester, NY: University of Rochester Press.

McArthur, Tom 2003. World English, Euro-English, Nordic English. *English Today* 19 (1). 54–58.

Meierkord, Christiane & Bridget Fonkeu. 2013. Of birds and the human species – communication in migration contexts: English in the Cameroonian migrant community in the Ruhr area. In Nils-Lennart Johannesson, Gunnel Melchers & Beyza Björkman (eds.), *Of butterflies and birds, of dialects and genres: Essays in honour of Philip Shaw* (Acta Universitatis Stockholmiensis/Stockholm Studies in English, 104), 271–287. Stockholm: University of Stockholm.

Meierkord, Christiane, Bridget Fonkeu & Eva Zumhasch. 2015. Diasporic second language Englishes in the African communities of Germany's Ruhr area. *IJEL* 5 (1). DOI:10.5539/ijel.v5n1p1 (accessed 22 November 2019)

Mesthrie, Rajend & Rakesh M. Bhatt. 2008. *World Englishes: The study of new varieties*. Cambridge: Cambridge University Press.

Mufwene, Salikoko. 2010. Globalization, Global English, and World English(es): Myths and facts. In Nikolas Coupland (ed.), *The handbook of language and globalization*, 31–55. Malden, MA: Blackwell.

Okpewho, Isidore & Nkiru Nzegwu (eds.), 2009. *The New African diaspora*. Bloomington IN: Indiana University Press.

Tejuoso, Olakunle. 2007. *Lagos: A city at work*. Lagos: Glendora Books.

Tsagué Assopgoum, Florence. 2011. *Migration aus Afrika in die EU*. Wiesbaden: VS Verlag für Sozialwissenschaften.

Wilson, Guyanne. 2021. Language use among Syrian refugees in Germany. In Edgar W. Schneider & Christiane Meierkord (eds.), *World Englishes at the grassroots*, 211–232. Edinburgh: Edinburgh University Press.

Francis O. Egbokhare
Chapter 3
The accidental lingua franca: The paradox of the ascendancy of Nigerian Pidgin in Nigeria

Introduction

Language is emblematic of the stability, transitions and transformations in society. The nature and structure of society, and its fundamental principles of culture generate social and interactional networks which manifest in attitudes that are in turn mirrored as ideological currents and templates for identity formation. Human societies are continuously being dynamized by socioeconomic, political and technological forces. These forces have implications for the perception and image of self thereby determining identities. Power relations affect the fortunes of a language. The power position of a people and consequently their language is determined by socio-political and historical forces (Liberson, 1982). The profile of a language therefore, depends on dominance in culture, science and technology and education among other things.

The contending ideologies in society are sometimes replicated as linguistic choices and behaviour. It follows therefore that by giving accurate interpretations to the language use patterns, not merely as purely quantitative and qualitative linguistic expressions, but also in terms of deeper currents and movements in society, we may in fact provide a better explanation of socio-political forces underlying the linguistic realities. If we follow this line of thinking, it will mean that there are non-linguistic concomitants of socio-political forces and by understanding them, we can better elucidate what we see ordinarily as attitudes and choices forced upon speakers of a language as part of a larger ideological unity. Consequently, we may be able to connect the apparently disparate events in popular culture, politics, social movements and language attitudes, acquisition and use patterns in terms of deeper ideological unity. What would the mixing of language in popular culture and language, code switching, mixing and language interlarding, as well as syncretism and hybridizing in arts and fashion tell us as a prevailing ideological bent? There would seem to be three contending ideologies dominant in Nigerian society. We may represent these as negation, negritude and adaptation. Pidgin represents the ideology of integration, adaptation and convergence, an amalgam of tradition and modernity, an aspiration for glocalization.

Negritude is reflected in the arguments for conservatism, ethnoreligious revivalism while negation drives the tendency that promotes the emergence of English as first language and promotion of colonial culture. The explosive spread of NP is evidence of the predominance of the ideology of convergence and integration. Convergence or adaptation is a youth phenomenon promoted by social media and popular culture. The ascendancy of pidgin in the Nigerian space may therefore be seen as an ideology of accommodation. The pidgin identity defines a liberal identity, while the language is simply emblematic of both conditions. Only languages with the capacity, resources and affiliations to the new media, ideology and identity would benefit from the new digital environment. Nigerian Pidgin provides the only credible language in the Nigerian space.

Language may be used to project identity, define boundaries and thereby serve exclusionary and inclusionary purposes. Social identity theory offers some perspectives in terms of linguistic concomitants of identities and identity formation. The whole idea of identities is built on inclusion of the in-group against the backdrop of negation of the other. Tajfel (1978) introduces the concept of secure and insecure identities as cognitive alternatives. It is opined that "In insecure situations, dominant groups regard their superiority as legitimate and tend to intensify the existing differences to maintain their psychological distinctiveness and resulting positive identity. This intensification of differences is usually manifested by a heightened sense of identity amongst the dominant groups and increased discrimination against minority outgroups. For a minority group, it may manifest as rejection of subordinate status leading to efforts to improve status and generate positive identity through social creativity, social competition and social mobility (Tajfel & Turner, 1986: 19–20). The notions of soft and hard boundaries may be culled up to emphasize the tendency for ethnic boundaries to reject or permit assimilation or integration. Ethnic boundaries in Nigeria are hard. Citizenship is derived from ethnicity and the allocation of political constituencies, privileges and advantages are derived from ethnic membership.

Cultural capital and linguistic capital relate to advantages and benefits that accrue to speakers of a major language such as prestige, honour, educational advantages, etc. Speaking the right language is a form of capital investment which can consolidate and enhance one's credibility in a non-material sense (Craith, 2007). The ideological system, the foundation principle and fundamental component of a group's culture can be conceived as its core value. A language can become a core value of a culture if it serves as its instrument of communication and solidarity (Smolicz, 1983: 75–77). Critical to understanding the reasons for the spread and negative attitudes to NP is the fact that it has no cultural capital, although it has extensive linguistic capital. NP has no ethnic affiliation, that is, it is ethnically neutral and no identifiable geopolitical territory, therefore no political constituency around which it can serve as a core value for identity, solidarity and patronage. Whereas this characteristics of pidgin reinforces its negative attitude and non-recognition by government, because it is a no-man's language it serves well as a catalyst for its spread because it is not perceived as being in competition with indigenous languages.

Diversity, globalization and ICTs, especially social media provide the context for the spread of NP. Diversity has created the need for a lingua franca, globalization on its part has created a liberal, democratic ideology in negation of prevailing ideologies of resistance and dis-integration. ICTs, Mobile Phone, Radio and social media provide new patterns of social connections. It was the association of NP with popular culture, comedy, music, Nollywood and through these the linkage with mainstream youth movements of protest, later hip hop, and rap that tipped Pidgin. The pop stars, Fela Kuti destigmatized and transformed pidgin into a "cool" language. Driven by the ideology of syncretism, hybridization, adaptation and convergence and a need for a national identity, Pidgin became a natural candidate in a market of linguistic multitudes. One other area of digital influence on language is the area of the contribution of technology to common parlance and the popularization of hitherto technical terminologies. There is a widening convergence between the formal and informal spaces and the creation of a common pool of lexical items from which languages draw freely to enrich their repertoire. The permeability of NP to lexical and grammatical borrowing and adaptation has made it an interlanguage, a sociocultural bridge as well as a transactional resource.

1 The paradox of the ascendancy of pidgin in the Nigerian space

What do we mean by the ascendancy of pidgin in Nigeria and why is this a paradox? Pidgin has become a lingua franca across social, geopolitical and socioeconomic spaces. It has gained more functions in defining a Nigerian youth identity and characterizes an emerging ideology of nationalism. In this regard, Nigerian Pidgin is more than a linguistic phenomenon, it defines a consciousness. It is an accidental lingua franca because it is not recognized in the laws. It is stigmatized and discriminated against, notwithstanding, it has gained enormous status.

Nigerian Pidgin studies generally agree that there is a negative attitude towards the language (Agheyisi, 1983; Elugbe and Omarmor 1991; Jubril, 1995). In fact, the status of pidgin as a full-fledged language is a matter for debate. This is attested to by the reference to it as 'broken', bastardized and marginal variant of English. The lack of official recognition and distinguished mention in the Nigerian language policy and laws is seen as the ultimate evidence of the negative attitude towards it. Some other reasons are: 1. Its perceived negative influence on the learning of English; 2. Its association with so-called marginal social class and illiterate population; 3. Lack of accepted standard variety and orthography.

The paradox comes from two factors. First, the fact that Nigerian Pidgin is doing everything that it is not expected to do. In spite of all the baggage associated with it, including, its exclusion from the formal school system, Nigerian Pidgin has moved from a linguistic underdog to a top dog. It is a stigmatized language that is now regarded as "cool", a language without obvious association with formal business becoming the dominant language of advertising and radio broadcast. In addition, it is a language without political capital which is now functioning as the most credible language for national political campaigns and discourse. Although it is not used in teaching and formal education it is dominant in interactions in tertiary institutions and is preferred for public education. Pidgin confers no economic advantage as a language of a so-called marginal group. Notwithstanding, it is displacing other languages with all the perquisites of power and influence. NP has spread to new domains, new territories and spaces, contrary to received wisdom.

Second, all that is said to be wrong with pidgin is everything that is right with it. The very reasons adduced for its stigmatization and negative attitude towards it are the ones responsible for its increasing profile. These are: a. its relationship with English and Nigerian Languages; b. its association with a so-called marginal group; c. the very fact that it lacks a prescribed standard variety as well as official government spelling. This last point is very significant to the extent that the lack or official spelling and formal regulatory control of NP not only democratizes access but enhances participation, by limiting the tyranny of being regimented to formal situations and constrained to a social class. Absence of a standard enhances innovation, linguistic production and mass participation in shaping the language.

The idea that there is no standardized orthography may in fact require modification for two reasons. First, Nigerian English is undefined and is as yet uncodified. Notwithstanding, scholars have accepted as a matter of course its existence. Second, there is an orthographic practice in Pidgin that has emerged from crowd wisdom and participation enabled by social media. It is left for scholars to find it out and accept its reality instead of forcing a particular spelling on it. The fact that intelligibility and communication is not undermined by orthographic flexibility points to a convention and practice. The NP situation is a classic case of what happens when users of a language take over the formal side of language development from so-called experts.

The lack of official recognition by government is mocked by the deployment of the language by the same government as the language of mass mobilization, public education and youth engagement. The language is fast assuming the rallying point of national consciousness and identity. As a matter of fact, the reality of the Nigerian Languages policy shows that there is no value to the recognition of any language by Nigerian government. It cannot therefore be the case that the lack of mention for pidgin in the laws is something to worry about. The real area of exclusion of pidgin worthy of mention is the fact that it is not used in the education process. This is because academics still treat is as a mere exotic specimen for research.

2 Nigerian linguistic space

Let us begin with what we now generally know about pidgins. Although popular beliefs may lead one to think that pidgins are restricted codes and marginal languages, studies have shown that we cannot circumscribe speakers of pidgins to a lower social class, not even at their points of origin, although recent history of slavery may mislead one into such faulty assumptions. We also know that
a) Pidgins can develop a considerable amount of stability and complexity.
b) Simplification, i.e. greater grammatical regularity is confused with impoverishment, i.e. lack of referential and non-referential quality.
c) Substantial changes in meaning and pronunciation occur in the lexical items from the originating languages. The way the words are used are often very divergent from their meanings in the original language.
d) The fact that a substantial part of the vocabulary of the English language comes from several other languages in the world does not lead one to conclude that English is a pidgin.
e) The use of expressions such as English-based pidgin or Spanish-based pidgin assumes a principal originating language spoken by the socially dominant group. This ignores the "mixed or compromise character of pidgin lexicon" and erroneously assumes that the lexicon is the foundation of a language (Mühlhäusler 1986).

The linguistic ecology of a multilingual setting is always changing, even if imperceptibly. Where the dynamic forces endure for a sustainable length of time, it is easy to identify notable currents and movements. However, observation of change and their analyses may be hampered by absence of reliable quantitative data on a significant scale over a period of time. Such data reveal the sociolinguistic concomitants of forces in different milieus across epochs. The absence of national census data on Nigerian linguistic behaviour proves a limitation to the credibility of our conclusions. We therefore are constrained to rely heavily on anecdotal and inferential evidence and projections of qualitative studies by credible linguists.

Hansford *et. al.* (1976) puts the number of languages in Nigeria at 500. English is the official language being the language of the bureaucracy, formal/organized business, education and governance. Arabic and French are the two foreign languages. The remaining languages can be classified as major, state and local languages based on their status as dominant languages, their territorial spread and population of speakers. Thus, we have three major languages made up of Hausa, Yoruba and Igbo, thirteen state languages, over forty-four local languages and numerous others unclassified. Nigerian Pidgin is neither named as a Nigerian language nor is it represented in the linguistic map in addition to being ignored in official documents. However, in Glottolog, it is captured as ISO 639-3. If it is not a language, one wonders what it is.

The North West Zone has the highest level of diversity with 176 languages. Bauchi is the most linguistically diverse state accounting for about 80 languages. The North East is the next most diverse area with about 133 languages followed by the North Central which has 125 languages. This is very interesting because of the dominance of Hausa which gives people the impression of a monolithic North. The South West and South East have about 8 and 7 languages respectively while the South-South (Niger Delta) has 116 languages. The number of languages in Northern Nigeria is about 439 as against about 131 in the south. The five most diverse states in Nigeria are Bauchi (80), Plateau (74), Taraba (54), Adamawa (46) and Kaduna (43). Apart from Edo (30) and Cross Rivers (34), Southern Nigeria states are fairly linguistically homogenous. It is necessary to note that the figures do not represent the fact of urban diversity and the existence of linguistic enclaves. About 90% of Nigerians can be reached with Pidgin, English, Hausa, Yoruba and Igbo.

2.1 Nigeria's language policy

The policy may be collated from the National Policy on Education (1981) and the language provision of the respective Nigerian constitutions. The policy recognizes the following five categories of language (Bamgbose, 1992, 2000):

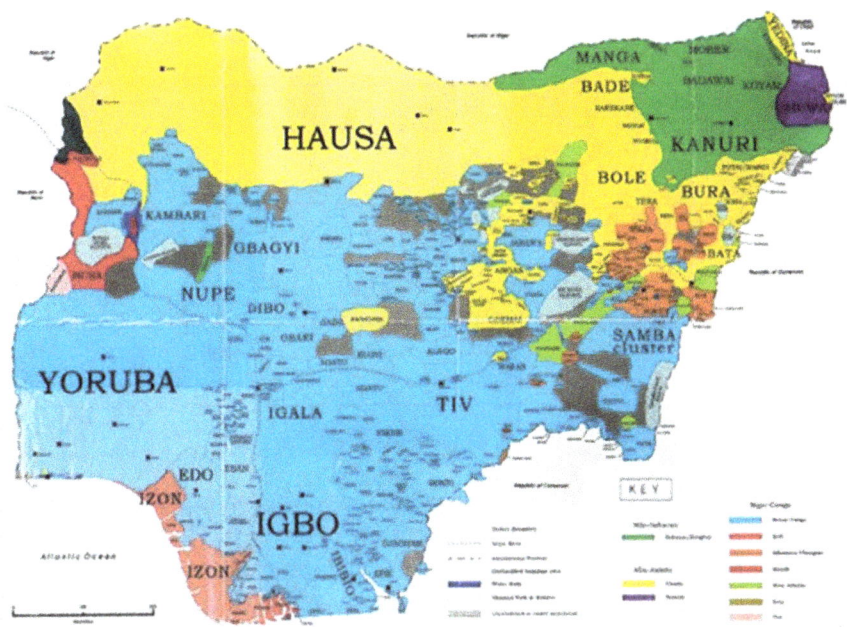

Figure 1: Language map of Nigeria (cf. Hansford et. al.1976).

a. The mother tongue (i.e. child's first language)
b. A language of immediate community (i.e. a language spoken by a wider community) and generally learnt and used as a second language by those mother tongue is a smaller language)
c. A major Nigeria language (i.e. Hausa, Igbo and Yoruba)
d. English
e. A foreign language (i.e. French and Arabic) (Bamgbose, 1992)

In the table in (1) below, Bamgbose summarizes the integration of these languages in the school system (p. 71).

The constitutional provision of the policy can be found in section 55 of the 1999 constitution. It states: "The business of the National Assembly shall be conducted in English, and in Hausa, Igbo and Yoruba when adequate arrangements have been made thereof. In 1979 constitution, a parallel provision was made in the State Houses of Assembly for the conduct of government business in English as well as one or more other languages spoken in the State as the House may by resolution approve (p. 91).

Table 1: Nigeria: Language in the school curriculum (cf. Table 6).

	Level	Medium	Subjects
1.	Pre primary	MT/LIC	MT/LIC
2.	Primary	MT/LIC 1–3 English 4–6	MT/LIC
3.	Junior Secondary	English	MT/LIC MNL$_2$ (FL)
4.	Senior Secondary[1]	English	English MNL$_1$ MNL$_2$ (FL)

It is clear from the above that the policy is restricted to assigning status and functions to different languages. Also, in spite of the inclusion of Nigerian languages, English holds sway as the official language, medium of education and is in fact creeping into domains hitherto reserved for local languages. Official pronouncements do not always translate to action. Consequently, some provisions of the policy are in abeyance. The point here is that there is no value to the recognition of any language by Nigerian government. It cannot therefore be the case that the lack of mention for NP is something to worry about. The real area of exclusion of pidgin worthy of mention is the fact that it is not in the education process. This is because academics still treat it as a mere exotic specimen for research. The table in 2 below shows the level to which Nigerian Languages are accorded recognition in tertiary institutions.

2.2 Founding principles of the language policy

Bamgbose (1992: 8–9) summarizes the founding principles of the policy and gives us useful insights on the problems of implementation. According to him, the rationale for this practice is that "English as the official language and language of technology is needed more especially at the secondary and tertiary levels; hence the need to acquire its mastery as early as possible in the educational cycle."

---

[1] MT (Mother tongue), LIC (Language of the Immediate Community), MNL$_1$ (Minor Nigerian Language as First Language), MNL$_2$ (Major Nigerian Language as Second Language), FL (Foreign Language), 1–6 (Primary Classes).

Table 2: Nigerian Language Programs in Tertiary Education/Examinations Subjects.

Nigerian languages examined at School certificate level	Languages examined at the University matriculation entrance	No of Languages offered as University Degree Programs/Subjects (31)									
		English	Hausa	Yoruba	Igbo	Fulfude	Ibibio	Efik	Urhobo	Edo	Tiv
Hausa, Yorub, Igbo, Edo, Efik, Ibibio	Hausa, Yoruba, Igbo	All/	17	10	09	02	02	01	01	01	01
06	03	165									

He outlines the following as problems associated with the possible use of the mother tongue as a medium.
i. multiplicity of languages and problem of choice,
ii. existence of small group languages in which education is hardly feasible, since there are a few children of school-going age who speak the languages,
iii. lack of suitably trained teachers,
iv. lack of suitable texts – in fact several languages are yet to be reduced to writing
v. lack of technical terminology for use in teaching mathematics, science and other subjects,
vi. lack of political will,
vii. negative attitude towards local languages'

Whereas i. and ii. above make a case for Pidgin, Table in 1 above shows why iii., iv. apply, because NP is not being taught in any Nigerian Tertiary institution. The fact that it has a significant population of creole and second language speakers and is the largest language in Nigeria has not encouraged its listing as a course in any tertiary institution in Nigeria.

Elugbe (1995:251) lists the following in support of NP: ethnic neutrality, national spread, utility as the language of education in areas where many local languages would make it difficult to implement the language policy, utility as the bridge language in the teaching of English. I think the real problem here is lack of academic will and absence of ethno-political constituency for NP. Pidgin lacks its own independent cultural and political capital, has no ethnic loyalty and therefore has no value in the negotiation of citizenship in Nigeria. In the Nigerian state, citizenship is by ethnicity and constituencies are delineated along ethnic lines. Being primarily a second language with recent origins from contact situations, it has no claims to land/territory, no exclusive culture and therefore lacks political legitimacy within the Nigerian realities of politics and power. Pidgin is primarily a second language spoken by people who have ancestral roots in another living culturally authentic language. One could also point to the elitist concerns of a mass language, ideological resistance due to its relationship with English and fears that it will displace the major Nigerian languages as factors which undermine the potentials for the formal recognition and adoption of pidgin.

3 The nature of the Nigerian state and the growth of Nigerian Pidgin

The critical questions would be, what is NP telling us about the Nigerian society? How has the Nigerian society provided the context for the emergence of NP as a lingua franca? The clue lies in looking at the structuring of society through socioeconomic and political forces, the role of technology, especially ICTs and social media in defining what it means to be human, the influence of globalization and the associated mentalities, ideologies and philosophies and the convergence in the fundamental principles of human culture and civilization.

The other thing we need to look at is the nature of the Nigerian Federation. Citizenship is by ethnicity and there is a bifurcation between citizens and settlers. National identity is through ethnic affiliation. Political constituencies, allocation of privileges as well as educational opportunities are based on ethnic

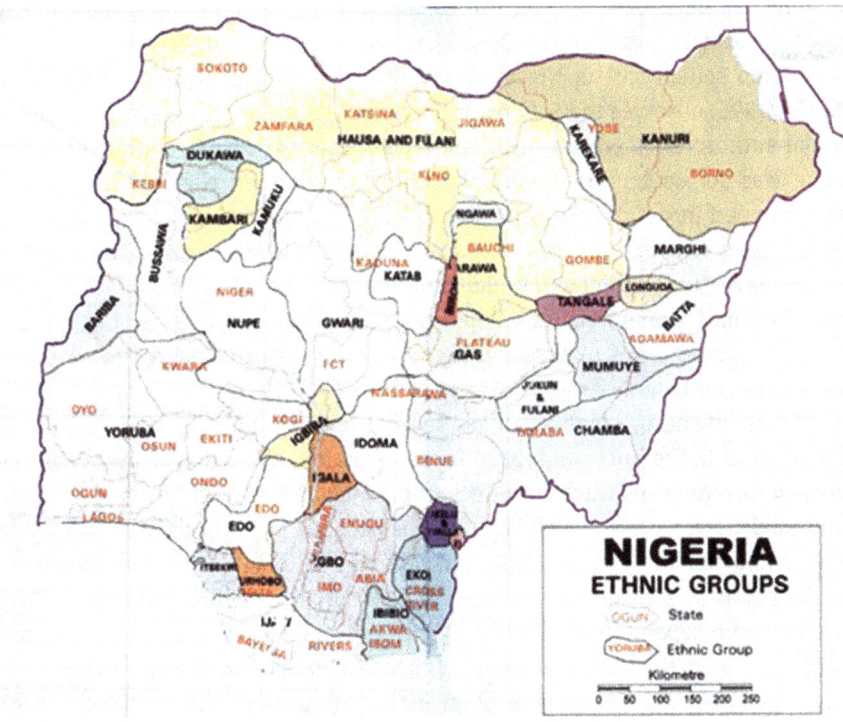

Figure 2: Map of Nigerian Ethnic Groups. (http://www.onlinenigeria.com/population/?blurb=135#ixzz4KMYiOaU1)

affiliation. Consequently, there is a hardening of ethnic boundaries against integration, thereby creating a fractious diversity. Thus, there are 500 languages in 250 ethnic groups, 36 states and 794 local government areas competing for space, defined by excessive domination by the majority groups and unmanageable minority agitation.

3.1 Urban settlement patterns

There is a large volume of internal migration in the country induced by scarcity of land, impoverished soil, declining crop yields, poor harvests, soil erosion, mass unemployment, violence and conflicts, creation of new states and Local Government Areas among others. The most significant form of movement is from rural areas to urban centres. "Rural-urban migration is responsible for the depopulation of some rural areas and the influx of people into towns and cities. The rapid rate of increase in the population of large urban centres through migration has been of great concern to successive governments in the country since the second half of the 1950s".

Urban settlements in Nigeria are segregated along class and ethnic lines. Albert (1996) observes the Sabongari phenomenon which was created by the colonial authorities to preserve the sanctity of Islam (p5). Thus, a stranger settlement was set up for the dominantly Christian southern Nigerian immigrants who trooped into Northern cities to serve the colonial masters. Stranger settlements have remained a feature of many Nigerian cities to date. These settlements have "unique demographic configurations, social orientation, religious and economic characteristics". Whereas the stranger communities in Northern cities are made up of diverse southern minorities, in the south, they contain mainly Hausa-Fulani elements (Albert, 1996).

Complementing neighbourhood segregation is trade specialization along ethnic lines in the informal sector. These taken together with the bifurcation of society into natives and non-natives, indigenes and settlers, 'sons of the soil' and foreigners, we see a social fracture disincentive to cultural assimilation and integration. Settlers are second class citizens who have little rights to employment in the public sector, state or local government service or public institutions. They are therefore separated from the indigenes at a particular social class and may function only in the private sector or informal sector of the economy. This sector is therefore characterized by mixed populations with each striving to maintain their identity.

3.2 Bifurcation of the Nigerian economy

The Nigerian economy is divided into the formal/ organized and informal sectors. If we take data on the amount of currency outside the banking sector as a cue, the informal sector has at least 70% of the business. Take this with the literacy rate of about 54%, defined as those who have some understanding of English, coupled with unemployment figures in excess of 25%, under employment raising the figure to as much as 40%, poverty levels of 70% defined as those who live below $2 per day, we can appreciate the level of significance of the informal sector. If we consider that internal migration is significant and that individuals who reside outside their state of paternal ancestry have very little chance of working in the formal sector or public service, we get some idea of

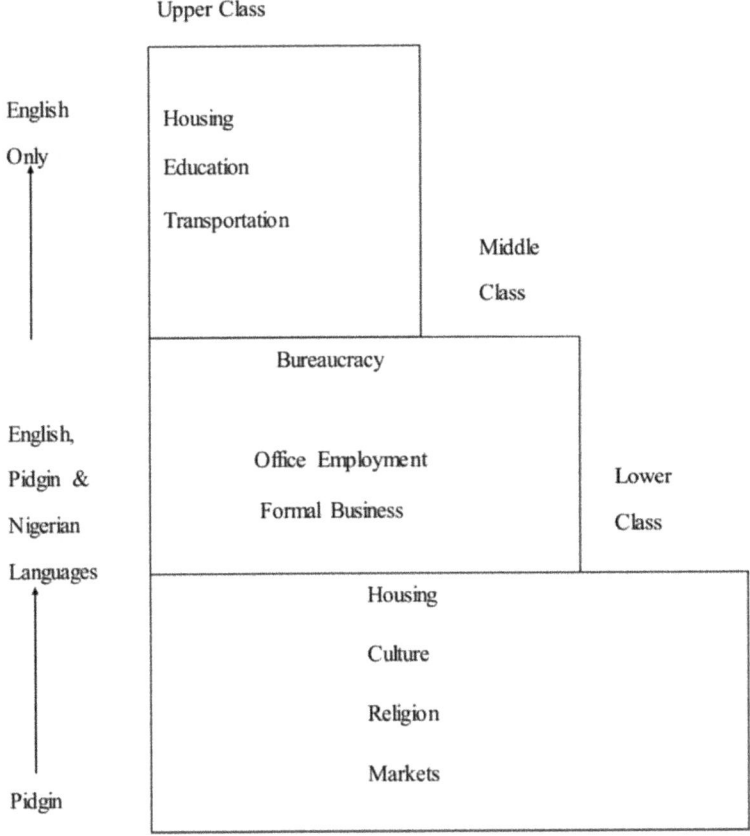

Figure 3: Convergence of Class and Language Use Patterns.

the significance of the informal sector. The population of Nigerians who operate in the formal sector is about 25%. English is the language of the formal/organized sector. The informal sector therefore is large, highly diverse and has the capacity of dominating the formal in terms of social and interactional dynamics. The informal sector creates a large common, economic, social, cultural and religious convergence point between the different social classes and ethnic groups.

The implication of the above is that we end up having the language associated with the lower class, i.e. the lingua franca, as the dominant language forced upon the upper and middle classes as a matter of necessity. This is a clear example of how economics may impact on language. Conventional wisdom would suggest that English being the language of economic opportunity, and the main languages being the emblems of political power would dominate and drive the aspirations of the larger populace. However, as we have argued, other socioeconomic factors have created a new set of dynamics that appears to give advantage to Nigerian Pidgin. Whereas the upper class resides in exclusive estates and their children attend exclusive schools, they converge with other classes in the markets, services, religious and cultural spaces which are by far dominant. The middle class only converges with the upper class in employment. It however shares housing and education with the lower class. The above leaves us with a need; i. a language connector between the formal and informal domains; ii. A language of intergroup interactions which is neutral enough not to confer any advantage in the power equation; iii. A language that bridges the class demarcations and allows the diverse classes to converge. That language is NP.

3.3 Citizenship: Indigenes vs settlers

Citizenship is variegated in Nigeria. It is based on ethnicity and a division of society into natives and non-natives, indigenes and settlers, 'sons of the soil' and foreigners. This categorization is legitimized by the principle of representation and the demarcation of constituencies along ethnolinguistic lines. Appointments, promotions, revenue allocation, educational opportunities and official business patronage are based largely on one's ethnicity and status as a citizen or settler. This has tended to promote the hardening of ethnic boundaries, minority agitations, social fracture which are disincentives to cultural assimilation and integration. Settlers are second class citizens who have little rights to employment in the public sector, state or local government service or public institutions. They are therefore separated from the indigenes at a particular social class and may function only in the private sector or informal sector of the economy. Language, as an emblem of identity becomes both instruments of resistance and solidarity.

4 Functions of Nigerian Pidgin

We do not intend to restate the findings of earlier works on Nigerian Pidgin. We should draw attention however to very important works such as Omamor (1990a&b), Elugbe and Omamor (1991), Elugbe (1992, 1995) Dueber (2005), Mafeni (1971), Agheyisi (1983), Faraclas (1983, 1996), Igboanusi (2008), (1993, 1998). Studies that are particularly related to the spread of Nigerian Pidgin are Egbokhare (2001, 2003, 2010), Schaefer and Egbokhare (2006). The points of convergence in these works are many. These point to the negative attitudes towards NP, lack of official recognition, its exclusion from being a language of formal education and organized business, its enlarging functions, spread and displacement of local languages, among other things. Where disagreements occur relate to matters of definition, nomenclature, origin, orthographic practices and relationship with English and the exact population of speakers. The last point is understandable given the fact that language data is not captured in population census in Nigeria. The issues are trivial and will not affect our focus in this presentation. What has come to be accepted is that Pidgin is the most widely spoken language in Nigeria today. We still need to disaggregate this population according to relevant linguistic and demographic variables. However we may hazard a guess that there are about a 100 million speakers organized into the categories below.

Table 3: Classification of Pidgin Speakers.

Creoles	About 10million and increasing
1st Language Speakers	30 million
2nd Language Speakers	40 million
Marginal Users	Remaining Urban & Semi-Urban dwellers

Jubril (1995: 233) points out that the functions of NP have become more extensive. It has expanded and spread as a lingua franca beyond its traditional domains such as ethnically-heterogeneous areas such as Warri, Sapele, Port-Harcourt, Lagos, Abuja and other large cities, motor parks, markets, university campuses and among the lower ranks of the security forces.

It is now used extensively in radio and television broadcasts, popular culture, comedy, advertisement, and online, social, media and in poetry and drama. NP is the language of stand-up comedy in Nigeria. Because there is a myth that it is

Table 4: Major Languages, Minority Languages and Lingua Francas in Nigeria's 36 States and Federal Capital (cf F O Egbokhare 2004, Language and Politics in Nigeria, fig 3, pp. 518–8).

S/N	STATE	MAJOR CITIES	MAJOR LANG.	MINORITY LANG.	LINGUA FRANCA
1	ABIA	ABA, Umuahia	Igbo	–	Igbo/Pidgin
2	ADAMAWA	Yola, Mubi	Hausa/Fula Kamw'e' Many	Bacama, Kilba, many	Hausa/Fula
3	AKWA IBOM	UYO	Ibibio	(many)	Pidgin/Ibibio (Efik for writing)
4	ANAMBRA	AWKA	Igbo		Igbo/Pidgin
5	BAUCHI	BAUCHI	Hausa/Fula	(many)	Hausa
6	BAYELSA	YENAGOA	Ijo		Ijo/Pidgin
7	BENUE	MAKURDI, Gboko, Otukpo	Idoma	(many)	English/Pidgin
8	BORNO	MAIDUGURI, Biu	Kanuri, Bura, Marghi, Shuwa	(many)	Kanuri/Hausa
9	CROSS RIVER	CALABAR	Efik, Ibibio	(many)	Efik/Pidgin
10	DELTA	ASABA, Warri, Ughelli	Itsekiri, Urhobo, Igbo, Isoko	Ukwuani, Igbanke, Igala	Pidgin/English
11	EBONYI	ABAKALIKI	Igbo		Igbo
12	EDO	BENIN, Auchi	Edo	Many	Pidgin
13	EKITI	ADO EKITI	Yoruba		Yoruba
14	ENUGU	ENUGU, Nsukka	Igbo		Igbo/Pidgin
15	FCT	ABUJA, Suleja	Gwari, Hausa, Pidgin	(many)	English/Pidgin/Hausa
16	GOMBE	GOMBE	Hausa	(many)	Hausa
17	IMO	OWERRI, Okigwe	Igbo	–	Igbo/Pidgin

Table 4 (continued)

S/N	STATE	MAJOR CITIES	MAJOR LANG.	MINORITY LANG.	LINGUA FRANCA
18	JIGAWA	DUTSE, Birnin Kudu	Hausa	–	Hausa
19	KADUNA	KADUNA, Zaria	Hausa, Gwari, Kaje	(many)	Hausa/pidgin
20	KANO	KANO	Hausa	–	Hausa/pidgin
21	KASTINA	KASTINA	Hausa	–	Hausa
22	KEBBI	BIRNIN KEBBI, Argungu	Hausa, Gwari	Several	Hausa
23	NASSARAWA	LAFIA	Hausa	Many	Hausa
24	KOGI	LOKOJA, Okene	Ebira, Igala,	Several	Yoruba /Igala/ Ebira/Pidgin
25	KWARA	ILORIN, Offa	Yoruba	Several	Hausa/Yoruba
26	LAGOS	IKEJA, Lagos	Yoruba	Several	Yoruba/ English/Pidgin
27	NIGER	MINNA, Bida	Nupe, Gwari	Several	Hausa
28	OGUN	ABEOKUTA, Shagamu	Yoruba	–	Yoruba
29	ONDO	AKURE, Okitipupa	Yoruba,	Several	Yoruba, Ijaw, Pidgin
30	OSUN	OSOGBO, Ede, Ilesha	Yoruba	–	Yoruba
31	OYO	IBADAN, Ogbomosho	Yoruba	–	Yoruba/Pidgin
32	PLATEAU	JOS, Lafia	Angas, Birom	(many)	Hausa/Pidgin
33	RIVERS	PORT-HARCOURT	Nembe, Kalabari, Khana, Izon, Ikwere	(many)	Pidgin
34	SOKOTO	SOKOTO	Hausa, Fula,	Several	Hausa
35	TARABA	JALINGO	Fula, Jukun, Tiv, Mumuye, Chamba	Very many	Hausa
36	YOBE	DAMATURU, Potiskum	Kanuri, Hausa, Fula, Bada	(many)	Hausa
37	ZAMFARA	GUSAU	Hausa	–	Hausa

funnier to deliver comedy in it. The "Night of a Thousand Laughter" Brand and other comedy programs are delivered entirely in Pidgin.

4.1 Pidgin in mass media

The economics of language use is clearly to the advantage of NP as reflected in its use in advertising and explosive presence in Radio. There is hardly any radio station in Nigeria today that does not have a program in Pidgin. A trend started in 2013 with the introduction of Pidgin mainly radio station, which broadcast almost entirely in Pidgin. WAZOBIA FM brand in five states of Nigeria launched this trend which is now being replicated by other stations. The yielding of state control of the radio and television media to private investors has led to the emergence of pidgin as a top broadcast language brand in Nigeria. The listenership statistics clearly bears out the demand for and popularity of pidgin in Nigeria. A new pidgin-based television station has been established in the national capital by WAZOBIA brand on Star Times and DSTV Satellite media. Online following of Pidgin programs cut across demographic variables and across the diaspora. To further emphasize the relevance of Pidgin, Banks and telecoms companies have pidgin prompts and support desks at their respective call centre operations. Only Hausa, Igbo, Yoruba and English can boast of similar opportunity.

Recently in 2017, BBC has incorporated a Pidgin service to its Nigerian language programming. What will be interesting would be to see the user profiles for these facilities and the language preferences in order to properly understand the directions of change in the Nigerian linguistic space.

Table 5: Use of Pidgin in Radio Medium. This is original from my survey as part of the research leading to this work.

Approx. no of Radio stations	Location	Nigerian Langs. Mainly	English Mainly	Pidgin Mainly	Pidgin+others	Main Nig. Lang. of Zone
42	North West	NIL	NIL	1	16	Hausa
21	North East	NIL	NIL	NIL	9	Kanuri, Hausa, Fulfude
36	North Central	NIL	NIL	NIL	24	Tiv, Igala, Idoma, Nupe

Table 5 (continued)

Approx. no of Radio stations	Location	Nigerian Langs. Mainly	English Mainly	Pidgin Mainly	Pidgin+others	Main Nig. Lang. of Zone
53	South West	1	NIL	NIL	46	Yoruba
35	South East	NIL	NIL	NIL	33	Igbo
47	South South	NIL	NIL	1	33	Ijaw, Efik, Ibibio, Edo, Urhobo
27	Lagos		NIL	1	21	Yoruba
17	Abuja		NIL	1	14	
279	Total		NIL	4	195	

4.2 Some Wazobia FM data

The best example that illustrates the dynamism of Pidgin in the media is presented by the Wazobia FM Brand. Below, we present data on the spread, user profile and demand statistics as far back as 2013. Current data is unavailable. Figures 4–7 below provide evidence of the trend of Pidgin use in the media. Consider that just two decades ago, pidgin was considered as some form of oddity in the media.

Figure 4: Wazobia FM and Pidginmania.

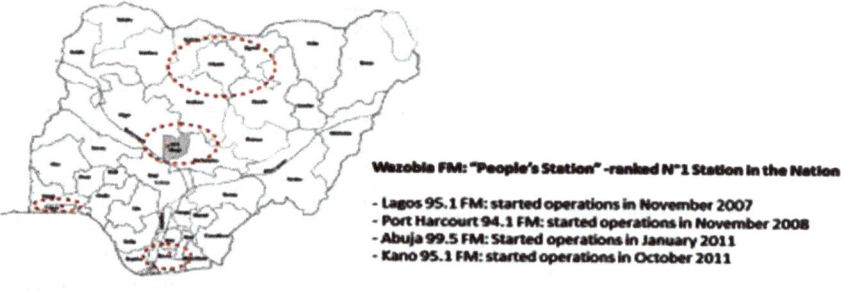

Figure 5: Spread of Wazobia Radio Brand.

Figure 6: Pidgin Penetration in Social Media.

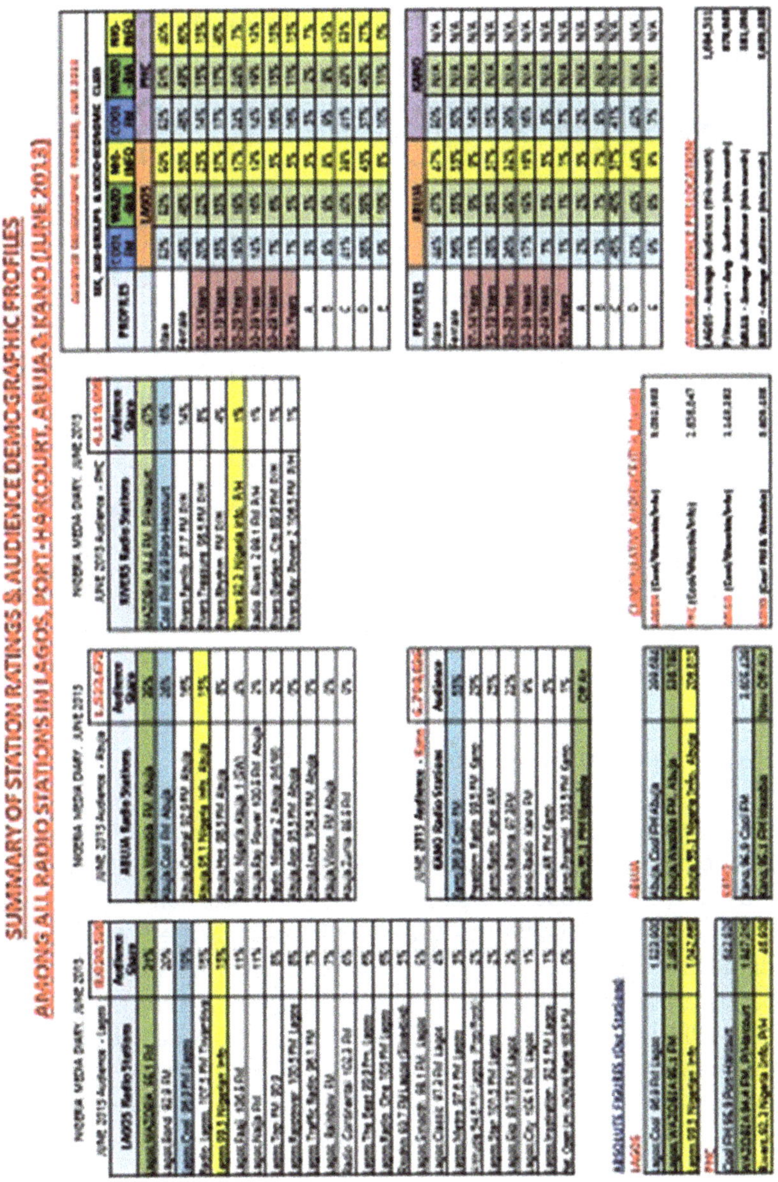

Chapter 3 The accidental lingua franca — 87

Figure 7a: Audience Demographics in Radio Stations in Lagos.

MONTHLY AUDIENCE SHARES (RATINGS) OF RADIO STATIONS IN LAGOS STATE (JAN 2013 – MAY 2013)

LAGOS Radio Stations	JAN	FEB	MAR	APR	MAY	JUN	JUL	AUG	SEP	OCT	NOV	DEC	CUMM. TOTAL	AVRG. TO DATE
Monthly Audience Base -->	6,918,999	6,959,543	6,424,194	7,448,603	7,622,526								35,372,865	7,074,613
Lagos, Cool 96.9 FM Lagos	32%	25%	23%	24%	25%								129%	26%
Lagos, Eko 89.75 FM Lagos	22%	25%	28%	26%	5%								106%	21%
Lagos, Inspiration 92.3 FM Lagos	3%	3%	4%	3%	3%								16%	3%
Lagos, Radio One 103 FM Lagos	6%	6%	7%	6%	6%								31%	6%
Lagos, Metro 97.6 FM Lagos	4%	5%	4%	4%	3%								20%	4%
Lagos, Bond 92.9 FM	20%	19%	21%	22%	21%								103%	21%
Lagos, Radio Lagos, 107.5 FM Tinsertsea	5%	15%	18%	15%	15%								68%	13%
Lagos, Raypower 100.5 FM Lagos	7%	0%	0%	0%	0%								7%	1%
Lagos, Rhythm 93.7 FM Lagos (Silverbird)	5%	5%	5%	5%	5%								25%	5%
Lagos, Star 101.5 FM Lagos	7%	6%	7%	6%	6%								32%	6%
Lagos, Unilag 105.1 FM	2%	2%	2%	2%	2%								10%	2%
Lagos, Radio Continental 102.3 FM	13%	13%	14%	11%	11%								62%	12%
Lagos, WAZOBIA 95.1 FM	26%	29%	29%	28%	32%								144%	29%
Lagos, Top FM 90.9	11%	11%	12%	10%	9%								53%	11%
Lagos, Classic 97.3 FM Lagos	5%	5%	5%	4%	4%								23%	5%
Lagos, The Beat 99.9 FM, Lagos	7%	8%	6%	6%	6%								33%	6%
Lagos, Smooth 98.1 FM, Lagos	5%	5%	6%	4%	5%								25%	5%
Lagos, Rainbow FM	7%	7%	7%	8%	7%								36%	7%
Lagos, City 105.1 FM, Lagos	1%	1%	1%	1%	1%								5%	1%
Lagos, Nat. Open Uni. (NOUN) Radio 105.9 FM	0%	0%	0%	0%	0%								0%	0%
Lagos, Altitude 94.8 FM Lagos (Pop/Rock)	3%	3%	3%	3%	2%								14%	3%
Lagos, Naija FM	10%	10%	12%	0%	0%								32%	6%
Lagos, 99.3 Nigerian Info	13%	15%	13%	14%	15%								60%	14%
Lagos, Lagos Traffic Radio 96.1 FM	6%	11%	11%	11%	9%								48%	10%
Lagos, Faaji 106.5 FM	8%	12%	17%	15%	15%								67%	13%

Figure 7b: Monthly Audience Share of Radio Stations in Lagos.

4.3 Pidgin in advertising (Pidgin is trending)

Pidgin is represented in all advertising media from radio, television, billboard, newspaper to the internet. The advertisers range from local and multinational producers of consumer products, telecoms, pharmaceuticals, building materials, banks, breweries, political parties, governments, development agencies, etc. However, educational organizations and service providers do not use pidgin. Small scale businesses do not have their sign boards in pidgin even in areas where pidgin is endemic, although advertising content may be in pidgin. A detailed study of the locationalization of billboards and advert placement pattern in Nigeria will certainly show that main Nigerian languages are marginal when compared with pidgin. A recent trend relates to the use of pidgin as the language of wedding invitation cards.

   Pidgin adverts represent both national and socioeconomic spread depending on product and message. Contrary to this, main Nigerian languages are restricted to their ethnic domains and are seldom used in print and billboards. The national appeal of pidgin as a language of intergroup communication, mass

PIDGIN BILLBOARD ADVERTS 1

Figure 8a: Advertising Billboard 1.

mobilisation and youth engagement, informs its use in public service campaigns, public education, political advertisements.

PIDGIN BILLBOARD ADVERT 2

Figure 8b: Advertising Billboard 2.

The advert images show pidgin as "cool" (see Gulder, Pepsi ads.). Its social appeal as a language of cosmopolitan and urbanized person, for the expression of peer intimacy and *belongingness* makes it a preference when advertisement targets youth identity in its message. Pidgin is considered a fun language, with a quality of slanginess which recommends it to the pop culture youth identity. On the contrary, English is considered as too formalized, incomprehensible, lacking expression and incorporating too much grammar in local parlance. This point is made clearly in the lyrics of Lagbaja and Fela's *Vernacular*.

PIDGIN ADVERT 3

Figure 8c: Advertising Billboard 3.

There is code switching between pidgin and English on billboards. The practice is to deliver the message in pidgin for the stickiness factor, provide the key message, the brand logo or product label and technical information in English (see Hollandia Evap, Orijin and Pepsi ads.).

PIDGIN ADVERT 4

I call my bobo for free with you and me
I called my boyfriend free of charge with you and me (package)

I dey save money bcos my okada dey chop better oil
I am saving money because my motorbike is consuming good lubricating oil

Figure 8d: Advertising Billboard 4.

Figure 8e: Wedding Invite in Pidgin.

5 Pidgin in education and literature

Pidgin is not a language of education, but it is much used for informal interaction by students in tertiary institutions in Nigeria. There is a progressive growth in the use of pidgin as a language of literary expression in novels, poetry and drama. Dan Izevbaye (personal communication) talks about a remarkable presence of pidgin in the Nigerian novel, from Carey's Mr Johnson, Soyinka's Interpreter, Achebe's *A Man of the People* to Ken Saro Wiwa's *Sozaboy*. In the majority of literary works, pidgin is used as a marker for lower class individuals, based on its function at the time as a motor park or market lingo. Sozaboy is the best effort so far at producing a completely pidgin novel. In poetry we can readily identify the following: Vatsa (1981), *Tori for Geti Bow Leg*; Aig Imoukhuede's (1982), *Pidgin Stew and Sufferhead*; Oribhabor (2011), *Abuja na Kpangba an Oda Puem-dem*. Ken Saro Wiwa's *Dis Nigeria sef* (1985b). Tunde Fatunde's full length plays in pidgin, *No food for Country* (1985), *Oga na Tief Man*, (1986) as well as numerous poems in Lagos Life, a weekly gossip newspaper published by The Guardian. Pidgin publishing online is very vibrant and diverse. This goes to show that there is a credible literate and creative community of pidginites in cyberspace.

6 Pidgin in music

Table 6 contains artists who sang mostly in straight pidgin or Nigerian Languages. They represent earlier generations of musicians who adopted Pidgin. There is no central ideology to match the group. Nevertheless, one may single out the music of Fela Kuti as distinctly protest or Yabis in the language of the Shrine.

Table 6: A List of Some Popular Songs in Nigerian Pidgin.

s/n	Song title	Artist
1	She Go Run Away	Fatai Rolling Dollars
2	Na My Own You Dey See	Fatai Rolling Dollars
4	No Time	J. Martins featuring Psquare
5	Face Me	Sunny Nneji
6	If He No Love You	Sunny Nneji
7	Tolotolo	Sunny Nneji
8	2010	Sound Sultan
9	If To say	Timaya
10	Good or bad	J. Martins
11	No Be lie	Banky W
12	Na You Sabi	2shot
14	If You Ask me	Omawumi
15	I Go Always Pray For You	Nosa
16	Them Mama	Timaya
17	No Do Gragra	Lagbaja
18	Zombie; Original Sufferhead Trouble Sleep and many more	Fela
19	Bosigbangba	Eldee

Table 6 (continued)

s/n	Song title	Artist
20	Dance for me	Dunce mighty
21	If You Love Somebody	African China
22	No be Mistake	9ice
23	Kokoroko	Kefee feat. Timaya
24	If you see mamiwater, Joromi	Victor Uwaifo
25	Sweet Mother	Nico Mbanga

The following are mainly hip hop and rap artiste whose use of Pidgin is characterized by code mixing with English and Nigerian Languages, depending on the artiste. This tendency clearly sets the modern Nigerian youth performer from earlier ones showing an ideology that is more integrative and an identity that is more national if not global. Observe that the musicians come from diverse ethnic backgrounds.

Table 7: Contemporary Musicians.

Artiste	Ethnicity	Albums	Code-mixing
Olubankole Wellington (Banky W)	Yoruba (African American)	– 2003: Undeniable (EP) – 2005: Back in the Building – 2008: Mr. Capable – 2009: The W Experience – 2013: R&BW	Yoruba and English
Ayodeji Ibrahim Balogun (Wizkid)	Yoruba	2011: Superstar 2013: Chosen 2014: Ayo 2015: In Love With a Lie	Yoruba and English
David Ayodeji Adeleke (Davido)	Yoruba	– Omo Baba Olowo (2012) – The Baddest (TBD)	Yoruba and English
Tuface Idibia	Benue?	– Only me, Implication	
Azubuike Chibuzo Nelson (Phyno)	Igbo	– No Guts No Glory (2014) – 2Kings (2015) (with Olamide)	English, Pidgin and Igbo

Table 7 (continued)

Artiste	Ethnicity	Albums	Code-mixing
Olamide Ayodeji (Baddo)	Yoruba	– Rapsodi (2011) – YBNL (2012) – Baddest Guy Ever Liveth (2013) – Street OT (2014) – Eyan Mayweather (2015) – Compilation albums – 2 Kings (2015) (with Phyno)	Yoruba, Pidgin and English
Bukola Elemide (Asa)	Yoruba	2007: Asa (Asha) 2009: Live in Paris 2010: Beautiful Imperfection 2014: Bed of Stone	Yoruba and English
Chidinma Ekile (Ms. Kedike)	Igbo	2012: Chidinma	English, Pidgin and Igbo
Panshak Zamani (Ice Prince)	Hausa	– Everybody Loves Ice Prince (2011) – Fire of Zamani (2013)	English and Hausa **(Pidgin faintly)**
Jude Abaga (Mr Incredible M.I)	Igbo	– Talk About It (2008) – M.I 2 (2010) – The Chairman (2014)	English (Yoruba Pidgin faintly)
Innocent Ujah Idibia (2face Idibia)	Igbo	– 2004: Face 2 Face – 2006: Grass 2 Grace – 2008: The Unstoppable – 2010: The Unstoppable International Edition – 2012: Away & Beyond – 2014: The Ascension	English, (Igbo, Pidgin and Yoruba faintly)
Oladapo Daniel Oyebanjo (D'banj)	Yoruba	2005: No Long Thing 2006: RunDown Funk U Up 2008: The Entertainer	English and Yoruba
Duncan Wene Mighty Okechukwu (Duncan Mighty)	Igbo	– Koliwater (2008) – Ahamefuna (Legacy) (2010) – Footprints (2012) – Grace & Talent (2014)	English and Igbo **(Pidgin)**

Table 7 (continued)

Artiste	Ethnicity	Albums	Code-mixing
Enetimi Alfred Odon (Timaya)	Igbo	– True Story (2007) – Gift And Grace (2008) – De Rebirth (2010) – LLNPLong Life N Prosperity (2011) – Upgrade (2012) – Epiphany (2014)	English and Igbo **(Pidgin)**
Eedris Turayo Abdulkareem Ajenifuja (Eedris Abdulkareem)	Yoruba (Hausa) Adopted Kano State as his state of origin	– P.A.S.S (2002) – Mr. Lecturer (2002) – Jaga Jaga (2004) – Letter to Mr. President (2005) – King Is Back (2007) – Unfinished Business (2010)	English
Adigun Adegbola Abolore (9ice)	Yoruba	– Certificate (2007) – Gongo Aso (2008) – Tradition (2009) – Versus (2011) – Bashorun Gaa (2011) – Deluxe Version Versus & Bashorun Gaa (2011) – CNN/GRA (2014)	Yoruba and English
Jeremiah Gyang	Hausa	– NA BA KA ! – The Love Album – The Christmas Singles	English and Hausa
Da Grin(Oladapo Olaitan Olaonipekun)	Yoruba	– Pon Pon Pon – Kondo Majic	Yoruba and Pidgin/English
Lord of Ajasa (Olusegun Osaniyi)	Yoruba	– I dey 4 party 2010 – Oti ya 2010 – Koleyewon 2016	Yoruba and Pidgin
Reminisce (Remilekun Abdulkalid Safaru)	Yoruba	– Asalamalekun – Feego – Where I come from	Yoruba and Pidgin

7 The spread of Nigerian Pidgin

We are going to try to answer two questions. Why is Pidgin spreading and not any other Nigerian Language, including English? The second question is how is it spreading? Language exists in a socio-political, economic, geospacial, technological and temporal milieu. It is therefore affected by these forces. Thus, the fortunes of a language are tied up with and are reflections of the history of peoples and nations.

The fortunes of a language are inextricably tied to the fortunes of its speakers. Thus according to Liberson, 1982, "languages do not differ among themselves in their inherent power, but users of language differ in their ability to alter existing language usage patterns thereby affecting the fortunes of their language. The power position of a people and consequently their language is sometimes not under conscious control but is determined by subtle socio-political and historical forces. The profile of a language may improve positively if it becomes associated with a thriving culture, religion, trade, science and technology and education, or if it is associated with a dominant political or economic power (Liberson, 1982). On the contrary, ecological disasters, war, conquest, labour migrations, urbanization, conflicts and prejudices may impact negatively on a people and their language. In multilingual societies, competition for power often leads to unwholesome intervention in the normal course of change of language usage patterns through language planning and policies.

We draw useful insights from Malcom Gladwell's (2000) *The Tipping Point* in explaining the spread of NP. He identifies three agents of change in (social) epidemics. These are *The Law of the Few*, *The Stickiness Factor* and *The Power of Context*. He also identifies the Tipping Point in the process of change, which is when it boils over, trends or becomes contagious. Following his argument, change depends on a few influential people with a rare set of social gifts. Stickiness refers to the quality of the message that makes it linger and have impact. The conditions, circumstances, times and places that catalyse it are its context.

7.1 The process of spread

Explaining the process of spread of NP requires a fair amount of understanding of the complex socio-political events in Nigeria. The origin of NP is put around the 15th century in the South East coast. The first contact was made by the Portuguese around 1469. The Dutch followed at about 1593 but soon faded away to be replaced by the English who dominated trade from 1650 onward. Taking that date up to 1914 when Nigeria was created as a colonial state and then up to 1960 when she gained independence, it would have taken 500 years for NP to establish a foothold and creolize in the coast. English-based variety has been around for about 300 years. There are indications that there was a demand for English even before the arrival of missionaries in the Niger Delta in the 18th century. This was restricted however only for the purposes of measurement, accounting and trade. The people only wanted English to enable them gauge palm oil, manufacture gun powder or sugar or build boats. The demand was not really for Education. "When the United Presbyterians arrived in 1846, there was already an indigenous tradition of literacy in English (Isichei, 1995). Many of the natives could write English: an art first acquired by some of the traders' sons who had visited England. Apart from schools run by missionaries, there was an evidence of a secular school run on behalf of Jaja of Opobo by an American, Emma White around 1869 (Isichei, 1995). "The children at Creek Town, said Waddel in 1848, are taught in English, not merely from necessity on our part, nor solely because *some knew our tongue a little* and all wished to learn it, but also from a conviction of the great importance ... of promoting among them the knowledge of our language. Broken English, he said, was already spoken along the coast from Gambia to Gaboon" (Ajayi, ed. 1965). There is conclusive evidence of a thriving pidgin. Oko Jombo said to Livingstone about Jaja, in Pidgin: *He be one of ourselves, we no want to crush him* (Dike, 1956: 188). Also, men of Calabar in early 19th century explaining why girls are excluded from schools said: *They no can saby book ... they no want go for ship make trade. Suppose they sabi book, they saucy book. It no fit they pass bos* (Isichei, 1995: 176). The last point explains why pidgin was consolidated and spread in the South East coast but not in Lagos where at least 20% of its population in 1865 were Sierra Leoneans (Huber, 1999:120). According to Huber, "there is evidence that the Saro (Recaptives) spoke a restructured English that was different from the local jargons/pidgin: The missionary Adolphus Mann called Hugo Schuchardt's attention to two kinds of Negro English in the Lagos of 1870s, Sierra Leone English on the one hand and the purely African type on the other ... " (p.120). Pidgin in Lagos and environs could have gone dormant or underground because "the freed slaves (Saro) were regarded as cultural lepers" (Ayandele, 1974). This is a case of negative attitude. Moreover, the linguistic heterogeneity of the Delta provided the initial impetus for the consolidation and spread of NP. Unlike Lagos and environ which was almost entirely Yoruba, "the Niger-Delta is a linguistically diverse area, where at least 25 languages, representing no less than six (6) distinct sub-branches and four (4) distinct branches of {Benue-Congo} of Niger-Congo) are spoken in close proximity to one another (Faraclas, Ibim and Worukwo (n.d..i)). Dike (1956:29–30) states that in the peopling of the Delta no one Nigerian tribe had a monopoly. Benis, Ijaws, Sobos, Jekris, Ekoi, Ibibios, Efik, and even the northern elements cohabited. Dike emphasizes that the different communities "developed the independence and individualism so typical of island dwellers" (p.30). Furthermore according to Faraclas *et.al.*, the various people of the Delta have traditionally maintained important relationships of exchange at all levels . . . such relationships . . . would have required the acquisitions by members of many different language groups of a common language to be used in the market place. Indeed, bi-and multilingualism are the norm rather than the exception in the Delta and such languages as Igbo and Pidgin English have been used by Delta peoples as trade languages as well as to meet the other communication needs of people of diverse linguistic origins living together (p.i).

The following represent the phases in the spread of Nigerian Pidgin:

Indigenization phase
I. Origin and Consolidation in the Delta: 15th-18th century (300 years)
II. Seeding in Lagos by recaptives and renewal of Delta by missionaries, national seeding by labour mobility to commercial and administrative centres, military barracks: 18th century to 1960s (about 100 years)

Lingua franca phase
III. Spread to hinterland in the Delta areas and adjoining territories following the creation of the Midwestern Region from Western Region in 1963 and the Civil War between1967–70 and subsequent creation of 12 states in 1968 including 2 from the Eastern Region.
IV. Nationalization of Pidgin through state creation led to massive labour mobility, urbanization catalysed by the oil boom of 70s, improved communication, mixed school system, sports development: 1968–80

Ideology phase
V. De-stigmatization and adoption as a language of youth movements, protest, youth solidarity, popular culture, especially by Fela Kuti. Pidgin gained popularity in the schools: mid 1970s-90s

Identity and globalization phase
VI. Digital Era. Aligning with social media, explosion in electronic media, hip hop and rap, advertising, political campaigns: 2000 to date

Below, we shall provide more details on the factors that led to the spread of NP.

Bamgbose (1992) states clearly that the Nigerian language policy is restricted to assigning status and functions to different languages. Thus, in spite of the inclusion of Nigerian languages in the policy, English holds sway as the official language, medium of education and is in fact creeping into domains hitherto reserved for local languages. Official pronouncements do not always translate to action. Consequently, some provisions of the policy are in abeyance. He also observes negative attitude towards indigenous languages thereby showing such

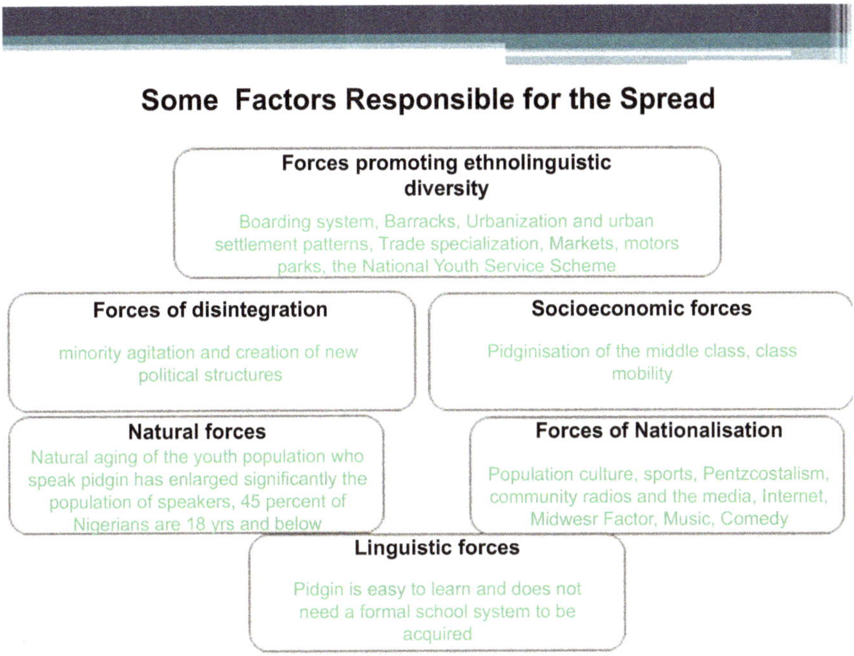

Some Factors Responsible for the Spread

Forces promoting ethnolinguistic diversity
Boarding system, Barracks, Urbanization and urban settlement patterns, Trade specialization, Markets, motors parks, the National Youth Service Scheme

Forces of disintegration
minority agitation and creation of new political structures

Socioeconomic forces
Pidginisation of the middle class, class mobility

Natural forces
Natural aging of the youth population who speak pidgin has enlarged significantly the population of speakers, 45 percent of Nigerians are 18 yrs and below

Forces of Nationalisation
Population culture, sports, Pentzcostalism, community radios and the media, Internet, Midwesr Factor, Music, Comedy

Linguistic forces
Pidgin is easy to learn and does not need a formal school system to be acquired

Figure 9: Spread of Nigerian Pidgin (Egbokhare, F.O. 2003).

recognition to be irrelevant. In fact, the main languages that have official recognition are receding, experiencing diminishing vitality, decreasing government patronage and facing diverse degrees of endangerment. Pidgin is taking over their traditional functions as Schaefer and Egbokhare (2006) show clearly. It appears that we are dealing with new realities which we are yet to accommodate.

The spread of NP involved the interaction of several forces. We can group these into Political, Socioeconomic, Natural, Linguistic and Technological. Whereas political forces created a need for a language of intergroup and interclass communication by promoting and sustaining diversity; through war, creation of new political structures, urban segregation, variegated citizenship and hardening of ethnic boundaries; socioeconomic forces deriving from politics led to internal migrations, labour and class mobility, trade specialization, bloating of the informal sector and attendant economic segregation. While diversity created the need for a common language for intergroup and interclass engagement, segregation fed the need for a language of solidarity by oppressed populations.

Pidgin as language of intergroup relations in the South East Coast, the language of receptive slaves in the South West Coast, the Language of labour migrant servants of colonial masters in Northern Nigeria, the language of protest music of Fela Kuti, the identity of new heroes of pop culture fit the requirement. Pidgin tipped because of its natural linguistic characteristics and value, its ethnic/political neutrality, its convergence with Nigerian Languages and English (which made it adaptable to the new technology environment), without losing the cultural essence of what it means to be a Nigerian.

7.1.1 Linguistic forces: Nature of NP

Why does Pidgin have such a mass appeal? Many individuals point to the slanginess, simplicity, ease of learning and fun factor as recommending NP. What does this mean in real linguistic terms since we know conclusively that pidgins are not a less complex form of language? In fact, in translating any of the indigenous languages to English, it has often been observed that the weight, flavour, originality and intended message get lost. This point is emphasized in Lagbaja and Fela's duet, *Vernacular*. We shall reproduce part of the lyrics below.

Observe the free switching between Yoruba and NP as evident of the fact that NP is considered as not different from indigenous languages. Unlike English, it lends itself to "expression". English is considered obscure and inefficient, often employed by the oppressive class as clearly demonstrated in Lagbaja's *200 million Mumu*. When Nigerians have difficulty comprehending you or believe that you are talking over their heads, they say you are *Speaking Grammar*. Only those who speak English speak grammar. The point here is that the meaning in Nigerian languages also exists in NP and it takes *grammar* from English and transforms it into *expression*.

> **I speak, you hear**
> **When you speak, I understand,**
> **Ọ̀rọ̀ wa ti yera wa idea lo jù**
> **We understand each other**

7.1.2 Relationship between NP, English and Nigerian languages

Majority of Nigerian languages are Benue-Congo of Niger Congo. This means that there is a significantly basic structural reference for these languages from which NP can draw for a basic substrate structure and grammatical frame, no matter the original language of contact. This congruence has a dejavu effect and minimizes language learning effort. Consequently, the process of language learning will involve the insertion of lexical frames into the common grammatical frame.

LAGBAJA AND FELA: VERNACULAR

Chorus: I speak, you hear
When you speak, I understand,
Òrò wa ti yera wa idea lo jù
If I fire and you dodge, I don't care,
'Na the beginning of craze be that.
Fela: That's the trouble I have with my country.
So, it's until somebody speaks English...
Lagbaja: Mi ò mò fún won
Fela: and he speaks well

Lagbaja: Hen-en
Fela: Have you listened to deep oyinbo
Lagbaja: Dem no dey listen o, kòló people
Fela: Do you listen to deep Yoruba language talk
Lagbaja: Ó tì o! Dem no dey appreciate am
Fela: Talk Philosophy... Deep meanings...
Lagbaja: ìjìnlè
Fela: Deep meanings...

LAGBAJA AND FELA: VERNACULAR

Lagbaja: Òwe ńláńlá
Fela: That the meanings don't even exist in English
Lagbaja: Oh Yes! O ya, take oyinbo translate 'Ó yínmú sími'
Fela: Hen-hen
Lagbaja: 'ó mó mi lójú'
'Ẹ káàbò' na 'Welcome', wetin be 'Ẹ kúulé o'?
Fela: Yes, what are we talking....
English is not expression!

Lagbaja: Mba, láéláé!
Fela: Expression is in Yoruba
Expression is in all languages all over Nigeria
English, English,
Lagbaja: No, No.
Fela: English is not expression...

Figure 10: Vernacular. (https://lyrics.az/lagbaja/abami/vernacular.html).

The second issue relates to lexical selection for the NP vocabulary. We believe that there is a common core or popular vocabulary that defines the NP lexicon. This is made up of a share of items from the lexifier languages including English. We need to look at the predominance of English vocabulary items in terms of a popular lexicon. It is popular because these items also occur and is accessible to indigenous languages as part of their common parlance for communication. We need to understand how ICTs, technologization of life and democratization have restructured modern societies to accommodate this view point.

The technical-vocabulary gap between the literate and illiterate, experts and non-experts has been bridged significantly by the insertion of hitherto technical vocabulary into the informal space through ICTs as a result of public education, entertainment, community development, democracy and governance, technological diffusion, among other things. While there is a convergence in terms of access, medium, information content the primary divergence is in technical registers and expert knowledge.

The repertoire which is part of everyday conversation is huge and ever increasing, even in areas of economic development. Community Radios are very significant in the dissemination of these terms. What is the significance of this? (I) Improvement of mutual intelligibility between English and Pidgin; (II) functional levelling resulting from widening convergence between the formal and informal domains of language use; (III) class levelling as a result of the collapse of the middle class in Nigeria and its merger with the lower class. Substantial influence of the middle class interaction with the lower class is the booming of enlarge presence of English-based terms in pidgin discourses; (IV) the negative downside is the tendency to begin to define pidgin in terms of its relationship with English, as the debate of the pidgin continuum suggests.

I would like to suggest that we stop seeing the English-based words in Pidgin as English. Reason being that in terms of meaning, pronunciation and grammatical use, they are anything but standard English. Ability to draw lexical repertoire from diverse sources is an adaptive capacity of NP and gives it leverage over Nigerian languages in its capacity to modernize without conscious formal intervention. The figure in 11 below illustrates the relationship between NP, Nigerian languages and English.

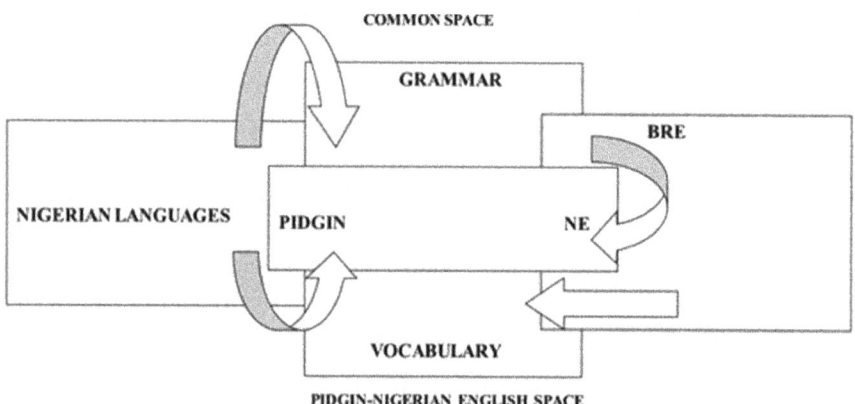

Figure 11: Convergence between Pidgin, English and Nigerian Languages.

7.1.3 Forces of dis-integration and diversity

Hard ethnic boundaries and perceived neutrality of Nigerian Pidgin

The notions of soft and hard boundaries may be culled up to emphasize the tendency for ethnic boundaries to reject or permit assimilation or integration. Ethnic boundaries in Nigeria are hard. Citizenship is derived from ethnicity and the allocation of political constituencies, privileges and advantages are derived from ethnic membership. This idea will be interesting later in understanding how political constituencies can affect the spread and shrinkage of languages.

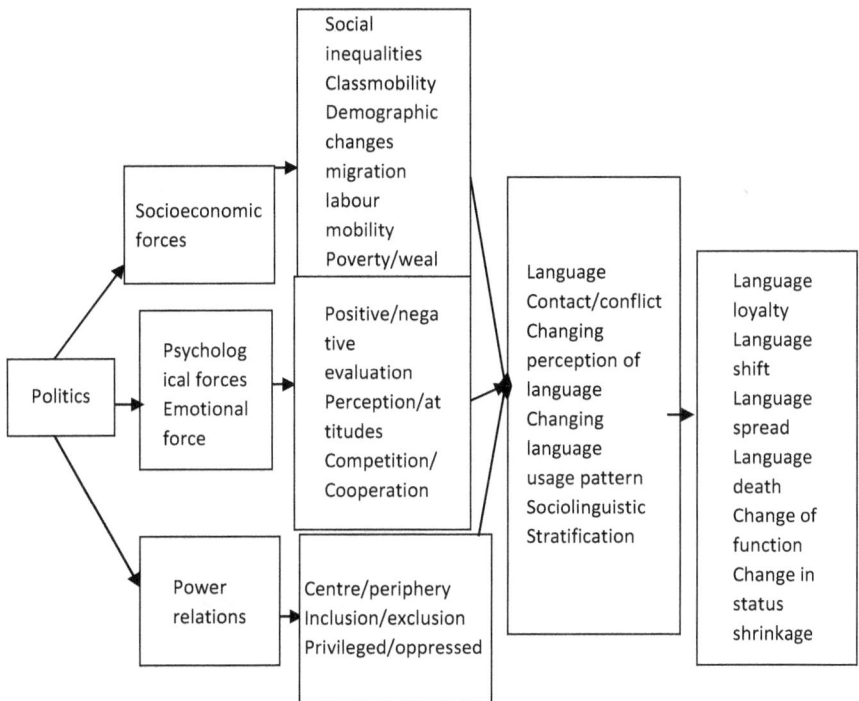

Figure 12: Dynamics of Politics and Language Spread (cf. F O Egbokhare 2004, Language and Politics in Nigeria p.510).

7.1.4 Civil war, minority agitations, politics and creation of new political structures

Some relevant events in Nigeria's history are the Fulani Jihad of 1803–30, Richard's constitution of 1954 that created the regional structure, the creation of the Midwest Region in 1963, the civil war of 1967–70, the creation of new political and administrative structures in 1968(12 states), 1979 (19 states), 1989 (21 states) and 36 states to date. Added to these is the multiplication of Local Government Areas, about 774 in all. The Fulani Jihad entrenched Hausa in Northern Nigeria as the lingua franca to the extent that it is difficult for people to believe that Northern

Nigeria is by far more diverse than the South. The Richards Constitution created the regional structure, the Northern, Western and Eastern Regions, thereby creating platforms for domination of minorities in the Midwest by the Yoruba in the west, the Eastern Minorities of Rivers, Cross Rivers and Akwa Ibom who were under the Igbo in the East and the position of Hausa was further deepened as the dominant language in the North. The creation of the Midwest in 1963, and more states across the country as stated above as well as the civil war caused the major languages to either recede completely to their ethnic homelands or begin a process of receding as is the case of Hausa in Northern Nigeria. Brann (1992) contends that the 36 state structure endeavoured to satisfy the territorial unity of the first and second tier languages, i.e., major and network groups, whereas the previous four regions and later twelve state structure satisfied only the major ones (pp1–2). Bamgbose (1992:3) puts it succinctly. "With the creation and recreation of states, languages which were formerly called minority languages have now attained a dominant status". The new political entities gave administrative, economic and territorial spaces to hitherto minorities, provided opportunities for state patronage at different tiers, eliminated the pressure to assimilate and integrate. In terms of politics, citizenship, is by ethnicity and political constituencies coincides with ethnolinguistic boundaries thereby making them useful platforms for political and citizenship negotiations. Ethnic boundaries were hardened, a bifurcation between indigenes and settlers put paid to possibilities of integration thereby leading to the receding of major languages of former regions in new states. Contrarily, new dominant state languages gained in function and status. A common national lingua franca became a pressing necessity, since English was restricted to formal bureaucracy and the education process. The collapse of Nigeria's public school system, huge illiterate population, burgeoning informal economic sector undermined the promise of English as a lingua franca. Amfani (2001) decries the loss of official recognition of Hausa by the Hausa states since the demise of the Northern Region, especially in states such as Kebbi, Kaduna, Niger, Adamawa and Taraba which have other ethnolinguistic groups. The loss of status of Hausa is even more pronounced currently as a result of numerous religious, ethnic and resource conflicts in Northern Nigeria. Three logical gaps arise from the foregoing. These are linguistic, identity and ideological. They create a need for a lingua franca and a language of nationalism.

8 ICTs and linguistic opportunities

Although Anderson's (2009) piece is not exactly about language, there are insights to gain from his submission. The digital environment is characterized by

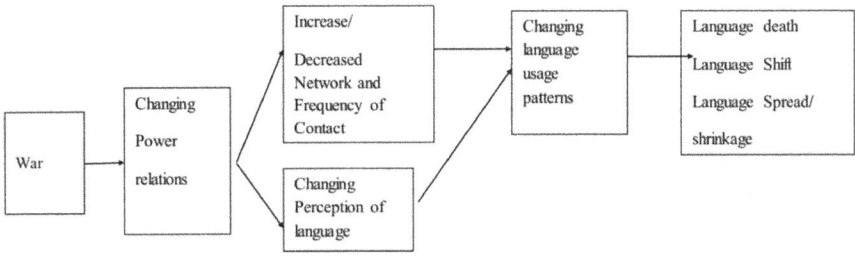

Figure 13: War and Language. This is original to this paper.

(a) The democratization of tools of production, (anyone can make content, including language content); people can make content freely unhindered, unconstrained.
(b) Democratization of distribution which has led to cut in the cost of production, understood here also to imply that the dissemination of linguistic innovations is now cheaper; individuals have greater control of their linguistic choices as opposed to formal prescription.
(c) Connecting supply and demand (through search engines, blogs, recommendations lists, etc.). Governments and organized regulatory environments no longer have monopolies of standards and channels of language flow. Formal recognition of language and power of regulatory control are whittling in the new digital environment.
(d) Democratization of participation (wisdom of the crowd)

Modern environment of ICTs is characterized by mass participation, "wisdom of crowds" in content creation (represented by Wikipedia for instance,) or collaboration in knowledge production (in form of professional networks and ideology of Open Source). The market is now a market of multitudes where size and geography no longer constitute limitations. The democratization of tools of production and the bridging of time and space through the internet, interoperability of media, etc. means that demand is no longer filtered by the economics of scarcity and supply is not limited by the tyranny of geography or size of market. By increasing the pace and intensity of human communication, providing new windows of orality, deemphasizing the influence of face-to-face physical contact, redefining literacy, through speech synthesis and speech recognition as new technologies of reading and writing, the value of the printed text and literacy as defined in language contact, standard setting, linguistic markers or barriers is minimized (See Adegbola, 2006).

One lesson to learn from this is that diversity is no longer a problem and size is no longer a disadvantage in the digital environment. Other significant lessons are the redefinition and configuration of power/influence, benefits and disadvantage, with implications for linguistic behaviour. The issue of government recognition of a language no longer matters to speakers of a language. The issue of varieties and standards are actually creations of the linguist since there is no apparent problem with communication. Besides, the pidgin spelling controversy is simply a prescriptive one that has arisen from traditions of learning as regards how a language should be spelt. Until we yield these instincts and connect with what users are doing in reality and not assume that we have legitimate control of knowledge, we shall not analyse events as they truly are.

8.1 Shift in cultural production

In all these, the centre of cultural production and language of cultural production has shifted from the local to the global and from physical to cyberspace. Linguistic creativity and innovations is no longer under organized and conscious control of expert knowledge but is driven by crowd wisdom. Cultural entrepreneurs are no longer in the village neighbourhood but in cyber neighbourhood. The vectors of language and culture are no longer traditional media but digital. In addition, the irrelevance of the local economy tied to cultural production which drives vocabulary development means that local languages are no longer enough to meet the needs and aspirations of globalized man. Only languages that key into the new global movement have a chance of being relevant. While the shift in cultural production has negatively affected other Nigerian languages, it has boosted the growth and spread of NPby freeing it from limitations of human control and regulation.

9 Globalization, youth movements and ideology

According to Egbokhare (2014), 'globalization and ICTs are creating new forms of identities and image of self. New forms of relationships and new social networks are emerging, coupled with new definitions of community, changing expressions of fraternity and loyalty. Old orders on which social fabrics and identities are built are crumbling due to the blurring of private and public space, merging of formal and informal space, wavering boundaries of loyalties and identity, shrinking of space and time. The endangerment and loss of language and culture is complicating the issue of identity. New and transcendental identities generated in form of new forms of religion and fundamentalism are overriding ethnic, and national loyalties. There are digital natives, culture communities, communities based on sexual orientation and a global convergence of youth aspirations driven by social media. How these may relate to, override or strengthen patrimony and primordial instincts are still being understood. Nevertheless, the blurring of boundaries and cultural norms of morality has been accentuated by social media to the extent that traditional taboos are no longer off limits.

In a sense, citizenship rights are often engraved in laws and state structures, institutions, customs and traditions which assume that identities are static and exist only along ethno-religious lines. It becomes difficult to admit and give recognition to new identities that are constantly being dynamized in the global environment. The other issue is that laws and institutions tend to imbue identities with permanence (contrary to the dynamic nature of social formation processes), thereby limiting man's capacity to respond to new realities, besides ascribing normative value to conservative elements and legitimizing claims of cultural entrepreneurs and status quo-opportunist to moral high ground. The bottom-line is that states end up with wrong premises for identity classification, or may sustain anachronistic divisions and in fact fail to be conscious of new identities thereby having within it citizens without status. Such citizens are the new internally displaced individuals in a sociocultural and legal sense.

Part of the socio-political crisis of modern states has been an attempt to define and constraint freedom of expression in the digital environment. The loss of control of national geographical boundaries in the digital world has its consequences of limiting the ability of state agents to control the ideology of nationalism. There is a push and pull between the individual's assertion of their individuality, groups' insistence on their pre-eminence and the state's exertion of coercive force to rein in what it considers to be unconventional and unacceptable norms of behaviour with severe implications for citizenship rights and responsibilities.

9.1 NP and ideology

The contending ideology in society is sometimes replicated as linguistic choices and behaviour, in terms of language use patterns. It follows therefore that by giving accurate interpretations to the patterns, not merely as purely quantitative and qualitative linguistic expressions, but also in terms of deeper currents and movements in society, we may in fact provide a better explanation of socio-political forces underlying the linguistic realities. If we follow this line of thinking, it will mean that there are non-linguistic concomitants of socio-political forces and by understanding them, we can better elucidate what we see ordinarily as attitudes and choices forced upon speakers of a language as part of a larger ideological unity. For instance, we may be able to connect the apparently disparate events in popular culture, politics, social movements and language attitudes, acquisition and use patterns in terms of deeper ideological unity. What would the mixing of language in popular culture and language, code switching, mixing and language interlarding, as well as syncretism and hybridizing in arts and fashion tell us as a prevailing ideological bent?

There would seem to be three contending ideologies dominant in Nigerian society. We may represent these as negation, negritude and adaptation. Pidgin represents the ideology of integration, adaptation and convergence, an amalgam of tradition and modernity, an aspiration for glocalization. Negritude is reflected in the arguments for conservatism, ethnoreligious revivalism while negation drives the tendency that promotes the emergence of English as first language and promotion of colonial culture. The explosive spread of NPis evidence of the predominance of the ideology of convergence and integration. Convergence or adaptation is a youth phenomenon promoted by social media and popular culture.

9.2 Negritude, negation and adaptation

In order to achieve some level of clarity in terms of the behaviour of language in society, we must understand the ideological currents and the nature of society that produces these currents. For instance, the Nigerian society may be characterized in terms of three ideological currents which are both sequential and coterminous. These are negation, negritude and adaptation. Negritude defines Afrocentricism, a resistance to external influence. The independence movement was powered by this philosophy and it retains various shades in economic, political and social movements. Linguistically, it drives loyalty to local languages and culture. Negation is the flip side that characterizes a Eurocentric orientation, an acceptance of colonial and foreign ideologies without question, reflected in the dominance of western culture, English language and Americanisms as a version of this. In sections of Northern Nigeria, it is reflected as *Arabicization*, promotion of Arabic language and schools, hardening against western values, sometimes interpreted as Islam. English language as the emblem of western culture is resisted giving room for Hausa to dominate (simplistic, not farfetched).

Adaptation is the new ideology that defines youth aspirations for integration and globalization, propelled by popular culture, media and urbanization. It is a movement towards convergence with emblems in every area of Nigerian life.

9.3 Popular culture and ideology of protest and Yabis

What kind of image, social statement or personality statement do pidgin speakers wish to make? Given the fact that ethnic boundaries are hard and impenetrable in the Nigerian environment, what kinds of opportunities does the use of pidgin offer? In order to answer these questions, we need to look at the role of popular culture movements and their associated identities engraved in Nigerian Pidgin.

Adetunji Adegoke's (2011) paper on *Language and Identity Representation in Popular Music* focuses on the role of popular music and significant features of language in the creolization/indigenization of popular music and representation of national identity. This is foregrounded by the active deployment of music in African colonial struggle, resistance and preservation of self, identity, philosophies, ideologies and culture (p.1) In understanding the ideological currents and how pidgin keys into this, it is important that we examine music and within this context, popular culture as a most conspicuous vector of new identities and ideologies (Fabian, 1978). There is a polarity between popular and high culture in many societies and the music and arts, 'provide spaces or sites between the resistance of subordinate groups and forces of incorporation operating in the interest of dominant groups. Music as a medium serves as a terrain of exchange and negotiation between ideological polarities, with popular culture representing a mass ideology. Two critical characteristics of popular music are represented by two personalities who represent different milieu. These are Fela Anikulapo Kuti, whose genre is ideologically characterized as Yabis, i.e. protest and Lagbaja who is an Archivist (Olatunji, 2007). The main features of contemporary popular music are syncretism, appropriation, hybridization, borrowing to form new cultural forms and spaces. The linguistic embodiment of this strategy consists of code switching, language mixing, language interlarding, creolization (use of Nigerian Pidgin) (Babalola and Taiwo, 2009:6). Code switching is an identity marker showing on the one hand an affinity with cultural roots and on the other an accommodation of the other. Nigerian pidgin is emblematic of this ideology of convergence, adaptation and integration.

Popular culture as a vector of Nigerian Pidgin has three main milieus that stand out. There is the Patois revival defined by the dominance of Reggae as a music genre in Nigeria in the late sixties and seventies. It defined a Rasta subculture of ganja smoking individuals who were rebels of conventional norms and practices, with a hippie-like lifestyle, laisse fair, deviant lifestyle. This movement had as the heroes Jimmy Cliff, Bob Maley, U-Roy, I-Roy and many Jamaican and local musicians of the genre. In a sense, it defined the emergence of a global awareness and diasporan connection, of an identity bigger than the local.

Following this was the **Yabis** movement characterized by the music of Fela Ransome Kuti whose primary language of musical expression was Nigerian Pidgin. Fela's music was essentially protest music with a large youth cult following. Whereas Reggae Patois opened up the media pipeline for parameterization of the pidgin stigma, Fela's music not only popularized it but also keyed it into a positive identity with revolutionary and progressive ideology of protest and change. It is difficult to tell, if pidgin made Fela or Fela made pidgin. What is essentially true was that while Fela's music provided a credible medium for de-stigmatization and respectability, pidgin provided him with mass opportunity and loyalty of those who connected with his musical ideology. Fela held sway in the late 70s to 80s. By the late 80s, a new youth movement influenced by visual, media, television, and video had taken hold. New forms of expression, creation of niches, ideologies of choice and opportunities provided for new ways of doing things culminating with the digital revolution peaking in the 2000s with Web 2.0. This was the era of globalization. Globalization was both aggregating and disintegrating. It aggregated youth aspirations but led to disintegration of control at individual and group levels followed by reconfiguration and redefinition and new realities.

The overall effect of the new image associated with pidgin is a *coolness factor*. Use of NPconfers on one an urban cosmopolitan personality, a certain legitimacy. In this regard, we see a transition from stigma to prestige. The conversion achieved in this final phase is creditable to the role of community radio, advertising, comedy, Nollywood, political campaigns and improved communications through the GSM. Pidgin is the language of stand-up comedy in Nigeria. Aside from English, no Nigerian Language has as much presence in the media as pidgin. Of all the languages in Nigeria, Pidgin is perhaps the only language that has a Television Station devoted entirely to its use.

Whenever attempts are made to address Nigerians as a whole, pidgin is deployed as the language of intergroup and cross-cultural and class communication. It is obvious that more Nigerians drawn from different strata are beginning to recognize the unifying nature of the language (Osisanwo, 2012). This is not by choice but by necessity and accident of history. Today, pidgin is trending. The new heroes, the stars speak it. Politicians portray an image of cross-cultural and class identification by using it. It is perhaps the incursion of pidgin as the dominant language of interaction among students in Universities that has succeeded in breaking its taboo as a bastardized and broken language.

9.4 NP identity

Identity is not monolithic but is highly dynamic and is dynamized by numerous socio-political and economic forces. "we cannot reduce questions of language to such social psychological notions of instrumental and integrative motivations, but must account for the extent to which language is embedded in social, economic and political struggles" (Pennycock, 1994: 15). The use of myths and stereotypes to reinforce distinctness and positive identity has a corollary in the use of stigmatization to and self-condemnation as a derivative (Ogbuagu, 2013). Tajfel (1978) introduces the concept of secure and insecure identities as cognitive alternatives. 'In insecure situations, dominant groups regard their superiority as legitimate and tend to intensify the existing differences to maintain their psychological distinctiveness and resulting positive identity. The notions of soft and hard boundaries may be culled up to emphasize the tendency for ethnic boundaries to reject or permit assimilation or integration. Ethnic boundaries in Nigeria are hard. Citizenship is derived from ethnicity and the allocation of political constituencies, privileges and advantages are derived from ethnic membership.

10 Conclusion: WAZOBIA, Naija in NPIdentity construction

The search for a national consciousness has involved conscious linguistic enterprises in language policy and planning and as well as attempts to create artificial languages out of the dominant Nigerian languages. Two such efforts are WAZOBIA and GUOSA. Like Esperanto before them, both efforts failed. This notwithstanding, a new national consciousness is emerging from youth culture, propelled by the new media and popular culture. It is the Naija consciousness (also written 9ja). It is derived from the root word *Niger* in the word Nigeria. It is difficult to determine when it was first used and who first used it. It is a term used mainly in popular culture and youth parlance to refer to Nigerian people. It is an evolving nomenclature, an identity undergoing construction and revision. It is a term that has evolved out of informal conversations, diaspora solidarity and popular culture. Naija defines the commonality and essence of the culture and practices that define Nigerians as a distinct people. In essence, in the multilingual, pluralistic and fractured society it is a nomenclature that expresses or otherwise captures the aspiration for a common identity. Naija may also be seen as a statement by the youths, a popular movement, a culture, a mindset, a Nigerianness. Naija provides a basis for unity and nationalistic sentiments, cultural and behavioural convergence as well is a philosophical and ideological rallying point. There is a Naija spirit that defines a Nigerian personality or a personality that Nigerians aspire to as definitive of resilience and a can do spirit. Naija represents an ethos that is aggregative of the diverse cultures and peoples. NP defines the linguistic concomitant of this consciousness, the essence of a national convergence, the preference of the youth for adaptation and integration. This term is now being suggested by some researchers and writers as the new name for Nigerian pidgin in order to destigmatize it, accommodate it as a bonafide Nigerian language and legitimize it as an authentic lingua franca.

References

Adegbola, Tunde. 2006. Globalization: Colonizing the space of flows. In Francis Egbokhare & Clement Kolawole (eds), *Globalization and the future of African languages*, 1–12. Ibadan: Ibadan Cultural Studies Group.

Adegoke, Adetunji. 2011. Language and Identity Representation in Popular Music. *International Journal of Innovative Interdisciplinary Research*, No. 1, 150–164

Agheyisi, Rebecca. 1971. *West African Pidgin English: Simplification and simplicity*. Stanford: University of Stanford Ph.D. dissertation. Ann Arbor: University Microfilms.

Agheyisi, Rebecca. 1983. Linguistic Implications of the Changing role of Nigerian Pidgin English. Paper read at the 14th Annual Conference on African Linguistics. University of Wisconsin, Madison.

Agheyisi, Rebecca & Frank Aig-Imoukhuede. 1982. *Pidgin stew and sufferhead*. Ibadan: Heinemann Educational Books.

Ajayi, Ade J. F. 1965. *Christian missions in Nigeria, 1841–1891: The making of a new elite*. Evanston: Northwestern University Press.

Albert, Isaac Olawale. 1996. Ethnic Residential Segregation in Kano, Nigeria and its Antecedents. *African Studies Monograph* 17(2), 85–100.

Amfani, Ahmed. 2001. Unifying the Orthographies of the Languages in North-West. In Francis Egbokhare and Solomon O. Oyetade (eds.), *Harmonisation and standardisation of Nigerian languages*, 56–69. Cape Town: Centre for Advanced Studies of African Society.

Anderson, Chris. 2009. *The long tail: Why the future of business is selling less or more*. New York: Hyperion.

Ayandele, Emmanuel Ayankanmi. 1974. *The educated elite in the Nigerian society*. Ibadan: Ibadan University Press.

Babalola, Emmanual T. & Rotimi Taiwo. 2009. Code-switching in Contemporary Nigerian hip-hop music. *Itupale online Journal of African studies* 1 (1), 1–26.

Bamgbose, Ayo. 1992. Speaking in Tongues: Implication of multilingualism for Language Policy in Nigeria. Merit Award Winners Lecture Kaduna: The Board of Trustees of the Nigerian Merit Award.

Bamgbose, Ayo. 2000. *Language and exclusion: The consequences of language policies in Africa*. Hamburg: Literature Verlag.
Bamgbose, Ayo, Ayo Banjo & Andrew Thomas. 1995. *New Englishes: A West African perspective*. Ibadan: Mosuro.
Cooper, Robert. 1982. A Framework for the Study of Language Spread. In Robert Cooper (ed.), *Language spread*, 1–4. Bloomington: Indiana University Press.
Craith, Máiréad Nic. 2007. *Language, power and identity politics*. New York: Palgrave Macmillan.
Hansford, Keir, John BendoSamuel & Ronald Stanford. 1976. *An index of Nigerian languages*. Accra: Summer Institute of Linguistics.
Deuber, Dagmar. 2005. *Nigerian Pidgin in Lagos: Language contact, variation and change in an African urban setting*. London: Battlebridge.
Dike, Kenneth. 1956. *Trade and politics in the Niger Delta: 1830–1885*. London: Oxford University Press.
Egbokhare, Francis. 2004. Language and politics in Nigeria. In Owolabi D K O and A Dasylva (eds), Forms and Functions of English and Indigenous Languages in Nigeria. Ibadan: Group Publishers.
Egbokhare, F. 2003. The Story of a Language. Nigerian Pidgin in Spatiotemporal, Social and Linguistic Context. In Lucko, P., Peter, L. Wolf, H. (eds.) Studies in African Varieties of English. Frankfurt: Peter Lang. 21–40.
Egbokhare, Francis, Solomon O. Oyetade, Eno-Abasi E. Urua & Ahmed H. Amfani. 2001. *Language clusters in Nigeria*. CASAS Monograph Series No 12. Cape Town: South Africa.
Egbokhare, Francis. 2003. *Breaking barriers: ICT, language policy and development*. Ibadan: Postgraduate School.
Egbokhare, Francis. 2010. Language Flows through Pipeline: Nigerian Pidgin and its Spread. In Michael Oladejo Afolayan (ed.), *Multiculturalism in the age of the mosaic: Essays in honour of Rudolf G. Wilson*. New York: Nova Science Publishers.
Egbokhare, Francis and Solomon Oyetade. 2002. *Harmonisation and standardization of Nigerian languages*. CASAS Book Series No 19, Cape Town: South Africa.
Elugbe, Ben. 1992. *The scramble for Nigeria*. Unpublished Inaugural Lecture.
Elugbe, Ben. 1995. Nigeria Pidgin: Problems and prospects. In Ayo Bamgbose, Ayo Banjo & Andrew Thomas (eds.), *New Englishes: A West African perspective*, 284–299. Ibadan: Mosuro.
Elugbe, Ben & Augusta Omamor. 1991. *Nigerian Pidgin: Background and prospects*. Ibadan: Heinemann Educational Books Plc.
Fabian, Johannes. 1978. Popular culture in Africa: Findings and conjectures. To the Memory of Placide Temples (1906–1977), *Journal of the International African Institute* 48(4), 315–334.
Faraclas, Nicholas. 1996. *Nigerian Pidgin*. London: Routledge.
Faraclas, Nicolas & Ibim Worukwo. *A Language Synopsis of Rivers Pidgin English*, ms. N.d.
Faraclas, Nicolas, O. Ibim, G. Worukwo, A. Minah & A. Tariah. 1983–84. Rivers State Pidgin English. *Journal of Language Association of Nigeria 2*, 187–198.
Gladwell, Malcolm. 2000. *The tipping point: How little things can make a big difference*. London: Abacus.

Huber, Magnus. 1999. *Ghanaian Pidgin English in its West African context*. Amsterdam: John Benjamin.

Igboanusi, Herbert. 2008. Empowering Nigerian Pidgin: Challenge for Status Planning. *World Englishes* 27(1), 68–82.

Isichei, Elizabeth A. 1995. *A history of Christianity in Africa: From antiquity to the present*. Grand Rapids: William B. Eerdmans Publishing.

Jibril, Munzali. 1995. The elaboration of the functions of Nigerian Pidgin. In Ayo Bamgbose, Ayo Banjo & Andrew Thomas (eds.), *New Englishes: A West African perspective*, 232–247. Ibadan: Mosuro.

Lieberson, Stanley. 1982. Forces Affecting Language Spread: Some Basic Propositions. In Robert Cooper (ed.), *Language spread*, 5–36. Bloomington: Indiana University Press.

Mafeni, Bernard. 1971. Nigerian Pidgin. In John Spencer (ed.), *The English Language in West African*, 95–112. London: Longman.

Mann, Charles C. 1993. The Sociolinguistic Status of Anglo-Nigerian Pidgin: An Overview. *International Journal of Sociology of Language* 100–101, 167–78.

Mühlhäusler, Peter. 1986. *Pidgins and creole linguistics*. New York: Basil Blackwell, 1986.

Olatunji, Michael. 2007. Yabis: A Phenomenon in the Contemporary Nigerian Music. *Africology: The Journal of Pan African Studies* 1(9), 26–46.

Omamor, Augusta. 1990a. Towards extricating Nigerian Pidgin (NP) from a straight jacket: A Preliminary Study. Paper presented at the XIV Annual Conference on African Linguistics (CAL) University of Wisconsin, Madison.

Omamor, Augusta. 1990b. Pidgins and Pseudo Pidgins: A Case Study of the Nigerian Situation. *Research in African Languages and Linguistics* 1(1), 43–55.

Oribhabor, Eriata. 2012. *If you Hie Se A De Prizin. Antologi of Puem-Dem Fo Naija Langwej*. Abuja: Something for Everybody Ventures.

Osisanwo, Ayo. 2012. A morphological analysis of Nigerian Pidgin: The example of selected advertisement jingles. *The Journal of the Linguistic Association of Nigeria* 15(1&2), 41–54.

Pennycook, Alastair 1994. *The cultural politics of English as an international language*. London: Longman.

Schaefer, Ronald & Francis Egbokhare. 2006. On Profiles of Use for Majority Language in Southern Nigeria. In R. Elangaiyan, Nicholas Ostler, McKenna R. Brown & K. Mahandra (eds.), *Vital voices: Endangered languages and multilingualism*, 105–110. Bath: Foundation for Endangered Languages.

Smolicz, J. J. 1983. Meaning and Values in Cross-Cultural Contacts. *Ethnic and Racial Studies* 6(1), 33–49.

Tajfel, Henri. (1978) The achievement of group differentiation. In Henri Tajfel (ed.), *Differentiation between social groups: Studies in the social psychology of intergroup relations*, 77–98. London: Academic Press.

Tajfel, Henri & John C. Turner. (1986). The social identity theory of intergroup behavior. In Stephen Worchel & William G. Austin (eds.), *Psychology of intergroup relations*, 7–24. Chicago: Nelson-Hall.

The Federal Republic of Nigeria. 1981. *National Policy on Education*. Lagos: NERDC Press.

The Federal Republic of Nigeria. 1999. *The Constitution of the Federal Republic of Nigeria*. Abuja: Federal Ministry of Justice.

Vatsa, Mamman J. 1981. *Tori for geti bow leg and other Pidgin poems*. Lagos, Nigeria: Cross Continent Press.

Idom Inyabri and Eyo Mensah
Chapter 4
Nigerian Pidgin, identity and national re-invention in Naija stand-up comedy

Introduction

Stand-up comedy in Africa is one of the most powerful youth-based art forms that has established itself as an agency for the African youth in this millennium. In Nigeria, stand-up comedy has successfully appropriated the facilities of indigenous traditional performances, along with the technological innovations and cultural impulses of its time to install a genre that has become very influential in the country. In fact, with regard to the circumstances of its growth and impact, one can liken and link its emergence to *Naija* hip hop and the Nollywood home video phenomenon. To establish our discourse more properly, it is important to state from the onset that for us, stand-up comedy is an electronic media-specific, socially conscious comic performance genre in which a comedian takes centre stage to make humour for the pleasure of an audience. As a performative genre, stand-up comedy has gradually established itself as a global commoditized product that involves live delivery of comic materials on a stage before an audience. By the implication of its name, the stand-up comedian is often compelled by his art to stand and perform to their audience. The art is predominantly performed by a solo comic artist who takes charge of the stage and manages proxemics to suit their act. Although we stated that the genre is defined by a solo performer, this is not the rule as stand-up comedians may go into *collabo* (collaborations) with other colleagues to capture certain themes that demand elaborate characterization. In the context of the rise of electronic media and their influence on the development and dissemination of the art form, it is only apt to also describe *Naija* stand-up comedy in the words of Adejunmobi (2014: 178) as an electronically "mediated" performance through which the comedian interrogates "the ethics [. . .] surrounding the different ways in which individuals perform their subjectivity" (176). Indeed, as Bergson (2003: 5) would have it, "the humour in *Naija* stand-up comedy is truly culture-specific, because the mirth that arises from its performances is only transmitted through a Nigerian idiom, especially Nigerian Pidgin and it speaks to "the customs and ideas of [Nigeria]".

However, it should also be understood that generally, the art form is distinguished by an individual performer who by their comic iconicity invests a stamp of identity and difference on their own performance, and through that act, develops a folk image and a fan base. We use the qualifier *Naija* in this paper to delineate a unique post-structural adjustment Nigerian youth character to the genre as it has been established in the Nigerian cultural space. Taking into consideration the larger circumstance of post-independence Nigerian youth cultural production and identity creation in the last quarter of the 20th century, the term *Naija* stand-up comedy seems apt to capture the character of this comic genre and the varied youth-based cultural agencies around it, namely, graffiti, pose, fashion rap. The name – *Naija* – is a unique Nigerian Pidgin coinage, which probably emerged in the early 1990s to capture the character and cultural identity of the Nigerian postcolony in all its desperation, creative ingenuity and resilience. In the popular domain, the word also functions as a signifier for the Nigerian citizen and the nation state at the same time. It is important to state here that since the early 90s, "Naija" has been widely used in Nigeria by its youth population predominantly. In fact, the establishment now identifies with the term whenever it wishes to carry out any form of social mobilization to include the youth.[1]

Although stand-up comedy as an art form, in the mode that we discuss here, started taking shape and became more prominent in the mid-1990s and at the turn of the millennium, it has its roots deep in a plethora of oral traditions that can be considered their own "embryonic form of *dramatic art*" (authors' emphasis, de Graft 1976: 9) coupled with other precursor diasporic/Western and urban performances before it. We shall account for these creative antecedents to *Naija* stand-up comedy later but it is important at this point to elaborate the connection that our discourse has with similar intellectual pursuits in the stand-up comedy performance as an academic discourse. In this regard, it must be noted that stand-up comedy has not attracted much scholarly engagement in its own right as a Nigerian Pidgin cultural phenomenon and art form with a peculiar text. In an intriguing essay which studies Wole Soyinka as a popular artist, especially with the release of his famous music record "Unlimited Liability Company", Adelugba (1987) makes one of the earliest hints at studies on popular art genres such as stand-up comedy. Picking on *yabbing*, the popular Nigerian Pidgin practice of mutual jibes and criticism, Adelugba (1987) critiques Soyinka's musical satire as a popular art form that lyrically signifies "*love* [for] one's country" and a committed form of "patriotism" (authors' emphasis, Adelugba 1987: 194). In this way, he nudges at the form and guiding

---

[1] The National Orientation Agency under President Goodluck Ebele Jonathan used the word *Naija* in its radio and television jingles for mass mobilization towards encouraging a work ethics in the country.

principle of a postmodern oral art that would blossom in our time. Indeed *yabing* or *yabies* (in its Nigerian Pidgin form) is what *Naija* stand-up comedians have developed into a complex popular art form. Barber (1997) would later draw our attention to the integrity of popular arts genres, which obviously include stand-up comedy, when she defines them as hybrid forms that defy simplistic categorization. In an insightful exposition, Barber (1997) reasons that the "vast domain of cultural production" emerging as popular arts cannot be schemed into the usual binaries of "traditional" or "elite", "oral" or "literate", "indigenous" or "Western", because "they make use of all available contemporary materials to speak to contemporary struggles" (Barber 1997: 2). Here, again, lies a critical discourse that provides an aesthetic paradigm within which we can squarely locate Naija stand-up comedy. But our study responds in a more specific way to Barber's (1997) seeming challenge to scholars of African popular arts to investigate the ramifications of globalization with regard to cultural production in Africa. According to her, "though much has been written about 'globalization', more attention could be paid to the specific ways it works through local African scenes of cultural production and consumption, and to the question of what African audiences actually do with, or make of, imported cultural products" (Barber 1997: 7).

As it is, African scholars seem to have been making cautious and cursory inquest into stand-up comedy as a formidable popular art genre. Calling for a radicalization of the curriculum of English studies to suit the needs of contemporary society in Nigeria, Oha (2014) uses the moral import of folk tales and the ethics of stand-up comedy to emphasize "the need for a dynamic view of the literary studies, a more socially-relevant English studies in our time" (Oha 2014: 15). What is of interest to us is the fact that he shows that humour can be a discursive strategy of ensuring social stability, while equipping and positioning students in a knowledge economy (Oha 2014: 8). Apart from Oha's intriguing reference to stand-up comedy, Adejunmobi (2014) has also demonstrated that stand-up comedy can be used to uncouple the subtle nature of performance in everyday life, especially in what he refers to as a "media-saturated environment" (Adejunmobi 2014: 179). Hence, through a deft application of sociological/cultural theories he problematizes performance in the context of a collective African culture, which is coming to terms with the vagaries of mediation, yet bedevilled by the challenges of failed economies. Using the arts of Nigerian stand-up comics as an anthropological fulcrum, Adejunmobi (2014) interrogates the liminal boundaries that divide, yet fuse different levels of performances as acts and arts of daily survival. While we benefit from Adejunmobi's exquisite interrogation of the ethics of performance in mediatized everyday setting, we focus on particular performance texts to show that *Naija* (Nigerian) stand-up comedy is "self-referential" and "overtly political" in their criticism of both political postures and policies, which are inseparably embodied in what Adejunmobi (2014: 179) would refer to as "occupational performance".

In this study our aim is to demonstrate through an ethnographic approach how a generation of young Nigerians exploits the art of stand-up comedy in Nigerian Pidgin to establish a self-critical identity and engineer a liberal sense of nationhood. This paper is presented in seven major sections. The first section is the introduction where the background of the study on stand-up comedy as an art form performed in the Nigerian cultural context is delineated. In section two we account for the pieces scholarship, which have fore-grounded stand-up comedy as a global phenomenon. In section three we uncouple the theoretical positions through which we engage the performance of stand-up comedy in Nigeria. Thus, we are discursively located in a web of postcolonial, postmodern and dialogic theories which sharpen our critical and interpretive perspectives. Since this is an ethnographic study, we specify and describe our research methodology and participants in the fourth section. In section five we are preoccupied with tracing the precursor of stand-up comedy as comic performance in the heterogeneous Nigerian cultural context. The critical examination of stand-up comedy in Nigeria is carried out in section six, where we have identified and analysed in four sub-sections the broad theme of identity and national re-invention. In our conclusion, we present a summary of our discussion and contemplate on the kind of identity and nationality that is signified by stand-up comedy in Nigeria.

1 Stand-up comedy as an emerging global phenomenon

Stand-up comedy as a performative genre has been studied and theorized from a wide range of academic disciplines; theatre (Donkor 2013; Pype 2015), gender studies (Foy 2015; Finley 2016), politics (Sinéad 2008; Donkor 2013; Gillota 2015), linguistics (Katayama 2008; Moriarty 2011; Githatu and Chai), and sociology (Perez 2013; Vigouroux 2015). Beyond its humorous and entertainment value, a variety of other social functions in Western societies provides a voice or a platform to challenge dominant hegemonic norms, beliefs and perceptions that are widely stereotyped (Finley 2016; Lockyer 2015). Vigouroux (2015) shows how comedy performers of North and Sahara African descents utilize stand-up comedy as a forum to make their way of being French heard. This is achieved mainly through their display of heteroglossic repertoires which challenge the social and cultural homogeneity of the French establishment. This evidence reveals that stand-up comedy is a strong tool for indexical inclusion, thus conferring identity and ethnicity to people whose sense of belonging has been threatened or emasculated. Stand-up comedy has also been used as a resource for the promotion and sustenance of a country's minority languages. According to Moriarty (2011), stand-up comedy is an important strategy that favours the use of minority languages in performative genres. Based on an Irish case study, this study reveals that stand-up comedy has increased the potential of language maintenance and planning which "favours the possibility for language revitalization and renewal" (Moriarty 2011: 557). This state of affairs reveals that stand-up performance can broaden our understanding of the cultural context of language use in the everyday interactional experience of its speakers, and could lead to the preservation of linguistic heritage, particularly of minority languages.

Stand-up artists have also used their performance space to subvert and challenge some stereotyped social norms which are deeply entrenched in their societies. Foy (2015: 711) demonstrates how female comedians in America incorporate "sexually transgressive materials" to defy "the cultural values of modesty and passivity for females". Through such subjectivities, female comedians discuss the subject of sex openly, display their homosexual identities, and attempt to "dismantle or appropriate the male gaze" (2015: 703). This position shows that stand-up comedy is not just a forum for self-expression but a platform to accentuate one's social beliefs and orientations. Lockyer (2015) similarly reports how disabled comedians use their performances to resist and renegotiate hegemonic norms about disability, and to counteract disabling practices. In this way, comedy is explored as a discursive strategy to condemn and criticize the cultural stigma and social ideology about disability. According to Moynihan (2008), a popular Irish American comedian, Des Bishop asserts his comic persona to establish himself as a mediating figure between white and non-white immigrants in Ireland. He uses comedy to negotiate class and racial privilege, and to condemn pre-existing Irish identity. In this connection, the artist utilises comedy as "a site to manifest ideological struggle" (Stott 2005: 105). By so doing, he confers class and racial privileges to people who were hitherto subjected to racial abuse.

Many countries of the world have embraced stand-up comedy as an authentic resource for entertainment and for giving voices to emerging contemporary social issues. The impacts, mode of delivery and intentions, may vary from one comic community to another. Studies in the American tradition of stand-up comedy (Katayama 2006, 2008; Perez 2013; Gillota 2015; Finley 2016) have critically interrogated the engagement of humour in reconceptualising the notions of politics, sexuality, racism, and current affairs. Gillota maintains that "American stand-up comedy resonates not only with the classic model of the individual vs. society but also with more contemporary conversations about identity politics"

(2015: 102). On its effect on racism, Perez (2013: 478) argues that "the use of humour allows the 'constraints' on current racial discourse, on whites in particular, to be broken, suggesting a new phase of colour-blind racism may be underway"

The context of comedy performance in Africa varies thematically from the ideological struggle of the West to its functions in ritual performances, politics and mainstream criticism of the establishment. Pype (2015) discusses the emergence of funerary comedies as cultural forms where young people use burial or funeral events as performance space for comedy. Based on this study, funerary jokes emphasise the personal connection between the joker and the deceased. The comedian's role is "to cheer the bereaved and relieve them of the polluting duties of burial" (Pype 2015: 474). In Ghana, stand-up comedy has been enacted to as a tool for political propaganda and mobilization. Donkor (2013) reports that the Ghanaian government recruited the services of a stand-up comedian to launder the president's image and restore his integrity after a mass protest that claimed the lives of protesters was linked to the government's poor handling of the crisis. This was in the wake of a presidential election in which the incumbent president was a candidate. The comedian eventually emerges as "a politrick (trickster) whose indirection allowed him to navigate the minefields of social expectations and unpredictable interpretations" (Donkor 2013: 276). This evidence reveals that if properly harnessed as a mass communication tool, stand-up comedy could be a source of public enlightenment, political mobilization, and information dissemination. In Kenya, comedy jokes range from themes such as tax evasion, greed (by the political class), and ethnicity to social class differentiation, and other social commentaries (Githatu and Chai 2015). These usually form the comedy routine in the culture of comedy in Kenya.

In Nigeria, a number of factors: social, economic and political have contributed to the emergence and growth of stand-up comedy as a performative genre particularly among young people who employ shared cultural knowledge and life experiences in comic entertainment (Brodile 2008; Katayama 2006). The majority of the audiences are equally younger people who consume comedy narratives and humour as forms of emotional relief, expression of social identity, and transportation of their social bubbles into a different world (Mensah 2016). Importantly, stand-up comedy in the Nigerian cultural context is an essential component of ideological becoming, and a new way of gathering new experiences and exhibiting differing social dynamism (Mensah 2016; Mensah and Inyabri 2016). The performance of comedy is therefore a subcultural capital for youth survival and engagement of socio-cultural and political realities. In the sections that follow, we identify and discuss the varied facets of experiences that the performance idiom engages.

2 Theoretical reflections

Considering the socio-cultural, political and technological circumstances of its emergence and sustenance, it is only appropriate to comprehend the phenomenon of *Naija* stand-up comedy through the postcolonial and postmodern perspectives. Arising from its cultural foundations of indigenous performances and dominant Western (American) precursors, *Naija* stand-up comedy is not just a hybrid form but an agency created by a dispossessed youth population to signify presence, establish an identity and engage the challenges of everyday living in a desperate economy. In itself, *Naija* stand-up comedy is yet another example of the resilience and triumph of a marginal group in the hegemony of an odd postcolony. To this extent, the art form in all its varied formation can be said to be a dialogic "folkloric" or "semifolkloric" (Bakhtin 1981: 158) art that has arisen to confront dominant socio-political principalities in the Nigerian state. At the same time, the genre is acting as a performative strategy to surreptitiously redefine that 'queer' nation-space and empower its practitioners. In interpreting the function of this postcolonial art form, we are obviously rooted in Bakhtin's dialogic explication of the role of the "clown" along with the "fool" and "rogue" in their pristine function of exposing the "hypocrisy", "falsehood" and under-belly of humanity through the privilege of mask, metaphors and allegory (1981: 162). Hence, in that Bakhtinian term, we see performers of *Naija* stand-up comedy as part of the heritage of the so called "dregs of society" (Bakhtin 1981: 158) to force what Bakhtin (1981: 263) again calls "heteroglossia" into a space where successive generations of self-seeking "internal bourgeoisie" (Fanon 1967: 120) or "new colonist" (Fanon 1967: 124) have usurped the apparatus of state for self-aggrandisement, stifle expression and perpetrate a culture of ignorance and dispossession. In their tensioned filled art, therefore, *Naija* stand-up comedians are involved in the signification of a new sense of nationhood, which in the perspective of Homi Bhabha is a metaphoric (2004: 200–201, 212), narrative or performative sense of nationality. Deriving insights from Gelner, Jameson, Anderson, Frued and many other kindred postcolonial/postmodern theorists, Bhabha (2004: 201) would want us to see "this cultural construction of nationness as a form of social and textual affiliation." In their radical disruption of the seemingly stable propaganda of the state, these voices from the margins use their own idiom as a "cultural force" and "a narrative strategy" (Bhabha 2004: 201) to perform a national identity they wish to install.

However, it is the manner in which this collective social imaginary or what Appadurai (1996: 8) calls "a community of sentiment" has transcended its status as a non-canonical popular art to dominate the nation space that we are interested in. But what is even more intriguing is how the postmodern/postcolonial perspective gives insight to the dynamics and character of *Naija* stand-up comedy. In this regard, Appadurai's (1996: 9) classic thought on the momentous constellation of "electronic mediation and mass migration" in the making of a new form of modernity in what he also calls "the postelectronic world" (Appadurai's (1996: 5) is quite helpful for us. From the foregoing account on the emergence of the art form under discussion, the roles of migration and different forms of electronic technology in the evolution and influence of this comic art cannot be underestimated. In this paper, we affirm the power of electronic media in rupturing the false duality that have circumscribed popular performance to the margins as it has also levelled the interactive/creative spaces in the society. Appadurai (1996: 5) puts it more succinctly when he states that "the imagination in the postelectronic world [. . .] has broken out of the special expressive spaces of art, myth, and has now become a part of the quotidian mental work of ordinary people in many societies". It is the business of this paper to explain how the cultural and technological revolution that the world has been witnessing since the late 20th century has given birth to a truly globalised art form and a "sodality" or imagined cultural collective (Appadurai 1996: 8) which in their varied manifestations inscribe a new form of identity and perception of the nation in the Nigerian postcolony.

3 Methods and participants

Data for this study were obtained through a nine-month ethnographic fieldwork that took the researchers to Lagos, Abuja, Enugu, and Calabar to interact with comedians, radio producers, television producers and directors in an attempt to investigate the precursors of stand-up comedy in Nigeria. We employed mainly oral interviews, informal conversations and participant observations where we assumed the role of subjective participants and objective observers with our subjects to elicit information on the ideological intentions and motives of comedians in enacting individual and differentiated identities. We also aimed to trace the evolution of stand-up comedy in the Nigerian socio-cultural and media contexts. According to Jorgensen (1989: 63) participant observation strategy is an approach to data collection that involves "penetrating and gaining experience of a form of human life. It is an objective approach insofar as it represents in the accurate, detailed description of the insiders' experience of life". This approach also enabled us to give depth to the linguistic and non-linguistic import of stand-up comedy performances and facilitated a close text reading of the selected performances.

To be more focused, we utilized commercially produced audio visual discs of live comedy performances of Gordons, and other contemporary Nigerian popular comedians who have been serialised in the Opa Williams "Night of Thousand Laughs" show. Given the fluid and dynamic forms that characterise the apprehension of cultural activities in our time, it was also necessary to access virtual archives on YouTube and other internet bases for performances. In this study, Gordons' performances form the discursive fulcrum upon which we connect other stand-up comedians co-referentially in terms of thematic preoccupations. The choice of Gordons as our major touchstone is informed by his creative enterprise, popularity, industry, bold metaphors and innuendoes which characterize his performances. All recordings were transcribed and annotated. The transcribed interview scripts and performance recordings were analysed within the framework of postcolonialism, which is based on the concepts of otherness and resistance, and an attempt to articulate and celebrate the cultural identities of hegemonized people and reclaim their past from the colonizers (Lye 1993). Our position in this study is that *Naija* stand-up comedy is a youth-based performance that widely indexes identity, a new sense of nationhood, and agency through Nigerian Pidgin in a digital age.

4 Comic precursors

By virtue of their roles in established mornachies in Nigeria – the Yoruba and Bini, for instance, – we observe that court jesters are not just mirth-makers for the Obas' court; they are sources of humour and indeed the moral centre for the entire community. In Northern Nigeria, in spite of the strictures of Islam, the itinerant griot with his string instrument is a figure who performs the role of a poet/musician and comedian in the community. He, the griot, freely lampoons individuals and throws indicting metaphors and innuendoes at the system. Among the Igbo of eastern Nigeria there thrives, till date, a robust tradition of collective/interpersonal humour and gibes called *Njakiri*. In fact, the Igbo example stands as one of Africa's most established indigenous folk forms of inter-personal and communal comic art. Oha (2014) sees *Njakiri* as an "ancient Igbo lore [. . .] a seemingly less too-serious way that indigenous Africans, specifically the local Igbo, would, engage objectionable behaviour" (Oha 2014: 7–8). As he goes further to indicate, *Njakiri* is one of the critical manners in which the Igbo show "how to make discourse confront serious issues while pretending to be humorous and simple", it is indeed a "psychologically oriented approach to problems in human conduct, especially transgressions"

(Oha 2014: 8). Kadimo Oqua, a stand-up comedian and Master of Ceremony (MC), opines that the Efik/Qua people of Cross River State, South-eastern Nigeria had an indigenous one-man itinerant comic masquerade performance called *Ekporoko* (Stock-fish), which picked on deviances, ills and follies in the community[2] (personal interview 6/9/16). As a show of appreciation for patronage to his performance, *Ekporoko*, the masquerade comedian, would usually cut out a piece from his stock-fish and offer it to his host(s) – an act of reciprocal patronage and benevolence. For Kadimo Oqua, as he is popularly called, *Ekporoko*, who is his own personal inspiration and model in the stand-up comedy art, represents an indigenous source to what has now become modern, digital and urban.

Beyond the aforementioned "traditional" forebears of the stand-up comedy genre in Nigeria, it is important to account for some modern precursors that have contributed to the emergence of the art as we know it today. In this regard, the monopoly of public television services provided Nigerians who had the aptitude for this form of comic performance to experiment, express themselves and reach out to their audiences. As a public media broadcaster established to galvanise the multi-ethnic people of the Nigerian state, the Nigerian Television Authority (NTA) with channels in the different regions in Nigeria hosted the earliest artists who we may identify as harbingers of today's stand-up comedy. For Ndubuisi Osuagwu and Chike Ikeokpara (personal interview 2015), the legendary Mazi Ukonu (Anyaogu Elekwachi Ukonu) and Nwelekebe are representative examples of stand-up comedians in the 1960s through the '70s (personal interview 2/9/16). Mazi Ukonu, for instance, ran a show on NTA Channel 6 Aba, Eastern Nigeria, which was known as the "Ukonu's Club – Teenagers Playtime", where he interlaced comics and gybes with moral/inspirational exhortations for young people. Because of his fame and contribution to social life in Eastern Nigeria and indeed as a cultural icon in Nigeria generally, Alexander Iheke has written a biography in his honour entitled *Mazi Ukono: Journey from Medicine to Theatre Arts* (2010). But many respondents, including Akpausoh A. Akpausoh and Teniyi Ajayi of NTA Headquarters, Abuja, and Kadimo Oqua, remember John Chukwu as a television personality who presaged today's stand-up comedians in the art. For Akpausoh and Mrs Ajayi, John Chukwu was a "versatile" artist who, apart from comics, was an MC and musician (personal interview 28/9/16). John Chukwu also had a TV show on NTA Lagos, which ran life on that national TV from the late

---

[2] The symbol of Ekporoko (the masquerade) is the stock-fish; a delicacy imported from Europe, especially Norway. As Kadimo tells us, the Ekporoko, by association, became the name of the masquerade.

1960s through the 70s. Of course, much after these personalities, we also remember Mazi Mperempe of the "Mazi Mperempe Show" and his fame in the late 1970s through the 80s on Radio Nigeria and Anambra Broadcasting Corporation (ABC) Television, UHF Channel 50 Enugu, Eastern Nigeria, who also thrilled his audience with dance, motivational speeches and ultimately "jokes that left rib cracking and had people beating themselves so hard" (Dee Fash Blog 2013).

From the foregoing, it can be observed that the precursors of the art mentioned above were employees of public television and in some cases, as it was with Mazi Mperempe, they were limited to their own region/state because of the poor signal coverage of television at the time.[3] More so, as was observed by respondents, the Mazi Ukonus, Nwelekebes, Chukwus and Mperempes were not known for satires that took up the establishment and functionaries in government, which may be suggestive of the consciousness of government presence and control on their art and duties as employees. Their shows, as some have said, were basically meant for humour and general entertainment. But we must add that the above constraints did not take away the ingenuity of their art and the fame which they acquired therefrom. Although comedians John Chukwu and Jude Edesiri Onakpoma (Away-Away), who started as a stand-up comedians in their university days at the University of Benin, Mid-western Nigeria, have been identified as having had some finesse in the art, it is generally acknowledged that it was Alleluia Akporobome (Ali Baba) who gave the art visibility, dignity and positioned it as an entertainment business (Ayakoroma 2020: 4). Ali Baba, who said he started out in the Bendel State University (now Ambrose Ali University) as a "heckler" (CNN African Voices 2015), moved to Lagos, which is Nigeria's, and perhaps West Africa's biggest economic nerve centre, after graduation from the university. Aware of the economic potentials of the ever bustling Lagos city in the late 1990s, Ali Baba recounts that he had paid for publicity through billboards at three strategic positions in high-brow business avenues, where he announced himself and his art in an unprecedented manner: "Ali Baba - being funny is big business" (CNN African Voices 2015). Building on the corporate posture of his comic forbear, Away-Away, and cashing in on the emerging private TV and Frequency Modulation (FM) radio stations, which coincidentally had become more dominant and influential than public radio by the 1990s, Ali Baba became the official modern father of Naija stand-up comedy. Till date, he is the most outstanding performer and a classic of the genre in

---

[3] Public television channels in Nigeria are predominantly localised. Every state has a state-owned TV and a channel of the national television station NTA. Signals are often limited and people from other states depend on national network time or stories to know what is broadcast on stations outside their states.

a space where a community of professionals in the field have arisen and become international youth icons with a large fan base across the Nigerian social strata.

However, we cannot underestimate the influence of the West on the emergence and character of stand-up comedy in Nigeria. Although few Naija stand-up comedians have unequivocally acknowledged the influence of American stand-up comedians and show hosts such as Jon Stewart and Eddy Murphy on their arts, we can see impressions of many other Western media personalities in other Nigerian stand-up comedians. Besides his indigenous comic masquerade performance model *Ekporoko*, from whom he got his signature tone "Abasi",[4] Kadimo tells us that the old videos of Eddy Murphy's comedy shows "brought from abroad by one big man pikin"[5] in the 1980s inspired him greatly with regard to making humour for audiences. Mr. Rudolf Okonkwo (Dr. Njakiri Damages), who is a career journalist but whose show, like that of his colleague Adeola Fayehun, has all the trappings of stand-up comedy, also confesses that he is a great fan of the David Letterman and The Jon Stewart Show, after which he fashioned his own comic news show "Dr. Damages Show" (Okonkwo 2013). The point here is that these Western show hosts/comedians also represent early models and true modern media icons that enchanted the imagination of ambitious young Nigerians and helped them re-imagine and re-position themselves to confront the challenges of everyday life, and the contradictions thrown up to them by vicious self-seeking post-independent bourgeoisie.

By the mid-1990s, Opa Williams, a media businessman, had already harnessed the dispersed talents in the industry and started touring major Nigerian cities with his heavily packaged entertainment event entitled "Night of a Thousand Laughs". With the death of government-managed cultural centres, theatres and cinemas, Night of a Thousand Laughs emerged as a befitting and timely replacement, providing occasions for another form of urban night-life entertainment. But more importantly is the fact that Opa William's Night of a Thousand Laughs with its media hype became a formal endorsement for a struggling youth-based art form. For many young Nigerian stand-up comedians, being invited to take up the microphone at any of the shows marked a turning point in their fortunes. In what we may refer to as "jokes of the Rise from Grass to Grace" theme, Nigerian stand-up comedians constantly acknowledge the power of Opa William's

---

[4] The literal meaning is "God!" or "God almighty". The word is used as an exclamation to express surprise, alarm, or excitement in the Akwa-Cross region of south-eastern Nigeria. Its origin is Efik/Ibibio.

[5] 'A rich man's child'.

show over their status. We find this in different versions by the likes of Gordons, I Go Die, AY, and Youngest Landlord, among many others.

Today, we can say that stand-up comedy as described above is an established distinct genre of comedy and entertainment in Nigeria. The art form as practised in Nigeria has a peculiar Nigerian flavour and has also remained a multi-media technology-driven event. Among the stars of Nollywood home videos and Naija hip hop, we also have stand-up comedians such as Gordons, Basket Mouth and Akpororo as telecommunication companies' ambassadors and advertisement personalities. What then is it that makes Naija stand-up comedy in the millennium more popular and visible than its comic precursors in the 1950s, 1960s, 1970s and 1980s? What is it, also, that accounts for its astronomical rise and influence? The reasons, for us, lie in a consilience of postmodern forces, vectors of fundamental changes in the world and in the popular language use – Nigerian Pidgin, which has proven to be a uniting linguistic force in the Nigerian postcolony.

5 Expressiveness, agency and the nation-space

> "... a take on everything under the sun ... Apart from the Holy Spirit
> ... Everything ... everything ..." – Ali Baba (CNN African Voices 2015)

Nigerian stand-up comedians in the millennium are perhaps some of the most daring and creative in the world. Although the country has come out of decades of military dictatorship – one in which there were records of censorship and fatal consequences for freedom of expression – we cannot take for granted the fact that stand-up comedians still work within an unpredictable circumstance, which Soyinka (2005: 1) aptly refers to as a "climate of fear". In 2002, a jocular suggestion by a journalist with regard to Prophet Mohammed's fancy for contestants in a world beauty pageant engendered a violent fundamentalist response that caused the pageantry to be rescheduled from Kaduna, in northern Nigeria to Cross River and Lagos, in south-eastern and south-western Nigeria. Even though that happened within a democratic era, the young Nigerian comedians discussed here are still working in the same sensitive space to make commentary on the human condition and redefine their generation. In the succeeding sections, we shall proceed by engaging some topical issues that preoccupy Naija stand-up comedians and delineate what their creativity implies to identity and nationality.

6 Everything holy: Religion, God and Men-of-God

The Pew Research Center has shown that Nigeria is one of the countries in the world that ranks highest in citizens' religious commitment at several levels; between 85–95 percent of Nigerians reveal that religion is very important in their lives (Pew Reseaech Center 2013, 2018). The data as released by the World Economic Forum states that Nigeria is one of those religious countries where nine in ten people attest that religion is a major determinant factor in their lives. This indeed is true given the proliferation of churches, mosques, traditional and sundry spiritual centres all over the country. Ironically the country is also said to be one of the world's most corrupt nations. Apart from the traditional African cosmology, which makes it almost impossible for many Nigerians to be atheists, unreligious or, as it is also categorised in modern terms, secular, the factors of poverty and ignorance in a bastardised economy breed fertile ground for this paradox to thrive in post-civil war Nigeria.

Years of sustained military dictatorship which abhors depth and rigour to deprecating socio-economic problems installed a culture of desperation and mediocrity in the country. With a deepening economic crisis, disregard for the intellect, and in some cases incarceration of professionals and academics, the country began to witness an exodus of its most treasured human resources to the west; this situation known as "brain-drain" has been going on from the 1980s till date. In this situation, a culture of thuggery and superstition was installed, and as the middle class was suffocated, the margin between the very rich and poor was only expanded. To mediate this gap, sharp practices, drug trafficking, ritual or what Enwerem (2003: 189) calls "money-magic" becomes the path to achievement and 'arrival'. Accordingly, spirituality and religiosity also became the most plausible modus for explaining what seem to be imponderable in an enchanted public space.[6] In this context, therefore, the Imam, Spiritual Master, Pastor or Bishop becomes an omnibus counsellor and Father or Mother (popularly and intriguingly referred as Daddy-in-the-Lord or Mummy-in-the-Lord). While religion has played a fundamental role in inspiring many Nigerians, especially the youth, its apocalyptic grammar has also been utilized by acclaimed "Men-of-God" to exploit and deprecate the ignorant and vulnerable.

---

[6] In an insightful study, Harry Garuba provides a theoretical exploration for the tendency of dispossessed postcolonial people to spiritualize "social relationships, economic activities and political actions" (2003: 283). The psychical root for this impulse is what he refers to as the "animist unconscious" (2003: 270). Located in the alternative animistic cosmology of postcolonial peoples, particularly Nigerians, this alternative world view of "[generating] meanings that

Naija stand-up comedians are awake to the realities of religion in the context of their country. Being conscious citizens themselves, they have continually lampooned the sham religiosity in Nigeria without taking away its functionality among the people. This level of sensibility is what we have in many of the performances of Gordons, who displays a high level of Bible knowledge and Pentecostal verve in his comic rhetoric. In fact, it is instructive that apart from eulogising himself as the "Berlusconi of Nigerian comedy", Gordons often introduces himself as the "beloved son of Pastor Ayo, the begotten son of Idahosa, the loving son of Adeboye, accepted son Oyedepo, the prodigal son of Pastor Paul Adefarasin and the *rejected* son of Okotie".[7] His rejectedness with regard to Okotie emanates from Gordons' unequivocal but humorous indictment of the "Man-of-God" who had divorced his wife on the grounds of alleged immorality and was, at the time of the performance, getting ready for a second marriage to a younger woman. Critical of the charismatic pastor's claim, Gordons makes bold to comically question the pastor's own saintliness. Thus, he says in Nigerian Pidgin:

> E no matter the kind spirit wey your wife get . . . .
> [It doesn't matter, the kind of spirit that your wife has . . .]
> Whether na marine spirit[. . .], bush spirit, desert spirit, forest spirit or even computer spirit . . .
> Every spirit . . . you no suppose drive am
> [you are not supposed to divorce her]

Referring the Man-of-God to Fela Kuti, who, by Nigerian Christian standards, is an unbeliever and a polygamist, Gordon's asserts that the Afrobeat musician, with his multiple wives and their legion of spirits, still remained married to all of them till his death:

> Na today we dey see spirit?
> [It's been long since we started seeing spirits]
> Even with the legion of spirits wey Fela wives dem get . . .

---

cast an otherworldly veil over natural phenomena as much as over human activities" (283) has been exploited by both "traditional elites" and "the new elites who control economic and political power" to rip off their people and "to bolster their authority and legitimacy" (2003: 285).

[7] The Pastors mentioned are among the most influential and richest in Nigerian Pentecostalism. Some have established universities and own private jets (another point of humour for Gordons (see "Night of a Thousand Laughs", vol. 29). Pastor Chris Okotie on whom the selected performance is directed is a rich and controversial musician-turn-pastor. He owns a big church in Lagos, Nigeria and has been a presidential aspirant.

[In spite of the legion of spirits that possessed Fela's wives]
Fela still marry dem until him die
[Fela still remained married to them until his death]

Typical of his depth and insights to biblical instances, Gordons makes cryptic references to biblical examples of long-suffering marriages. He ends up admonishing the musician-turn-pastor Okotie to take back his first wife before "people go tink say you get the Spirit-of-taking-and-leaving [before people will think you have the Spirit-of-taking-and-leaving]" (Comedy Clinic Ward 4).

Considering the supernatural image of pastors, their wealth and large cult following in Nigeria, Gordons' criticism of Pastor Chris Okotie was an instant sensation. The bit was applauded by Nigerians who thought he was apt and exposed the vanity of pastors but it was dismissed by fans and members of the Pastor's church, who think the comedian is disrespectful to his elders and has contravened God's injunction of reverence to His "anointed". In fact, one of Okotie's pastors – Rev. Mrs Grace Funmi Paul – in an interview berated the comedian for going against his own Christian calling by satirizing the Man-of-God (pulsing.com). For us, Rev. Mrs Funmi's defence of her boss and her logic in berating the comedian are perhaps demonstrative of one of Adejunmobi's (2014: 180) theories of comic performances in the society – the performance of the "social self" in a culture where, as Smith (2007: 222–223) would have it, "obligation to kin and clients are rooted in a moral economy that privileges reciprocity, sharing, and interdependence" (qtd in Adejunmobi 2014: 182). Thus for Rev. Mrs Funmi, rising in defence of her over-seer may be an act of performing relationship even when it may be against high (individual) moral standards (Adejunmobi 2014: 182).

It is not only the lasciviousness of the Men-of-God that Gordons and Nigerian stand-up comedians indict. The obsession with money in Nigerian churches has also been held to ridicule. Gordons for instance says that the drive for financial benefits is the major corruptive factor in churches in Nigeria today. According to him:

Take it or leave it!
The problem of the church, I make bold to declare, is tithe and offering
If you remove tithe and offering from church
Some of these people wey say na God call them
[Some of these people who claim they are called by God]
They will have another call
Na there you go see people go talk say I be engineer before o
[That's when you'll see people confess that they were engineers]
I thought the Lord called me

Ehmm . . . [sighs]
Him no know say na miss-call na 'im him hear
[He didn't know that he heard a missed call]
That's just the way it is . . .
The problem of the church has been tithe and offering
If una want criticise me make una criticise me I no fear . . .
[You people can criticize me, if you wish, I'm not scared]
[pause]
It has been tithe and offering
Let this monetary spirit be taken from the church
You now see people who will worship God in spirit and in truth

In the same performance, Gordons gives a long fictive narrative of a seminar "conducted" by President Jonathan (immediate past President of Nigeria), where His Excellency invited three Nigerian pastors, namely Pastor Ayo (Orisejafor), Paul (Adefarasin), and Omobudin. In the said seminar, the President informed the Men-of-God of his "purposeful" ratification of the anti-homosexual bill and his plan to ban prostitution the coming year. The Men-of-God excitedly applauded and lavished encomiums on the President. However, when the President unveiled his plan to ban tithe and offering in churches, because of the obvious corruptive tendencies of the practice, the pastors objected with vehemence that is not only a shift from their virtuous position against the earlier "vices" (homosexuality and prostitution) but a betrayal of their selfish motivations with regards to pecuniary gains in the conduct of Christianity. It is their vehement and near militant objections to the President's plan that heightens the humorous satire intended by the comedian:

I no know wetin make Jonathan come go say:
[I didn't know what made Jonathan say]
"Ladies and gentlemen next year we are declaring tithe and offering in the church illegal!"
[pause]
There was silence
And then Pastor Ayo reacted
F-o-r w-h-a-t!! [emphatically]
Is tithe and offering the problem of the country?
Is tithe and offering Boko Haram?
Is tithe and offering terrorism?
Before I know it Pastor Omobudin replied Jonathan with the Scripture:
If you t-r-y it! If you t-r-y it!
I tell you "if the foundation be broken what can the righteous do"
Na him Jonathan say
[Jonathan answered back]:
"the righteous will do something . . . what will they not do?"

Na him pastor Ayo ask Pastor Paul
[translation]
"what do you have to say concerning this matter"
You know say Pastor Paul na polished pastor
[You know that Pastor Paul is a polished pastor]
Na him Pastor Paul say
[Pastor Paul said]:
"for this reason was the son of God made manifest!"
"He will destroy the work of Satan . . . I tell you the truth!"

The one wey finish everybody na pastor Omobudin
[It was Omobudin's response that alarmed everybody]
Na him dem ask Pastor Omobudin "what do you have to say"
[And they asked Omobudin what he had to say]
Na ím him say
[Then he said]: "Ehehe
[laughs and sighs in Urhobo]"
I've been waiting for my turn . . . If you try it! Darkness will be upon the nation
and gross darkness upon the people"
And Jonathan said: "But I've not banned it yet"
And they said "we know but your plans towards us are plans of evil and it will not take us to the expected end!"
"Leave our tithe and offering o! This has been the foundation . . . you want to break it!"

The humour in this performance is not just in the ludicrous fictive representation of the mannerisms of the pastors but also their purposeful twist of the Bible's message to re-enforce and sustain a system of exploitation. Akpororo, another favourite Naija stand-up comedian and media icon, in one of his performances for "AY Live" (Lagos 2014) has shown the hypocritical excitement with which Nigerian Pastors betray their "divine calling" at the instance of money:

So na him I dey tell people if winch dey press you for mid night
[So I tell people, if you get pressed by a witch at midnight]
You call pastor e go look your call e no go pick o!
[And you call the Pastor . . . he'll look at your call and won't pick it]
Because you no fit dey pay tithe
[Because you can't pay your tithe]

So na him I dey tell people if you sow seed to Man-of-God like that kin' one million
[So I tell people . . . sow a "seed" to a Man-of-God to the tune of one million]
As you give the envelope wetin you go hear na
[As you present the envelope . . . What you'll hear is . . .]
Raaaaahhh . . . Reeeehhh . . . Keeeehhh . . . Teeeeeh . . . Sokota! Rorororo . . .
[Speaking in tongues amid general laughter from the audience]
[Pastor gestures to fall face down in excitement of the huge amount of money]
Na you go ask Pastor wetin be that!

[It is you that will ask the pastor what's going on]
Him go say na 'in-tongues . . .'
[He will reply "it's speaking in tongues"]
[General laughter from the audience]
"Go down on your knees as I pray for you
[Prays with feverish excitement and enthusiasm]
"My God will enlarge you . . .!
My God will increase you! . . . will . . . . Raaahhh . . .!

[Pastor goes into another session of sustained loud speaking-in-tongues, which ends with his mouth agape in amazement. General laughter and applause follow from the audience.]

To further heighten the lampoon on greedy men-of-God in Nigeria the comedian goes on to represent what happens when the pastor receives ten million Naira in a Ghana-must-go.[8] As the bag of money opens the comedian shows that the already mesmerised pastor would get into a greater feat of excitement and speaking-in-tongues, while performing versions of *Naija* hip hop dance for the payer of the tithe. At the climax of this joke the comedian tells his audience that when the excited Pastor regains consciousness, he reverses role and poise, and in the same feat asks the tithe payer to stand on their feet instead of kneeling as a supplicant would do in humility, while he himself kneels down to pray for the tithe payer. Although Akpororo begins the joke in form of admonition to his audience to take care of Pastors, the performance ends up in a humorous lampoon on the ludicrous worship of money and vanity by today's men-of-God in Nigeria. His ascription of *Naija* hip hop dance style to the clergy is a dialogic performance that further heightens the satire on the pretentious superstructure in society. But in a more interesting manner, Akpororo seems to also perform a subtle cultural link between stand-up comedy and hip hop in a way that portrays both performances as part of a youth cultural politics.

In spite of the exception specified by the doyen of *Naija* stand-up comedy, Ali Baba, in the prefatory note of this section, it seems that *Naija* stand-up comedians do not see any bounds in their characterisation of the Nigerian everyday experience. There abound instances of parodies of God in relation to humans, Men-of-God in their deliverance sessions and even more rib-cracking instructive characterisation of Christians in Holy Spirit "possession" feats. For these, it will be revealing to watch the performances of Gordons (Comedy Clinic Ward VI) and Funny Bone (Night of Thousand Laughs vol. 23). But here again, it would be instructive to note the manner in which *Naija* stand-up comedians use their own

---

8 Ghana-Must-Go is a popular utility bag of different sizes in Nigeria. It derived its origin from the mass deportation of Ghanaians from Nigeria in 1983.

art to uncouple the contradictions inherent in what Adejunmobi identifies as "performance of the occupational self" (2014: 180), which is a nontheatrical performance "connected to professional life" (Adejunmobi 2014: 179). However, even more revealing is the fact that in a mediatized context, this form of professional performance is given to sustaining a culture of corruption and exploitation, which intriguingly is tacitly approved by a dispossessed society that has habituated compromise (Adejunmobi 2014: 183).

6.1 Naija politics, government and the political class

The phony politics, politicians and system of governance in post-independent Nigeria are major themes in Naija stand-up comedy. Since the disengagement of the military from the politics of the country in 1999, the tensions and contradictions that characterise democratic politics in the Nigerian postcolony have generated conflicts, disenchantment, and divisions in some regard. The follies that define politics in Nigeria have not escaped the comic imaginary of *Naija* stand-up comedians mostly relayed in Nigerian Pidgin. In some cases, as it is with Olusegun Obasanjo, Nigeria's second democratically-elected President and Adams Oshiomhole, labour leader turned politician and Governor of the oil producing mid-western state of Edo, it is their physical disposition that have been the subject of much humour amongst *Naija* stand-up comedians. President Obasanjo, fondly referred to in Nigerian Pidgin as "Baba", "Shege", "Baba Iyabo" or "Baba Shege" is himself a comical fellow in terms of his speeches laced with comic rhetoric. However, in our opinion, he remains Nigeria's most comically represented President till date. Many a Nigerian comedian has produced narratives that liken Obasanjo with an ape or a monkey. In a subtle allusion to Obasanjo and Oshiomole, Gordons tells of an instance when he was asked to act the part of a monkey in a movie, he rejected the role and directed the producer to Edo or Ogun State. The humour in this innuendo is not lost on the Nigerian audience who comprehend it readily as a pointer to Governor Oshiomole (at the time the Governor of Edo State, Nigeria) and ex-President Obasanjo (an indigene of Ogun) (Night of a Thousand Laughs, vol. 29).

Representing the general superstition of Nigerians and mimicking the speech mannerism of President Obasanjo, Gordons tells of "Shege's" reaction to an alleged prophesy by the radical Nigerian Pastor, Tunde Bakare, with regard to the impending death of a president. According to the joke, when Obasanjo heard of this ominous situation, he relented in his ambition to re-run the post of the President. Instead, Obasanjo called Atiku Abubakar, his Vice President at the time and one of Nigeria's business moguls, to rather contest for the position. If Obasanjo is Nigeria's most comically represented President, for us Patience Jonathan, the wife of President Goodluck Ebele Jonathan, is the most caricatured first lady that Nigeria has ever had. Although Mrs Jonathan has acquired certificates up to tertiary level and has even been conferred with an honorary doctorate degree by the University of Port Harcourt, Nigeria, her grammatical errors, penchant for Nigerian Pidgin usage, and public mannerisms leave much to be desired. It is on account of her public slips and seemingly uncouth self-presentation, especially with regard to the missing Chibok girls, that Ali Baba has raised questions on the quality of her education and used the same opportunity to make bold statements about the poor quality of education that the Nigerian (girl) child receives (interview with Hip Tv 2015). The personality of Mrs Jonathan is indeed a comic resource for Naija stand-up comedians generally. In one of Gordons' performances, he staged a quarrel between the President, fondly called Jona in comic circles, and his wife Patience, also fondly called "Mama P", where the president in irritation threatened to stop taking the first lady in his company on account of her embarrassing flawed English grammar. Gordons goes further to say that in her condolence speech on the occasion of the funeral of Emeka Odumegwu Ojukwu, secessionist leader of Biafra, Mrs Jonathan, in praise of the dead warrior, said "Ojukwu has died but his manhood lives on!" (Night of a Thousand Laughs, vol. 29)

However, it is Ali Baba and Seyi Law, who in the stand-up comedy circle have presented the most dramatic and viral representations of the first lady's public disgrace. Employing the deft mimicry of Ambassador Wahala (Oni Lukman Olarewaju), both comedians on two different performances have used the hubris of Mrs Jonathan to make satiric statements (Hip TV 2015). In fact, it is in disenchantment with her public posture and abuse of the privileges of the position of the first lady that Wole Soyinka suggested in an interview that the former first lady lacks the poise, grace and dignity to be called a "lady" (TV 360, Nigeria July 2013). In this regard, while we agree with Adejunmobi (2014) that in Nigerian stand-up comedy, policies are not particularly taken up as much as the topicality of under-performance of the roles expected of powerful men and women in the society, it would be misleading to state that "we do not however see overtly political criticism of those in power" (Adejunmobi 2014: 185–186). This is because *Naija* stand-up comedians have been unprecedented in their political satire. Perhaps it should also be said that Nigerian politics in itself has not really been identified with policies as it has been defined by postcolonial elites who are derided for endemic corruption. In terms of the representation of politics, politicians and government functionaries thereof, this generation of comedians are phenomenal. From interactions with Nigerians who have been following the dynamics of stand-up comedy in the country, we know that this boldness is unprecedented. While Akpausoh Apkausoh says emphatically that

John Chukwu was not casting satire on the government, Teniyi Ajayi cannot remember instances where Chukwu in the 1970s and '80s would take up politicians to ridicule (personal interview 28/9/16). Sam Udekwe could not also recall that Mazi Imperempe in the 1980s was taking up politicians and government functionaries. For him Mazi Imperempe "was simply an entertainer" (personal interview 6/10/16). In this regard, therefore, *Naija* stand-up comedians have gone beyond the reach of their predecessors.

6.2 The Dogs' play: Self-mockery, peers and the family

> "Dog say: 'if I fall for you and you fall for me na play.
> But if I fall for you, you no fall for me . . ., e don turn another thing"
>
> [The dog says: 'if I fall for you and you fall for me it's a play
> But if I fall for you and you don't fall for me . . ., it has become something else.']
>
> Nigerian proverb in Pidgin

We begin our discussion in this section by drawing discursive verve from the metaphors in an African proverb that has accent in different languages in Nigeria. However, it is the Nigerian Pidgin version that is apt for us here. The dog is known for its playfulness. But among many Nigerian people there are also proverbs that suggest that to play with a dog is also to court dirt. This is perhaps because dogs in 'traditional' African homes are not confined within fences but are free to range. Thus, they are susceptible to attracting dirt that can soil anybody that meddles with them. In that sense, to play with the dog, especially a puppy, is to court dirt.

The metaphor of the dog here is of great import to our appreciation of the potentials of stand-up comedy to radicalise the public space, and bring in parody and playfulness in the reinvention of the self and the other. Nigerian stand-up comedians have not only found in their art a creative mirror through which to self-criticise their private oddities but also a playful paradigm through which truths and hard facts can be co-referentially or self-referentially expressed. In this context, it is also difficult to ignore the import of another African proverb which in Nigerian Pidgin states: "na laf-laf dem dey take talk true [It is through humour that truth is told]".

Almost all *Naija* stand-up comedians have represented themselves as personae that have arisen from penurious conditions. In line with this, there is the motif of the once-poor-condition in the oeuvre of *Naija* stand-up comedy. Gordons tells of his father's painful attempt at mediating the constraints of his family's poor living condition with the desire to make love with his wife after three months of working off shore. But within the depravity of a one-room apartment, love-making can be fraught with embarrassing obstacles. Just after his father thought he had succeeded in forcing his children to a night's rest and immersed himself in the conjugal act, the comedian plays the mischievous child and truncates his father's libido. The little Gordons woke up on the flimsy excuse that he needed to use the bathroom:

> Just at that point when Asokoro will meet Maitama[9]. . . I woke up
> [Just at the point my father was about to penetrate his wife . . . I woke up]
> I shock when my papa say "who be that!"
> [I was shocked when my father asked "who is that"]
> I say "na me"
> [I said "it's me"]
> Who be you
> ["Who are you"]
> I be your pikin
> ["I'm your child"]
> Which of my pikin? [General Laughter]
> ["Which of my child"]
> I say "na Godwin"
> [I said "It's Godwin"] [General Laughter]
> "E-h-h! Na wetin!"
> ["E-h-h! What is it?"]
> I say "Daddy I wan' piss"
> [I said "Daddy, I want to urinate"]
> "For dis hour?"
> ["At this hour"]
> "You know dem tell me say you be wintch I no believe"
> ["You know they told me you are wizard I didn't believe"]
> "With this singular act . . . I believe [general laughter]"
> (Night of a Thousand Laughs, vol. 28)

For Youngest Landlord, his family was the poorest of the poor: "People dey say their papa poor . . . their papa poor . . . me my papa no poor . . . [pause] . . . . my papa wretched!" [People say their fathers are poor, as for me . . ., my father isn't poor . . . my father is wretched!] (Night of a Thousand Laughs, vol. 27)

To keep her children from exposing their deprived condition and bringing disgrace to the family, one of Nigeria's stand-up comedians, Elenu, says that his mother hatched a mischief before Christmas day. The comedian tells his audience that his mother fed them with a meal of sleeping pills that sent them to

---

[9] Asokoro and Maitama are upper-middle class and elite suburbs in Nigeria's Federal Capital Abuja. Here they are used as sexual metaphors.

sleep till it was January 4th. Upon waking, she cautioned them not to shout the usual "Happy Christmas!", as Nigerian children would in excitement, because they were already in the New Year (Night of a Thousand Laughs, vol. 27). These instances of family related comic representations speak humorously to the palpable hardship that post-civil war Nigerians are all too well aware of. Particularly, for this generation of young Nigerians, using this mediatised comic performance is to heuristically come to terms with egregious socio-economic realities that were inaugurated by the Structural Adjustment Programme (SAP) of the 1980s. This, in fact, further characterises stand-up comedy as a post-structural adjustment art form that bears the anxieties of the time. Making mirth of the different penurious conditions of their imagined family in stand-up comedy is a way through which the comedians are also healing themselves and their audiences of deep social strive. In the process of this mutual social healing, Nigerian Pidgin equally becomes a common linguistic tool for that catharsis. This is because beyond its capacity to produce humour, Nigerian Pidgin for different audiences of stand-up comedy is a mutually intelligible cultural heritage.

Beyond the incision of personal "bad condition", as it would be said in popular Nigerian parlance, *Naija* stand-up comedians are known for inter-personal "yabbies" (ridicule). Gordons, for instance, picks on Daddy Showkey (iconic popular Nigerian musician) over his dread-locks (called *Dada* in Nigeria). In a string of yabies, he has also made allusions to his colleague I Go Die's inability to speak the English language "I Go Die wey wan' speak English . . . na him sabi o!" ["I Go Die who wants to speak in English has himself to blame"] (Comedy Clinic Ward 2). On account of her body size, he thinks that the female comedian Lepascious Bose (Bose Ogunboye) will not make heaven. He admonishes her to stop trying to lose weight because her fate is already decided: "as for Lepascious Bose stop doing all-night [vigil prayer session], because we know where you dey go [we know where you're going] . . . the Bible says broad is the way . . .!" (Comedy Clinic Ward 2).

The award-winning *Naija* hip-hop artist, Tuface Idibia (Innocent Idibia), who reportedly has children from different women, is another favourite subject matter for *Naija* stand-up comedians. But interestingly, the musician has intertextually played on the numerous lewd jokes on him to create mirth upon himself. For example, as preamble to entertaining an audience on Night of a Thousand Laughs show, he told of a certain girl who was rebuked for getting pregnant to some nonentity instead of making herself available to Tuface (Night of a Thousand Laughs, vol. 21)

As it is with Tuface, so it is with another world class *Naija* hip-hop diva D' Banj and the pretty Nollywood actress Genevieve Nnaji. Their alleged secret love affair has been the source of much fun for stand-up comedy audience. In fact, I Go Die has even gone the extra mile to make a joke of D'Banj's genitalia. Playing on the imagery in the artist's song "I'm so endowed", the comedian announces that the musician is far from being "endowed". In the same vain, Bovi thinks that Genevieve is still tangled with D'Banj as she is featured in his new single (Night of a Thousand Laughs, vol. 23). Tuface's self-parody noted above is intriguing. It confirms what Oha (2014: 8) says about the mutual disposition of "folks" to accommodate the sting of Njakiri; a communal/interpersonal humorous way through which the Igbo engage objectionable behaviour" on one another. The significance of the reciprocal "yabies" that is promoted by the art of *Naija* stand-up comedy has deep implication on the comedians' collective identity and the kind of nation they seem to envision with their performances. With regard to their self-parody and mutual caricatures, even if in many cases they are performed ironically, *Naija* stand-up comedians have again surpassed their forebears in public exposure and criticism. It is to this extent that we think Adejunmobi (2014: 180) has generalized and ignored some details when she suggests that Nigerian comedy performers "have not yet become 'self-reflexive performing subject[s]'" who obsessively comment about their own experiences of mediation and mediated performance".

6.3 Identity and national reinvention

As an agency, Naija stand-up comedy provides the Nigerian youth with a creative facility for individuation. The art of naming the self, some of which are self-deprecating, is an index to private pain and aspiration and a signifier of collective socio-cultural and political angst. By their art, therefore, this generation of comedians is performing a political imaginary; a sense of nationhood that is ambivalent. Its "ambivalence" (Bhabha 2004: 211) lies in the very nature of its liberal polyglossia, which promotes self-criticism and the aptitude to contain the other's satire, however bitter. This is a more creative, convivial and dialogic nationality; one which many countries in postcolonial Africa have not yet achieved since imperial balkanization and disengagement. In a country that is sitting at the edge of ethnic bigotry and religious extremism, the metaphoric nationality that is performed by Naija stand-up comedy, expressed linguistically through Pidgin, a language associated with the lowly, is an alternative force from the margins of society.

When Ali Baba, the acclaimed father of *Naija* stand-up comedy, took the decision to use billboards in projecting an art form hitherto considered vernacular or unserious, he was keying into a new impulse of modernity/nationality that is now global. Indeed he was dexterously showing Nigerians that platforms such as billboards along with "T-shirts, graffiti, rap music, street dancing and slum housing" are conduits through which global images of "the media" can be re-contextualised "into local repertoires of irony, anger, *humor*, and resistance" (Appadurai 1996: 7, emphasis added). Indeed, in identifying Ali Baba's dexterous utilization of global media, we have discursively answered the call by Barber (1997: 7) two decades ago to pay "more attention [. . .] to the specific ways [that globalization] works through local African scenes of cultural production and consumption." More so, our field work only confirms that like physical migration, technological migration, however slow in the Nigerian media space, has radicalised the socio-political and cultural life of Nigerians. The movement from more analogue forms of recording and broadcasting (U-matic tapes, reel-to-reel, and VHS) to high speed resolution audio-video digital system (CD, DVD) and ultimately the hyper-reel World Wide Web facility meant that power and control over production and "dissemi-*nation*" (Bhabha 2004: 212) has been democratised. This liberalization in itself has implications on creativity, which can only be appreciated in the words of Appadurai (1996: 7–8), when he states that in the context of the new global reality, "the imagination is today a staging ground for action and not only for escape", and that now the imagination (creativity) has become a "property of collectives [. . .] not merely [. . .] a faculty of the gifted individual."

7 The value of Nigerian Pidgin

Nigerian Pidgin also known as Naija is the most popular means of communication in Nigeria in terms of population of speakers and degree of acceptance by speakers of other languages. Mann (1983: 167) describes the language as "an interethnic lingua franca" and Mensah (2011) sees it as the most efficient interethnic language among the densely culturally and linguistically heterogeneous people of Nigeria. Nigerian Pidgin has well over 70 million speakers (Egbokhare, 2021) as either first, second or third language speakers. The diverse sociolinguistic ecology of Nigeria has favoured Nigerian Pidgin as the bridge builder between the demands of English and those of the country's indigenous languages by virtue of its neutrality, flexibility and simplicity. It is the most neutral national language because it does not have any cultural affiliations; it is elastic and adaptable to any communicative situation; and can be easily learned. As part of its social expansion process, Nigerian Pidgin has a central place in the appropriation of youth subcultural capital like hip hop culture, Nollywood video film industry and the

Naija stand-up comedy performances, where it has been established as the most prominent medium of comic production and consumption in Nigeria.

Nigerian Pidgin, as a language of wider communication, is best suited to attract mass production and consumption of comedy materials. Mensah and Ndimele (2014: 232) submit that Nigerian Pidgin "has a level of creativity that allows it to be ever-expanding and ever-changing. It carries the distinctive Nigerian flavour, and acts as the bridge between the global (English) and the local (Nigerian indigenous languages). In this way, it provides a clear understanding of the symbolic value of comedy performance, and facilitates the fusion of elements of local culture with global comedy consumption thus creating the glocalisation of comedy culture in Nigeria. For the stand-up comedian, Nigerian Pidgin provides the resource for self-expression, identity and authenticity. He or she uses the language to navigate the complex linguistic diversity, connect with a broad range of audience interests, and negotiate multiple cultural boundaries within their performance space and community of practice. Nigerian Pidgin is the most creative tool to attack archaic cultural practices, unpopular government policies, religious fanaticism and obnoxious sexual practices. In this connection, the comic artist laces comedy with the realities of everyday life.

For the audience, Nigerian Pidgin is a unifying factor, and facilitates the construction of a sense of identity. It also facilitates the peculiar Nigerianness of the comedy materials which are consolidated as unique and valuable. The vast majority of the patrons of stand-up comedy in Nigeria are the youths, who have already established Nigerian Pidgin as the main transporter of their subcultural capital. It is an authentic representation of their interests and desires, and the distinct language of their era. Nigerian Pidgin facilitates the flow and understanding of specific performance style in appreciation of the meaning of comedy materials. Based on the indispensability of the NP medium, we claim that it sensitively offers "cognitive and moral legitimacy" (Authur 2006: 144) to stand-up comedy performance in Nigeria. Cognitive legitimacy is concerned with the interpretation of meaning and moral legitimacy is based on the benefits that the audience derives from the performance.

8 Conclusion

In this paper, we have attempted to trace the emergence of stand-up comedy as a mediatised and commoditised comic performance in Nigeria. To do this, we have accounted for indigenous comic performance among different Nigerian people that may be considered precursors to stand-up comedy in Nigeria. However, we have also squarely placed the art form as genre that has been directly birthed by a global electronic media performance that has its root in America. Using an ethnographic method, our study has shown predominantly through the performances of Gordons, a foremost contemporary Nigerian stand-up comedian that the art has been deployed by Nigerian youth to project a peculiar youth politics. Within this ideology is a sense of national engineering and interpersonal criticism that is unprecedented by precursor arts in the Nigerian postcolony. Hence for us, beyond the entrepreneurial slant to the art, this generation of stand-up comedian is performing and projecting a regime of liberal democracy that is counter to the predominant hegemony in Nigeria and Africa generally.

But it is important to note that in the course of this research, it was stunning to find out, as Akpausoh, Ajayi and Udekwe would tell us, that powerful government-owned media houses do not have recordings of the early productions of the creative ancestors of stand-up comedy in Nigeria. Today, not only do hundreds of thousands of people around the world watch and participate real-time in audio visual productions of Naija stand-up comedy, but they also carry with them audio visual skits of such productions, which in turn are readily available in private blogs and websites. Hence, the gap between audiences and performers has been bridged by the virtual facility of the internet and more young people are envisioning themselves in new ways. The incarnation of Naija stand-up comedy performances in the millennium, therefore, inscribes an identity that is not only radical, but also a sense of nationhood that is tenuously liberal, self-interrogative and "collective" (Appadurai, 1996: 7). That collectivism in Naija stand-up comedy is further given force through the use of the Nigerian Pidgin which it has, by default, prioritized and exploited to give expression to the striving of a dispossessed generation. But researching stand-up comedy in Nigeria also challenges us to confront the impact of technological dynamics and interrogate the implications of nationhood in the millennium.

List of interviewees

Akpausoh A. Akpausoh: Executive Director Programmes, Nigerian Television Authority, headquarters, Abuja, Nigeria
Dr Chike Ikeokpara: Reader, Department of Religious and Cultural Studies, University of Calabar, Nigeria.
Dr. Ndubuisi Osuagwu: Senior Lecturer, Department of English and Literary Studies, University of Calabar, Nigeria.
Mr. Sam Udekwe: Programmes Department Enugu State Television (ETV), Enugu, Nigeria.
Mr. Kadimo Oqua: Stand-up comedian, Master of Ceremony (Mc) and lecturer, University of Calabar, Nigeria

Mrs Gloria Agu: Librarian, Federal Radio Corporation of Nigeria, Enugu, Nigeria
Mrs Teniyi Ajayi: Assistant Director of Programmes, Nigerian Television Authority (NTA), headquarters, Abuja, Nigeria

References

Adejunmobi, Moradewun. 2014. Standup comedy and the ethics of popular performance in Nigeria. In Stephanie Newell & Onookome Okome (eds.), *Popular culture in Africa: The episteme of the everyday*, 175–194. New York: Routledge.

Adelugba, Dapo. 1987. Yapping – A Form of Patriotism. In Dapo Adelugba (ed.), *Before our very eyes: Tributes to Wole Soyinka*, 183–211. Ibadan: Spectrum.

Akpororo, Apororo. 2014. *Best of Akpororo*. Obaino Music. Lagos. Vol. 2 VCD.

Appadurai, Arjun. 1996. *Modernity at large: Cultural dimensions of globalization*. Minnesota: University of Minnesota Press.

Authur, Damien. 2006. Authenticity and consumption in Australian hip hop culture. *Qualitative Market Research: An International Journal* 9(2), 140–156.

Ayakoroma, Foubiri. 2020. The Rise of Stand-up Comedy in Nigeria: from Nothing to something in Artistic Entertainment. https://www.nico.gov.ng/index.php/category-list-2/1151-the-rise-of-stand-up-comedy-genre-in-nigeria (accessed 11 Juni 2020)

Baba, Ali. 2016. January 1st Show. URL http://www.youtube.com/watch?v=MwPfenJHxlw 2015. (accessed 19 September 2016).

Baba, Ali. https://www.youtube,com/watch?v=60HfRH30dzg (accessed 19 September 2016)

Bakhtin, Mikhail. 1981. *The dialogic imagination: Four essays*. Austin: University of Texas Press.

Barber, Karin. 1997. Introduction. In Karin Barber (ed.), *Readings in popular culture*, 1–12. Bloomington: Indiana University Press.

Bergson, Henri. 2003. *Laughter: An essay on the meaning of the comic*. New York: Temple of Earth Publishing.

Bhabha, Homi. 2004. *The location of culture*. London: Routledge.

Brodile, Ian. 2008. Stand-up comedy as a genre of intimacy. *Ethnologies* 30(2), 153–180.

Bovi, Bovi. 2013. *Night of a Thousand Laughs*. Opa Williams, Lagos. Vol. 23 VCD.

CNN African Voices. 2015. Cnn/videos/world/2015/03/06/spc-african-voice-atunyota-alleluya-akporobomere-a.cnn/videos/playlists/intl-african-voices (accessed 19 September 2016)

de Graft, Joe. 1976. Roots in African drama and theatre. In Elred Jones (ed.), *African literature today 8: Drama in Africa*, 1–25. London: Heinemann.

Egbokhare, Francis. 2021. The accidental lingua franca: The paradox of the ascendancy of pidgin in the Nigerian linguistic space. In Akinmade T. Akande & Oladipo Salami (eds.), *Current Trends in Nigerian Pidgin English: A Sociolinguistic Perspective*, 67–114. Berlin/Boston: De Gruyter Mouton.

Fash, Dee. 2013. deefash.blogspot.co.za/2013/11/right-from-popular-mazi-mperempe-comedy.html. (accessed 15 Oktober 2016)

Donkor, David. 2013. Selling the president: Stand-up comedy as the politricks of indirection in Ghana. *Theatre Review* 54(2), 255–281.

Eble, Connie. 1996. *Slang and sociability: In-group language among college students*. London: The University of North Carolina Press.
Elenu, Elenu. 2015. *A night of a thousand laughs*. Opa Williams, Lagos. Vol. 27 VCD.
Enwerem, Iheanyi. 2003. Money magic and ritual killing in contemporary Nigeria. Jane Guyer, LaRay Denzer & Adigun Agbaje (eds.), *Money magic and city life: Devaluation in Ibadan and other urban centers in Southern Nigeria 1986–1996*, 189–205. Ibadan: Book Builders.
Fanon, Frantz. 1967. *The wretched of the earth*. Harmonsworth: Penguin.
Finley, Jessyka. 2016. Raunch and redress: Interrogating pleasure in Black women's stand-up comedy. *The Journal of Popular Culture* 49(4), 780–798.
Foy, Jennifer. 2015. Fooling around: Female stand-ups and sexual joking. *The Journal of Popular Culture* 48(4), 703–713.
Bone, Funny. 2013. *Night of a thousand laughs*. Opa Williams, Lagos. Vol. 23 VCD.
Garuba, Harry. 2003. Exploration in animist materialism: Notes on reading/writing African literature, culture, and society. *Public Culture* 15(2), 261–285.
Gillota, David. 2015. Stand-up Nation: Humor and American Identity. *The Journal of American Culture* 38(2), 102–112.
Githatu, Mary & Chai Furaha. 2015. Discursive structure of humour in stand-up comedy in Kenya: Discourse topics and stylistic devices in Churchill's performances. *International Journal of Language and Linguistics* 3(6), 409–415.
Gordons, Gordon. 2016. *Night of a Thousand Laughs*. Opa Williams, Lagos. Vol. 29 VCD.
Gordons, Gordon. 2015. *Night of a Thousand Laughs*. Opa Williams, Lagos. Vol. 28 VCD.
Gordons, Gordon. 2010. *Comedy Klinic Ward 2*. Obaino Music, Lagos. VCD.
Gordons, Gordon. 2012. *Comedy Klinic Ward 4*. Obaino Music, Lagos. VCD.
Gordons, Gordon. 2014. *Comedy Klinic Ward 6*. Obaino Music, Lagos. VCD.
Idibia, Tuface. 2012. *Night of a Thousand Laughs*. Opa Williams, Lagos. Vol. 21 VCD.
Jorgensen, Danny. 1989. *Participant observation*. Newbury Park: Sage.
Katayama, Hanae. 2006. *A cross-cultural analysis of humour in stand-up comedy in the US and Japan*. Pennsylvania: Pennsylvania State University PhD Thesis.
Katayama, Hanae. 2008. Humor in Manzai stand-up comedy: A historical and comparative analysis. *The International Journal of the Humanities* 6(1), 213–223.
Landlord, Youngest. 2015. *Night of a Thousand Laughs*. Opa Williams, Lagos. Vol. 27.
Law, Seyi & Ambassador Wahala. URL https://www.youtube.com/watch?v=mYGQLErKG2Q (accessed 19 September 2016)
Lockyer, Sharon. 2015. From comedy targets to comedy-makers: Disability and comedy in live performance. *Disability and Society* 30(9), 1397–1412.
Lye, John. 1993. Contemporary literary theory. *Brock Review* 2(1), 90–106.
Mann, Charles. 1993. The sociolinguistic status of Anglo-Nigerian Pidgin: An overview. *International Journal of the Sociology of Language*, 100/101, 167–178.
Mensah, Eyo. 2011. Lexicalization in Nigerian Pidgin. *Concentric: Studies in Linguistics*, 37(2), 209–240.
Mensah, Eyo. 2016. The dynamics of youth language in Africa: An Introduction. *Sociolinguistic Studies* 10(1–2), 1–14.
Mensah, Eyo & Roseline Ndimele. 2013. Linguistic creativity in Nigerian Pidgin advertising. *Sociolinguistic Studies* 7(3), 321–344.
Mensah, Eyo & Idom Inyabri. 2016. The ideological significance of metaphors in sexualized discursive practices among Nigerian youth. *Critical Multilingual Studies* 4(2), 10–34.

Moriaty, Mairead. 2011. Minority languages and performative genre: The case of Irish language stand-up comedy. *Journal of Multilingual and Multicultural Development* 32(6), 547–559.

Moynihan, Sinéad. 2008. Stand(ing) up for the Immigrants: The Work of Comedian Des Bishop. *Irish Studies Review* 16(4), 403–413.

Nyingifa, Theodore. 2013. My leaving Stephine was God's instruction- Pastor Chris. www.pulse.ng/gist/my-leaving-stephanie-was-gods-instruction-pastor-chris-okotie-comedian-gordons-gets-some-bashing-as-well-id2507922.html (accessed 14 September 2016)

Oha, Obododimma. 2014. Of cunning-mouth and postcolonial bad conditions. In Grace Okereke (ed.), *Currents in African Literature and the English Language*, 5–18. Calabar: University of Calabar Press.

Okonkwo, Rudolph. 2013. www.premiumtimesng.com/arts-entertainment/145107-profile-enter-dr-damages-the-man-behind-one-of-africas-most-popular-comedy-show.html (accessed 14 September 2016)

Perez, Raúl. 2013. Learning to make racism funny in the 'color-blind' era: Stand-up comedy students, performance strategies and the (re)production of racist jokes in public. *Discourse and Society* 24(4), 478–503.

Pew Research Center. 2013. https://www.pewforum.org/2018/06/13/how-religious-commitment-varies-by-country-among-people-of-all-ages/

Pew Research Center. 2014. https://assets.pewresearch.org/wp-content/uploads/sites/11/2014/01/global-religion-full.pdf

Pyle, Katrien. 2015. Funerary comedies in contemporary Kinshasa: social differences, urban communities and the emergence of a cultural form. *Africa* 85(3), 457–477.

Stott, Andrew. 2005. *Comedy*. New York: Routledge.

Soyinka, Wole. 2005. *Climate of fear: the quest for dignity in a dehumanized world*. New York: Random House.

Soyinka, Wole. 2013. URL https://www.youtube.com/watch?v=faBgpuT7Ff8 (accessed 19 September 2016)

Transparency International. 2015. www.transparency.org/cpi2015?gclid=clq7u5H27M8CFW0ADwodDpsO21o (accessed 14 September 2016)

Vagourous, Cecile. 2015. Genre, Heteroglossic performances, and new identity: Stand-up comedy in modern French society." *Language in Society* 44(2), 243–72.

Mirka Honkanen
Chapter 5
Nigerian Pidgin in authenticating immigrant identities

Introduction

A key characteristic of globalization is the increased movement of people, information, capital, ideologies, and other cultural objects, such as language (Appadurai, 1996). This mobility significantly affects West Africa through, for instance, the "brain drain" of qualified individuals emigrating (Adegoke, 2019), and concerns even non-standardized contact languages (Mair, 2013a), such as Nigerian Pidgin (NP). There are millions of people of Nigerian heritage living outside of Nigeria: official statistics put the number slightly below 400,000 for the United States by 2013 (Migration Policy Institute, 2015) and slightly above 200,000 for the United Kingdom by 2018 (Office for National Statistics, 2019), but these figures only account for legal immigration and the two most popular destinations.

Intense migration and technologies of disembodied communication may create additional leeway for negotiating and contesting belonging to ethnic, national, racial, or other social groupings. Nonetheless, people continue to strive for and value authenticity and authentic cultural membership. Adopting a constructivist and relativist view of authenticity as "authentication" (Bucholtz, 2003) and "enoughness" (Blommaert and Varis, 2011), the current chapter zooms in on the nexus between migration, authenticity, and computer-mediated communication in the Nigerian context. Acknowledging the intimate connection between authenticity and language, this study examines the role of NP in the construction of authentic Nigerianness and in other discourses of authenticity, inauthenticity, and deception, particularly among Nigerians abroad. In an ethnographically inspired corpus-linguistic study, I analyze interactions taking place on a Nigerian web forum between Nigerians in Nigeria and in the global diaspora.

The paper addresses three aspects of NP usage in connection with authenticity and immigrant identities. First, it provides an overview of NP vocabulary related to the themes of authenticity and migration. Second, diasporic Nigerians' attitudes toward their pidgin will be examined based on metalanguage on the web forum. Third, a collection of instances of NP being used strategically to claim Nigerian identities will be analyzed.

Earlier treatments of NP have tended to take an interest in its historical development, structural aspects, contexts of use, and status, as well as attitudes toward this traditionally overtly stigmatized oral vernacular. Lexicological studies, however, are more recent and still scarce. Mensah discusses NP proverbs (2013) and word formation (2011). The part most pertinent to this study is the dozen metaphorical ways of referring to dishonest behavior, mainly bribery, listed by Mensah (2011: 227). This chapter also shows some overlap with Heyd's work on NP ethnoracial vocabulary (2014) and metacommunicative lexicon (2015). The former paper explores ethnic and racial labels and categories salient in diasporic encounters, while the latter is relevant for its discussion of words depicting linguistic accommodation and assimilation. However, there is still lexicological ground to cover, as the scope of this project extends beyond linguistic authenticity to the (de-)authentication of identities, behaviors, and objects, and to migration topics beyond gentilic words. Moreover, the study contributes to mapping the role of pidgins and creoles in globalization as "mobile resources" (Blommaert, 2010); this line of work has been undertaken previously at the University of Freiburg (Hinrichs, 2006; Mair, 2011, 2013a; Mair and Pfänder, 2013; Heyd and Mair, 2014; Moll, 2015; Heyd, 2016a). My investigation of Nigerian immigrants' and their descendants' perceptions of their pidgin extends the old interest in language attitudes to a new context – the diaspora. Finally, analyzing the use of NP in diasporic Nigerians' identity statements joins the topics of immigrant identities, authentication, and NP on the micro-linguistic level.

After this introduction, I will first present the constructivist understanding of authenticity implemented in this study, and then the web forum corpus and corpus tool the investigation relies on. In the main body of the chapter, findings will be discussed in three thematic sections, focusing on lexicon, attitudes, and strategic authentication respectively, followed by a short conclusion.

1 Authenticity in globalization

While heritage languages lose much of their communicative value in the diaspora, they "remain highly important for processes of identity construction, since members of cultural diasporas often employ transplanted varieties of their 'home languages' in order to index ethnic affiliation", as Moll (2015: 1) puts it in her study on Jamaican Creole on a Jamaican diasporic web forum. However, this is not a straightforward process, as "in diasporic settings, including virtual ones, [. . .] the linguistic resources chosen to index ethnic identity do not necessarily correlate with native speaker competence", making authenticity and identity work in these contexts particularly "precarious" (Moll, 2015: 30). As a reaction to this,

I suggest embracing a flexible and relative approach to authenticity, espoused in Bucholtz (2003) and Blommaert and Varis (2011).

Bucholtz (2003) puts forward a constructivist understanding of authenticity in the context of sociolinguistic enquiry. Viewing authenticity as non-essential and emergent from jointly negotiated practices, she proposes that "authenticity is not there to be discovered [. . .]; rather, it is conferred – by language users and their audiences" (2003: 408). Hence, the target of sociolinguistic investigation should be the concrete "authenticating practices" that produce "authenticity effects" (Bucholtz, 2003: 408). Bucholtz focuses on people being seen as authentic members of social groups or as authentic speakers of varieties, and that is my main interest too, but I argue that other (non-linguistic) behaviors, objects, and properties can be "authenticated" or "deauthenticated" as well. Therefore, the glossary of authentication (Section 3.1 and Table 1 in the appendix) includes not only metacommunicative terminology (cf. Heyd, 2015) but also vocabulary related to other types of inauthenticity (e.g., Coupland, 2001; Gill, 2013).

Blommaert and Varis's (2011) take on post-modern identity construction provides another productive way of looking at authenticity in globalization. The scholars see identity practices as "discursive orientations towards sets of features that are seen (or can be seen) as emblematic of particular identities" (2011: 3). However, in order for an identity claim to be accepted, it need not fulfill all the criteria associated with the identity; instead, authenticity emerges as relative "enoughness", where "[o]ne has to 'have' enough of the emblematic features in order to be ratified as an authentic member of an identity category" (Blommaert and Varis, 2011: 4). This view is compatible with the concept of authentication: social agents choose to highlight in interaction those factors that (so they hope) make them seem sufficiently authentic in the specific context, and their audience either confers or rejects the identity claim. This paper examines linguistic authentication moves by mainly diasporic Nigerians. The first empirical part introduces the vocabulary needed for authentication and deauthentication in NP, while the third one looks at concrete, explicit identity claims, focusing on national and ethnic identities. The second part in between contextualizes the use of Pidgin in the light of diasporic Nigerians' language attitudes.

2 Data and methods

This is a qualitative study that relies on corpus linguistic tools combined with a touch of virtual ethnography (Hine, 2000; Androutsopoulos, 2008) and discourse analysis. The data were downloaded from the Nigerian web forum Nairaland (www.nairaland.com) by computer scientist Daniel Alcón López in a research project at the University of Freiburg (Mair and Pfänder, 2013). They comprise over 800 million words from 2005 to 2014 of multilingual, interactive, stylistically heterogeneous online writing, full of narratives of belonging (Heyd, 2016b), rich metalanguage (Jaworski, Coupland, and Galasinski, 2004), and intentional as well as unintentional non-standard orthography, grammar, and lexis. The primary language of the forum is English, but NP plays a significant role, and other Nigerian and world languages occur occasionally (Honkanen, 2020). What makes Nairaland a particularly suitable data source for this project is that its member base is globally dispersed, consisting of not only Nigeria-based participants but also Nigerian immigrants and their offspring in various diasporic locations.

The corpus can be accessed via a web-based search interface, Net Corpora Administration Tool (NCAT), developed at the University of Freiburg for the purpose of querying and visualizing such web forum data. NCAT allows searching for words or parts of words in the data, and restricting the search to certain forum members or time periods. Links are retained between messages and their authors on the one hand, and messages and the preceding and following text in the same thread on the other hand. Therefore, the researcher can focus on interesting individuals, or consider the larger interactional context when interpreting messages. This enables discourse analysis as well as averts the problem of "loss of context", typical of "sampling by phenomenon" that targets "particular linguistic features or patterns of language use" (Androutsopoulos, 2013: 238–239).

The methodological details of how each of the three topics was approached will be clarified below in the respective sections, along with the findings.

3 Analysis

3.1 Nigerian Pidgin lexicon of authenticity and migration

This section takes a look at the concrete words used for discussing topics of authenticity and migration in NP. It discusses two glossaries included in the appendix, the first on authenticity and the second on migration. During my previous qualitative work on Nairaland (Honkanen, 2020), I became aware of many of these lexemes as well as the prominence of these topics in Nigerian online communication. Further items were harvested from various existing – primarily non-professional – sources of lexicographic information, published as online dictionaries or word lists in blogs or on Nairaland. The most comprehensive resources are *Babawilly's dictionary of Pidgin English words and phrases*, a one-man project documenting the lexicon of NP as spoken in the Lagos metropole (Babawilly, 2000), and the crowd-sourced *naija lingo* website with over 1,600 entries (naija lingo, 2019). These and other resources were surveyed, and potentially relevant items were checked against my corpus.

Table 1 in the appendix details the NP vocabulary of authentication and inauthenticity, providing for each word some possible translations and alternative spellings, its etymological origin if known, and a usage example from Nairaland, translated when unobvious. Entries are not assigned to parts-of-speech as most items can be used in various syntactic positions; besides, NP is usually said to not possess a separate word class of adjectives (Faraclas, 1996: 214). For information about ethnic Nigerian languages, I rely on Mensah (2011), *A dictionary of the Yoruba language* by the Church Missionary Society (1913), and the kind help of Professor Akinmade Akande and Dr. Adesoji Babalola (both from Obafemi Awolowo University). Some important tendencies and interesting cases will be discussed below.

This collection of words shows how rich the Nigerian vocabulary of authentication is. There are several synonyms for *authentic* or *original*, which occur prominently in identity statements (see Section 3.3). However, apart from these, the list shows a distinct negativity bias: there are many more words, especially nouns and verbs, for describing inauthentic or fraudulent activities, people, and objects. Some lexemes are culturally relevant in the Nigerian society, notoriously grappling with corruption and fraud, while others are useful in discourses of global mobility for describing undesirable cultural/linguistic accommodation. Along with semantically widely applicable lexemes, there are items with narrower meanings, such as *panda* for fake gilded jewelry, or *toronto* for fake educational degrees.

Etymologically, most items can be traced back to either English or one of the major Nigerian languages. However, the borrowed morphemes may have been modified further through clipping (e.g., *ote* from *authentic*, *fabu* from *fabulous* or *fabulate*), reduplication (e.g., *boju boju, yahoo yahoo*), or compounding (e.g., *wayo man, corner corner love*). Some of them originate from specific events or things, such as *toronto* from politician Salisu Buhari's scandalous fake certificates "from the University of Toronto", *jankara* from the famous Lagos market where everything can be bought, or *419* from the Nigerian Criminal Code relating to fraudulent practices.

As NP is an English-lexifier language, many more English words are employed in Pidgin discourses of authenticity than are given in Table 1. The glossary only includes English-origin items that differ from their standardized use either formally (e.g., *bold face* 'bald-faced', *cunny* 'cunning'), semantically (e.g., *chance* 'to trick', *form* 'to pretend, show off'), or syntactically (e.g., *claim* directly followed by an adjective or a noun related to the claimed identity). Further words such as *fake, wannabe, pretend, proper,* or *correct* occur very frequently (see Example 1 and Section 3.3), but they are used to confer or deny identities much in the same way as in English, and are therefore not discussed here.

(1)   *[singer] na propa delta babe n she no de fake accent*   (male, Nigeria)
'[singer] is an authentic Niger Delta girl and she does not fake an accent'

The next extracts feature several of the discussed words each, showing which ones of them are seen as close synonyms and how they must possess notable expressive power as they are used in such seemingly redundant ways.

(2)   *I am over 1000000000% sured that [name] is a*   (male, Ireland)
SCAMMER/419/jibiti/Gbajue.

(3)   *Why everything with naija elections be mago*   (male, USA)
mago, wayo and wuru wuru to the answer?

(4)   *Na me be the original/authentic/ogbonge*   (male, Nigeria)
Ibadan persin.

If this glossary were to be extended, one could add terms related to scamming (e.g., words for fraud victims), corruption, or bribery (cf. Adegoju and Raheem, 2015). These have, however, been excluded for reasons of scope, and attention will be turned next to the Nigerian lexicon of migration, an overview of which is again presented in a table format in the appendix.

    The words in question depict foreign or diasporic locations or people, the concept of abroadness in general, or in some cases, are derogatory terms for those who have not been able to enjoy the mobility of the privileged in globalization. Non-standard toponyms may serve the function of expressing affiliation to, dissociation from, or at least familiarity with places (Heyd and Honkanen, 2015). More items could be added to the glossary if one were to include informal place names at the city-level (e.g., Jos as *J-Town*, Houston as *H-Town*, Lagos as *Lasgidi*, Abuja as *ABJ*).

    These items, too, represent various word-formation strategies from abbreviation (*JJC*) and clipping (*overs, loki*) to compounding (*bushman*) and affixation (*Southie, janded*). *Yonda* ('abroad') from English *yonder* exemplifies the very Nigerian tendency to localize archaic English expressions (cf. Kperogi, 2015: 11). One also witnesses lexical borrowing and accompanying semantic change – many items have more specific meanings in their source language but have undergone semantic extension upon entering NP. This is visible in the following metalinguistic comments.

(5) E.g. *my broda dey for overseas, overseas here* (male, Nigeria)
could mean, UK, America or Benin republic

(6) *akata just describes an African American* (female, USA)
and we call white people oyibo or bekee
in Igboland. Akata is sometimes used as
name for imported things. I've even
heard expressions like 'I dey go akata'
meaning, I'm going abroad.

(7) *i thot jand is abroad not just london.* (female, USA)

The most multilayered items are *akata* and *tokunbo*. Negatively connoted, *akata* is a complex term of "othering" (Heyd, 2014: 43), which Nigerians in the United States seem to employ overwhelmingly in reference to African Americans (Example 6) but which may in other contexts refer to foreigners of any ethnicity, or even to emigrated Nigerians. "Go akata" does not occur in my data. *Tokunbo*, then, is a word of Yoruba origin with two basic meanings: 'second-hand', or 'from abroad'. These two senses come together in its most common usage: tokunbos are used cars imported from abroad, reputed to be in better shape than vehicles driven on Nigerian roads. However, *tokunbo* may also be used in reference to a person born abroad, or even given as a first name to a foreign-born child, or according to Mensah (2011: 222), a child whose father is abroad.

Containing several items from Tables 1 and 2, the final example of this section connects the themes of migration and linguistic authenticity. It is a reaction to Nigerians' high ranking in a CNN poll of the world's sexiest accents.

(8) ☻ *maybe the JJC wey don land for Jand will* (female, UK)
no more xerox yankee lingo now oh, una dey
hear ur own accent be segzy ☻
'maybe the newcomers who've arrived in England will
no longer imitate American ways of speaking now [that]
you hear your own accent is sexy'

3.2 Diasporic Nigerians' language attitudes

Some research has been conducted into attitudes toward NP in Nigeria (e.g., Mann, 1996, 2009; Akande and Salami, 2010; Obi, 2014), but there have been hardly any substantial contributions addressing attitudes in diasporic contexts. In my work on Nigerians in the United States (Honkanen, 2020), I conclude that due to their high levels of educational attainment and English competence, U.S.-Nigerians' use of NP is likely to be dissociated from former connotations of illiteracy, poverty, and lack of schooling even more so than in Nigeria, where many educated people and media sources now also increasingly employ Pidgin. Hence, the language has been freed to acquire new indexicalities, and now carries a significant expressive, aesthetic, symbolic, and authenticating force (Honkanen, 2020: 231). This section explores attitudes toward NP in the Nigerian diaspora, based on expatriate Nigerians' metalanguage on the Nairaland forum.

NCAT was used to locate relevant metalinguistic comments, or in the first instance, diasporic users. A considerable portion of the data by the most frequent forum contributors has been manually tagged for geolocation by our Freiburg research team (Honkanen, 2020: 56–57). NCAT creates for every query a list of users who produce the most posts containing the search term(s). I searched for "Pidgin" and names of major migrant destinations until I had identified 300 diasporic forum members who self-identify as Nigerian. NCAT queries can be limited to chosen members, so in the next step, I searched for "Broken English",[1] "Pidgin", and orthographic variants in this sample of 300. This yielded 1,106 posts by 180 members, which were read through and coded for language attitudes expressed. The findings of this qualitative investigation are described next.

One can only speculate that those 40% who never explicitly refer to NP in their online writing might not have particularly strong feelings about it in either direction. Other diasporic Nigerians' attitudes toward their pidgin can be divided into positive, negative, and conflicted ones. Those with favorable attitudes often use emotional language to describe their pleasure upon speaking or hearing NP, whether they are competent users of the language themselves (Example 9) or not (Example 10).

(9) *OMO!!! even to ma friends here* (female, France)
if den tell me sontin wey I no like
I go jus tell dem 'na una sabi'

---

[1] *Broken English* usually denotes NP, though it may in some cases refer to learner English that deviates significantly from internationally accepted standards.

Den go dey look me like mumu
but wettin be ma own? if u no undastand
na ma problem? Na ur own cup of kunu be that o!
seriously, witout pidgin I no go fit communicate well.
I need to express maself well well!
se una get? 😊
'[vocative]! [I speak NP] even to my friends here.
If they say something that I don't like
I'll just tell them 'na una sabi'
They'll be looking at me like idiots
but what's that got to do with me? If you don't understand,
is it my problem? That's your own problem!
Seriously, without Pidgin I cannot communicate well.
I need to express myself fully!
Do you understand?'

(10) *oh wow i guess ive been off nl for wayy too long.*   (female, USA,
nawa [name] u no even fit tell me about this one   subscript in original)
ehn 😊 *dude i jus totally spoke pidgin it felt friggin awesome !!* 😊

(11) *There is life in pidgin, english grammar is stern*   (male, USA)
and dry . . . too formal.

There is also another strand of pro-Pidgin thinking, one that focuses on various practical, political, and ideological reasons for favoring the language. The proponents of NP see it as a useful, ethnically neutral, and authentically African language.

(12) *Anyway, to involve everytribe in Nigeria, Pidgin En-*   (female, USA)
glish will be a perfect main language in Nigeria.
Every tribe in Nigeria speaks it.

(13) *INFERIORITY COMPLEX IS A BIG SICKNESS THAT CANNOT BE*   (male,
CURE IN ANY HOSPITAL [. . .] who on earth has made speaking   Sweden)
English the better way of doing things. When u are proud of what
you have, you see others join you. Please [hip-hop artist] speak
ONLY pidgin and IGBOOOOO. [. . .] Please nigeria should adopt
pidgin as official language. some piple prefer to be inferior.

Those with negative attitudes tend to lack competence in NP, and view it not as an independent language but a ruleless, corrupt form of English, or might even blame it for some Nigerians' imperfect command of the English language. These are linguistically uninformed standpoints that ignore the systematicity of pidgin and creole languages and the great human potential for competent multilingualism under the right conditions.

(14) *I don't the understand the pidgin crap so it fine. That a flaw I'm proud of. It wont help me compete in a global economy and not original.* (female, USA)

(15) *I can't speak pidgin. But, I never considered the language anything other than poorly educated Nigerians struggling to learn English.* (male, USA)

(16) *In my opinion, pidgin distorts regular English. This is apparent in graduates getting their tenses mixed up, and other grammatical blunders.* (male, UK)

Some expatriates seem torn between these two positions. I will present only one lengthy extract to exemplify conflicted attitudes. This member speaks NP and recognizes its "coolness" and usefulness in Nigeria but also associates it with working-class professions and worries about its negative impact on English if learned first.

(17) *I grew up speaking grammatically correct English at home because my parents were very particular about it. I am grateful for that. We may say that pidgin English is more widely spoken within Nigeria, but then Nigeria is not the whole world. It has always been a source of irritation when I see Nigerians over here struggling to knit sentences together in the same language that they were actually taught in school with. While in my last two years in the university, I learnt how to speak pidgin English and can now smoothly switch between both. So I can converse with the Queen as well as the tomato seller at Uselu Market in Benin. The issue here is that I got solidly drilled in universally spoken English BEFORE venturing into learning pidgin English. Whether we want to admit it or not, learning both languages the other way round is not very wise. Pidgin English may sound cool, but what seems cool isn't always cool. I* (male, Germany)

can't have my kids jabbering away like bus-conductors plying the Ugbowo-Ring Road route in Benin while they are still in their formative years. Finally, pidgin to my parents? Never. My parents to their kids? Never. My parents to the neighbours back then? Sometimes. Us to the neighbours? Sometimes. All in all: I have the best of both worlds, but still prefer speaking correct English.

Moreover, many seem to react to NP with strong amusement. It seems to be the preferred language for joking and humorous storytelling, and some primarily use it for jocular purposes (Example 20). Although this certainly is a non-hostile reaction to NP, it does put the language in a fairly narrow box. But for many, the non-seriousness and playfulness of Pidgin seem to be its main connotations.

(18) *Your broken English makes it real & fun, keep up the comic relief on here.* (female, USA)

(19) *ahahahahahahaha abeg that story is too funny. even the fact that he wrote it in pidgin is what makes it better* (female, Italy)

(20) *i speak pigdin a little to my mom, grandma, uncle, and anut and that's it, nut usually when we are joking or when we are in public and i don't want people to know what i am saying. i never speak pidgin to my dad because he hates pidgin. he only speaks pidgin when he has to, like when every single person in the room is speaking it.* (female, USA)

Finally, the most interesting metalinguistic statements are those that offer glimpses into potential differences between attitudes in Nigeria and the diaspora and/ or changes in the situation. In this regard, my data suggest a generational shift that contrasts with Mann's (2009) survey findings, where the youngest cohort had the most negative attitudes toward Pidgin. Numerous Nairalanders comment on their parents being unable to speak NP, unwilling to teach it to them, and/or discouraging its use altogether. However, many of these young Nigerians themselves have more competence in and more positive attitudes toward the language than the previous generation has.

(21) *i love pidgin. i wish my mom let me speak it n 9ja.* (female, UK)

(22) *my mom cant even speak pigin. and she was born* (female, USA)
and raised in naija. she understands it a little.
she only speaks good english. lol i know more
than her!! 😊 😊

Some posters explicitly reflect on these developments and the changing indexicalities of NP.

(23) *But in naija's case today, not only the poverty-stricken* (female, USA)
people speak pidgin these days, it's more like being in-
formal not uneducated to me.

(24) *Social attitudes toward pidgin have changed for the* (male, USA, 2012)
better in the last 12 years however it is still considered
an informal language. Some decades ago it was con-
sidered a faux pas to use it amongst the middle and
upper classes (who would only use it when talking to
people from lower classes), but now its often used in
everyday conversation.

In some narratives, these changes are tied to the experience of migration, which supports the idea that attitudes may be more lenient in the diaspora, where associating NP with lack of education is certainly not justified. Instead, Pidgin may signal, for instance, authentic Nigerianness (Example 26).

(25) *Growing up in Naija. In our house Pidgin English was for-* (female, USA)
bidden. My mama and my father can speak it but they
didn't teach it to us. Atleast they taught us Igbo. My sister
and brother learnt how to speak it from friends. Me on the
other hand i'm slowly learning. I can read and understand
it but i can't speak it or write it yet. My parents don't care
anymore if we speak broken english in the House. My
mother even agreed that pidgin should be Naija main
language. Maybe in the future i'll know how to speak
and write it. So i can confuse yankee people. not only
with Igbo but with broken english also.

(26) *being in the UK makes me appreciate Yoruba and Pidgin*   (male, UK)
1000 times more, because you realise it is a unique part
of your identity!

In sum, diasporic Nigerians display a variety of attitudes towards NP, building on differing underlying beliefs about linguistic realities, some of which we discovered. The social indexicalities of NP may vary and change, but generally, there appears to be a shift toward more tolerance, or in many cases even enthusiasm, for speaking Pidgin in the diaspora – on the internet, with family and the wider Nigerian expatriate community, as well as upon visits to the homeland. I speculate that one of the main functions of NP in the diaspora is to authenticate (Bucholtz, 2003) the speaker/writer as a Nigerian. Akande (2011: 229) links codeswitching into Pidgin with "index[ing] national identity" in Nigeria as well. This topic will be explored in the third and last part of the analysis below.

3.3 Nigerian Pidgin in strategic authentication

This section brings together once more the different topics of the current paper – the lexicon and functions of NP, the Nigerian diaspora, identity construction, and authenticity – and explores the role of NP in authenticating Nigerian immigrant identities through an analysis of identity statements on Nairaland.

NCAT was used to locate potential NP identity statements in the data. I chose one simple structure that yields a sufficient sample of identity statements. The search string was "I be" (and orthographic variants), as *bì* has been identified as "the most commonly used copular element in copular sentences with nominal complements" in NP (Faraclas, 1996: 44). The query was restricted to the same 300 diasporic Nigerians (see Section 3.2), to target identity work among immigrants. I focused on national, ethnic, and geographical belonging though the whole identity spectrum on Nairaland is infinitely more varied and complex. Of course, the search string massively truncates all potential data, but this structure can be discussed as one example of how identity negotiation may play out in NP. The following are representative examples (for more, see also Table 1).

(27) *chei which kain yawa be this, oyibo ke?, abeg i be serious*   (female, USA)
naija pikin, born and bred.
'[exclamation] what nonsense is this, a Caucasian? Please!
I am an authentic Nigerian, born and bred.'

(28) *i thought u be iGBO, but i be yoruba sha, omo Ibadan* (male, USA)
'I thought you're Igbo, but I'm Yoruba [emphasis],
a person from [the city of] Ibadan'

(29) *I BE CONFIRM NAIJA EMI NI CONFIRM OMO, CONFIRM* (male, China)
BOBO ☻ *ITS GREEN WHITE GREEN TILL I DIE!!!!* ☻ ☻
'I'm an authentic Nigerian. I'm an authentic person, an authentic guy. It's green-white-green[2] till I die!'

Most of the minimal identity statements with "I be" display a strikingly consistent formal and semantic pattern also beyond their identical start. In its maximal form, the structure can be schematically represented like this:

I be (authenticating adjective) identity label (noun) (authenticator) (emphasis marker)

Minimally, the construction could consist of "I be" followed by an identity label, but it is often expanded with elements that strengthen or elaborate the identity claim, and hence, as I claim, strive to authenticate it. Firstly, the identity label is often preceded by an adjective. Table 1 contains various Nigerian authenticating adjectives; additionally, many English adjectives are used. The most common ones are *proper, correct*, and *real*, but one encounters in this position also, for instance, *true, full blooded, confirm*, and *original*.

The identity label may indicate belonging to any cultural or geopolitical group or entity. Most commonly, an ethnic label is chosen. The African continent has always been primarily divided along ethnic lines, while borders imposed by European colonizers as well as Pan-African sentiments deriving from, for example, racial identification play a smaller (though not insignificant) role. These preferences hold in the diaspora as well. Apart from ethnic labels, many diasporic Nairalanders choose to self-identify as Nigerians, calling forth the political unit of the Federal Republic of Nigeria. Most commonly, the local variant *Naija* ('Nigerian') is used. Moreover, one frequently finds geographical terms in this position, at a precision ranging from states to cities to even neighborhoods. For instance, Mushin in Example 30 is a suburb in the metropole of Lagos, while Sapele and Warri (<warfy> in Example 31) are cities in the Niger Delta region, known as the heartland of NP. *Jappa*, however, in Example 31, is not an actual place but a Yoruba word meaning 'to leave, escape', which, in fact, here refers to the emigrant experience. The word is not included in Table 2 because it is very rare

---

[2] Green and white are the colors of the Nigerian flag. This reference is, hence, a further authenticating move and highlights nationality over ethnic and other forms of identity.

in my data, but it is currently becoming increasingly popular in NP as well (Adesoji Babalola, personal communication, 18 August 2019).

(30) *i be lagos girl, mushin girl to be specific. but am igbo* (female, USA)

(31) *am familiar with warfy ways, lol i be proper sapele pikin, jappa town for lyfe* ☺ (female, UK)

As with non-standard toponyms in Table 2, one sees here the importance of place and space for identity construction in disembodied, diasporic online communication (cf. Heyd and Honkanen, 2015).

The next position in the schema is optionally but frequently filled by a person-referring noun. Most of these are gendered items (e.g., *guy*, *babe*, *girl*, *man*, *boi*, *broad*) that hence add another layer of identity – gender identity – and often carry implications of age as well. There are also some gender-neutral options with a local flavor, such as *persin* (NP 'a person'), *pikin* (NP 'a child'), or *omo* (Yoruba 'a child'). *Omo* is syntactically unique in that it always precedes the identity label.

(32) *I be omo Yoruba too to make it worse, i be Omo eko.* (female, USA)
 'I am a Yoruba person, too. To make matters worse, I am a Lagosian.'

The next slot in the structure may be taken up by different strengthening and elaborating phrases which I call authenticators because they reinforce the identity claim made. Some examples from my data include "born and bred", "through and through", "for lyfe", "no be small" ('very'), "to the marrow", "100%", or "inside-out". Such phrases imply an understanding of ethnic/national/local belonging as a gradual phenomenon, which an individual may embody more or less thoroughly and permanently. Another noticeable aspect of these phrases is that, apart from "no be small", they would all be coded rather as English than as NP if one insisted on making such a distinction. In fact, this is typical of writing practices on Nairaland: NP and English are often mixed intimately, even within individual phrases.

Finally, many of these identity statements close with an emphasis or emotion marking discourse particle, such as *oo*, *sha*, or *sef*. Such semantically and pragmatically flexible markers are very common in Nigerian computer-mediated communication (Honkanen, 2020). In these "I be" constructions, one could argue their role to be, on the one hand, to add expressive and emotional force to these important interactional turns[3] and, on the other hand, to further authenticate these utterances as Nigerian. Mair (2013b: 25) has identified *oo* as the minimal marker of Nigerianness among aspiring though not fully competent writers of NP. The idea that such simple elements can index ethnic belonging in the diaspora is precisely what Blommaert and Varis's understanding of authenticity as "enoughness" (2011) can mean on the linguistic plane. This can be seen in the next extract, which contains a minimal performance of NP by a diasporic Nigerian in a thread that asks "How Many Of You Speak Pidgin To Your Parents?"

(33) *Hello. I be a Nigerian oo. Lmfao !* (female, Belgium)

This user has no real competence in NP (as she willingly admits elsewhere) beyond familiarity with the marker *oo* and some basic verbal morphology, but she wants to participate nonetheless and claim a Nigerian identity using the limited resources at her disposal. The abbreviation ('laughing my fucking ass off') again shows the connotation of NP with jocularity especially among less competent speakers, as well as mitigates this immigrant's desperate attempt to sufficiently authenticate her identity statement.

Pidgin's role as an authenticator can also be seen in how frequently one finds identity statements realized in NP within passages otherwise in English. In Example 34, the author declares her racial and ethnic identity in NP, but then turns to English for the "serious", on-topic part of the message.

(34) *I no be whity ooo. I be omo yoruba . . . Biko make una save* (female, USA)
me ooo. Oh and seriously, no taboos. There's never being a
concrete reason as to why one shouldn't kiss/make out or
marry one's cousin.
'I am not a white person. I am a Yoruba. Please spare me.
[. . .]'

(35) *anywhere with basketball court is utopia for me. i love to* (male, USA)
play. and ermm i am not ajebo by any stretch of the imagi-
nation. i be ajepaki no be small sef. ol boy the traffick here
in chicago on lake shore drive in the morning is the same.

---

[3] This function can be carried out by emojis as well, which are another type of resource to commonly fill the utterance-final position in identity statements.

so whats ya point ⊕ *try driving on lake shore drive going downtown from the northside every morning. trAFFICK jam dey everywhere my brother. no where in the world is utopia. you just have to make ya sorroundings work for ya*

Example 35 contains two insertions of NP amidst English discourse. The first one supports a claim to a specific Nigerian class identity – that of a street-smart and resilient *ajepaki* (literally, 'one who eats cassava') from a rough background, as opposed to a more refined, spoiled upper-class *ajebo*, or *ajebota* ('one who eats butter') – for which NP is the most appropriate linguistic code. The second minimal insertion, of the NP existential verb *dey*, occurs within a statement expressing solidarity with the addressee. The evidence discussed in this section suggests that Pidgin may play a prominent role in identity statements and in authenticating different Nigerian identities on this diasporic web forum.

4 Conclusion

This chapter has addressed the use of Nigerian Pidgin in connection to the topics of authenticity and migration. It reported on a qualitative corpus-based study, which targeted three aspects of the topic: NP lexicon, attitudes toward NP among diasporic Nigerians, and their use of NP in identity statements.

The lexical semantic analysis of Pidgin words of authentication and the migrant experience revealed the richness of Nigerian vocabulary related to these topics. NP vocabulary is extended through borrowing from English and local languages, and often affected by semantic change or word-formation processes such as clipping or affixation. The high number of lexemes depicting inauthentic and fraudulent behaviors suggests that there might be more different ways of being untrue than there are of being true, fitting with the well-known psychological principle of negative differentiation. The high degree of nuance in the lexicon related to these topics testifies to their significance for Nigerians worldwide.

I analyzed diasporic Nigerians' language attitudes based on their metalanguage on a Nigerian web forum. While their competence varies greatly, many young Nigerians have positive attitudes toward their pidgin. Such favorable views may be either emotionally or pragmatically based, whereas negative attitudes tend to stem from linguistically ungrounded ideas about pidgins as learner English or as a hindrance to learning English. One also encounters more nuanced, conflicted attitudes, as well as the simplistic view of Pidgin as a code for humor. Although such genuine, unsolicited metalinguistic statements may well be analyzed for the language attitudes they reflect, for a more systematic investigation of language attitudes and changes in them, interviews or questionnaires represent a more effective method of data collection. However, a corpus of the size of ours certainly offers enough material for a first exploration of the issue.

The investigation of identity statements in NP was restricted to exploring one construction – "I be" followed by different Nigerian identity labels – but already from this, some interesting tendencies emerged. Even in the diaspora, ethnic identity seems to remain highly relevant, though many also self-identify as Nigerians, or verbalize feelings of belonging to specific geographical places in Nigeria. The category of gender is prominent as well. The "I be" construction is often expanded with various authenticating expressions in NP and even more commonly in English, showing an understanding of Nigerianness as something gradable and negotiable. Combining NP with English seems to be accepted as authentic linguistic practice in the Nigerian online context. These exciting data offer a first glimpse into how NP plays a role in the strategic construction of different Nigerian identities, whereby authenticity is actively created through processes of "authentication" (Bucholtz, 2003). Migrant identities are complex and precarious, and often negotiated and relativized through language.

References

Adegoju, Adeyemi & Saheed Raheem. 2015. Gone are the days of 'kola(nut)': New trends in language habits and coding of corrupt practices in Nigeria. *Marang: Journal of Language and Literature* 26, 155–172.

Adegoke, Yemisi. 2019. Does Nigeria have too many doctors to worry about a 'brain drain'? *BBC News*. https://www.bbc.com/news/world-africa-45473036 (accessed 6 August 2021)

Akande, Akinmade. 2011. Codeswitching and identity. In Inyang Udofot & Juliet Udoudom (eds.), *English usage in Nigeria since 1842: Patterns and changes: A festschrift for Prof. David Eka*, 218–233. Ikot Ekpene: Devconsont Services.

Akande, Akinmade & Oladipo Salami. 2010. Use and attitudes towards Nigerian Pidgin English among Nigerian university students. In Robert Millar (ed.), *Marginal dialects: Language varieties on linguistic boundaries in Scotland, Ireland and beyond*, 70–89. Aberdeen: Forum for Research on the Languages of Scotland and Ireland.

Androutsopoulos, Jannis. 2008. Potentials and limitations of Discourse-Centred Online Ethnography. *Language@Internet* 5, 1–20.

Androutsopoulos, Jannis. 2013. Online data collection. In Christine Mallinson, Becky Childs & Gerald Van Herk (eds.), *Data collection in sociolinguistics: Methods and applications*, 236–249. New York: Routledge.

Appadurai, Arjun. 1996. *Modernity at large: Cultural dimensions of globalization*. Minneapolis: University of Minnesota Press.

Babawilly. 2000. Babawilly's dictionary of Pidgin English words and phrases. *NigeriaExchange*. http://www.ngex.com/personalities/babawilly/dictionary/ (accessed 6 August 2021)

Blommaert, Jan. 2010. *The sociolinguistics of globalization*. Cambridge: Cambridge University Press.

Blommaert, Jan & Piia Varis. 2011. Enough is enough: The heuristics of authenticity in superdiversity. *Working Papers in Urban Language & Literacies* 76, 1–13.

Bucholtz, Mary. 2003. Sociolinguistic nostalgia and the authentication of identity. *Journal of Sociolinguistics* 7(3), 398–416.

Church Missionary Society. 1913. *A dictionary of the Yoruba language*. Lagos: Church Missionary Society Bookshop.

Coupland, Nikolas. 2001. Stylization, authenticity and TV news review. *Discourse Studies* 3(4), 413–442.

Faraclas, Nicholas. 1996. *Nigerian Pidgin*. London & New York: Routledge.

Gill, Martin. 2013. Authentication and Nigerian letters. In Susan Herring, Dieter Stein & Tuija Virtanen (eds.), *Pragmatics of computer-mediated communication* (Handbooks of Pragmatics 9), 411–436. Berlin & Boston: De Gruyter Mouton.

Heyd, Theresa. 2014. Doing race and ethnicity in a digital community: Lexical labels and narratives of belonging in a Nigerian web forum. *Discourse, Context & Media* 4–5, 38–47.

Heyd, Theresa. 2015. Beyond 'grammar' and 'phonetics': The metacommunicative lexicon of Nigerian Pidgin. *World Englishes* 34(4), 669–687.

Heyd, Theresa. 2016a. Global varieties of English gone digital: Orthographic and semantic variation in digital Nigerian Pidgin. In Lauren Squires (ed.), *English in computer-mediated communication: Variation, representation, and change* (Topics in English Linguistics 93), 101–122. Boston & Berlin: De Gruyter.

Heyd, Theresa. 2016b. Narratives of belonging in the digital diaspora: Corpus approaches to a cultural concept. *Open Linguistics* 2(1), 287–299.

Heyd, Theresa & Mirka Honkanen. 2015. From Naija to Chitown: The New African Diaspora and digital representations of place. *Discourse, Context & Media* 9, 14–23.

Heyd, Theresa & Christian Mair. 2014. From vernacular to digital ethnolinguistic repertoire: The case of Nigerian Pidgin. In Veronique Lacoste, Jacob Leimgruber & Thiemo Breyer (eds.), *Indexing authenticity: Sociolinguistic perspectives*, 244–268. Berlin & Boston: De Gruyter.

Hine, Christine. 2000. *Virtual ethnography*. London, Thousand Oaks & New Delhi: SAGE.

Hinrichs, Lars. 2006. *Codeswitching on the web: English and Jamaican Creole in e-mail communication* (Pragmatics & Beyond New Series 147). Amsterdam: John Benjamins.

Honkanen, Mirka. 2020. *World Englishes on the web: The Nigerian diaspora in the USA* (Varieties of English Around the World G63). Amsterdam: John Benjamins.

Honkanen, Mirka. 2020. 'This word no get concrete meaning oo': Pragmatic markers in Nigerian multilingual online communication. *Journal of Pragmatics*.

Jaworski, Adam, Nikolas Coupland & Dariusz Galasinski (eds.). 2004. *Metalanguage: Social and ideological perspectives*. Berlin: De Gruyter.

Kperogi, Farooq. 2015. *Glocal English: The changing face and forms of Nigerian English in a global world*. New York: Peter Lang.

Mair, Christian. 2011. Corpora and the new Englishes: Using the 'Corpus of Cyber-Jamaican' to explore research perspectives for the future. In Fanny Meunier, Sylvie De Cock, Gaëtanelle Gilquin & Magali Paquot (eds.), *A taste for corpora: In honour of Sylviane Granger* (Studies in Corpus Linguistics 45), 209–236. Amsterdam: John Benjamins.

Mair, Christian. 2013a. The World System of Englishes: Accounting for the transnational importance of mobile and mediated vernaculars. *English World-Wide* 34(3), 253–278.

Mair, Christian. 2013b. Corpus-approaches to the new English web: Post-colonial diasporic forums in West Africa and the Caribbean. *Covenant Journal of Language Studies* 1(1), 17–30.

Mair, Christian & Stefan Pfänder. 2013. Vernacular and multilingual writing in mediated spaces: Web-forums for post-colonial communities of practice. In Peter Auer, Martin Hilpert, Anja Stukenbrock & Benedikt Szmrecsanyi (eds.), *Space in language and linguistics: Geographical, interactional, and cognitive perspectives* (Linguae & Litterae 24), 529–556. Berlin & Boston: De Gruyter.

Mann, Charles. 1996. Anglo-Nigerian Pidgin in Nigerian education: A survey of policy, practices and attitudes. In Tina Hickey & Jenny Williams (eds.), *Language, education and society in a changing world*, 93–106. Philadelphia: Multilingual Matters.

Mann, Charles. 2009. Attitudes toward Anglo-Nigerian Pidgin in urban, southern Nigeria: The generational variable. *Revue roumaine de linguistique* 3–4, 349–364.

Mensah, Eyo. 2011. Lexicalization in Nigerian Pidgin. *Concentric: Studies in Linguistics* 37(2), 209–240.

Mensah, Eyo. 2013. Proverbs in Nigerian Pidgin. *Journal of Anthropological Research* 69(1), 87–115.

Migration Policy Institute. 2015. RAD diaspora profile: The Nigerian diaspora in the United States, rev. edn. Washington, DC: Migration Policy Institute. www.migrationpolicy.org/sites/default/files/publications/RAD-Nigeria.pdf (accessed 6 August 2021).

Moll, Andrea. 2015. *Jamaican Creole goes web: Sociolinguistic styling and authenticity in a digital 'yaad'* (Creole Language Library 49). Amsterdam & Philadelphia: John Benjamins.

naija lingo. 2019. Naijalingo: The Nigerian Pidgin English dictionary. *Naijalingo: The Nigerian Pidgin English dictionary created by you for you!* http://naijalingo.com/ (accessed 6 August 2021).

Obi, Edith. 2014. Language attitude and Nigerian Pidgin. *International Journal of Arts and Humanities* 3–4(12), 34–46.

Office for National Statistics. 2019. Population of the UK by country of birth and nationality: Individual country data. https://www.ons.gov.uk/peoplepopulationandcommunity/populationandmigration/internationalmigration/datasets/populationoftheunitedkingdombycountryofbirthandnationality (accessed 6 August 2021)

Storch, Anne. 2017. Ruination and amusement – dialect, youth and revolution in Naija. In Reem Bassiouney (ed.), *Identity and dialect performance: A study of communities and dialects* (Routledge Studies in Language and Identity), 303–320. Oxon & New York: Routledge.

Chapter 5 Nigerian Pidgin in authenticating immigrant identities — 167

Appendix

Table 1: Nigerian Pidgin lexicon of (in)authenticity.

Lexeme	Meaning	Etymology	Example	Comments
419, 4-1-9, 419er	'scam, advance fee fraud', 'scammer'	Criminal Code Section 419	"pls i beg i no be 419 ooooooo" 'please, please, I am not a scammer'	from the section of the Criminal Code on fraud
aba-made	'fake (product)'	Nigerian city (proper name) + English	"aba made has it's place even America get aba made" 'fake products have their place; even America has fake products'	Aba is the commercial center of the Southeast, known for its craftsmen and -women
baruf	'fake'	Hausa	"wetin concern baruf with origo if no be Alaba" 'I don't care fake or real unless it's at the Alaba market'	
bobo	'to lie'	Yoruba *bò* 'to cover, hide'	"i no fit dey BOBO u na . . . what will it profit me telling u lies" 'I cannot lie to you [. . .]'	unrelated meaning bobo 'guy'
boju boju	'deception', 'hidden', 'hide and seek'	Yoruba *boju* 'to veil'	"u can be allowed to see the product, no boju boju about dis"	
bold face	'bluff', 'bald-faced'	English *bald/bold-faced*	"no come dey use bold face for here" 'do not bluff here'	
bonafide, bonifide	'authentic, real'	Latin *bona fide*	"Me I be bonafide Nairalander na" 'I'm an authentic Nairalander'	more often spelled as one word 1,761 vs 662

Table 1 (continued)

Lexeme	Meaning	Etymology	Example	Comments
chance	'to trick, cheat'	English	*"Chinese too don begin dey chance us!"* 'The Chinese too have begun to trick us!'	
claim	'to claim to be'	English	*"u dey form/claim virgin abi wetin?"* 'are you pretending/claiming to be virgin or what?'	
conc, conc., konk	'authentic', 'strong', 'to hit', 'to concentrate'	English *concentrate(d)*	*"dis wan na conc. igbo gaaal"* 'she's an authentic Igbo girl'	
confirm, confam	'real, original'	English *confirmed*	*"me i be confirm Aj boy"* 'I'm an authentic Ajegunle boy'	
copy copy	'to plagiarize, copy', 'unoriginal'	English	*"not 1 artist is original, just dey copy copy"*	
corner corner	'to cheat', 'indirectly', 'diversion'	English	*"their straight forwardness, no corner corner"*	→ *corner corner love* 'extra-marital affair'
correct, korrect, correkt	'authentic, real'	English	*"i be correcccccccccccct igbo babe"*	
cunny	'dishonest, cunning'	English *cunning*	*"na cunny cunny love be dis o! Don't be deceived!"* 'this is deceptive love! [. . .]'	proverb *"cunny man die, cunny man bury im"* 'it takes one to know one'
dagbo	'fake, falsified', 'forgery'	Yoruba	*"That age 21 na dagbo age. I know the guy well he is about your age"* 'That age (21) is a falsified age. [. . .]'	

Table 1 (continued)

Lexeme	Meaning	Etymology	Example	Comments
fabu, faboo	'lie'	English *fabulous* 'having no basis in reality, mythical', or *fabulate* 'to relate invented stories'	"I nor gree. dat one nah fabu" 'I don't agree. that's a lie'	
feferity, feferiti	'showing off, pretending (to be fancy)'	Yoruba *féfé* 'bravado' + English *-ity*	"Every single thing, launching, cutting ribbon, etc. na jus to dey do feferiti everywhere." '[. . .] it's just for showing off.'	
follow follow, folofolo	'to copy', 'unoriginal behavior/person'	English	"I don forget say you be expert in this 'follow-follow', copy-cat business!" 'I forgot that you are an expert [. . .]'	cf. Fela Kuti song "Mr. Follow Follow" (1976)
fone, phone, phonetic(s)	'fake accent'	English *phonetics*	"hope say u no dey speak phone like most pple wey travel dey do?" 'I hope that you don't speak with a fake accent like most people who travel do?'	see Heyd (2015: 674)
form	'to pretend, fake, show off, be proud'	English	"[name] dey form black, but im white pass winter" '[name] is pretending to be black but she is whiter than winter'	
front	'to pretend, fake, show off'	English	"i'm frm 9ja.proud 2b me. i no dey form. i no dey front." 'I'm from Nigeria. [I'm] proud to be me. I don't pretend. I don't fake.'	

Table 1 (continued)

Lexeme	Meaning	Etymology	Example	Comments
gbajue	'scam'	Yoruba	"*are u sure this is real or is this a form of gbajue?*"	
guy man, *guyman*	'con man, scammer'	English	"*Na greedy people dey fall mugu & guy man go take dat opportunity chop*" 'Greedy people fall victim and scammers take the opportunity to make money'	
grammar, *grammer*, *grama*	'use of involved lexicon'	English	"*no be by force to blow grammar ooo because English na for oyinbos*" 'it is not necessary to use involved language. English is for white people'	see Heyd (2015: 677)
ibo-made	'fake (product)'	ethnic group (proper name) + English	"*IBO made Louis Vittton!!*" 'fake Louis Vuitton'	
jankara	'fake', 'second-hand'	Nigerian market (proper name)	"*not your nonsense kinda jankara education where all you need do is pay money and settle your lecturers*"	
jibiti	'deception, cheating'	Yoruba	"*All this jibiti people! Una no dey shame?*" 'All these fraudsters! Aren't you ashamed?'	
lai	'lie'	English *lie*	"*[name] said d story is not true, na lai*"	unrelated *lai*, *lailai* Yoruba 'never'
mago mago	'deception'	Hausa	"*I'm trustworthy, no mago mago!*"	

Table 1 (continued)

Lexeme	Meaning	Etymology	Example	Comments
odu	'cheat (in an examination)'	Yoruba	*"IF YOUR WAEC NA ODU, THEN DON'T WASTE YOUR TIME"* 'If you cheated in your WAEC examination, [. . .]'	
ogbonge	'authentic, original', 'solid'	Igbo	*"u be original ogbonge omo elepo pupa"* 'you're an original, authentic palm-oil seller'	
ojoro	'cheat (at a game)'	Yoruba òjóró	*"The refree that Liverpool-Chelsea game na pure Ojoro man"* 'The referee of that Liverpool-Chelsea game was a cheat'	
origo, orijo	'authentic, original'	English *original*	*"Even me dey trip for ur origo waffi flow"* 'I really like your authentic way of speaking Pidgin' *"trust me, na orijo i dey sell"* '[. . .] it's an original I'm selling'	see also *orijo*
orijo	'a cheat sheet (for an examination)'	English *original*	*"abeg anhy body get ORIJO (expo) for JAMB?"* 'please does anybody have the questions for the JAMB examination?'	see also *odu*; also *pampa, expo* (from *exposed*) (Adegoju and Raheem, 2015: 166)

Table 1 (continued)

Lexeme	Meaning	Etymology	Example	Comments
ote, authe	'authentic'	English *authentic*	"you resident in Milan? Make we yarn how you go fit help me arrange one 'authe' jersey now?" 'Let's talk about how you can help me get one authentic jersey!'	
panda	'fake gold jewelry'	Yoruba	"this na origo no be panda" 'this is original, not fake'	
shakara	'to show off, boast', 'pretense', 'arrogance'		"shakara no dey my vocab . . . na reality i dey base on" 'pretense is not in my vocabulary. I base on reality'	cf. Fela Kuti song "Shakara (oloje)"; also *shako* Yoruba 'show off'
toronto	'fake (educational degree)'	Canadian city (proper name)	"[name] na 2017 graduate of ingrish from d toronto university" '[name] will be a 2017 graduate in bad English from a fake university'	
wayo	'trickery'	Hausa	"wayo people na who una wan deceive?" 'fraudsters, who do you want to deceive?'	common in compounds, e.g., *wayo man*
wuruwuru	'deception, cheating'	Hausa *wúrú wúrú*	"Wuru-wuru pastors don full ground" 'Fake pastors are plenty'	cf. unrelated *wúruwùrù* Yoruba 'in confusion'

Table 1 (continued)

Lexeme	Meaning	Etymology	Example	Comments
xerox	'to copy', 'plagiarism'	company (proper name)	"Go write ya own stuff and no Xerox person own" 'Write your own stuff instead of plagiarizing someone else'	
yahoo yahoo, yahooz, yahooze	'scam, fraud (on the internet)'	company (proper name)	"why u dey change from male to female and to male again? u dey yahoo yahoo us?" '[. . .] are you deceiving us?'	→ yahoo yahoo boy 'scammer'
yanga, inyanga	'to show off, pretend'	Yoruba yangàn 'to brag' Igbo ínyángá 'to show off'	"as soon as they travel go one place like dat not even uk dey start to they do yanga and denies not to be a nigerian" 'as soon as they travel someplace like that, not even to the UK, they start pretending and deny being Nigerian'	

Table 2: Nigerian Pidgin lexicon of migration.

Lexeme	Meaning	Etymology	Example	Comments
abroadian	'diasporic Nigerian'	English abroad + -ian	"make we abroadian marry awaself na" 'let us diasporic Nigerians intramarry'	
aduro	'asylum'	Yoruba	"Why u nor wan chop aduro for Norway?" 'Why don't you want to seek asylum in Norway?'	
akata	'foreigner', 'African-American', 'Nigerian emigrant', 'returnee'	Yoruba akátá	"Even Nigerians here will tell you she be AKATA no be oyinbo" '[. . .] she's African-American, she's not Caucasian'	see Heyd (2014: 43–44)
Andrew	'person wishing to leave Nigeria'	English first name (proper name)	"Andrew don check out oh! Nigeria go better!" 'Andrew has emigrated! Nigeria will improve!'	from a government sponsored ad featuring a man named Andrew
away	'foreign'	English	"Now you don change gear, come begin look for 'away' wife?" 'Now you've changed gears and come looking for a foreign wife?'	
been to	'traveled person', 'returnee'	English	"All these 'Been tos' wey dey come hia begin dey talk of how dem leave 'quality of life' to make money for 9ja" 'All these returnees who come here talk about how they left 'quality of life' to make money in Nigeria'	see also *never been to*
born throw away	'person not in touch with their cultural heritage'	English	"yeah am a british born throw away and i fcking love it, u can keep ur corruption infested country for ur clueless self"	

Table 2 (continued)

Lexeme	Meaning	Etymology	Example	Comments
bushman, bushmo	'uninformed local person'	English	"u be confam bushman. which village u dey stay?" 'you are a true local. which village do you live in?'	
Jand, Jandon, JD	'UK, London', 'abroad'		"why you dey call am England? after all everybody know say na 'jand'!" 'why are you calling it 'England'? after all everybody knows that it's 'jand'!'	may undergo further affixation → janded, jander
JJC, JJD	'newcomer', 'to arrive'	English Johnny Just Come/Drop	"me na jjc for america" 'I am new in America'	
land	'to arrive'	English	"when i don land for jand" 'when I will have arrived in the UK'	
loki, loci, lokito	'local', 'uninformed local person'	English local	"sorry I don't accept loci gifts. Imported please"	
Naija, 9ja	'Nigeria', 'Nigerian'	English	"Na hard life we dey live for naija..." 'It's a hard life we live in Nigeria'	may also refer to Nigerian Pidgin (Storch, 2017)
never been to	'not-traveled person'	English	"make the 'never been tos' see say abroad no be paradise" 'let the locals see that abroad is no paradise'	see also *been to*
overs	'abroad'	English overseas	"So, na even 4rm overs u buy am direct. No wonder it cost so much" 'So you even bought it directly from abroad. [. . .]'	

Table 2 (continued)

Lexeme	Meaning	Etymology	Example	Comments
oyinbo, oyibo	'Caucasian'	Yoruba òyìbó	"all this time I been the think say you be oyinbo pikin" 'all this time I've been thinking that you're a white person'	
Southie, Southy	'South Africa', 'South African'	English south + -ie	"southy is good for vacation, okay? but no kom southy to husstle okay" '[. . .] but don't come to South Africa to make money, okay?'	
tokunbo, tokumbo	'from abroad', 'second-hand car from abroad', 'child born abroad'	Yoruba tókúmbò	"all my kids must be 'tokunbo'" "na tokunbo abi locally used" 'is [the car] from abroad or locally used?'	
Yankee, Yanki, Yankey	'USA', 'US American'	English	"MAKE WE COME CHOP SMALL FOR YANKEE BEFORE RETURNING TO MAKE NAIJA A GREAT NATION" 'Let us make some money in the USA [. . .]'	
yonda	'abroad, far away'	English yonder	"Make una no 4get ona brodas here 4 naija, when ona dey enjoy 4 yonda" 'Don't forget your brothers here in Nigeria when you're abroad enjoying life'	

Eyo Mensah, Eunice Ukaegbu and Benjamin Nyong
Chapter 6
Towards a working orthography of Nigerian Pidgin

Introduction

When Voltaire described writing as "the painting of the voice" (Stephens 1998:17), he provides a deep socio-historical outlook of writing as an essential aspect of human communication; a tool for the expression of ideas, thoughts and emotions in print. He reframes the relationship between writing and speech, and heightens awareness of sound-symbol correspondence which is crucial in shaping the architecture of reading. An orthography is a set of rules or conventions that is used to represent language in a standardized system of writing. It starts with developing symbols which correspond to the significant sounds of a language. The graphemes, in addition to a system of rules, constitute the orthography which represents a spoken language in writing. Designing an orthography for a language is an essential part of its status and corpus planning, and aims to improve the capacity to promote literacy (and numeracy) in the language. An orthography, therefore, plays important roles in human history and in everyday life of its users. However, the simplified dichotomization of standard has grossly hindered the development of a generally accepted system of writing a language like Nigerian Pidgin (NP).

Much fruitful research and a growing body of literature have emerged in the study of West African Pidgin English (WAPE), including varieties such as Sierra Leone Creole (Krio) (Skinner and Herrell-Bond, 1977; Goerg, 1995; Velupillai, 2015), Cameroon Pidgin (CP) (Bird, 2001; Ngefac and Sala, 2006; Sala, 2009; Nkwain, 2011), Ghanaian Pidgin (GP) (Huber, 1995, 1999, 2008; Dako and Yitah, 2012; Rupp, 2013) in addition to NP. CP, GP and NP are more closely related in terms of history of contact, demography, grammar and lexicon. Speakers of Krio were descendants of liberated African communities in West Indies, Britain and America (Skinner and Herrell-Bond, 1977), *and their language is quite isolated from other varieties of WAPE in terms of grammar and vocabulary.* The most authoritative work on NP is Faraclas (1996) who examines the grammar of NP taking into perspective its origin and development, sound system, phonotactics, lexicon, morphology and syntax. Mafeni (1971), Agheyisi (1984), Elugbe and Omamor (1991), Mann (1993), Oyebade (1993) Egbokhare (2003, 2011), Deuber (2005) and Igboanusi (2008) have discussed the state of the art in NP research taking into account its origin, structure, ethnolinguistic and sociolinguistic relevance in the linguistic landscape of Nigeria and beyond. Egbokhare (2001) investigates the expanding profile of NP and makes a case for designing a generally acceptable orthography for the language. Elugbe and Omamor (1991) cover a comprehensive analysis of NP and attempt to distinguish NP from Pidgin English (PE) in Nigeria. According to them, NP has been identified as a language with its unique linguistic structure and identity. It evolved within a known and specified time frame and undergoes stages of growth to attain some levels of linguistic refinement. PE, on the other hand, is " . . . a substandard attempt by a large proportion of ill-equipped, illiterate Nigerians to manipulate the English language" (Elugbe and Omamor, 1991: 66). NP has, therefore, proven to be a fertile ground with enormous potential for contemporary linguistic and sociological research.

NP shapes and navigates the multilingual environment in various ways, and is gradually becoming an essential part of Nigerian culture, politics and economy. In some Nigerian cities, such as, Ajegunle (Lagos), Warri, Port Harcourt, Ikom and Calabar, transcultural, economic and socio-political forces have shaped the use of NP: more citizens are having awareness of government policies and programmes; the grassroots have greater sense of belonging particularly in political participation and ethnic divide has been bridged, and a new form of identity for speakers of NP created (Mensah, 2011). NP has, therefore, indexed a more favourable response to multilingualism in these cities, which have multilayered linguistic ecological system where Nigerian English, NP and the various indigenous languages compete for space in the linguistic market (Mensah, 2011). In spite of the bias against NP and its negative projection, especially by the elites, the language still stands out as the bridge between the demands of English and those of the indigenous languages in these cities. It has provided Nigerians with a wide range of opportunities to promote interethnic communication. It has also removed transnational boundaries, especially along the coast of West Africa where other pidgins like Ghanaian Pidgin and Cameroonian Pidgin English flourish. NP helps to strengthen political, socio-economic and cultural ties, and also promotes ethnolinguistic and cross-cultural attitudes and identity (Mensah and Ndimele, 2014). This justifies the claim by Jowitt (1991) that NP aids in establishing relationships between national and transnational publics, and is proven to have more appeal than the use of Standard English in these public spheres.

Over the years, there have been suggestions by linguists, language scholars, and educators (Essien, 1990; Egboghare, 2001, 2003; Mensah, 2019) for the adoption of NP as the national language in Nigeria given its relative advantage above English and the country's indigenous languages. Mensah (2019) specifically argues that NP best suits the cultural and linguistic heterogeneous composition of Nigeria, as a language with a true national consciousness. He notes that it is structurally simple and flexible and is already a known and familiar language among Nigerians. However, the single most constraining factor against the development of NP and its promotion as a national language in Nigeria is its lack of a cultural capital, that is, a specified ethnic affiliation and regional recognition like the major languages in Nigeria. This no-man's-island's status has impacted negatively on NP as, probably, the most resourceful and broad-based linguistic medium to galvanize Nigeria's common patrimony as a nation. Consequently, while its social functions are daily expanding, it is officially dwarfed by attitudes and ideologies that still project it as a bastardised variant of English. A significant effect of the official neglect of NP is its lack of standard in writing. Sadly enough, it is not one of the few Nigerian languages that have an approved orthography in spite of being the most widespread language spoken in the country.

Many authors and writers use arbitrary symbols to represent the sounds of NP. Some of these sounds are based on "the latest phonological fads of the day" (Powers, 1990: 496). While some prefer the alphabetic-based script, others use the phonetic-based script thus compromising consistency and harmonization as core principles of general orthographic development (Williamson, 1984). This chapter, therefore, sets out to propose a working orthography for NP. A working orthography, according to Burkhardt and Burkhardt (2019: 285) "is a revised orthography that is ready to be tested for widespread use". It is the last significant stage in the development of an orthography before it attains the status of being standardized. In our methodological approach, we draw the corpus from the various dialects that constitute NP in computer mediated communication (CMC) as we do not intend to recommend an orthography that is based on any particular variety of NP. Our approach is therefore multilectal in nature, and our focus is mainly to design a system that demonstrates faithfulness to the linguistic reality of NP where a single sound correspondingly reflects a single symbol in all its ramifications. The chapter is organized as follows: 6.0 introduces the research, 6.1 examines the socio-historical evolution of NP, 6.2 deals with the socioeconomic status of NP, 6.3 is concerned with the imperatives of NP orthography. 6.4 is the proposed working orthography of NP. 6.4.1 and 6.4.2 detail the consonants and vowels of NP. 6.5 deals with the orthographic strategies, and 6.5.1 describes the principles of orthographic choices and 6.6 is the conclusion.

1 Socio-historical evolution of NP

The socio-historical development of the NP spans across four separate periods of contact between the Western Europeans and the coastal people of Nigeria, mostly inhabitants along the Niger Delta regions of Port-Harcourt, Sapele, Warri, Calabar, and Benin. The Portuguese are considered the first set of European traders to arrive the Niger Delta area at about 1469 AD in search of gold, slaves and other valuables in West Africa (Nair, 1972; Osa, 1986; Faraclas, 1996). They journeyed through the coast and their search led them to meeting the Akan people (in Ghana) whose preoccupation was gold mining (Onwubiko, 1966). Elugbe and Omamor (1991: 3) indicates that the Akan tribe "preferred, or insisted on, receiving part of their gold in slaves".

Trade conditions at some points were not favourable with the miners from Akan thus leading the Portuguese merchants to further traverse along the Atlantic coast in search of more valuable items. They made contacts with the Beni people in present day Edo State, Mid-western Nigeria. Esizimetor (2010: 10) reports that their first contact was with the King of Benin who was the sole controller of activities in the region. This contact marked the beginning of trade between the Beni people and the Europeans. Aside from commerce, the Portuguese were also interested in education and religion. They took steps to introduce and establish Christianity in the Delta region of Nigeria and were involved in their legal system as well (Esizemetor and Egbokhare, 2012). There are evidence of the impact of the Portuguese on the NP lexicon with few lexical items having Portuguese root; *sabi* from '*saber/sabir*' meaning 'know', *pikin* from *pequeno/pequenino* meaning 'little child' *dash* from '*dash*' meaning 'to give freely'. After the Portuguese was the arrival of the Dutch. When the Dutch arrived in 1593 they immediately became trade partners with the Deltans. Unlike the Portuguese, their predecessor, they did not exercise total monopoly of trade in the entire region. Their concentration was on the Eastern part of the Niger Delta. The Dutch did not stay for a long period of time. They made business in the region for over 57 years. There is no trace of what could possibly be the linguistic contribution of Dutch language to NP. In the later part of the century the French had contact with the Niger Delta region even though it was less significant, their purpose on arrival was not trade, as Esizimetor (2010) puts it, "it was an expedition to verify the truth of the existence of a powerful wealthy kingdom at the heart of black Africa" Despite the short period some words in NP vocabulary today have French origin. Words like *boku* meaning 'many', 'much' is from beaucoup and *boku boku* meaning very many, very much also has the root beaucoup. By the time the English men arrived, It was around the beginning of the 17th century upon their contacts with the Nigerian indigenes, it was quite easy for them to communicate being that the British had previous trade relations with the Portuguese.

Overtime the Portuguese jargons were replaced by English words. The interests and concerns of the British broaden their contacts, from trade they made attempts to be involved in politics, religion and education. Few schools were built and some indigenes had formal training in Western culture and civilization (Elugbe and Omamor 1991). These developments were majorly in Calabar where the first recorded evidence of NP used in writing was documented. It was by Antera Duke a famous Efik Chief and merchant who documented events about the activities between the Efik and European traders. Scholars like (Forde, 1956; Elugbe and Omamor, 1991; Mensah, 2012) agree to an extent that the notes compiled into the famous Diary of Antera Duke (DAD) give evidence to the stock of NP words although there could be an argument that they are befitting only of a non-standard English form. Nevertheless, we can attest that bulk of the words in the compilation is used today as NP lexical items, pointing to the linguistic contribution and influence of English on NP. Words like *waya* for wire, *waka* for walk, *beta* for better, *veks* for vex, *baf* for bathe, *rait* for write among others clearly have English origin. The NP has gradually grown from a 'makeshift' language to a creole, historically, from being the means of communication between coastal ethnic peoples and the Europeans to a lingua franca in Nigeria. In this regard, many linguists (Emenanjo, 1985; Egbokhare, 2003) have called for the adoption of NP as the national language in Nigeria.

2 The socioeconomic status of NP

NP, otherwise known as *Naija*, is the Nigerian variant of the English-based pidgin along the West African coast. NP draws its linguistic resources primarily from English, Portuguese and Nigeria's indigenous languages. It is often stigmatised particularly by the elites as a language of the lower class status; a code for the non-literate as well as a bastardized form of English. Contemporary realities have however shown that NP is dynamic and is dominating social platforms and cultural spaces, and uniting people from varying linguistic backgrounds in Nigeria. It is obvious that NP thrives more in highly heterogeneously populated setting like Nigeria. Speaking on its spread, Agbedo (2019) maintains that NP is used widely in metropolitan cities of Nigeria, tertiary institutions, military and para-military formations and the *Sabon-Gari* (New Town) areas in Northern Nigeria. Its impact is also greatly felt in the media and entertainment industries. NP is a marker of identity and solidarity; it is an inter-ethnic language available to Nigerians without a common linguistic code. In the university environment, for instance, NP has served as a unifying factor among students from diverse linguistic and cultural backgrounds, and a means of casual communication between lecturers and students.

NP is more readily available to and acceptable by the youths who have sufficiently harnessed it as a symbolic resource for the promotion of varied subcultural capital ranging from their involvement in the social media, hip hop culture, stand-up comedy and graffiti production and consumption. In the online community, NP is used for broad discursive engagements of contemporary sociopolitical issues in Nigeria and beyond. It bridges intercultural communication among speakers of divergent languages or dialects, and creates a sense of identity that defies class or social status distinction. In this way, users/writers overcome language barriers in the virtual community they would ordinarily encounter in face-to-face communication. The online space also facilitates the consumption and circulation of NP within the global digital community. The creative impulse of the language in casual, personal or off-colour interactions enables the coinage of new words which are useful in expanding its vocabulary. The online community is also valuable in the creation of trends, example, *Our mumu don do* 'Enough of our stupidity' which was created by a user and popularised by members of the online community. The expression reflects a symbolic resistance of the Nigerian masses to poor governance and misrule in Nigeria.

The hip hop culture is the most vibrant and popular form of music that represents a dominant youth culture in Nigeria. NP is the most effective driver of hip hop style and ideology. Hip hop artists create slang in NP to address social problems such as insecurity, poverty, infidelity, prostitution, drug abuse and unemployment. In this regard, they "codify and label their own realities with new expressions" (Sam, 2007: 3). An important scope of the creativity in hip hop is the gaining of new words and expressions into the lexicon of NP. This is mainly facilitated by the rapid growth of digital technology and communication systems. NP is also valuable in the construction of local identity and authenticity, and its appropriation in "crossing and styling" is equally evident in the hip hop brand (Cutler, 2007: 519). NP has also been established as the dominant language of comic entertainment, especially in stand-up comedy performance. Given its simplicity, it enables timely delivery and cadence, and aids the comic performer to expand his or her ability and comic routine based on one's ideological inclinations (Filani and Ajayi, 2000). NP offers the comic entertainment industry a medium to reconcile business with laughter (pleasure) by reaching a wide range of audiences/patrons and enhancing the marketability of comic products. It is the most creative and influential language to attract the desired profit margin.

In the electronic media, there has been an exponential growth in the number of radio and television programmes that are aired in NP. There are also stations that are exclusively NP-based like the Correct FM in Calabar, Cross River State, and Wazobia FM in Lagos State. In 2017, the BBC World Service also added BBC News Pidgin which is anchored in NP in its roster for its West African audience. According to de Freytas- Tamura (2017), it is part of efforts to capture a younger, more diverse and digitally savvy audience. This has been a significant attempt at launching NP on a global platform. Advertising communication is another viable platform to deepen the social utility and functional relevance of NP in the public space. Mensah and Ndimele (2014) maintain that advertising in NP commands enormous public appeal because of its spread, flexibility and the creative possibilities it allows. This evidence shows that NP attracts a wider prospect in a competitive multilingual market environment like Nigeria. In the banking sector, NP has become an essential commodity to facilitate transactions between bankers and customers, the automated teller machines of most banks (in Nigeria) provide subscribers/users the option of carrying out banking operations like cash withdrawal and transfer with NP programmed commands, thus signifying solidarity and amity with users of NP and on another hand marketing and promoting the institution's values and services to a specialized audience in a non-complex but familiar code. In the health sector, NP is used to simplify communication between patients and health professionals, and sharing the same contextual background allows for mutual understanding. Significantly, most health-related sensitisation campaigns such as COVID-19 pandemic, Ebola, Lassa fever and HIV/AIDS are conveyed in NP to reach the widest possible targets in both urban and rural settings.

From these accounts, it is evident that NP is daily expanding its scope and sociolinguistic functions. It has positively impacted every sphere of Nigeria's social life, politics and economy, and has the vibrant mechanism and resources to address the national language question in Nigeria. The implementation of a standard orthography for NP is therefore long overdue.

3 The imperatives of a NP orthography

Speech or spoken language is the most sophisticated system of auditory communication. It is a biological endowment, and is acquired by human infants as an essential aspect of the socialisation process. Speech qualifies human beings as "talking animals" (Fry, 1977: 1), which is one of the characteristics that mark off human beings distinctively from animals. Writing on the other hand, symbolically represents language in a storable graphic form O'Grady et al. (1988: 258). It conventionally relates with language and is consciously learnt usually within the framework of a school. This justifies the claim by Lupke (2011: 315) that the learning of writing requires "more regulated apprenticeship." The written language is important to every field of human enterprise especially in the wake of contemporary scientific innovation, technological development and information transfer. It facilitates inventions and interventions that are needed to solve human problems. This shows that writing, generally, improves the quality of life.

There is a general consensus among linguists that orthography development goes beyond linguistic decisions. The task is multi-layered, complex, and encompasses a wide range of social, practical, religious, historical and political considerations in addition to the linguistic factor (Grenoble and Whaley, 2009; Lüpke, 2011). Thus, an orthography of a language is not designed in a vacuum. The interests of every stakeholder: native speakers, community members, missionaries, government officials and linguists are usually taken into account. The demands of language speakers/users usually take precedent over those of the orthography designers/linguists. This will facilitate community ownership of the resulting writing system and encourages local understanding of the rationale underlying the decision made in establishing the orthography (Bow, 2013; Schroeder, 2008). In this concern, the linguists function as consultants and advisers with moral or ethical responsibility to the community (Rice, 2006).

The development of an orthography is an essential aspect of the corpus and status planning of a language. For a language like NP that is widely spoken but officially neglected, a standard orthography will strengthen its use as a medium of literacy, and empowers its speakers to read and write the language (Bow, 2013). It will also help to destigmatise the language as a "broken, bad or lazy English" (Oenbring, 2013: 342), and lend prestige to the language. Such an orthography will command a regime of respect to speakers of NP (Lüpke, 2011). An orthography will project the language as a standard of linguistic excellence, and guarantee permanence and authenticity (Jaffe, 2002). It will entrench a culture of linguistic loyalty amongst its speakers which may considerable reverse the stereotyped attitudes towards it (Mensah, 2002). NP will begin to attract high status, high demography and high institutional support (Mann, 2000). This evidence shows that an orthography can change the attitude and perception of speakers of a language.

For children who speak NP as their mother tongue, the development of an orthography in NP is a matter of linguistic right in the overall context of their human and civil rights (Riagain, 1999). Learning to read and write in their mother tongue is required to enrich their communicative capabilities and strengthen their identities. Such a recognition will facilitate access to mother tongue education in the light of the language-in-education provision of the National Policy on Education (NPE) in Nigeria which specifies that every child shall be taught in the mother tongue or the language of the immediate community for the first four years of basic education (NPE, 2013). The implementation of such a policy will bridge the gap of social and linguistic injustice, and expand the practical use of writing in NP. It will also foster a unique identity and self-esteem in the multicultural context where NP is used. Essentially, a standard orthography will qualify NP as a full fledge language. It may spur more academic interest in the language and witness greater intellectual engagements and theorisation. The rising profile of NP should necessitate its development as a written language in Nigeria. The drive for its promotion through a robust process of language planning and policy has often been defeated by its lack of a standard orthography, as well as discrimination among other complex social and political considerations. This is the gap language policy makers in Nigeria need to bridge as a matter of urgency.

4 A working orthography for NP

In this study, we propose a phonetic spelling system for NP in order to ensure a more consistent relationship between sounds and symbols. For most languages, a phonetic-based script makes it possible to have a pronunciation which is closer to the spelling. The choice of a phonetic-based script allows direct mapping from sound to symbol. A basic principle of phonetic transcription is that it should be applicable to all languages, and its symbols should be able to denote the same phonetic properties irrespective of where they are found (Ukaegbu, 2018). Examples of phonetic spellings are words like "pot", "dad", "yam", "pen" which are often spelt the same way they are pronounced. This ease and consistency should be key in any process of orthography development to enable even a non-speaker learn the language with ease.

In the quest for the standardization of NP, it should be understood that this is a speech form that is spoken by people from diverse linguistic backgrounds, therefore the orthography chosen for the representation of its sounds must be one that will pose little or no challenge to the learners, as the introduction of complexities would inadvertently discourage people from learning to write it. Elugbe (1995: 290) observes that the common practice is still what he calls the 'anglicized' spelling, which is characterized by the writing of most NP words exactly as in English. Based on the fact that most Nigerian languages are written following the phonetic-based script, it makes a proposed phonetic-based orthography easier to be learnt, as people prefer familiar ideas to totally strange ones. Therefore, the question of whether the NP should continue to be written with anglicized spellings should be tackled, given that NP deserves to merit a status of its own. An anglicized spellings would reduce NP to a poor form of English, rather than a language on its own right, Therefore, if the decision is to write NP following the phonetic-based script, the words should be written as they are spoken, thus, for example, instead of "See as everywhere is quiet", we will have *si as evri wia kwayet*. This is because some NP speakers are non-literate, who might succeed in possessing fluency in the spoken form, but still face challenges in writing if the anglicised spelling is maintained. A phonetic unit of orthography is phoneme based, and has the prospect of aligning sounds with symbols to make for easy comprehension.

One would therefore, only have to write down what one hears, the exact way one hears it, following just the same way one says it. This is supported by Elugbe and Omamor (1991) where they proposed a writing system for NP tailored to fit in to the traditions of writing Nigerian languages. They believe that such a writing system would make NP look less like a wrongly cloned or bastardized form of English language. A lot of scholars have supported a Nigerianised spelling pattern for NP, as opposed to an anglicised spelling pattern. Egbokhare (2001: 121) says that:

> A strong reason in support of the Nigerianised spelling is the rhythmical incompatibility of NP with English. . . . . if we take this together with the fact that a wrong impression of phono-semantic equivalent is suggested by such a spelling, we face an urgent need to adopt the nigerianised spelling.

A core goal of a Nigerianised spelling system will, therefore, be to represent the pronunciation of NP words unambiguously in an attempt to achieve a near perfect visual representation of what is spoken.

4.1 Segmental orthography: The consonants

The consonant inventory of NP draws its sounds from Standard English and Nigerian languages. It lacks phonological complications and aims to produce a phonemic orthography. It is not based on any particular Nigerian language but many. In this regard, Hausa, Igbo and Yoruba are more prominent (at least in our corpus). The Phonemic consonant chart of NP is demonstrated in Table 1 below:

Table 1: The consonant phoneme chart of NP (Based on our corpus).

	bilabial	Labiodental	alveolar	post-alveolar	palatal	velar	labio-velar	labialized velar	glottal
Stops	p b		t d			k g	kp gb	kw gw	
Nasal	m		n		ɲ	ŋ			
Fricative		f v	s z	ʃ					h
Affricate				tʃ dʒ					
Trill			r						
Lateral			l						
Approximant					j			w	

We identified 26 consonant sounds based on our corpus. Of these sounds, 21 are derived from the English phonemic chart, indicating the predominant influence of English on the phonology of NP. A case of preference of English over Nigerianised spelling is found in the representation of the velar nasal sound /ŋ/. Most Nigerian languages represent this sound with the symbol <ñ> while NP has it as <ng>, tilting towards English. This evidence reveals the impracticability of the so-called Nigerianised spelling (Egbokhare, 2001). An important observation here is the recognition of the overwhelming English origin of and influence on NP words. There should be uniformity, harmony and a direct correspondence between the English-derived sounds with NP symbols. 5 sounds are sourced from the phonemic inventory of Nigerian languages. These are /ɲ, kp, gb, kw, gw/. These sounds are mainly realised orthographically as diagraphs and are introduced to avoid the use of special symbols which may prove difficult to read, print and understand. The following English consonants are not attested in NP phonemic system: /θ, ð, ʒ/. Some phonological principles are adopted in representing these sounds which are presented in Table 3 below and analysed in the subsequent section.

4.2 Segmental orthography: The vowels

The vowels used in NP are derived from the basic primary vowels. NP has no diphthongs or triphthongs like Standard English, but rather takes the primary vowel segments that are akin to both English and Nigerian languages. NP vowels in our data are represented in Table 2 below:

Table 2: The vowel system of NP.

	Front		Back	
	rounded	unrounded	rounded	Unrounded
High		i	u	
Mid-high		e	o	
Mid-low		ɛ	ɔ	
Low				a

There are 7 phonetic and 6 phonemic vowel sounds in the vowel inventory of NP. The sounds are mainly sourced from the primary cardinal vowels. We have identified the quality and articulatory features of each vowel and assign appropriate symbols on the basis of representing them in writing.

Table 3: The proposed orthography.

Grapheme	Phoneme	Example	Transcription	Gloss
A	a	Abeg	/abɛg/	Please
B	b	Brọda	/brɔda/	Brother
CH	tʃ	Chacha	/tʃatʃa/	Gambling
D	d	Dash	/daʃ/	Gift
E	e	Egunje	/egundʒe/	Bribe
Ɛ	ɛ	Petrol	/pɛtro/	Petrol
F	f	Fọwọd	/fɔwɔd/	Forward
G	g	Gofment	/gɔfment/	Government
GB	gb	Gbedu	/gbedu/	Dance/Party
GW	gw	Gwongoro	/gwoŋoro/	Lorry
H	h	Haus	/haus/	House
I	i	Ibeji	/ibedʒi/	Twins
J	dʒ	Jeje	/dʒedʒe/	Gently
K	k	Kontri	/kɔntri/	Country

Table 3 (continued)

Grapheme	Phoneme	Example	Transcription	Gloss
KP	kp	Kpafuka	/kᵖafuka/	Die
KW	kw	Kwench	/kʷɛntʃ/	Put off (fire)
L	l	Lekpa	/lɛkᵖa/	A slim person
M	m	Mata	/mata/	Matter
N	n	Naija	/naidʒa/	Nigeria
NG	ŋ	Inyanga	/iɲaŋga/	Pride
NY	ɲ	Nyafunyafu	/ɲafu ɲafu/	Surplus
O	o	Ogogoro	/ogogoro/	Local gin
Ọ	ɔ	ọrọbọ	/ɔrɔbɔ/	A fat person
P	p	Pikin	/pikin/	Child
R	r	Raits	/raits/	Right
S	s	sọfa	/sɔfa/	Suffer
Sh	ʃ	Ashawo	/aʃawo/	Prostitute
T	t	Tori	/tori/	Story
U	u	Una	/una/	You (plural)
V	v	Veks	/veks/	Be angry
W	w	Waka	/waka/	Walk
Y	j	Yawa	/jawa/	Problem
Z	z	Zombie	/zombi/	A fool

5 Orthographic strategies

Data for this research were sourced from the social media, particularly from writers/users' interactions on Facebook "in order to give more considerations to users' practices as experts" (Deubar and Hinrichs, 2007: 44). This is following the tradition of contemporary data collection in the study of Pidgin and Creole languages. Oenbring (2013) maintains that computer mediated communication (CMC) is a major space to obtain creole-inspired spelling where "writers are doing it themselves" (Sebba, 2000: 185), and not based on any "prescriptive regime on how to write" (Juffermans, 2011:652). An implication of adopting online ethnography for this study is the resort to the concept of speech community (Gumperz 1993) for the more fluid notion of community of practice (Wenger, 1998; King, 2014; Oko, 2018) which articulates mutual engagement, joint enterprise and shared repertoire. The interactants in this study shared a common interest and desire in generating interactional discourses in NP in an online-driven community. Within this community, they mediate participation and negotiate identities in addition to other subjectivities.

We extracted data from naturally occurring interactions with users/writers of NP in different Facebook pages. These were open discussions and did not require permission or ethical approval. Anonymity of interactants was however maintained. We collected many excerpts from those interactions. Few of the excerpts have been reproduced here. The first extract bothered on a religious discourse. The second extract was about NP itself, while the third extract was a more general discussion involving younger people. The idea of using CMC corpus for this study was to depart from older tradition of relying on a particular variety of NP as the standard, interviewing speakers and eliciting their responses or extracting data from written sources like newspapers, story books and pedagogical materials (Elugbe and Omamor, 1991; Faraclas, 1996) but to rely on what Egbokhare (2021) popularly referred to as "crowd wisdom" which manifest in how speakers actually write the language. The interactants were speakers of NP across ethnic and linguistic divides. This will sustain the neutrality and broad national outlook of NP, and make the proposed orthography acceptable to every user. It is instructive to note that our proposal is based on the orthographic strategies employed by the interactants in this study based on CMC corpus.

Excerpt 1

[. . .]Na true talk my broda. E be like say na end time sign dey sele with full force. Make we stand gidigba inside Jesus make devil no enter our heart come use our hand do im evil work. The whole world don wọwọ. I go yank de door wey dey my heart open make you enter, so we go jolificate dey go. Tief come steal, kill make evritin pafuka, I don come make una live and jolly nyafunyafu.

[It's the truth my brother. It appears as if end time signs are manifesting clearly. Let us stand firm with Jesus so that the devil will not confuse us to do his biddings. The whole world is so corrupt. I will open the door of my heart for you to enter and make merriment. The thief comes to steal, kill and destroy but I have come to give you eternal life].

Excerpt 2

[. . .]Hu tak say pidgin no bi awa own. Na di only language wey unite us wey no bi English na. I no fit speak Dagbare, Twi or any oda language for Ghana but I sure say even people wey no fit speak English fit understand my pidgin. No bi only Naija Pidgin dey o. I wan say mak you no vex. Pidgin dey hard to rait but swit to talk. We like am like dat bikos e neva get im own orthography nah. De kain rapport wey pidgin dey bring no get mate wallahi! I go look fowod to ram Prof. mak l see how you go do am.

[Who says pidgin is not our identity? It's the only language outside English that unites us. I do not speak Dagbare, Twi or any other Ghanaian languages but I know that people who cannot speak English can understand my pidgin. It is not only Nigerian Pidgin that we have (in West Africa). I want to apologise, pidgin is difficult to write but easy to speak. We like it so. It does not have an orthography. The kind of rapport that we establish with pidgin is truly unprecedented. I am looking forward to engaging Prof. (verbally in pidgin) and see how he'll interact in it. It will happen].

Excerpt 3

[. . .]Lekpa wan do inyanga. No enta one chance for Koro. No tak say person no tell you. Kontri bad! Orobo abeg pak well. Yu tink say na only yu dey shak ogogoro? See beta pikin. We stil dey d mata jeje. We no get gofment fo dis kontri. I just dey vex for all d tori wey yeye men dey take force sleep wit women and even small pikin dem. I don sufa, yawa don gas. Egunje don finish fo gofment haus. Mama Ibeji, l don kwench. You wan kom make person dash you one naira afta yu go kom dey zombie? Wai yu no tak gwongoro enta Lagos? I don kpafuka. Mai Oga, e get as e be. Gbedu no dey today. Una no sabi say na Naija we dey? Ashawo and chacha no be work. Even nyakiri and 419 be de same. Na ya work? Yu drink petrol? Abeg waka wich one be ya own? Notin dey hapen

[Young slim woman, you are full of pride now. Stay safe with Corona virus pandemic. Do not say you were not warned. Everywhere is risky. You fat young man, kindly mind your business. Do you think you are the only drunk around? Look at a beautiful girl. We are still on the matter gently. We do not have a government in this country. I am really saddened by the spate of rape involving women and young girls. I have suffered, there is a problem. There's no more bribe in government houses. Mother of twins. You want someone to give you one thousand naira only for you to turn around and behave like a fool. Why don't you join a lorry to Lagos (if you are broke)? I am dead. My master, I am in a difficult situation. There is no party (in town) today. Don't you know that we are in Nigeria? Prostitution and gambling are not occupations. Duping and advanced fee fraud are the same thing. Are they your occupations? Are you foolish? Please get out, what is your business? There is no problem].

There are a few general observations about the way NP is written by its users in CMC. First, the orthography is based on the Roman alphabet modelled after the

English language. Most writers/users of NP still adhere to Standard English spelling convention or what Juffermans (2011: 652) calls "spelling in the presence of English". This brings about variation in the way the same word is written by different users as we can see in the examples below:

1. talk   tak
    you   yu
    us   wi
    come   kom
    our   awa
    make   mak

As pointed out by Sebba (1998: 227) "linguists almost unanimously favour a creole orthography which resists Standard English convention." We prefer the variant that are somehow distant from the English orthography in a bid to give NP spelling its authenticity. It is a more faithful representation of sounds with corresponding symbols. Potential users need to follow the phonemic principles underlying the orthography of Nigerian indigenous languages. This is achieved in two ways: first, some symbols are sourced from orthographies of indigenous Nigerian languages. For example, <kp>, <ny>, <gb>, and <gw> are derived from Igbo, Yoruba and Hausa as we can see in the following words:, *inyanga* 'pride' (Igbo), *gbedu* 'party', *gbosa* 'noisy cheers' (Yoruba), *gwongoro* 'lorry', *gworo* 'bitter kola'. The second instantiation of the influence of the orthography of indigenous Nigerian languages on NP is the use of diacritic by some writers. The case of *sele* /ʃele/ is patterned after the Yoruba orthography. Yoruba users of NP tend to represent the initial symbol in this word as <ṣ> while non-Yoruba writers represent the sound as <sh> which is also tailored after the orthographies of their indigenous languages. In our proposal, however, we recommend the use of <sh> to represent the sound /ʃ/ in order to avoid the use of the diacritic in the earlier form which may prove difficult to use by users who lack formal linguistic training. This will also ensure simplicity and convenience. There are some observable orthographic strategy in representing the consonant system of NP based on our corpus. Oenbring (2013) claims that many Creole languages substitute the voiceless and voiced dental fricative /θ/ and /ð/ with the voiceless and voiced alveolar plosives /t/ and /d/ respectively. This pattern is not always the case in NP. There is every manifestation of /ð/ as <d> but not every realization of /θ/ is <t>. Some are represented as <d> especially in the initial position as in *the*, *this that* and *then*.

Another obvious orthographic strategy in our corpus is the conscious attempt by users to achieve a direct sound-symbol correspondence. English spelling like *everything, country, government, house, because* and *sweet* has been simplified in NP to achieve a closer and more faithful connection between the symbols and the sounds they represent. Another strategy is that while some English derived words have the same meaning, others have different meaning in NP. For example, words like *Prof, evil, bring, vex* and *orthography* retain the same spelling and meaning in both English and NP while other words like *beta* (beautiful), *mak* (let), *tell* (warn), and *say* (that) are English-derived forms but have different meanings. Other creative mechanisms have been adopted by NP users in CMC. Many writers drop the last symbol ending with the suffix –ing in English to generate such forms as notin 'nothing', groovin 'enjoyment', fuckin 'sex'. This may be as a result of borrowing from American and British varieties of English. Some expert may want to evaluate this orthographic practice as deviant or unconventional. It is however, gaining popularity and acceptance especially with the younger population. This evidence shows the resourcefulness of NP especially in its adaptability to affixation processes.

In our proposed orthography, we prefer the symbol <ɛ> to <ẹ> to avoid the use of diacritics in the system as recommended by Elugbe and Omamor (1991). Our position is that since some Nigerian languages already have this symbol, it will not pose any difficulty to writers of NP. Faraclas (1996) has adopted this symbol in addition to other two diacritical tone marks in his proposed NP orthography. However, since most users were not aware of them, they were rarely found in our corpus. We have already explained why we avoided the adoption of symbols with diacritical or tone marks.

6 The principles of orthographic choices

In this section, we conceptually weigh our proposed orthography in the light of Williamson's (1984) and Barnwell's (2008) principles of a good orthography. They have separately proposed five criteria: accuracy, consistency, convenience, harmonisation and familiarity. Barnwell (2008) similarly has accuracy, consistency, and convenience. Williamson's harmonisation and familiarity correspond to conformity and acceptability/agreement respectively. According to Williamson (1984: 7–10):

> Accuracy means that an orthography must agree with the sound system of the language for which it is intended. An orthography is consistent if the same sound or word is always written the same way whenever it appears. An orthography is convenient if it is easy to write, type or print. Harmonization is similarity to other orthographies and familiarity requires acceptability to the people the orthography introduces.

In our proposed working orthography, we have designed thirty-three symbols which represent thirty-three distinct sounds of NP. In other words, there is a direct relationship between the symbols we proposed and the sounds they represent. In this way, the orthography has fulfilled the condition of accuracy. The understanding here is that if the sounds are perfect reflection of the symbols, the same sound will always be written the same way thus meeting the provision of the principle of consistency. By not introducing special characters, tones and diacritics, the proposed orthography will be easy to read, write and print thereby satisfying the principle of convenience. We have already established that NP orthography has its origin in the English alphabetic system which most users of NP have been exposed to given the role of English in the sociocultural life of Nigerians. The introduction of elements of Nigeria's indigenous languages such as <ny>, <gb>, and <gw> into NP orthography will also help to expand the practical use of the system because Nigerians are already familiar with these symbols. These will promote the harmonisation of the NP orthography with those of existing indigenous languages. Familiarity entails the acceptance and agreement with the proposed orthography. This principle can fairly be tested during fieldwork for the implementation of the orthography. The perception of the users of the system is significant here. If the majority of the symbols are contested, it shows that the system is not familiar, and if it is not familiar, it would not be accepted, but if the majority of the symbols are not contested, it signals an agreement with what has been designed. We suggest that our proposed orthography be put to test by the approving authority in Nigeria in order to measure the level of its acceptance and familiarity.

7 Conclusion

Writing is said to be an indispensable form of communication in the contemporary society (Coulmas, 2013). It is an attribute of power for the speakers of a language and confers a language with permanence and authenticity. In this chapter, we have proposed a working orthography for NP taking into perspective its phonetic/phonological adequacy, simplicity and appropriateness. We call it a working orthography because it is not an end in itself but a means to an end, with the expectation that it is subject to revision in the overall interest of standardising NP. Orthographic development is one way in which linguists can have the clearest and strongest impact on the speech communities that they study and/or serve (Bontrager, 2015: 11). In this study, however, we were not engaged with a speech community in the sense of Gumperz (1993) but rather we engaged with a community of practice in a virtual environment. We have not made any attempt to prescribe a writing system for NP but have keyed into the process which evolved by itself based on the language experience of actual users/ speakers of NP. We have also not imposed any particular variety of NP as the written standard as the usual practice is to select one variety as the basis for the written standard when a language has dialectal variation (Sebba, 2007). Our corpus has been based on randomly selected interactions by users and writers of NP in CMC, with special reference to Facebook. We believe that this practice-oriented approach which involves multilectal linguistic behaviour, is best suited to a wide range of users, and is open to greater neutrality and inclusiveness.

The working orthography has thirty-three symbols to represent the corresponding sounds we identified in NP thus displaying a closer relationship between the sounds and the symbols they represent. We have avoided the use of tone marks, special symbols and diacritics in a bid to keep the system simple and convenient. We recognised the creative impulse of users and writers of NP who have attached symbolic values to the way some letters and words are written. A few writers tend to align NP spelling with the English spelling convention and others seem to write NP outside the mould of English. We have weighed our proposed orthography against the backdrop of principles of orthographic choices (Williamson, 1984; Barnwell, 2008), and have met all the conditions except the principle of familiarity which requires an orthography to be tested and accepted by its potential users in the field. A different research undertaking is needed to complement our efforts at this point. Finally, we recognise that an orthographic design is a social practice that is complex and multi-layered. It requires the commitment of the language users/speakers, linguists and the significant others. We call on policy makers and government at every level to give NP a pride of place in the linguistic ecology of Nigeria by setting up its orthography development workshop through the Nigeria Educational Research Development Council (NERDC) in order to change the fortunes of the language.

References

Agbedo, Chris. 2019. *Multilingualism and national development in Nigeria: Issues and challenges*. Nsukka: University of Nigeria Press.

Agheyisi, Rebecca. 1984. Linguistic implications for the changing role of Nigerian Pidgin English. *English World-Wide* 5, 211–233.

Barnwell, Katharine. 2008. Luke Partnership training materials. Unpublished ms. SIL International.

Bird, Steven. 2001. Orthography and identity in Cameroon. *Written Language and Literacy* 4(2). 131–162.
Bontrager, Gregory. 2015. *Concept and issues in orthographic design*. Florida: University of Florida PhD dissertation.
Bow, Catherine. 2013. Community-based orthography development in four Western Zambian languages. *Writing Systems Research* 5(1),73–87.
Burkhardt, Jey & Jurgen Burkhardt. 2019. Developing a unified orthography for Berawan: An endangered Bornean language. *Written Language and Literacy* 22(2),280–306.
Coulmas, Florian. 2013. Writing reform. *In writing and society: An introduction*. 104–125. Cambridge: Cambridge University Press.
Cutler, Cecilia. 2007. Hip hop languages sociolinguistics and beyond. *Language and Linguistics Compass* 1(5),519–538.
Dako, Kari & Helen Yitah. 2012. Pidgin, broken and othering in Ghanaian literature. *Legon Journal of the Humanities* 1, 202–230.
Esizemetor, David. 2010. Historical Development of Naija. A paper presented at the Conference of Nigerian Pidgin, University of Ibadan, Nigeria, 8–9 July, 2009.
Esizemetor, David & Francis Egbokhare. 2012. Naija (Nigerian Pidgin). https://www.hawaii.edu/satocenter/langnet/definitions/naija.html (accessed 9 December 2020)
de Freytas-Tamura, Kimiko. 2017. The BBC in pidgin? People like it well-well. Retrieved January 10, 2020. https://www.nytimes.com/2017/12/30/world/africa/bbc-pidgin.html
de Freytas-Tamura, Kimiko. 2017. "The BBC in Pidgin? People like it well-well". The New York Times. (Link) (accessed 16 June 2020)
Deuber, Dagmar. 2005. *Nigerian Pidgin in Lagos: Language Contact, Variation and Change in an African Urban Setting*. London: Battlebridge.
Deuber, Dagmar & Lars Hinrichs. 2007. Dynamics of orthography development in Jamaican Creole and Nigerian Pidgin. *World Englishes* 26(1),22–47.
Egbokhare, Francis. 2001. The Nigerian linguistic ecology and the changing profiles of Nigerian Pidgin. In Herbert Igboanusi (ed.), *Language attitude and language conflict in West Africa*. 105–124. Ibadan: Enicrownfit Publishers.
Egbokhare, Francis. 2003. The story of a language: Nigerian Pidgin in spatiotemporal, social and linguistic context. In Peter Lucko, Lothar Peter & Hans-Georg Wolf (eds.), *Studies in African varieties of English*, 21–40. Frankfurt am Main: Peter Lang.
Elugbe, Ben. 1995. Nigeria Pidgin: Problems and prospects. In Ayo Bamgbose, Ayo Banjo & Andrew Thomas (eds.), *New Englishes: A West African perspective*, 284–299. Ibadan: Mosuro Publishers.
Egbokhare, Francis. 2021. The accidental lingua franca: The paradox of the ascendancy of pidgin in the Nigerian lingustic space. In Akinmade T. Akande & Oladipo Salami (eds.), *Current trends in Nigerian Pidgin English: A sociolinguistic perspective*, 67–114. Berlin/Boston: De Gruyter Mouton.
Elugbe, Ben & Augusta Omamor. 1991. *Nigerian Pidgin: Background and prospects*. Ibadan: Heinemann Educational Books.
Emenanjo, Emmanuel. 1985. Nigerian language policy: Perspectives and prospectives. *Journal of Linguistic Association of Nigeria* 3, 123–134.
Essien, Okon. 1990. *The future of minority languages in Nigeria*. In Nolue Emenanjo (ed.), *Multilingualism, Minority Languages and Language Policy in Nigeria*, 156–168. Agbor: Central Books.
Faraclas, Nicholas. 1996. *Nigerian Pidgin*. London: New York: Routledge.

Filani, Ibukun & Temitope Ajayi. 2000. Ideologies in Nigerian stand-up comedy. Linguistik Online 100(7), 141–158.
Lüpke, Friederike. 2011. Orthography Development. In Peter K. Austin & Julia Sallabank (eds.), *Endangered languages*, 312–336. Cambridge: Cambridge University Press.
Fry, Dennis. 1977. *Homo loquens: Man as a talking animal*. Cambridge: Cambridge University Press.
Goerg, Odile. 1995. Sierra Leonais: Creoles, Krio: La dialectique de l'identite / Sierra Leone: Creoles, Krio: The dialect of identity. *Africa: Journal of International African Institute* 65 (1),114–132.
Grenoble, Lenore A. 2009. Losing it in Siberia: Assessing the impact of language contact. *Chicago Linguistic Society* 45(1),143–159.
Gumperz, John. 1993. Types of Linguistic Communities. *Anthropological Linguistics* 35(1/4), 130–142.
Heyd, Theresa. 2015. Beyond grammar and phonetics: The metacommunicative lexicon of Nigerian Pidgin. *World Englishes* 34(4),669–687.
Huber, Magnus. 1995. Ghanaian Pidgin: An overview. *English World-Wide* 16(2),215–249.
Huber, Magnus. 1999. *Ghanaian Pidgin in its West African context*. Amsterdam: John Benjamins.
Huber, Magnus. 2008. Ghanaian Pidgin: Morphology and syntax. In Rajend Mesthrie (ed.), *Varieties of English* (Volume 4. Africa, South and Southeast Asia), 381–394. Berlin and New York: Mouton de Gruyter.
Forde, Daryll. 1956. *Efik traders of Old Calabar*. London: Routledge.
Forde, Daryll. 1968. *Efik traders of old Calabar*. London, International African Institute.
Filani, Ibukun & Temitope M. Ajayi. 2019. Ideologies in Nigerian stand-up comedy. *Linguistik-Online* 100(7),141–158.
Igboanusi, Herbert. 2008. Empowering Nigerian Pidgin: A challenge for status planning. *World Englishes* 27(1),68–82.
Jaffe, Alexandra. 2002. Introduction: Non-standard orthography and non-standard speech. *Journal of Sociolinguistics* 4(4),497–513.
Jowitt, David. 1991. *Nigerian English usage. An introduction*. Ikeja: Longman.
Juffermans, Kasper. 2011. Do you want me to translate this in English or in a better Mandinka language? Unequal literacy regimes and grassroots spelling practices in peri-urban Gambia. *International Journal of Educational Development* 31, 643–653.
King, Brian 2014. Tracing the emergence of a community of practice: Presupposition in sociolinguistic research. *Language in Society* 43. 61–81.
Lüpke, Friederick. 2011. Orthography development. In Peter K. Austin & Julia Sallabank (eds), *The Cambridge handbook of endangered languages*,312–336. Cambridge: Cambridge University Press.
Mafeni, Bernard. 1991. Nigerian Pidgin. In John Spencer (ed.), *English language in West Africa*, 95–112. London: Longman.
Mann, Charles. 1993. The sociolinguistic status of Anglo-Nigerian Pidgin: An overview. *International Journal of the Sociology of Language* 100, 167–178.
Mann, Charles. 2000. Reviewing the ethnolinguistic vitality: The case of Anglo-Nigerian Pidgin. *Journal of Sociolinguistics* 4(3),458–474.
Maybin, Janet & Joan Swann. 2007. Everyday creativity in language: Textuality, contextuality and critique. *Applied Linguistics* 28(4),497–517.

Mensah, Eyo. 2002. Writing and literacy development: A linguistic evaluation. *Global Journal of Humanities* 2(1),51–68.

Mensah, Eyo. 2003. A critique of the Efik orthography. *Kiabara: Port Harcourt Journal of Humanities* 9(2),203–212.

Mensah, Eyo. 2011. Lexicalization in Nigerian Pidgin. *Concentric: Studies in Linguistics* 37(2), 209–240.

Mensah, Eyo. 2012. Grammaticalization in Nigerian Pidgin. *Íkala, Revista de Lenguaje y Cultura* 17(2),167–179.

Mensah, Eyo. 2019. The new language policy of the Nigerian Army: National integration or linguistic imperialism? *Journal of Asian and African Studies* 54(3),331–345.

Mensah, Eyo & Roseline Ndimele. 2014. Linguistic creativity in Nigerian Pidgin advertising. *Sociolinguistic Studies* 7(3),321–344.

Nair Kannan. 1972. *Politics and society in South Eastern Nigeria 1841–1906*. London: Frank Cass and Company limited.

National Policy on Education (2013) (6th eds.). Lagos: NERDC Press.

Ngefac, Aloysius & Bonaventure Sala. 2006. Cameroon Pidgin and Cameroon English at a confluence: A real time investigation. *English World-Wide* 27(2),217–227.

Nkwain, Joseph. 2011. Complementing the face: A pragma-stylistic analysis of appraisal speech acts in Cameroon Pidgin English. *Acta Hafniensia* 43(1),60–79.

O'Grady, William, John Archibald & Mark Aronoff. 1998. *Contemporary linguistics: An introduction*. New York: Bedford/St. Martins.

Oenbring, Raymond. 2013. Bey or bouy: Orthographic patterns in Bahamian Creole English on web. *English World-Wide* 34(3),341–364.

Oko, Christina. 2018. Orthography development for Darma: The case that wasn't. *Language Documentation and Conservation* 12(1),15–46.

Onwubiko, Kenneth. 1966. *School certificate history of West Africa (Book One)*. Africana Educational Publishers & FEP International Private Limited.

Osa Osayimwense. 1986. English in Nigeria: 1914–1985. *The English Journal* 75 (3),38–40.

Oyebade, Francis. 1993. Aspects of the phonology of Nigerian Pidgin English. MA thesis University of Ibadan.

Powers, William. 1990. Comments on the politics of orthography. *American Anthropologist* 92(2),496–498.

Riagain, Donall. 1999. The importance of linguistic rights for speakers of lesser used languages. *International Journal on Minority and Group Rights* 6, 289–298.

Rice, Karen. 2006. Ethical issues in linguistic fieldwork: an overview. *Journal of Academic Ethics* 4, 123–155.

Rupp, Laura. 2013. The functions of Student Pidgin in Ghana: Why do Ghanaian students who are proficient in Standard English choose to speak Student Pidgin? *English Today* 29(4), 13–22.

Ryder, Alan. 1969. *Benin and the Europeans*. London: Longman.

Ryder, Alan. 1980. The Benin Kingdom. In Obaro Ikime (ed.), *The groundwork of Nigerian history*, 109–20. Ibadan: Heinemann.

Sala, Bonaventure. 2009. Writing in Cameroon Pidgin English: Begging the question. *English Today* 25(2),11–17.

Sam, Supriya. 2007. True to words: Hip hop and the English language. Ms. University of Madras.

Schroeder, Leila. 2008. Bantu Orthography Manual, *SIL e-Books*. Dallas TX: SIL International.

Sebba, Mark. 1998. Meaningful choices in Creole orthography: "experts" and "users". In Rainer Schulze (ed.), *Making meaningful choices in English: On dimensions, perspectives, methodology and evidence*. 223–233. Tubingen: Narr.

Sebba, Mark. 2000. Writing switching in British Creole. In Marilyn Martin-Jones & Kathryn E. Jones (eds.), *Multilingual literacies: Reading and writing different worlds*. 171–187. Amsterdam: Benjamins.

Sebba, Mark. 2007. *Spelling and society: The culture and politics of orthography*. Cambridge: Cambridge University Press.

Skinner, David & Barbara Herrell-Bond. 1977. Misunderstandings arising from the use of the term 'Creole' in the literature on Sierra Leone. *Africa: Journal of International African Institute* 47 (3),305–320.

Stephens, Mitchel. 1998. *The rise of the image, the fall of the word*. New York: Oxford University Press.

Ukaegbu, Eunice. 2018. Participatory communication as an essential tool in orthography development. *International Journal of Linguistics and Communication* 4(1),163–180.

Velupillai, Viveka. 2015. *Pidgins, creoles and mixed languages: An introduction*. Philadelphia: John Benjamins.

Wenger, Etienne. 1998. *Community of practice: Learning, meaning and identity*. Cambridge: Cambridge University Press.

Williamson, Kay. 1984. *Practical orthography in Nigeria* (African Languages). Ibadan: Heinemann.

Akinmade T. Akande and Saheed O. Okesola
Chapter 7
Morpho-syntactic features of Nigerian Pidgin on Radio programmes rendered in Naija

Introduction

Nigerian Pidgin, popularly being referred to as *Naija*, can be described as an English-lexifier contact variety which emerged due to the socio-economic and historical contact between Nigerians and the British (and other Europeans). According to Durodola (2013: 9) "Nigerian Pidgin is a variant of the larger group of English-based pidgin and creole languages, which developed in West Africa as a result of contact with colonialists". While Naija draws its lexicon from English, substrate languages (i.e., indigenous languages) supply its morphology and syntax. Nigerian Pidgin (NP), like most English-based pidgins around the world, is a blend of English and several indigenous languages of the people of Nigeria.

Today, NP has become the most widely used language among people of different ethnic groups and regions in Nigeria. Although reported to be a product of "necessity" developed as a communication tool for and among people who did not share a common language at the time, NP is today arguably the lingua franca in Nigeria. Some language scholars have argued that it is also Nigeria's "real" number one language in terms of the number of the population of speakers, geographical spread or reach, and inclusiveness of people from all strata of the social stratification in Nigeria (Olatunji, 2007; Deuber, 2005; Durodola, 2013). This is because while all other languages in Nigeria including English do not cut across geographical, ethnic and social boundaries, NP can be described as a language of the masses though it is gradually gaining social acceptability among the elites even in formal and semi-formal settings (Akande, 2008). Deuber (2005: 51) points out that NP "is the most neutral language in Nigeria: it has neither the elitist connotations of English nor the ethnic connotations of the indigenous languages" while Akande (2016: 41) remarks that "As a language, NP cuts across ethnic boundaries as it is being used by the literate and illiterate, North and South, the rich and the poor". Most Nigerians, irrespective of their level of education, their region or their ethnic affiliation are usually able to function and meet their linguistic needs in different domains of language use through NP.

Although it is difficult to give the actual number of speakers of NP, as it is not formally studied in schools and it is not officially recognised as one of the languages to be used in formal settings, there is no doubt that the language is, according to Faraclas (2021), spoken by well over 110 million people who reside mainly in Nigeria. Apart from Faraclas, other scholars have maintained that NP is the most widely spoken language in Nigeria as more than half of the population are not only proficient in it, they use the language for different purposes (see Akinnaso, 1991; Akande, 2016). The language is used by people from different socio-cultural backgrounds with varying degrees of proficiency. It is indeed naturally the second language of several millions of people with little or no formal education and consequently, no proficiency in English (Deuber, 2005).

Like all other creole languages, NP is characterized by different morphological and syntactic features. These features, many of which can be found in indigenous languages, mark NP different from English. It is necessary to reiterate here that the features this chapter focuses on are not in any way peculiar NP features on Radio programmes. In fact, the features can be found in any domain where NP is used. This is because, unlike lexical items which may be peculiar to or constitute the register of a particular NP domain, morphology and syntax which form the core of this chapter are universal. It is the treatise of these morpho-syntactic features that is central to this chapter. The chapter is divided into the following sections. After the introduction (Section 1.0), Section 2.0 briefly highlights the uses of NP in different domains while Section 3.0 deals with the data source. While Section 4.0 highlights and discusses the morphological and syntactic features in the data, Section 5.0 states the summary as well as the conclusion.

1 Uses of Nigerian Pidgin

In spite of its widespread use by millions of people, NP was limited to informal interactions alone for a very long time as the language's lack of official recognition robs it of adoption and use by many educated Nigerians in perceived 'formal' settings. Some see the language as inappropriate for formal communication and, thus, not suitable for use in several important domains of language use. The above narrative is however changing as there is practically no domain of language use today where NP is not being used for one reason or the other. The language, which used to be regarded as the language of the illiterates (Agheyisi, 1971: 30) has over the years gradually become a language being vibrantly used by people from different walks of life including graduates, professors, journalists, lawyers, market women, artisans and politicians. In fact, many scholars have highlighted the use of NP in domains such as barracks, media broadcast, market places, campuses and churches (Akande, 2016). Faraclas's (1996: 2) prediction that NP would be the medium of communication for the majority of Nigerians and his prediction that NP (Naija) will be the language of the future (Faraclas, 2021) are not out of place. Today, NP is making exploits in virtually all areas of human lives and playing important roles in the national scheme of things in Nigeria. The undeniable presence, growth, as well as possible signals to the continued relevance of NP in the conduct of human affairs in Nigeria cannot be overemphasised.

Even though English and three other indigenous languages (Hausa, Igbo, and Yoruba) are the officially recognised languages by the constitution, NP is the number one choice for interethnic interactions among and between people from different ethnic groups. Many scholars (Deuber, 2005; Akande, 2008) have argued that for a language to qualify as truly a lingua franca and to play the role of intergroup communication in a country such as Nigeria, such a language must be one that cuts across the diverse groups in the country. The only language that best qualifies for this purpose in Nigeria is NP (Olatunji, 2007). This is because according to these scholars, NP is the only language that unites the different groups and also serves as a marker of national identity and solidarity. NP is the most widely used language by operators in Nigeria's informal sectors. The absence of complex grammatical rules endears the language to most Nigerians engaged in small and medium-sized enterprises in major cities like Lagos, Aba, Kano, Kaduna, Onitsha.

Nigerian Pidgin is also a very prominent language in both electronic and print media. According to Deuber (2005: 53), "The use of NP in the media has a considerable tradition". The language is very popular in the media and has continued to grow from strength to strength from the days of its use for different radio drama, comedy series, and television jingles in the 1970s and 80s. The situation today is that many media outfits use the language in broadcasting different programmes such as news, sport, and advertisement. A lot of radio stations in Lagos, Abuja, Port Harcourt, and other major cities around the country broadcast news and render different kinds of news-related programmes in the language. Attesting to the popularity of NP among Nigerians in an audience study focusing on Wazobia FM, the first Nigerian radio station to broadcast all its programmes in the language, Durodola (2013: 1) reports the controller of marketing of a media outfit (Radio Nigeria News Network) as saying "Clients such as multinationals, world development agencies, advertising agencies, corporate Nigeria and government ministries, produced their adverts in Pidgin English in order to attract a larger audience and reach previously unreached audiences".

The popularity of NP is not limited to local media. This is evident in its adoption by international media organisations as a way of reaching wider audience in Nigeria as well as other nations across West Africa. In 2017 the British Broadcasting Corporation launched the BBC News Pidgin, an online news service in NP. According to the organisation on the BBC Pidgin official website, "The news service, which is based in Lagos, Nigeria started broadcasting in the language to its listeners because it is the most widely-spoken language across the West African sub-region." Similarly, in 2018, AS Roma, Italian club and a major European football club officially launched a new NP twitter account for its fans and lovers of football in Nigeria and other *neighbouring countries*. Launching the @ASRomaPidgin account, AS Roma said "it creates the official social media profile specifically to communicate directly with fans in Africa's most populous country". Some media outfits such as Wazobia FM and Pidgin Radio now render live commentaries in NP during the English Premier and UEFA Champions League matches and other important sporting events. This growing international recognition and use of the language by several media organisations is a confirmation of the power of NP to reach a wider audience than all other languages.

NP is also the dominant language in popular culture and the comedy industry in Nigeria. In music, especially relatively new brand of music such as hip-hop, the use of NP is very prominent. In some of his studies, Akande (2012, 2013, 2014) has argued that NP is the matrix language of hip-hop and that artistes do use it primarily to authenticate their music, express a distinct identity and sometimes for economic reasons since its use enables them to reach a wider audience. Durodola (2013) also remarks that the default language of comedy in Nigeria is NP. Commenting on the central place of NP in stand-up comedy, Raheem (2018: 80) notes that NP is used by almost all comedians in Nigeria and Nigerians generally have associated the use of NP with comedy. Many Nigerians display national consciousness and identity through the use of the language at multicultural events. Due to ethnolinguistic complexities in Nigeria, there is no other language, apart from NP, that can be truly described as the national language in the real sense of the word (Olatunji, 2007; Deuber, 2005; Akande, 2010; Durodola, 2013). Thus, NP is the defacto national language used by most Nigerians to display their collective bond to their motherland. It is the language seen by the different groups in Nigeria as the language capable of fostering unity and oneness among people divided along ethno-linguistic and other social considerations.

2 Data source

The data for this study were sourced from selected episodes of *Wetin Dey Shele*, a programme being anchored by a popular on-air personality in the person of Robbin Emmanuel Oluwafemi. Emmanuel is a young Radio presenter popularly known as MC Reo and a comedian from Abeokuta, Ogun State. He acquired his fluency in Pidgin in Lagos, using the language for almost all his linguistic needs and in different areas. His love for Nigerian Pidgin and radio programming started in his early years growing up in Lagos alongside other young people from different parts of the country. Living in Ajiliti, Mile 12 area of the cosmopolitan city of Lagos for many years, Mc Reo recalled in a telephone interview that "He and his peers from different ethnolinguistic backgrounds rarely communicate in any other language than Pidgin at the time". Lagos, being a melting pot of different ethnic groups makes the use of NP a natural choice and the language for "all" as everyone on the street speaks it. During his university days at Obafemi Awolowo University, Ile-Ife, Southwest, Nigeria, he uses Pidgin fluently on campus among friends, and this culminated in his debut programme "*Wetin Dey Shele?*" on Crown 101.5 FM radio in Ile-Ife. According to MC Reo, "Even though I have been broadcasting before this programme in English, I started the Pidgin programme in 2014 and the way it was received served as the motivation to stay on and be more innovative with the language."

He reports that he opted for NP for his programme because even though English is the official language in Nigeria, NP appeals more to the masses especially those in the grassroots. According to him, "it is easier for government at any level, brands and corporate organisation to communicate, preach or sensitise the people with the language. I had to abandon all my contents in English in order to focus on Pidgin". In just five months of airing "Wetin Dey Shele?", the initial thirty minutes allotted to the programme was extended to an hour as a result of the increase in contributions and responses from the listening public. Today, Mc Reo is in the commercial city of Lagos, presenting and anchoring different radio programmes to the delight of the over twenty million people of Africa's mega city on *Star 101.5 FM/Dstv Channel 869*.

In all, ten episodes were randomly selected from the programmes. Each of the programmes often lasts for an average of one hour. The selected recorded episodes were transcribed. We then identified and tagged all the morphological and syntactic features in them with a view to analyzing the identified features qualitatively.

3 Data analysis and discussions

Presented below is an analysis of both the morphological and syntactic features in the data under study.

3.1 Morphological features of NP on Radio programmes

Our data has shown that morphological features such as reduplication, clipping, blending and compounding abound in the NP adverts on Radio programmes. Each of these is discussed below.

3.1.1 Reduplication

Reduplication which consists in full or partial repetition is a common morphological device observed in the data under study. Examples of reduplication are as follows:

1) Base on one or two **polopolo**, base on one or two yarn we dey sambalawise.
   (Based on one or two issues, based on one or two issues we are getting to know)

2) ... but this wey dem dey talk say **nothing nothing** happen ...
   (... but this one that they said that nothing happened ...)

3) ... so only God know all these **billion billion** we see ...
   (... so only God knows all these several billions we see ...)

4) ... just make sure free education ehn he boku **well well** this country ...
   (... just ensure that free education is fully available to all in this country ...)

5) he say all these **poor poor** people there when he dey talk am
   (He said all these poor people were there when he said it)

In NP, reduplication is sometimes used to avoid the use of intensifier, the use of inflections or the quantifier *many*. For instance, instead of adding the plural inflectional morpheme –s to *billion* in example 3, plurality is indicated by repeating the word *billion* twice – *billion billion*. Similarly, in order to indicate that the people being referred to are many in example 5, *poor* is repeated twice. Hence, English equivalent of *"these poor poor people"* is *"these many poor people."* Also, the first *well* in example 4 functions as an intensifier similar to the word *very* in English. Thus, *well well* in NP is equivalent to *very well* in English.

3.1.2 Clipping

Clipping occurs when a part of a word is cut off and the remaining part becomes a new word. Examples of clipping are *photo* and *tele* from *photograph* and *television* respectively. Examples of clipping in the data under study are shown below.

6) Baba how far you don already take the position of the **Presido** of the country?
   (Old man, have you already taken the position of the President of the country?)

7) . . . Mr Akeem Adeyemi wey come from Oyo APC **rep** caucus . . .
   (. . . Mr Akeem Adeyemi who is of Oyo APC representative Caucus . . .)

8) Me country people, **informate** make reach us this morning o be say . . .
   (My fellow country people, information reaching us this morning is that . . .)

9) . . . he say that one know **tory** about her . . .
   (He said that somebody knew a story about her . . .)

10) AD dere na dem dey **kolabo** small small with the Labour Party
    (AD there is already collaboratiing with the Labour Party)

11) . . . the new **tech** era dere . . .
    (. . . the new technology era there . . .)

A shortening device which MC Reo uses a lot is clipping as evident in examples 6 to 11 above. In example 6, *President* is shortened to *Presido*, *representative* to *rep* in example 7 and *information* becomes *informate* in example 8. The English words *story* and *collaboration* are shortened to *tory* and *kolabo* in examples 9 and 10 respectively while *technology* is shortened to *tech* in example 11. Apart from the fact that NP permits the creation of new words just like any other natural language through clipping, most of the clipped words in NP make the language more appealing to the users as they sometimes sound musical and easier to pronounce.

3.1.3 Acronymy

Another shortening device often used by MC Reo is acronymy. Acronymy is the use of the first letter of every word in a long expression to form a new word. For instance, *WHO* is an acronym formed from *World Health Organisation*. Some of the acronyms have to do with politics and elections in Nigeria. There are several instances of acronyms for political parties.

12) Independence Electoral Commission, he say **INEC**.
    (Independent Electoral Commission, he says INEC.)

13) . . . but you see **APC** ehn no be dem win the election **AD** na dem talk say . . .
    (. . . but you see APC ehn, was not the winner of the election, it was AD that said . . .)

14) . . . dey say plenty of **PVC** wey be say dey . . .
    (. . . They said that a lot of PVC which were . . .)

The acronyms APC and AD in example 13 stand for the names of two political parties in Nigeria namely, *All Progressives Congress* and *Alliance for Democracy* respectively. While PVC represents *Permanent Voter's Card*, the electoral body responsible for conducting elections in Nigeria known as Independent National Electoral Commission is shortened to INEC.

Apart from the acronyms that deal with names of political parties, there are also those that represent institutions of higher learning as shown in the examples below:

15) Mashood Abiola Polytechnic wey den dey call **MAPOLY** dis one tanda gidigba dere . . .
    (Mashood Abiola Polytechnic also known as MAPOLY is also well established there . . .)

16) University dey for Ogun State before abi no be dere Olabisi Onabanjo University **(OOU)** dey dere and other university? You sure if you dey look Nigeria where school plenty pass, where higher institution plenty past dere

he be like say na Ogun state as dey see state you dey see federal, you dey see dis at least **FUNAB** dey for Abeokuta . . .
(There was a university in Ogun State before, or was it not there that we have Olabisi Onabanjo University (OOU) and other universities? One is sure that Ogun State is one of the states with a lot of schools. This is because as there are state-owned schools, so also are federal schools, FUNAB is at least in Abeokuta . . .)

17) The Mama wey be say she be prayer warrior dere for de ogbonge place wey be worship for **MFM** International headquarters . . .
(The woman who is a prayer warrior there in the place of worship at the MFM International headquarters . . .)

18) . . . carry better restructuring dere enter the Special Anti-robbery Squad dere of Nigeria police force dat na dem SARS
(. . . carry out a better restructuring of the Special Anti-robbery Squad of the Nigeria Police, also called SARS)

As shown in examples 16 and 17, MAPOLY, OOU and FUNAB are acronyms for names of specific tertiary institutions in Ogun State. FUNAB the full name of which is not indicated in example 16, unlike MAPOLY and OOU in examples 15 and 16, stands for *Federal University of Agriculture, Abeokuta*. Apart from institutions of higher learning, there are other acronyms for religious institutions. An example of this is MFM (i.e., Mountains of Fire and Miracles Ministry) as in example 17. Also a unit of the Police which is represented by an acronym is SARS (Special Anti-robbery Squad) as in example 18.

3.1.4 Affixation

Affixation is not very common in the data since NP rarely makes use of inflections. However, there are one or two cases worth discussing here.

19) Me country people, this morning very soon I go sambalawise **correctment** call to one ogbonge Mr John wey dey for ogbonge Ikorodu . . .
(My country people, very soon this morning, I will place an important call to one Mr John who lives in Ikorodu)

20) . . . the ogbonge **yarnment** wey come come this morning na say the ogbonge supreme court don talk yesterday . . .
(. . . the information that has come this morning is that the Supreme Court has given a verdict yesterday . . .)

21) . . . and it is programme wey accommodate plenty of **talktalment** dere . . .
(. . . and it is a programme that accommodates a lot of debates . . .)

As shown in examples 19 and 20, *correctment* and *yarnment* are instances of affixation while *talktalkment* combines both the processes of duplication and affixation. The root *talktalk* exemplifies reduplication; however, the suffix –*ment* added to it makes it qualify to instantiate affixation.

3.2 Syntactic features of NP on Radio programmes

Our data is replete with several syntactic features ranging from lack of inflection to mark past tense, present and past participle forms, plural nouns and the use of *me* and *we* as possessive pronouns to the use of Tense, Mood and Aspect (TMA) markers, the use of reiterative BE, the use of NP pronouns such as *una* and *am* and the use of complementizer *say*. Each of these is discussed under different categories.

3.2.1 Unmarked nouns

As it is typical of many pidgins and creoles, NP is characterized by lack of inflectional morphemes to indicate plurality. Thus, plurality in NP is often contextually marked through the use of number, quantifiers and the pronoun *them*. Below are some examples to illustrate this.

22) . . . country people there about ogbonge **eleven person** dere they don confirm . . .
(. . . fellow country people, there are about eleven important people there whom they have confirmed . . .)

23) . . . country people wetin Imo State governor talk you don do **two term** . . .
(. . . fellow country people, the Imo State governor says you have done two terms . . .)

24) Me country people so dem go fit motivate them no be say them dey come back **few month** later we go hear . . .
(. . . My country people so they can motivate them and not that they will come around a few months later to say . . .)

25) Fo dis next level hen lait mata go rish eleven tasand mega-watt, wi go rish tiri tasan market and komuniti **dem** wit lait wey no go dey go of at ol at ol (Adeuti 2020: 54).
(For this next level, electricity generation will go up to eleven thousand mega-watt, and uninterrupted electricity will get to three thousand markets and communities.)

As shown in example 22 to 24, the nouns *person, term* and *month* are not inflected for plurality. However, the modifiers *eleven, two* and *few* that occur before them clearly show that they are plural nouns. Lack of plural or tense inflectional markers has been widely reported in the literature on NP (see Faraclas, 1996, 2004; Deuber, 2005; Akande, 2008, Adeuti, 2020). Although Adeuti (2020) reports the use of post-nominal plural marker **dem** as in example 25 above, this special use of **dem** is rare in NP and it is not attested in our data.

3.2.2 Pronouns

Most of the pronouns in NP are also present in English. However, the functions and positions of occurrence of NP pronouns are sometimes radically different from what obtain in English. Our attention here is on pronouns which are either different from that of English or are used differently from the way they are used in English.

26) . . . we go hear pe person dey commit suicide because he be chairman for South Africa country before but when he come to **he own country**; o boy, they don turn **am** to do tuale sir.
(. . . we will hear that people are committing suicide because he was a successful person in South Africa but on getting to his own country (Nigeria) he has been reduced to a tout.)

27) . . . **Me** country people Obasanjo reply he say if I we be presido of South Africa . . .
(. . . My fellow countrymen, Obasanjo replied and said if he were the president of South Africa . . .)

28) . . . he say all these poor poor people there when he dey talk **am** I dey look **am** like haha . . .
(. . . he said all these poor people there, ... When he was saying it, I was astonished . . .)

29) . . . na sure that dis one na original he say make **una** catapult **am** make the whole world dere make dey hear.
(. . . It was sure that this was authentic and he said we should advertise it so the whole world get to know of it.)

30) . . . make foreigner go enter **we** country, come dey invest in our country so that **we** country will grow.
(. . . let foreigners come into our country to invest and help grow our economy.)

31) . . . so **una** no know the work wey **una** wan do to . . .
(. . . so you don't know the work that you are to do to . . .)

32) . . . he say abeg na dey beg **una** . . .
(. . . he said, please, I'm pleading with you . . .)

The first category of pronouns in the examples above consists of those that are not present in English: *am* and *una*. On the one hand, the pronoun *una* can occur at the subject position as in examples 29 and 31as well as at the object position as in example 32. On the other hand, *am* can only occur at the object or post-verbal position and never at the subject position as shown in examples 26 to 29. In example 26, *am* functions as the direct object to the verb phrase *don turn*, it is the object of the verb *dey talk* and *catapult* in examples 28 and 29 respectively. The second category comprises possessive pronouns *me, he* and *we*. In Standard English, these three pronouns cannot function as possessive pronouns but their high frequencies in NP as possessive pronouns can arguably suggest that the pronominal system in NP is different from that of Standard English. Thus, the expressions *he own country, me country* and *we country* in examples 26, 27 and 30 respectively are clearly NP expressions by virtue of the position of occurrence of the three pronouns.

3.2.3 Verb phrase

3.2.3.1 Preverbal markers

There are some syntactic features which are directly related to the verb in NP. The first of these features is the use of preverbal markers, otherwise called TMA markers (see Faraclas, 1996), which seems to be a universal feature of all Creole languages (see Bickerton, 1975; Faraclas, 2004; Deuber, 2005; Patrick, 2007). Preverbal markers in Creole languages can be analysed in terms of the completive versus incompletive and realis versus irrealis (Bickerton 1973; Bybee, Perkins and Pagliuca, 1994; Patrick 1999; Spears 1990). While realis mode refers to actions that actually occurred either in the past or in the present moment, irrealis mode refers to "all states and actions which have not actually occurred, whether these are expressed by future or conditional tenses or by modals" (Bickerton, 1975: 42) and as Patrick (2007: 133) put it, irrealis verb phrases "do not express any already accomplished or presently occurring event, state or action." Both completive and incompletive are aspectual and while "completive verb phrases refer to completed actions, incompletive verb phrases refer to actions that are on-going at any point in time" (Akande, 2008: 55). It is possible for a verb phrase to consist of a combination of irrealis mode and completive aspect or realis mode and incompletive aspect as shown below.

Preverbal markers that express irrealis actions

33) ... him come to tell dem say he say he **wan go** for senate so that he **go make** sure the kind relationship ...
 (... he told them that he wanted to run for the senatorial election so that he would ensure the kind of relationship ... .)

34) He **wan sack** plentiful of de ogbonge lecturer wey be say de be dey dere.
 (He wants to sack many of the lecturers who are there).

35) ... you **go know** say part of the ogbonge reason
 (... you will know that part of the important reasons)

36) ... Me country people he talk say he **go employ** like one thousand seven hundred of them wey be say they **go face** the ogbonge challenges
 (... My fellow countrymen, he said he will employ about one thousand seven hundred of them who will assist in addressing the challenges)

Preverbal markers that express realis mode and completive aspect

37) ... now they **don come** draw boundaries there for South Africa ...
    (... now they have drawn the battle line for South Africa ...)

38) ... Senator Sheu **don tell** Yemi Osibanjo ...
    (... Senator Sheu has told Yemi Osinbajo ...)

39) ... he say but now he **don happen** ...
    (... he said it has happened ...)

Preverbal markers that express incompletive aspect

40) If you still **dey sleep**, this bell na go wake you up.
    (If you are still sleeping, this bell will wake you up.)

41) ... while deputy governor of Edo State **dey carry** two hands up for Buhari ...
    (... while the Deputy Governor of Edo State is hailing Buhari ...)

42) ... they talk say den **dey calcufast** den **dey think** of wetin to do to regain their mandate komot from the hand of Governor-elect ...
    (... they say they are being calculative and thinking of what to do to regain their mandate from the Governor-elect ...)

Examples 33 to 36 consist of verb phrases that depict actions that may occur but have not actually occurred. For instance, the intention to sack many lecturers expressed through the verb *wan sack* in example 34 may never come to reality just as the willingness to employ 1700 workers in example 36 as shown by *go employ* may not be actualized. Contrary to what we observe in examples 33 to 36, examples 37 to 39 indicate that the action depicted by each of the verb phrases has not only occurred but it is deemed completed. The preverbal marker *don*, when it appears as the only auxiliary marker in a verb phrase, often depicts a completed and accomplished action. The actions expressed in examples 40 to 42 are realis by default but incompletive in that the actions are ongoing. The NP preverbal marker *dey* has the syntactic function of expressing progressive actions (Akande, 2008).

Another preverbal marker that does express past actions and events in NP is *been/bin* (Faraclas, 1996). However, *been* as a preverbal marker to indicate past events is very rare in our data as we found only two occurrences as indicated below.

43) ... dis one he **been sele** for de Ogbonge March 31ˢᵗ, 2019.
    (... this one happened on March 31ˢᵗ, 2019.)

44) ... but if they lose or draw he means Liverpool dey go still keep the number one wey be say dey **been** dey.
    (... but if they lose or play draw it means that Liverpool would still be at the top of the league table where they were.)

3.2.3.2 The use of reiterative BE

The reiterative *be* which Alim (2004) refers to as equative copula seems to be a common feature in African American Language (AAL) and some other creole languages. This features later crept into Hip Hop Nation Language; a variety that shares a lot of features with AAL.

45) ... because he **be** chairman ...
    (... because he is the chairman ...)

46) ... because say you **be** deputy governor ...
    (... because you are the Deputy Governor ...)

47) ... if he **be** the presido of South Africa wetin he for don do ...?
    (... if he was the President of South Africa, what would he have done ...?)

As shown in examples 45 to 47, the reiterative *be* is a syntactic feature which is attested in our NP data. This feature, as reported by Akande (2014), is very common in Nigerian Hip Hop Language whose default language is NP.

3.2.3.3 Serial verbs

The occurrence of serial verbs is characteristic of many creole languages and this feature, although rare, is attested in our data. Below are two examples of serial verbs in the data.

48) ... make una **follow hear** am.
    (... kindly also listen to it.)

49) . . . **get bring** correct machine
(. . . assist in bringing good machine)

The verb phrases in examples 48 and 49 are typical verb phrases in creole languages as they can rarely be found in Standard English. The occurrence of serial verbs is one of the syntactic features that NP shares with some indigenous languages in Nigeria as such verbs are common in Yoruba.

3.2.3.4 Negation
Negation is indicated generally in NP through the use of the nagator *no*.

50) . . . their matter **no** be from fry pan to fire . . .
(. . . their problem is not too complicated . . .)

51) . . . they **no** understand the kind impact wey Nigerian don make . . .
(. . . they do not understand the kind impact that Nigerians have made . . .)

52) . . . one leaf **no** fall down from one leaf wey Baba God Almighty **no** know about am.
(. . . not a single leaf can fall from a tree without the knowledge of God Almighty).

As can be seen from the examples above (examples 50 to 52), the negative marker *no* always appears after the subject and before the verb. Thus, it appears after *their matter* in 50, *they* in 51 and *one leaf* and *Baba God Almighty*, the subject of the relative clause "wey Baba God Almighty no know about am" in example 52. Sometimes, when TMA markers occur in a negative sentence, the negator *no* precedes such TMA markers as in:

53) . . . wey **no** dey sleep . . . (*no* occurring before the aspect marker *dey*)
(. . . who does not sleep . . .)

54) . . . me country people I **no** go dey selfish to hear this matter alone (*no* occurring before the modal marker *go*)
(. . . my fellow countrymen, I won't selfish by keeping this information to myself alone)

3.2.4 Complementizer

In NP, the word *say* is polysemous in that it can mean *to say something* as in "*Hin say hin no go come*" and it can also be used to introduce a dependent clause. Whenever it is used to introduce a dependent clause, it functions as a complementizer as in

55) ... South Africa go know **say** something komot inside their country.
    (... South Africa will realize that some important things have left the country.)

56) ... he talk **say** Buhari quick response to the incidence ...
    (... he said that Buhari's quick response to the incidence ...)

In each of examples 55 and 56, there is a dependent clause introduced by the complementizer *say*. In example 55, the dependent clause "say something komot inside their country" functions as the direct object of the verb phrase *go know* just as "say Buhari quick response to the incidence" functions as the direct object of *talk* in example 56.

3.2.5 Relative clause

57) Plentiful of Nigerians dey lead the riots now for the Ogbonge place **wey** we know as South African.
    (A lot of Nigerians are now leading the protests in South Africa as we speak.)

58) ... Mr John **wey** dey for ogbonge Ikorodu, he just come back from South Africa.
    (... Mr. John who is from Ikorodu just came back from South Africa.)

59) Person **wey** give you that kind project no tell am the number of days or months duration of how the work dey take be.
    (Someone who gave that type of project didn't tell you the number of days or months it would take.)

Our data show that relative clauses functioning as qualifiers abound in the programmes of MC Reo. Each of the relative clauses is introduced by the NP relativizer *wey* as shown in examples 57 to 59. The relativizer *wey* can be preceded by either an inanimate antecedent as in example 57 where the antecedent is *the ogbonge place* or by animate antecedents as in examples 58 and 59 where the antecedents are *Mr John* and *person* respectively.

3.2.6 Discourse marker *o*

Discourse marker *o* is referred to by Faraclas (2004: 852) as *the sentence-final realis modality particle* and according to him, it has different meanings which include its use to show solidarity and stress the truth value of a statement.

60) . . . he say they too dey carry fake tory **o**
     (. . . he said they also report fake news too)

61) . . . vote buying dey **o** he say they buy vote they sell vote . . .
     (. . . vote buying is real, he said they buy and sell votes . . .)

62) . . . another talktalment come **o**
     (. . . another news is here)

In examples 60 to 62 above, the use of the discourse marker *o* has shown clearly that the sentences are NP sentences. Akande (2008: 186) has reported that the use of the discourse marker *o* is criterial of NP.

4 Conclusion

In this chapter, an attempt has been made to investigate the morphological and syntactic features of NP as evident in the programmes of MC Reo. The analysis showed that MC Reo's presentation is replete with rich morphological features such as duplication, acronymy and clipping just as syntactic features such as lack of inflectional markers, the use of NP-peculiar pronominals, the use of TMA markers and the heavy occurrence of the complementizer *say* are evident in the data. The analysis further demonstrated that NP as evident in its use in the domain studied here provides a vibrant avenue for the study of morphology and syntax specifically and for the study of contact linguistics generally. The paper concluded that morphological and syntactic features being used on Radio programmes delivered in NP are not radically different from those NP features observed in other domains. This is probably so because the grammar of NP is universal irrespective of the domain or variety being studied.

References

Adeuti, Bukola Ariyike. 2020. *Morpho-syntactic analysis of Nigerian Pidgin advertisement in wazobia and Eko Radio stations*. Ile-Ife: Obafemi Awolowo University MA dissertation.
Agheyisi, Rebecca. 1971. *West African Pidgin: Simplification and simplicity*. Stanford: Stanford University PhD dissertation.
Akande, Akinmade T. 2008. *The verb in standard Nigerian English and Nigerian Pidgin English: A sociolinguistic approach*. Leeds: University of Leeds PhD dissertastion.
Akande, Akinmade T. 2010. Is *Nigerian Pidgin English* English? *Dialectologia et Geolinguistica*, 18, 3–22.
Akande, Akinmade T. 2012. The appropriation of African American Vernacular English and Jamaican Patois by Nigerian hip-hop artistes. *Zeitschrift fur Anglistik und Amerikanistik: A Quarterly of Language, Literature and Culture* 3(3), 237–254.
Akande, Akinmade T. 2013. Code-switching in Nigerian hip-hop lyrics. *Language Matters: Studies in the Languages of Africa* 44(1), 39–57.
Akande, Akinmade T. 2014. Hybridity as authenticity in Nigerian hip-hop lyrics. In Veronique Lacoste, Jacob Leimgruber & Thiemo Breyer (eds.), *Authenticity: A view from inside and outside sociolinguistics*, 267–284. Berlin: Mouton de Gruyter.
Akande, Akinmade T. 2016. Multilingual practices in Nigerian army barracks. *African Identities* 14(1), 38–58.
Akinnaso, Niyi. 1991. Towards the development of a multilingual language policy in Nigeria. *Applied Linguistics* 12(1), 29–61.
Alim, H. Sammy. 2004. *You know my steez: An ethnographic and sociolinguistic study of styleshifting in a black American speech community*. Durham, NC: Duke University Press.
Bickerton, Derek. 1973. On the nature of a creole continuum. *Language* 49, 640–669.
Bickerton, Derek. 1975. *Dynamics of a creole system*. Cambridge: Cambridge University Press.
Bybee, Joan, Revere R. Perkins & William Pagliuca. 1994. *The evolution of grammar: tense, aspect, and modality in the languages of the world*. Chicago/London: The University of Chicago Press.
Deuber, Dagmar. 2005. *Nigerian Pidgin in Lagos: Language contact, variation and change in an African urban setting*. UK: Battlebridge.
Durodola, Funke Treasure. 2013. *The rising popularity of Pidgin English Radio stations in Nigeria: An audience study of wazobia FM, Lagos*. Grahamstown: Rhodes University MA dissertation.
Faraclas, Nicholas. 1996. *Nigerian Pidgin*. London: Routledge.
Faraclas, Nicholas. 2004. Nigerian Pidgin English: morphology and syntax. In Bernd Kortmann, Kate Burridge, Rajend Mesthrie, Edgar W. Schneider & Clive Upton (eds.), *A handbook of varieties of English*, vol 2, 828–853. Berlin: Mouton de Gruyter.
Faraclas, Nicholas. 2021. Naija: A language of the future. In Akinmade T. Akande & Oladipo Salami (eds.), *Current Trends in Nigerian Pidgin English: A Sociolinguistic Perspective*, 9–38. Berlin/Boston: De Gruyter Mouton.
Olatunji, Michael. 2001. The Use of Pidgin English in Contemporary Nigerian Music: A New Approach Towards National Identity. *Humanities Review Journal* 1(1), 41–46.
Olatunji, Michael. 2007. Yabis: A Phenomenon in the Contemporary Nigerian Music. *Africology: The Journal of Pan African Studies* 1(9), 26–46.

Patrick, Peter L. 1999. *Urban Jamaican creole: Variation in the mesolect*. Amsterdam/Philadephia: John Benjamins.
Patrick, Peter L. 2007. Jamaican Patwa (Creole English). In John Holm & Peter L. Patrick (eds.), *Comparative creole syntax: Parallel outlines of 18 creole grammars*, 127–152. United Kingdom/Sri Lanka: Battlebridge.
Raheem, Saheed O. 2018. A sociolinguistic study of social-political activism and non-violent resistance in stand-up comedy performances in Nigeria. *Africology*: *The Journal of Pan African Studies* 12(6), 75–92.
Spears, Arthur K. 1990. Tense, mood, and aspect in the Haitian creole preverbal marker system. In John Victor Singler (ed.), *Pidgin and creole tense-mood-aspect systems*, 119–142. Amsterdam/Philadelphia: John Benjamins.

Macaulay Mowarin
Chapter 8
Emphasis, focalization and topicalization in Nigerian Pidgin

Introduction

All natural and contact languages accentuate grammatical constituents in sentences. This accentuation can occur through prosodic, lexical and syntactic operations. When sentences are structured according to the discourse status of their constituents, they constitute information structure and it is categorized into *topic* which is given information and *focus* which more often constitutes new information (Chafe, 1976; Ayafor and Green, 2017). As language universals, topicalization and focus construction occur in both natural and contact languages. This chapter addresses the syntactic processes of topicalization, focus construction and emphasis in Nigerian Pidgin (henceforth referred to as NP).

Focus construction in NP is achieved mostly through the syntactic process of clefting. The data on which the analyses of topicalization and focus construction are based are sentences taped-recorded from resource persons in the Warri/Sapele/Abraka speech communities. The resource persons are competent speakers of the Warri/Sapele variety of NP, which is also known as Waffi variety (Akande, 2008). In addition, they grew up in the speech communities. They speak mostly the mesolectal variety although the highly educated respondents speak the acrolectal variety which they sometimes code mix or code switch with English. English-NP code mixed and code switched sentences are sifted out from the data for analysis. There is a triglossic relationship between the languages spoken in the speech communities. While English is the high code, NP constitutes the mid code and the indigenous languages are the low codes (Romaine, 2012; Guy, 2012).

This chapter is structured as follows. After the introduction, Section 1 provides the background to the study. This section undertakes an overview of emphasis, topicalization and focus construction. Section 2 discusses dislocation and types of topicalization. This section undertakes a detailed analysis of base generation of topicalizers and left dislocation or external merge of topicalizers. Section 3 centralizes on focus and it discusses the three subtypes of focus construction in NP. They are presentational or specificational, identificational or contrastive and wh- focus. Section 4 is on discussion while Section 5 states the conclusion.

1 Background: Topicalization and focus construction

This section undertakes an overview of topicalization and focus construction

1.1 Topicalization

There are different definitions of topicalization by linguists. Some salient ones include that of Yu (2014: 2594) who asserts that "Topicalization is a process by which a constituent is made into the topic of a sentence by being moved into a more prominent position at the front of the sentence." During the 1960s when attention was being paid to topicalization as information structure, the definitions then are still in consonance with what it is as at today. Fillmore (1968: 57) defines topicalization as devices for isolating one constituent of a sentence as 'topic'. Halliday (1968) did not use the word 'topic' in his discussion; rather, he used 'theme' as a synonym for topic and 'rheme' for the comment when he states that topicalization is used to denote the process of both foregrounding of information and selection of the topic of information. He adds that topicalization singles out certain elements in a sentence which becomes the topic on which comment is made. So, the element which is moved to the beginning of the sentence expresses a general topic and the rest of the sentence represents comment on the sentence. So, linguists are of the opinion that the topic of a sentence is synonymous with the 'theme' and it is the foregrounded constituent of the sentence while the comment of the sentence is synonymous with its rheme and background.

In the literature on topicalization, three types are identified. They are 'Aboutness topic', contrastive topic and familiar topic (Lambrecht, 1994: 194). Haegemenon (2004) observes that since the 1970s, linguists have asserted that aboutness topic occurs mainly in root or matrix clauses. Haegemenon adds that if topic phrase occurs in embedded clauses, such clauses must have root clause links. *Contrastive topic* denotes contrast and Miyagawa (2017: 19) states that it induces alternatives since it creates oppositional pairs with respect to other topics. *Familiar topic* focuses on the given or accessible constituent in the sentence. Miyagawa (2017: 19) adds that familiar topic is always realized in a pronominal form.

There are three methods for the derivation of topicalization in the literature. NP has two which are the insertion of a particle that precedes the topicalized phrase and the dislocation to the left periphery or external merge.

1.2 Derivation of topicalisation in NP

In NP, there are two methods of deriving topicalization. They are:
i. Base generation of topicalizer particles.
ii. Left dislocation or external merge.

Faraclas (1996) identifies the two methods above for deriving topicalization in his study of NP. Huber (1999: 248) also states that only the two topicalizing methods identified by Faraclas also exist in Ghanaian Pidgin (GP). As for topicalization in Cameroonian Pidgin (CP), Ayafor and Green (2017: 243) state that only left dislocation exists in the contact language. They state that "The CP topic clause-initial position and (with exception of some topic pronoun constructions) required a co-referential pronoun lower in the clause". The resumptive pronoun that occurs lower in the CP topicalized clause proves that the derivation is a case of dislocation to the left periphery.

1.2.1 Topicalization through topicalizer particle

The topicalizer particles that are generated to topicalize the grammatical constituents that they follow or occur after in NP include *sha, sef, tu* (too) and *nko*. These topicalizer particles are different from the ones identified by Faraclas (1996). He identifies *kwanu* which is an Igbo word. The difference is most probably due to the fact that Faraclas collected his data from Port-Harcourt where Igbo is one of the most common substrate languages that influence this variety while we collected ours from Warri/Sapele/Abraka Area. As stated earlier, the topicalizer *nko* which is Yoruba is in the data for this study. The topicalizer can tropicalize a Determiner Phrase or a Noun Phrase, (DP/NP), a Verb Phrase (VP) and an Adjective phrase(AdjP). The topicalized constituent is highlighted in the examples below.

(1a) Una   no   sabi   Mathematics **sef**.+
      2PL.SUBJ   NEG   know   Mathematics TPC.
      You people don't know Mathematics TPC.

(1b) Una   no   dey   read   una   books   **tu**.
      2PL.SUBJ   NEG. COP   read   2PL.OBJ booksTPC. TPC.
      You don't read your books too.

Examples 1a&b above are part of the data collected from Primary 3 teachers and pupils in Alegbo Primary School, Effurun, Warri where NP is mostly spoken as a creolized form. One of the teachers used particles to tropicalize *Mathematics* and *books* to admonish the children to develop interest in Mathematics and to develop a reading habit generally. In the school, NP is neither taught as a subject nor is it usually used as a medium for teaching other subjects. NP is used mainly to explain a few points by the teachers who code mix NP with English. In 1a& b above, the topicalized constituents are DPs functioning as the object of the respective sentences. It is pertinent to state here that second person singular and plural pronouns are denoted with different lexical items in NP. While *yu* (you) represents second person singular number, *una* (you people) refers to second person plural number.

(2) The questions for   ELS 202 **sef**, had   welwel.
     DEF questions PREP ELS 202 TPC difficult very very.
     The questions of ELS 202 TPC are very difficult.

The topicalized constituent in example 2 above is the subject DP which is topicalized by "sef".

(3a) The food **sha** no   swit   o.
     DEF food TPC NEG sweet EMP.
     The food TPC is not delicious EMP.

(3b) Mai   mama bon   ejimetu o.
     1SG. POSS mother deliver twin(s) TPC EMP.
     My mother delivered of a set of twins TPC EMP.

In examples 3a&b, the topicalized constituents are DPs/ (NP) functioning as the subject and complement of the respective sentences. A peculiar feature of both examples is the inclusion of the emphatic marker *o* at the end of both sentences. The emphatic markers add more emphasis to the topicalized constituents in the examples.

Apart from the instances of DP/NP being topicalized with topicalizers, VP and AdjP can also be topicalized with topicalizers. Below are examples of VPs being topicalized with topicalizers.

(4) Yo   broda   dey   chop **sha**.
     2 SG. POSS brother IPFV eat   TPC.
     Your brother used to eat TPC.

In example 4, the topicalizer particle *sha* tropicalizes the MV *chop* (eat). Example 4 is an intransitive clause and the topicalized VP is in final position of the sentence.

(5a) To   do draiva wok   **sef** don taya me.
     PREP do driver work TPC PF   tired 3 SG.OBJ.
     To work TPC as a driver is uninteresting to me.

(5b) Di   goat neva   die **sha** o.
     DEF goat IMPF NEG   die TPC EMP.
     The goat has not died TPC EMP.

Examples 5a&b are instances of topicalizer particles topicalizing verb phrases. Each example has its peculiar features. Example 5a is a case of serial verb construction. Serial verb constructions are syntactic features of substrate languages in NP. The topicalizer in example 5a occurred in the medial position of the sentence. In example 5b, *neva* functions as both a present imperfective aspectual verb "has" plus a negative particle "not". The topicalizer particle topicalized the verb *die* and the topicalizer is followed by the emphatic marker *o* which emphasizes the topicalized verb. Below are examples of adjectives that are topicalized by topicalizers:

(6a) Politics doti   **sha** o.
     Politics is dirty TPC   EMP.
     Politics is a dirty game TPC EMP.

(6b) Di   wota no   belefu me,   e   no   plenty **sef**.
     DEF water NEG satisfy 3SG.OBJ. 1SG.SUBJ NEG plenty TPC.
     The water did not satisfy me. It is not enough TPC.

It is relevant to state here that there are rarely true adjectives in NP as attested to by Faraclas (1996: 25) when he states, "what might be called 'adjectives' in another language are in fact verbs, modifier nouns or pronominal objects in NP". Mowarin (2005: 88) also buttresses Faraclas' assertion above when he states that "There are few true adjectives in NP. Most adjectives in NP are stative verbs."

In example 6a above, the topicalized adjectives *doti* (i.e., BE dirty) is not a true adjective playing predicative function. Since the *BE* verb is intrinsically linked to the adjective, it can aptly be described as a stative verb. The emphatic marker in example 6a emphasizes the dirtiness of politics. *Dirty* as used in example 6a is a case of semantic extension or multi-functionality (see Mowarin,

2009: 57–67). In example 6b, the main clause that preceded the one with the adjective that is topicalized with a topic particle *sef* makes the context of the sentence explicit. So, 'plenti-plenty' in NP has undergone semantic extension since it can be used to modify both liquid and solid nouns. So, example 7 below is correct in NP

(7) Di   wota   no   plenti.
     DEF   water NEG   plenty.
     The water is not much.

In English *plenty* collocates with only (-LIQUID) nouns. In NP, it collocates with (+/-LIQUID) nouns.

The topic particle also topicalizes temporal adverbials in NP as shown in the example below.

(8a) Mai   broda   no   go   travel again tumoro   **sef.**
     ISG.POSS SUBJ   brother NEG FUT   travel again tomorrow TPC.
     My brother will not travel again tomorrow TPC.

In example 8a, the temporal adverbial is topicalized with the topic particle *sef*. If the temporal adverbial is extraposed to the initial position through internal merge to derive the sentence below, it is still grammatical in NP.

(8b) Tumoro   **sef,** mai   broda   nor   go   travel again.
     Tomorrow, TPC   ISG.POSS   brother NEG   FUT   travel again.
     Tomorrow, TPC my brother will not travel again.

Nko

Nko plays dual functions in NP. First, it functions as a *wh-in-situ* marker as attested to by Mowarin (2012: 105). Where *nko* functions clause final, such *wh-* interrogative functions as a content or information-seeking question unlike its preposed *wh-phrase* counterpart.

(9) "Mai   moni,   **nko**?"
     1SG. POSS SUBJ   money, what about/where?
     What about/where is my money?

In example 9, *nko* functions as a wh-in-situ marker. Secondly, *nko* also functions as a topicalizer as shown in the example below.

(10) Mai   meresin nko.
    1SG.POSS medicine TPC.
    My medicine TPC.

Although the respondents insisted that *nko* in example 10 above functions as a topicalizer, we can also adduce the fact that *nko* plays a dual function in example 10. It is instructive to state here that multifunctionality or polysemy of lexical items is one of the lexico-semantic processes in the language that is employed by NP speakers to meet their communicative needs (see Mowarin, 2009: 57–66).

2 Dislocation to the left periphery

The only type of movement that derives topicalized constituent is dislocation to the left periphery or external merge. A peculiar feature of left dislocation is the fact that the topicalized constituent leaves a resumptive pronoun in the object position from which the topicalized constituent was moved. An example of dislocation to the left periphery is illustrated below.

(11) Di   two thieves, police don catch dem.
    DEF two thieves, police PF catch 3PL.
    The two thieves, the police have arrested them.

Dem (them) is the resumptive pronoun that represents *Di two thieves* (the two thieves) and it is in the object position of the sentence from which the topicalized constituent was extraposed.
    Below is another example:

(12) Di fine car, A   don bai am.
    DEF fine car, 1SG.SUBJ PF buy 3SG.OBJ.
    The fine car, 1 have bought it.

From the data collected, it was noticed that the resumptive pronoun does not occur only in the object DP position as shown in examples 11 & 12 above. In examples 13a&b below, the topicalized constituent is followed by its possessive pronoun which is a reflexive of the topicalized DP.

(13a) Dis   fine gel im   mouth dey smell.
      DEM fine girl TOP 1SG.POSS mouth PF   smell.
      This beautiful girl TOP, her mouth smells.

(13b) For   my   Popsy,   he   too wicked.
      PREP ISG.POSS   father TOP 1SG.SUBJ   too harsh.
      As for my father, he is too harsh.

There are cases of left dislocation where the topicalized constituent is repeated either wholly or partly in the rheme of the sentence. In examples 14a&b below, the topicalised constituent is repeated.

(14a) For   water for   baf   TOP A   nor dey
      PREP   water PREP   bathe   TOP 1SG.SUBJ. NEG IMPF
      like   hot   water.
      like   hot   water.
      As for bathing water, I don't like hot water.

(14b) Dis   hostel TOP no   bi   fine   hostel.
      DEM   hostel TOP NEG   COP   fine   hostel.
      This hostel TOP is not a fine hostel.

In example 14a above, the topicalized constituent is a prepositional phrase and the DP which is the complement of the respective prepositional phrase is repeated in the object of the DP of the topicalised sentence. An adjective, (hot) is added to the noun that functions as the complement of the prepositional phrase as shown below.

(15a) For water   ⟶   hot wota
      Prep water   ⟶   hot water
      For water   ⟶   hot water

(15a) Addition of the adj. (hot) to the object of TP.

In example 14b which is a DP, the determiner in the topicalized constituent is not repeated in the object of the TP. However, an adjective (fine) is added to the object of the TP as shown below.

(15b) Dis hostel ⟶ fine hostel
DEM hostel ⟶ fine hostel
This hostel ⟶ fine hostel

(15b) Addition of the adj (fine) to the object of TP.

An interesting feature of the object of the TP is that the topicalised constituent is negativized as shown in (14b).

Verb phrases are also topicalized through left dislocation. In the example of the topicalized verb phrase below, the verb phrase is reduplicated and it is preceded by a prepositional particle. The topicalized verb is repeated in the sentence as shown below.

(16) For bakibaki,   Simba sabi bak wel wel.
     PREP bark barkTOP Simba know bark well well.
     For barking, TOP Simba really knows how to bark.

While the reduplicated verb phrase functions like a gerund in example 16 above, the single verb phrase in the TP of the clause is the VP of the TP.

There are also instances of reduplicated topicalized VP which are replaced by resumptive pronouns. The resumptive pronoun does not function as the object of the topicalized sentence but as double copula. Below is an example.

(17) Toku toku na   im   bi   Edesiri wok.
     Talk talk TOP COP 3SG COPE desiri work.
     Talking, TOP it is Edesiri's occupation.

The double copula are *na (im)* and *bi*. As stated earlier, *na im* also functions as a relativizer. Since the topicalized reduplicated verb has undergone nominalization, the pronoun (im) 'it' in example 17 functions appropriately as the resumptive pronoun. It is important to state here that the pronoun *im* (it) is not an explective in example 17 above.

Topicalized topic pronouns are also derived through left dislocation. The common instance is that of a first person pronoun which is always co-indexed with a referential subject in the sentence. While the topicalized pronoun is in the objective case, the co-referential pronoun is in the nominative case. Below are some examples.

(18a) Mi   A   nor   sabi cook banga rice.
      1SG.OBJ TOP 1SG.SUBJ NEG know cook banga rice.
      As for me TOP, I don't know how to cook palm oil rice.

(18b) Mi   A   sabi Mathematics well well.
      ISG.OBJ TOP ISG.SUBJ know mathematics very well.
      As for me TOP, I know Mathematics very well.

An example of topicalized pronoun which is derived through left dislocation is second person plural pronoun, *una* (you people). The non-topicalized second person plural pronoun is co-indexed with the topicalized one since both of them are co-referential as shown in examples 19a&b below.

(19a) Una   TOP A   nor   sabi una   mama.
      2PL.SUBJ TOP ISG.SUBJ NEG   know 2PL.OBJ mother.
      You people, TOP I don't know you people's mother.

(19b) Una   TOP police go   soon   catch una.
      2 PL.SUBJ TOP Police FUT   soon   catch 2PL.OBJ.
      You people, TOP Police will soon arrest you.

In examples 19a& 19b, *una* (You people) is a possessive pronoun which is realized as *your* (plural).

There are also instances of second person singular topicalized pronoun in the data as shown in example 20 below.

(20) You,   your   mama   go   kill you   today.
     2SG. TOP 2SG.POSS   mother   FUT   kill 2PL.OBJ today.
     You TOP, your mother will kill you today.

In example 20 above, the topicalized second person pronoun in the singular number is co-referential with the same pronoun which is the object of the sentence. In NP, the second person singular pronoun *you* and the second person plural pronoun *una* are denoted with different lexical items from the data collected as shown in examples 19a&b and 20 respectively above.

3 Focus

Focus is a sub-component of information structure and it is a linguistic universal. Two types of focus in the literature are new information focus and contrastive focus (Drubig, 1984).

A typological analysis of focus in the literature identifies simple or full focus and Wh- focus which is also known as pseudo-focus. The full focus is divided into specificational and the predicational or contrastive focus. Declerck (1984) calls the specificational focus the default because it ascribes a value to a variable. In NP, Faraclas (1996: 115) states that the specificational focus is the default one and it begins with the equative copula verb *Na* while the contrastive focus begins with *No bi*. Clefting is the syntactic method most commonly used for derivation of focus. According to Lambrecht (2001: 4), clefting is:

> A complex sentence structure consisting of a matrix clause headed by a copula and a relative or relative-like clause whose relativized argument is co-indexed with the predicative argument of the copula. Taken together, the matrix and the relative clauses express a logically simple proposition which can also be expressed in the form of a single clause without a change in truth condition.

Declerck (1984) states that new information focus is formalized thus: "It is X that did Y". Heads that contrastive focus can be formulated thus: "X but Y" or (X not Y). So, contrastive focus holds some proposition to be true while it excludes other possibilities.

3.1 The peculiar features of *Na*

The first constituent in a cleft construction is *Na*. In NP, *na* is a copula. Two other copulas in the contact language are *bi* and *dey*. Below are examples of each of them.

(21a) Efe na smol boy.
    Efe COP small boy.
    Efe is a small boy.

(21b) Ese dey house.
    Ese COP house.
    Ese is at home.

(21c) Mai   popsi   bi   mai   ticha.
      ISG.POSS father COP   ISG.POSS teacher.
      My father is my teacher.

Na however has certain unique characteristics which distinguishes it from the other two copulas in NP. Caron (2019: 5) mentioned some of the features and they are summarized below: First, *na* is the only copula used for focus/cleft construction and it carries an uninterpretable person feature. Second, if *no* (NEG) precedes *na* and they co-occur in a sentence, such a sentence is ungrammatical as shown in example 22a below. However, *no* can co-occur with the other two copulas and the sentences will be grammatical as shown in examples 22b & 22c below.

(22a) *Efe no   na   mai   frend.
       Efe NEG   COP ISG.POSS friend.
       Efe is not my friend.

(22b) Efe no   bi   mai   friend.
      Efe NEG   COP 1SG.POSS friend.
      Efe is not my friend.

(22c) Efe no   dey   house.
      Efe NEG   COP   house.
      Efe is not at home.

Third, *na* cannot be used in content or *Wh-* questions or *Q-word* questions as shown in examples 23a and 23b below. However, if the other two copulas co-occur with content or *Wh*-questions or *Q-word* questions, such questions are grammatical as shown in examples 23c and 23d below.

(23a) *Hu   na   dere?
       Who COP   there?
       Who is there?

(23b) *Wetin na   your   name?
       What   COP   2SG.POSS name?
       What is your name?

(23c) Wetin bi   your   name?
      What COP 2SG.POSS name?
      What is your name?

(23d) Hu   dey   dere?
      Who COP there?
      Who is there?

Fourth, *na* can however be used to introduce Yes/No questions in NP while *dey* and *bi* cannot be used for the same purpose as shown in examples 24a, 24b and 24c respectively below.

(24a) Na   rain bi   dat?
      COP rain COP DEM?
      Is that rainfall?

(24b) *Bi   rain be   dat?
      COP rain COP DEM?
      Is that rainfall?

(24c) *Dey   rain bi   dat?
      COP   rain COP DEM?
      Is that rainfall?

Fifth, *na* cannot be used in contrastive cleft as shown in the example below.

(25) *No   na   Toju thief di   money.
     NEG COP Toju steal DEF money.
     It is not Toju that stole the money.

Bi is however used to introduce contrastive cleft as shown in (26.) below.

(26) No   bi   Toju tif   di   money.
     NEG COP Toju steal DEF money.
     It is not Toju that stole the money.

Sixth, *na* is followed by the clefted constituent which is known as the cleft phrase. The clefted constituent is followed by the cleft clause. The cleft clause is always a relative clause and it has three types of relativizers. They are shown below.

$$\left\{\begin{array}{l}\text{Wey} \\ \text{Ø} \\ \text{Naim}\end{array}\right\} \left\{\begin{array}{l}\text{that} \\ \text{Zero} \\ \text{COP+3SG.POSS}\end{array}\right.$$

(27a) The three relativizers of the cleft clause in NP.

The relativizer is followed by a tense phrase (TP). Below is an example of a clefted biclausal sentence which is derived from a non-clefted monoclausal sentence.

Non-clefted monolingual sentence

(27b) A   buy   dis   car   yestade.
      1SG.SUBJ buy   DEM   car   yesterday.
      I bought this car yesterday.

Clefted Bilingual Clause.

(27c) Na   dis   CAR   wey   A   buy   yestade.
      COP   DEM   CAR   Foc REL   1SG.SUBJ buy   yesterday.
      It's this CAR that I bought yesterday.

The information strategy of this cleft sentence is analysed as follows. The copula *na* is a focalizer and it introduces the cleft phrase which is *DIS CAR*. The focused phrase is the foregrounded information in the sentence. The cleft clause *wey A buy yestade* is less informative compared to the cleft phrase. In the clefted sentence, the rheme of the non-clefted sentence *DIS CAR* now precedes the theme which is *wey A buy yestade*. So, there is a theme-rheme reversal (Caron, 2019; Cornish, 2012).

3.2 Types of focus construction in NP

'Na' or simple focus is divided into presentational or specificational and identificational or predicational or contrastive focus. These two sub-types of focus are known as simple focus in the literature. Declerck (1983) calls specificational focus the default because it ascribes a value to a variable. Faraclas (1996) corroborates Declerck's (1983) assertion when he states that in NP the specificational focus is the default one and it begins with the copula *na* while the contrastive focus begins with *No bi*. In the literature, there is also wh- focus which is also known of pseudo-focus in English.

3.2.1 Presentational or specificational focus

The salient feature of presentational or specificational focus is that it is always a declarative sentence. The focus constituent in utterances with presentational focus can function as subject, adjunct, prepositional phrase, functioning as adjunct and predicate focus.

3.2.1.1 Subject
Focus constituents functioning as subject can be sub-divided into two. The first is the focused subject which does not involve the movement of the DP while the second is the focused subject which involves the movement of the DP since the direct object of the sentence is in its non-focused state.

Subject (without movement)

Non-focused

(28a) Efe tif di moni.
Efe steal DEF money.
Efe stole the money.

Focused

(28b) Na EFE wey tif di moni.
COP EFE REL steal DEF money.
It's EFE that stole the money.

Non-focused

(28c) Mai pikin go sweep church tomorrow.
1SG.POSS child FUT sweep church tomorrow.
My child will sweep the church tomorrow.

Focused

(28d) Na   my   PIKIN   wey go   sweep church tumoro.
     COP 1SG.POSSL CHILD REL FUT sweep church tomorrow.
     It's my CHILD that will sweep the church tomorrow.

Subject (with movement)
In the case of a focused subject that is derived through movement, the focused DP was the direct object of the sentence in its non-focused form. The movement is from its object position to its new position as the FocP functioning as the subject of the sentence. Below are some examples.

Non-focus sentence

(29a) A   kill di   fawol   yestade.
     1SG.SUBJ kill DEF chicken yesterday.
     I killed the chicken yesterday.

Focused sentence

(29b) Na   di   FAWOL   wey A   kill   yestade.
     COP DEF CHICKEN Rel 1SG.SUBJ killed yesterday.
     It's the CHICKEN that I slaughtered yesterday.

(30a) Fire burn di   dog dis   morning.
     Fire burnt DEF dog DEM   morning.
     Fire burnt the dog this morning.

(30b) Na   di   DOG   O   fire burn   dis   morning.
     COP DEF DOG (zero) fire burn   DEM morning.
     It's the DOG fire burnt this morning.

In examples 28b&d the subject DPs which are 'EFE' and 'mai PIKIN' remained in the canonical subject position. The insertion of the focalizer *na* in their respective left periphery resulted in their transformation from DP to FocP and the respective DP occurred in spec FocP position in order to check the uninterpretable features of Foc^o. FocP then becomes a phase subject to Phase Impenetrability Condition (PIC). The constituents after the cleft phrase are then relativized and it is now realized as the cleft clause. An example is the cleft clause of example 30b which is 'wey tif di moni" (that stole the money). In examples 29b & 30b, the object DP that has been moved to the subject position is focalized through the occurrence of COP (i.e., *Na*) functioning as focalizer. The respective FocP, *di FAWOL* and *di DOG* constitute a phase and with the application of PIC, no movement can operate on each of the phases again.

A peculiar feature of examples 29b & 30b is the fact that each of the two examples is also known as contradictory focus because the FocP contradicts an earlier assumption. Below is an example:

(31) Na   di   DOG wey fire burn dis   morning (nor bi   di   cat).
     COP DEF   DOG REL fire burn DEM morning (NEG COP DEF cat).
     It's the DOG that fire burnt this morning (it was not the cat).

The contradiction is premised on an earlier false assumption that it was the cat that got burnt.

3.2.1.2 Adjunct focus

An adjunct focus is presentational. Adjunct focus in cleft constructions involves the movement of the adjunct from the final position of the clause to the initial position before the focalizer 'na' occurs in the left periphery of the adjunhct phrase. The adjunct has then transformed to a cleft phrase. Then all constituents after the cleft phrase become the cleft clause through the process of relativisation as shown in examples 32a and 32b below.

(32a) Na   NEXT YEAR wey Delt State university go   increase school
      COP NEXT YEAR REL Delt State university FUT increase school
      fees
      fees
      It's NEXT YEAR that Delta State university will increase school fees.

(32b) Na   NEXT WEEK Ø   mai   pikin go   go Canada.
      COP NEXT WEEK (zero) ISG.POSS   child FUT go Canada.
      It's NEXT WEEK Ø my son will travel to Canada.

Examples 32a and 32b did undergo the same process enumerated for examples 29b and 29b above.

Prepositional phrase

Prepositional Phrases are also engaged in leftward movement to function as XP (+FOC) once the prepositional phrase is preceded by the COP functioning as focalizer. Below is an example of *prep phrase* in its normal position as the adjunct in the final position of the sentence and in its focalized form after its movement to the left periphery.

(33a) Mai   mama   buy   di   olive oil from   church.
      ISG.POSS mother buy   DEF   olive oil PREP church.
      My mother bought the olive oil from church.

(33b) Na   from CHURCH wey mai   mama   buy di   olive oil.
      COP PREP CHURCH REL ISG.POSS mother buy DEF olive oil.
      It's from the CHURCH that my mother bought the olive oil.

Below are examples of prepositional phrases playing instrumental and locative functions that have been moved to play focused functions at the left periphery of their respective sentences. Pied piping and preposition stranding are also discussed based on the focusing of prepositional phrases below.

Locative (pied piping)

(34a) Na   from RIVER wey A   draw di   wota.
      COP PREP RIVER REL 1SG.SUBJ   draw DEF water.
      It's from the RIVER that I fetched the water.

(35a) Na   for   LECTURE HALL na   im   mai   fred   for
      COP PREP LECTURE HALL COP 3SG.POSS 1SG.POSS friend PREP
      faint.
      faint.
      It's in the LECTURE HALL that my friend collapsed.

Locative (prep stranding)

(34b) Na   RIVER wey   A   draw di   wota   from.
      COP RIVER COMP ISG.SUBJ   draw DEF water PREP.
      It's the RIVER that I fetched the water from.

(35b) *Na LECTURE HALL na   im   mai   fred   for faint
      COP LECTURE HALL COP 3SG.POSS 1SG.POSS friend PREP faint
      for.
      PREP.
      It's at the LECTURE HALL that my friend collapsed for.

The second copula *na* is italisized above and it precedes third person singular pronoun *im*.

Instrumental (pied piping)

(36a) Na   with GUN wey di   hunter kill di   snake.
      COP PREP GUN REL DEF hunter kill DEF snake.
      It's with a GUN that the hunter killed the snake.

(37a) Na   with KOBOKO   wey di   solda   flog   di   agbero.
      COP PREP HORSE WHIP REL DEF soldier flog   DEF thug.
      It's with HORSE WHIP that the soldier flogged the thug.

Instrumental (prep stranding)

(36b) *Na GUN wey di   hunter kill di   snake with.
      COP GUN REL DEF hunter kill DEF snake PREP.
      It's a GUN that the hunter killed the snake with.

(37b) *Na KOBOKO   wey di   solda   flog   di   agbero with.
      COP HORSE WHIP REL DEF soldier flogged DEF AGBERO PREP.
      It's HORSE WHIP that the soldier flogged the thug with.

It is important to state at this point that NP has few prepositions in its lexical inventory. (See Mowarin, 2009: 5).

A contentious argument among some NP linguists is the argument that *from* is a verb and not a preposition in NP. Caron (2019:13) corroborates Faraclas (1996) assertion that *from* is always a verb in NP when he states that "It could be argued that, as in Nigerian Pidgin *from* is always a verb and not a preposition in Naija".

We disagree with Caron and Faraclas' assertions that *from* is a verb in NP. It is a preposition. So, the example that Caron (2019: 13) provides when he asserts that *from* is used as a verb is.

(38a) *'I   from   Kano'.
      1SG.SUBJ PREP   Kano.
      I from Kano.

Example 38a is not a grammatically correct NP sentence because it lacks a predicator. The correct NP sentence is supposed to be:

(38b) I   come   from   Kaduna.
      1SG.SUBJ come   PREP   Kaduna.
      I came from Kaduna.

Caron gave another example made by the resource person which gives one the impression that the resource person is correcting himself thus:

(38c) Na   from   Kaduna > + I   come   from.
      COP   PREP   Kaduna > + ISG.SUBJ   come   PREP.
      It's from Kaduna I came from.

Example 38c is a grammatical sentence in NP because it has a predicator which is 'come'.

Based on our data for this study, *from* is a preposition in NP and not a verb. In the examples of focused locative and instrumental prepositions, there are instances when the preposition is pied piped with the noun functioning as the complement of the preposition to the left periphery of the clause. So, the cases of the pied piped prepositions in examples 34a, 35a, 36a & 37a are grammatical. From the examples, it is observed that while some prepositions like *from* accepts preposition stranding, with 36b as an example, when the DP is preposed to the left periphery, preposition like *for* and *with* do not accept preposition stranding as shown in examples 36b and 37b above.

The reason why examples 36b and 37b are ungrammatical is due to what Radford (2002) calls violation of chain uniformity principle. This is due to the fact that the preposition is not pied piped along with its complement. The stranding of the preposition *from* in (36b.) can be regarded as an exception to the rule. So, from our data, it is only *from* that accepts preposition stranding.

It is also germane to state here that example 35b involves a case of double clefting since COP *na* occurred clause initial as *Na* occurs twice in the sentence. The first COP [*na*] occurred clause initial. The second COP [na] is followed by third person possessive in the singular number *im*.

3.2.1.3 Predicate focus

This is the third type of presentational focus. There are two cases of predicate focus which are derived through clefting. They are *reduplicated predicate focus* and *double predicate focus*.

3.2.1.3.1 Predicate focus through reduplications

In this sub-type of predicate focus, the verb phrase is reduplicated. Below are some examples.

(39) One wayorist call me for fone yestade dey yan opata about one million naira
wey im wan put for my account. Na laf A jos dey laf di wayorist.

[One scammer called me yesterday and was telling me about the sum of one million naira
he wanted to deposit in my account. It is derisive laughter I just laughed at the scammer.]

(40) Na   LAF   wey A   jos dey laf di wayoist.
     COP LAUGH   REL ISG.SUBJ. just IMPF laugh DEF scammer.
     It is LAUGH that I just laughed at the scammer.
     I just laughed incessantly at the scammer.

(41) Na CRY wey you cry mek   you get headache.
     COP CRY REL 2SG. cry made   2SG. get headache.
     It is the cry that you cried that resulted in you having headache.

Predicate focus through reduplication

(42) Na   yor   TOKU TOKU na   im   dey taya me.
     COP 2SG.POSS   TALK TALK COP   3SG. POSS IMPF tired 1SG.OBJ.
     It's your INCESSANT TALK that makes me fed up with you.

In examples 40 and 41, the VP *LAUGH* and *CRY* are respectively the cleft phrase and the VP of the cleft clause. The difference is that while the first predicator is in focused XP, the second predicator is not focused. It is apposite to state here that the focused predicator is playing a nominalised role. So, it can be termed as a gerund.

In example 42, the predicator *toku* (talk) is reduplicated. The first predicator intensifies the next one. It is also germane to note that the reduplicated predicate has undergone nominalization; so, it plays a nominal role in the focused phrase. The reduplicated predicate also has a case of double clefting. Double clefts in focus construction involve the presence of two COPs (i.e., *na*) in the focus sentence. Caron (2019: 13) states that:

> The double cleft strategy repeats the copula *na* before the focus-frame. *Na* is followed by the expletive 3s pronoun *im* which is co-indexed to the identifier and functions as antecedent of the backgrounded in the form of a bare relative.

In example 44, *dey taya mi* is the back-grounded clause. Double cleft functions as the third sub-type of relativizer of the cleft clause. These relativizers function respectively as COMP of the relative clause. Each of them occurs in *Co* position since each of them constitutes a lexical head.

3.2.2 Identificational or contrastive focus

A peculiar feature which distinguishes identificational focus from presentational one is that the focalizer of the former is *No bi*. Sudhoff (2010: 145) distinguishes between presentational and identificational focus thus:

> Contrastive focus in its narrow sense as opposed to new information focus imposes specific restrictions on the alternatives. Contrastive focus has a special pragmatic function: it interrupts sequential extension of the common ground for speaker and hearer and corrects an explicit or implicit assumption of the latter while all foci are contrastive in the sense that their interpretation involves a set of alternatives.

The structural position of '*no bi*' (it's not) within a contrastive focused construction is analyzed in the example below.

(43) No   bi   TORITSEJU   wey   break   de   plate
     NEG   COP   TORITSEJU   COMP   break   DEF   plate.
     It was not TORITSEJU that broke the plate.

The restriction that contrastive focus imposes on example 43 above is that it excludes Toritseju from the possible alternative of people that broke the plate.

Two types of contrastive focus in the data collected are subject and adjunct focus. Below are examples.

Subject focus

(44) No   bi   SAPELE   wey   dem   for   kill   the   thief.
     NEG COP SAPELE   REL 3PL.POSS PREP kill   DEF   thief.
     It was not in SAPELE that they killed the thief.

Adjunct focus

The common type of contrastive focus functioning as adjunct is temporal adverbial which is moved to + Foc XP. Below is an example.

(45) No   bi   NEXT YEAR   na   im   mai   pikin   go
     NEG COP   NEXT YEAR   COP 3SG.POSS 1SG.POSS child   FUT
     graduate.
     graduate.
     It is not NEXT YEAR that my child will graduate.

The adjunct contrastive focus in example 47 has double cleft as exemplified by *No bi* and *na im*.

3.2.3 Wh- focus construction in NP

Wh- interrogative focus is also known as pseudo-focus in English-based pidgins and creoles and it occurs frequently in contact languages. In NP, it does occur. Finney (2004: 63) defines *wh-*interrogative clefting in NP thus: "In wh-interrogative clefting, a focused *Wh- interrogative phrase* is introduced by <u>na</u> and like in nominal clefting the use of overt complementizer is prohibited". So, the complementizers like <u>wey</u> and *na im* are not accepted in wh-cleft construction in NP. Below are some examples:

(46a) Na   { wetin mek } RAIN   no   fall   tode?
      COP   what thing   make RAIN NEG fall   today?
            FOC WHY RAIN   not fall today?
            Why was there   no rainfall today?

(46b) Na   which   time   di   train   go   come?
      COP   what   time   DEF TRAIN   FUT   come?
      It's WHAT TIME THE TRAIN will come?

As stated by Finney (2004:63) above, an ungrammatical structure will evolve once an overt complementizer (i.e., *wey na im*) is added to a *wh*-interrogative cleft clause as shown below:

(47a) *Na which kind meat <u>wey</u> your mama buy for
     COP WHICH TYPE MEAT 2SG.POSS REL mother buy PREP
     market?
     market?
     Emp WHAT TYPE of MEAT that your mother bought from the market?
     WHAT TYPE OF MEAT did your mother buy from the market?

(47b) *Na WETIN MEK wey you de cry?
     COP WHAT MEK REL 2SG COP cry?
     WHY that you are crying?
     Why are you crying?

So examples 47a & 47b are ungrammatical because of the inclusion of the relative clause which is introduced by *wey*. However, Ø (zero) complementizers can be accepted in wh- interrogative clefting in NP.

3.2.4 Focus in embedded clauses in NP

Focus construction in embedded clauses were also found in our data although they did not occur frequently. Below are some examples.

(48a) Mi   A   know sey na   OVIE wey chop the moimoi.
     1SG.OBJ 1SG.SUBJ know REL COP OVIE REL eat DEF moimoi.
     Me I know that it's Ovie that ate the beans cake.

(48b) You know se   na dat MEDICINE wey kill di dog.
     2SG. know REL COP DEM MEDICINE REL kill DEF dog.
     You know that it's that MEDICINE that killed the dog.

In examples 48a & 48b, the focalized constituent, OVIE and MEDICINE are in the embedded clauses because FocP is in the embedded clause and not in the matrix clause.

4 Discussion

The chapter notes that topcalization is derived in NP through two syntactic operations. The first is the base generation of focus particles which precedes the topicalized constituents. The focalizers which include *sha, sef, tu* and *nko* can also have emphatic markers occurring in the final position of the sentence as shown in (5b.). The study notes that while *kwanu* is a topicalizer in Faraclas (1996) analysis of focus, it is *nko* that is found in the present study. The difference is due to the fact that Faraclas collected his data from the eastern or Port Harcourt variety of NP which is influenced by Igbo while the variety of NP spoken in Warri/Sapele speech community is influenced by Yoruba. *Nko* is a Yoruba word. So, the fact that substrate languages still play important role in the lexical inventory and syntactic processes of NP is a finding of this study. The constituents that are topicalized by topicalizer particles include: DP/NP in examples 3a & 3b, VP in examples 5a & 5b and AdjP in examples 6a & 6b. A peculiar feature of adjectives noticed in examples 6a & 6b is the fact that the so called adjectives are actually stative verbs as shown in example 6a: *Politics doti sha o* (Politics is very dirty). Based on (6a) above, one may also argue that NPE has adifferent kind of grammar which does not require a verb as the head of the predicate phrase when the semantic head is an adjective. *Nko* also plays a dual function as a topicalizer and a Q-word constituent as shown in example 10. The dual functions of *nko* and adjectives in the data highlight the fact that semantic extension and multifunctionality are some of the lexico-semantic processes in NP.

Dislocation to the left periphery or external merge is the other method employed in NP to derive topicalization. A major finding of this process is that apart from the common case of resumptive pronoun found in the final position of the topicalized sentence as shown in examples 12a & 12b, there is also a case of co-indexation of topicalized DP where the co-indexed pronoun is a reflexive of the topicalized DP as shown in examples 13a & 13b. There are also cases of repetition of topicalized DP as shown in examples 14a & 14b. For the cases of topicalization of VPs, there is always a reduplication of the DP as shown in example 16.

With regards to focus construction, the study notes that clefting is the main method of derivation of focus constituents. Although there are three types of copula in NP which are *na, bi* and *dey*, it is only *na* that functions as a focalizer. The peculiar features of *na* in NP are identified and they include the fact that *na* does not accept negation as shown in examples 23a & 23b. *Na* cannot be used for contrastive focus as shown in example 25. In the discussion of a cleft biclausal clause, it was observed that there are three types of relativizers which are *wey, zero* and double cleft, *na im*. In the discussion on presentational focus, we noticed that the focused constituent can be subject (examples 28a & 28b), adjunct (examples 32a & 32b.) and prepositional phrase (examples 33a & 33b). The unique syntactic phenomenon of preposition pied piping and preposition stranding for focus construction are identified. The study notes that the preposition *with* does not accept preposition stranding as shown in example 36b. However, the preposition *from* accepts preposition stranding as shown in example 34b. The study notes that example 36b is ungrammatical due to what Radford (2002) calls violation of chain uniformity condition. The essay also adds that example 34b is grammatical because it is an exception to the chain uniformity condition. That after the phase of each of them has been constituted, PIC will make it impossible for any syntactic processes to occur in the sentence in which they occur.

5 Conclusion

In conclusion, this study has highlighted some of the salient syntactic processes of the internal structure of topicalization and focus construction in NP. There is an intrinsic relationship between NP and contact linguistics in the Nigerian linguistic ecology since the study of NP has generated interest in contact research in complexly multilingual and multicultural Nigeria. Topicalizers and emphatic markers are unique features employed by NP speakers to foreground already topicalized constituents. The three types of focus in NP which are presentational, contrastive and wh-focus are discussed and the unique features of each of them are identified. There is no gainsaying the fact that NP has now evolved as a neo-Nigerian language; however, the language is not homogenous in the country even in the Niger Delta region.

Finally, the study has laid a foundation for further research into information structure in particular and syntactic analysis of the language in general. There is the need for further research on the influence of substrate languages, lexifier or superstrate language and universal processes of second language acquisition in the derivation of topicalization and focus construction in NP. It is hoped that this study will stimulate further research in the syntactic processes of NP.

References

Agheyisi, Rebecca. 1984. Linguistic implications of the changing role of Nigerian Pidgin English. *English World-Wide* 5, 211–33.
Akande, Akinmade T. 2008. *The verb in standard Nigerian English and Nigerian Pidgin: A sociolinguistic approach*. Leeds: University of Leeds PhD dissertation.
Akande, Akinmade T. 2010. Is Nigerian Pidgin English English? *Dialectologia et Geolinguistica* 18, 3–22.
Ayafor, Miriam & Melanie Green. 2017. *Cameroon Pidgin English: A comprehensive grammar*. Amsterdam: John Benjamin.
Bamgbose, Ayo. 1971. The English language in Nigeria. In John Spencer (ed.), *The English language in West Africa*, 303–308. London: Longman.
Chafe, Wallace. 1976. Givenness, contrativeness, definiteness, subjects, topics and point of view. In Charles N. Li & Sandra A. Thomson (eds.), *Subject and topic*. 25–55. New York: Academic Press.
Caron, Bernard. 2019. Clefts in Naija: A Nigerian Pidgincreole. Paper presented at the *International Naija Symposium* (ms.). University of Ibadan, 27–29 June.
Chomsky, Noam. 1995. *The minimalist program*. Cambridge, MA: MIT Press.
Chomsky, Noam. 2008. On Phases. In Jean-Roger Vergnaud, Robert Freidin, Carlos Peregrin Otero & Maria Luisa Zubzarreta (eds.), *Foundational issues in linguistic theory: Essays in honour of Jean- Roger Vergnaud*. 133–166. Cambridge, MA: MIT Press.
Cornish, Francis. 2012. Micro-syntactic, macro-syntactic, foregrounding and backgrounding in discourse. *Belgian Journal of Linguistics* 26, 6–24.
Declerck, Renaat. 1984. The pragmatics of it-cleft and wh-clefts. *Lingua* 64, 251–289.
Drubig, Hans Bernhard. 1984. Towards a typology of focus and focus constructions. *Linguistics Analysis* 13(2), 63–113.
Durrleman-Tame, Stephanie. 2008. *The syntax of Jamaican creole (A Cartographic perspective)*. Amsterdam/Philadelphia: John Benjamins Publishing Company.
Elugbe, Ben. 1995. Nigerian Pidgin: Problems and prospects. In Ayo Bamgbose, Ayo Banjo & Andrew Thomas (eds.), *New Englishes: A West African perspective*. 284–299. Ibadan: Monsuro Press.
Faraclas, Nicholas. 1996. *Nigerian Pidgin*. New York: Routledge.
Finney, Malcolm Awadajiin. 2004. Substratal influence on the morphosyntactic properties of Krio. <http://membersaol.com/afripalavaz/podgin.html>.
Fillmore, Charles. 1968. The case forcase. In Emmon Bach & Robert Thomas Harms (eds), *Universals in Linguistic Theory* 6, 527–539. Cambridge: Cambridge University Press.
Gilman, Charles. 1976. Cameroonian Pidgin English: A neo African language. In Ian F. Hancook et al (eds.), *Creole and contact language*. 43–74. Cambridge: Cambridge University Press.
Guy, Gregory R. 2012. Language, social class and status. In Rajend Mesthrie (ed.), *The Cambridge handbook of sociolinguistics*. 159–185. Cambridge: Cambridge University Press.
Hancook, Ian F. 1987. A Preliminary classification of the Anglophone Antlantic Creoles with Syntactic data from thirty-three representative dialects: In Glen G. Gilbert (ed.), *Pidgin and Creole languages. Essays in memory of John E. Reinecke*. 264–333. Honolulu, HI: University of Hawaii Press.
Holm, John. 1988. *Pidgins and creoles*. Cambridge: Cambridge University Press.

Horvath, Julia. 2010. "Discourse features": Syntactic displacement and the status of contrast. *Lingua* 120 (6), 1346–1369.
Halliday, Michael. 1968. Notes on transitivity and theme in English. *Journal of Linguistics* 3. 37–81.
Haegerman, Lilliane. 2004. Topicalization, CLLD and the left periphery. *ZAS Papers in Linguistics* 33, 157–192.
Huber, Magnus. 1999. *Ghanian Pidgin English in its West African Context: A sociohistorical and structural analysis*. Amsterdam: Benjamins.
Kachru, Braj, Yamuna Kachru & Cecil L. Nelson. 2012. Introduction: The world of World Englishes. In Braj Kachru, Yamuna Kachru & Cecil L. Nelson (eds.), *The handbook of World Englishes*. 1–16. Oxford: Wiley Blackwell.
Lambrecht, Knuk. 2001. A framework for the analysis of cleft construction. *Linguistics* 39, 463–516.
Lambrecht, Krud. 1994. *Structure and sentence form: Topic, focus and mental representation of discourse referents*. Cambridge: Cambridge University Press.
Marchese, Lynell & Anna Schnukal. 1982. Nigerian Pidgin English of Warri. *Journal of the Linguistic Association of Nigeria* 1, 213–219.
Miyagawa, Shigeru. 2017. Topicalization. *GengoKenkyu* 152, 1–29.
Mowarin, Macaulay. 2005. A contrastive analysis of determiners and adjectives in English and Nigerian Pidgin. In Ozo-Mekuri Ndimele (ed.), *Trends in the study of language and linguistics in Nigeria: A festschrift for Philip Ajukobi Nwachukwu*. 79–94. Port Harcourt: Ombi Publishers.
Mowarin, Macaulay. 2009. Aspects of Lexico-Semantic Processes in Nigerian Pidgin. *Journal of the Linguistics Association of Nigeria* 12, 57–66.
Mowarin, Macaulay. 2012. Q-Word in Nigerian Pidgin. *Journal of the Linguistic Association of Nigeria* 15(1&2), 95–109.
Marchese, Lynell & Anna Schnukal. 1982. Nigerian Pidgin English. *Journal of the Linguistics Association of Nigeria*, 213–219.
Oyeleye, Lekan. 2005. The new linguistic order: A critical examination of the impact of globalisation on the English language. In Moji Olateju & Lekan Oyeleye (eds.), *Perspectives in language and literature*, 3–13. Ile-Ife: Obafemi Awolowo Press.
Rizzi, Luigi. 1990. *Relativized minimality* Cambridge: MIT Press.
Radford, Andrew. 2002. *Syntactic theory and the structure of English*. Cambridge: Cambridge University Press.
Romaine, Suzanne. 2012. The Bilingual and Multilingual Community. In Rajend Mesthrie (ed.), *The Cambridge handbook of sociolinguistics*, 445–465. Cambridge. Cambridge University Press.
Schneider, Edgar W. 2011. *English around the world (An introduction)*. Cambridge: Cambridge University Press.
Singler, John Victor. 1992. Nativization and Pidgin/Creole Genesis: A Reply to Bickerton: *Journal of Pidgin and Creole Languages* 7(2/3), 391–33.
Sudhoff, Stefan. 2010. Focus particles and contrast in German. *Lingua* 120 (6), 1458–1475.
Yu, Haopeng. 2014. The syntax of ND/ DP after 'DE' in Chinese theory and practice. *Language Studies* 4(12), 2594–2596.

Adesoji Babalola
Chapter 9
Metalanguage of football commentary in Nigerian Pidgin

Introduction

This chapter explores the metalanguage of football commentary in Nigerian Pidgin (NP). By metalanguage of football commentary in NP, we mean the peculiar grammatical choices used by commentators to describe football actions and football related phenomena in the language. That is, they relate to linguistic choices deployed by the NP commentators to make sense of sport events in a systematic manner such that the listeners could also make sense of their expressions. We are therefore interested in how several meanings through different linguistic choices are embedded and foregrounded at the lexical, phrasal and clausal levels in NP football commentary. Commentary is generally defined as the verbal account of essential occurrences or happenings. Various types of sports have their commentary which projects certain metalanguage. Focusing on the radio commentary of baseball, Ferguson (1983) points out that sports commentary is a social genre that exhibits highly specialized linguistic structures and organization with preponderance use of simple present tense and aspectual functionalities. Whannel (1992: 25) also hints that the essential intricacies of commentary must maintain interest with suspense, provide accurate explanation and interpretation, give logical narration and vocally sustain pace with spontaneity.

Several studies have focused on NP from different engaging viewpoints and some of these studies can be broadly grouped into three – (a) those that dwell on the sociolinguistics of NP (e.g., Akande and Salami, 2010; Egbokhare, 2003; Elugbe and Omamor, 1991; Igboanusi, 2008), (b) those that focus on the grammar and lexis of NP (e.g., Deuber, 2005; Faraclas, 1996; Ihemere, 2006; Mensah, 2011, 2012; Mowarin, 2012), and (c) those that examine variation in English and NP (e.g., Akande, 2008; Osoba, 2004). While all these studies are engaging, there is still a huge lacuna in the area of carrying out thorough research on the linguistic features of NP football commentary. It is against this backdrop that this chapter attempts to investigate the metalanguage of NP football commentary. The main thesis of this chapter is that NP commentary has some metalanguage that requires adequate description for the good understanding of the commentary itself. In other words, if the NP commentary is to be clearly understood linguistically, a description of its metalanguage is necessary. Given this background, the specific objectives of this study are to: (i) identify and establish the linguistic resources in NP that serve as metalanguage of football commentary, and (ii) examine the peculiarity and classify the identified metalanguage lexically and syntactically. It is strongly believed that if these objectives are rigorously addressed, this study will provide new insight on the linguistic properties of NP in sports domain.

1 The rising status of Nigerian Pidgin

Since the inception of NP as a contact language, it has been considered as a 'bastardised', 'debased' and 'illiterate' form of expression used merely for trade communication between Nigerians and the Europeans (Elugbe and Omamor, 1991; Egbokhare, 2003; Ihemere, 2006; Mensah, 2011; Ofulue, 2004). This negative perception towards the language continued to linger even during the postcolonial era when Nigeria had secured her independence and could put in place her own sovereign language policy. However, in present-day Nigeria, NP is steadily shedding its stigmatic skin of negativity, bastardization and lowlife form of expression, and wearing an apparel of prestige, honour, appreciation, and positive identity especially among the youthful Nigerian population. The language has transcended all various forms of marginalization and continued to gather momentum and relevance in different social space of linguistic functionality and practicality. NP has therefore out-grown its mere language of trade designation and metamorphosed into a popular code of cross-ethnic communication, youth socialization and identity construction, expanding its linguistic resources through its utilization in various social functions, institutions, workplaces and homes; and gradually becoming a vibrant instrument of communication in major Nigerian cosmopolitan cities where ethnic diversity and linguistic plurulingualism are the norm.

Dwelling on the national and international signification of NP, Mair (2016: 32) observes that NP has a 'strong covert prestige abroad [and it is] a suitable index of group solidarity'. It is evident therefore that NP is a symbol of group solidarity and a linguistic pride for most Nigerians at home and in the diaspora. As NP continues to enjoy high sociolinguistic patronage among Nigerians, the language begins to venture into diverse socio-cultural domains that can further project the essence of the code. Such domains include entertainment, politics, media, campus life, literature, security and sports.

In the Nigerian entertainment industry, particularly Afro-pop and hip-hop, NP is one of the dominant languages deployed by Nigerian artistes to reach out to a wider audience, thereby making their music more endearing to the populace. The acceptance of music largely in pidgin is usually hinged on the fact that the songs produced in the language are often characterized by lyrical simplicity, easy lyrical learning and ethnic neutrality. One of the reasons the music of the Nigerian Afro-pop pioneer, late Fela Anikulapo-Kuti, witnessed a huge revolution in terms of popularity across the country was his adoption of NP as one of the major forms of expression (Ofule, 2004). Fela's success was premised on the reality that majority of the general public could easily relate with his activism and satire based on his language choice. In the actual words of Ofulue (2004: 270), 'when the late Fela Anikulapo-Kuti changed his medium of singing from Yoruba, his mother tongue, to Nigerian Pidgin in the late seventies, his music became more popular'. What this suggests is that NP plays an essential role in the popularity of any good music genre in Nigeria especially if the target is geared towards ethnic deterritorialisation.

Broadly speaking, current Nigerian hip-hop artistes such as Tu face, Davido, Wizkid, Burna Boy, Naira Marley and many more who are also making waves on both national and global scenes, collaborating with local and international acts, and winning international awards have adopted NP as a major lyrical vehicle of expression in their songs. Thus, while Nigerian hip-hop blossoms on multilingualism, the efficacy of NP in driving the music industry cannot be downplayed (Akande, 2012). Regarding the value of NP in Nigerian hip-hop music, Mensah (2011: 214) hints that

> In the Nigerian music scene, particularly with the emerging Naija pop culture, NP is a predominant language of expression and a form of solidarity or a mark of identity among the various multi-ethnic youth groups who crave to create their respective urban culture given their group dynamics and social orientation.

NP could as a result be perceived as a marker of 'national identity' on a global market of cultural diversities and identity negotiations. In the area of stand-up comedy, NP is at the forefront, breaking ethnic barriers as it is the leading language of humour in the country. Many great comedians including Alibaba, Basket Mouth, AY, I Go Die, Kenny Black, I Go Save and others have used and are still using NP to achieve huge success in the field of comedy, and carving a niche for themselves in the entertainment world.

In media broadcast and advertisement, political campaign, and public enlightenment, NP is one of the prominent languages utilized to perform such social functions, helping to reach out to the inhabitants without any inclination of social stratification. In this regards, the two popular radio stations that conduct all their activities and programmes in NP are Wazobia FM and Naija FM, and this has tremendously helped the stations in registering huge success and audience in the major cities of their establishment across Nigeria. Another landmark in the globalization of NP was evident when Google launched its search engine in Pidgin in 2011. Also, in 2017, NP witnessed an unprecedented media boost as the British Broadcasting Corporation (BBC) launched pidgin digital services in West Africa to attract more audience on the continent and consequently promoted the language transnationally, having realised its huge potentiality in the area of mass orientation. With the headquarter in Lagos, it is evident that the BBC Pidgin online service is pushing for the internationalization of the language especially across West Africa since countries like Nigeria, Ghana, The Gambia, Sierra Leone, Cameroon and Equatorial Guinea share pidgin varieties that are largely mutually intelligible. Similarly, since the boost in global Information Technology and the Internet, NP is spreading and globalizing through its deployment on the social media platforms such as Facebook, Instagram and Twitter (Babalola, 2019: 224). In corporate advertisement, for instance, NP is essential for marketing goods and services. For instance, in addition to running some of their TV and radio adverts in NP, most of the telecommunication companies in Nigeria often name many of their tariff plans in pidgin such as Glo Jollific8, Glo Yakata, Glo Amebo, MTN Awuf4u, MTN Beta Talk, and MTN Yafunyafun. To summarise the value of NP in corporate commercials, Osisanwo (2012: 52) remarks that the language accommodates "the demands of both the literate and the illiterate".

In public enlightenment involving immunization, grassroot mobilization and campaigns against diseases such as Polio, HIV/AIDS and COVID-19, NP plays an active role in information dissemination to the Nigerian Public. A very popular poster written in NP and pasted across Nigeria in 2008 in the campaign against HIV/AIDS reads thus: *Aids no dey show for face, if you no fit hold body, make you use condom* (Aids does not show on the face, if you cannot exhibit self-control, use condom), (Ofulue, 2004). In educational domains, especially on Nigerian public university campuses, NP has been alluded to play significant role in youth bonding and socializing especially in informal students' gatherings (Abdullahi-Idiagbon, 2010; Akande and Salami, 2010; Amao, 2012; Balogun, 2013). Nigerian youth segmentation is like a fraternity in which language is a marker of identity recognition and acceptability. To navigate this social boundaries and exhibit a sense of belonging requires one's ability to stylistically and freely participate, relate and interact in NP which is the code of youth affinity, association and friendship. However, while NP has strong affinity with the majority of Nigerian students, the language is educationally marginalized. Thus, Faraclas (1991: 511) hints that 'as long as NP [NP] is not accorded the place it deserves in Nigerian education, an invaluable tool for the teaching of English will continue to be wasted and unused'. Well, the debate on whether NP should be deployed to teach English is not within the scope of this paper but the assertion essentially foregrounds how the status of NP can be educationally promoted.

Within the security institutions in Nigeria, NP is a popular linguistic instrument of communication. It is the mostly widely used language in Nigerian Army Barracks particularly "among the rank and file" (Akande, 2016: 43). It is also predominantly used in various Nigerian Police Stations, Police Colleges and Police Staff Quarters throughout Nigeria (Babalola, 2017: 79). Reacting to the incessant reports of police brutality, killings and human right violation particularly in Lagos, the Head of the Nigeria Police Force's Public Complaint Rapid Response Unit (NPF-PCRRU), ACP Abayomi Shogunle, reechoed the popularity of NP in the police workforce as he advised Nigerians to speak pidgin to police personnel at road checkpoints and avoid Queen's English so as to evade police harassment (Pulse.ng, April 17, 2019). Below is the actual tweet of the police officer as reported by the aforementioned online newspapers:

Abayomi Shogunle
✓@YomiShogunle

cc: @PoliceNG_CRU#YSGuide: For now, don't go and be speaking Queen's English with them on the road. For proper understanding talk to them in Pidgin, another way to avoid kasala.

Within the purview of sports which is the major concern of this paper, NP is gradually gathering momentum and finding its relevance. NP, in recent time, has become a favoured language of football commentary. Majority of football fans in Nigeria such as okada riders (commercial motorcyclists), danfo drivers (commercial bus drivers), mechanics, plumbers, electricians, tailors, and barbers are illiterates or semi-literates who may struggle to understand perfectly football commentary in English. As a result, when major football matches such as the FiFa World Cup and the Africa Cup of Nations are played and aired on DSTV and local TV stations, commentaries are usually run in NP in addition to the English commentary on different TV channels in order to make sport discourse easily accessible and better understood by football supporters. With this, the fans are not only entertained by the actions of football and the linguistic choices in the commentary but also able to relate with the linguistic resources deployed to describe the actions in the games.

2 Methodology

The data for this study consisted of about five hours of NP commentary drawn from the two semi-finals and the final of the 2018 World Cup that were aired on DSTV. The two stages are recorded because they are usually considered the most exciting in any World Cup. The data were tape-recorded during the live matches, using an Olympus audio tape recorder. After this, the data were transcribed on Microsoft word for easy navigation during analysis. The data were closely studied to identify, classify, and describe the peculiarity of the metalanguage of NP commentary based on the theoretical framework of Systemic functional linguistics metalanguage as espoused by Halliday (1985). This designates that methodically, the study is qualitative in orientation.

3 Data analysis and discussion

The analysis of data is presented in this section. The identified instances of the metalanguage of NP commentary are classified into lexical, phrasal and clausal items. Specifically, the lexical items are broken down into word classes such as nouns, verbs, adjectives and adverbs. It is after this that the phrasal and the clausal items are carefully considered. The actual instances of usage of some of the identified items are also presented for thorough discussion.

Table 1: Lexical Metalanguage of Football Commentary in NP (Nouns).

S/N	Nouns	Meaning
1	Shagalo	bicycle kick
2	Ororo	C.Ronaldo nick name in Pidgin
3	Collabo	collaboration/close contact
4	Smally	a player with a small physique
5	Coachy	Coach
6	Headmaster	a player that is good at using header to score
7	Opportunate	Opportunity
8	Otumoporo	Tactics
9	Jambody	collision/close contact

Table 1 (continued)

S/N	Nouns	Meaning
10	Skillashy	Skills
11	Agbakara	Force/strength
12	wayo-falling	Dive
13	Sabiness	Experience/performance
14	Skipo	Skipper
15	Ogologo	a tall player
16	Wahala	trouble/problem/bias
17	Domot	at home (literally means door-mouth)
18	Wayo	Robbery/fraud
19	Bossy	Boss
20	Ginger	Motivation
21	Posi	Position
22	Capito	Captain
23	Kasala	Problem
24	Awuf	free ball
25	Igwe	Thierry Henry's nick name in Pidgin
26	Bros	a player

As shown in Table 1, there are 26 nouns out of the lexical metalanguage of NP commentary identified in the data analysed. Each of the identified nouns has its own separate meaning. However, whereas some items are typical NP terms such as *shagolo, wayo, kasala, ogologo, awuf and wahala*, without any morphological orientation, some are NP or superstrate terms that have undergone some morphological processes of clipping (*collabo, posi, capito, and skipo*), affixation particularly suffixation (*smally, coachy, bossy, skillash, sabiness*), hyphenated compounding with suffixation (*wayo-falling*), and close compounding (*jambody*). Instances such as *collabo, posi, capito and skipo* are considered as examples of clipping in that one or two of their final syllables have been deleted from their original English forms (i.e. *collaboration, position, captain and skipper*) to form NP words. This is in line with Mensah (2011: 225)'s assertion that 'clipping or truncation is another morphological process that is viable in NP'. Also, in examples like *smally, coachy* and *bossy*, the *–y suffix* is attached to the bases to form NP words and thus, projecting them as good examples of affixation. In the word *skillash*, the *suffix –ash* is added to the English base *skill* while in *sabiness*, the English nominal suffix *–ness* is attached to the pidgin verbal root *sabi* to form a nominal pidgin item *sabiness*. Although it has been reported that affixation is not a popular feature of NP (Osoba, 2004: 245), this analysis indicates that NP is now gradually and systematically adopting affixation as a viable word formation process to expand its lexicon.

The only instance of blending is the use of *domot* which is formed from the fragments of *door* and *mouth*. This is in accordance with Osoba (2004: 241)'s examples of blending such as "comot (come+out), troway (throw+away) and sidon (sit+down)". A critical look at the meaning of the word *headmaster* as used in NP commentary shows that the linguistic item exhibits a different meaning from its source language. This demonstrates that while the compound word is borrowed from English and designates 'a man who is in charge of a school', it has undergone a semantic change in NP within the domain of football to mean 'a player that is good at scoring goals with headers'. The most complex lexical item among the nouns identified is *wayo-falling* in that it exhibits two morphological processes. First, there is compounding in the formation of the base *(wayo-fall)* and second, the *suffix –ing* is attached to the root to indicate a process of affixation. Thus, while *wayo-fall* could be described as a verb as in (He don wayo-fall: he has dived), the addition of the *suffix –ing* to the base makes it a noun as in (That one na wayo-falling: That is a dive). What this implies is that the *–ing* suffix is a derivational morpheme in that contextual usage in that it changes the word class from a verb to a noun. In addition, *ororo* is a Yoruba word, making it a substrate term which typically denotes 'vegetable oil' but the word is often borrowed and deployed as C. Ronaldo's nick name in NP to mean 'a fantastic goalscorer' or 'a great finisher'. The use of ororo in this context is similar to what Mensah (2011: 221) calls metaphorical extension. As noted by Mensah, 'metaphors are used to extend the meaning of words or forms as single symbolic formation' (pp. 222). Thus, while 'ororo' is used to fry food items into edible forms or finished products, C. Ronaldo is often seen as a 'finisher' who is good at scoring goals. Interestingly, within the context of football, *ororo* is peculiar only to C. Ronaldo, and that makes it a nick name. Another word worthy of mention is *Igwe* which designates 'a king' in Igbo language but in sports especially among Nigerian youth, it is used as a Thierry Henry's nick name in NP to mean 'a football superstar'. At this juncture, let us consider some actual examples of some of the identified nouns from the data:

1. Now with that **ginger**, the kind noise wey dem go come dey make for stadium here fit blind person ear.
   (With that *motivation*, the ovation/noise in the stadium can make someone deef).

2. Make I no lie you, I dey enjoy the **collabo** wey dey that England back.
   (Let me not deceive you, I am enjoying the *collaboration* at the England's defence).

3. the bros don really show better **sabiness** for dis world cup.
   (The player has shown great *performance* in this World Cup).

4. This England team ehn, the **sabiness** wey them take bring come this world cup, no be small thing o.
   (The England team came to this World Cup with great *experience*).

5. Giroud want try one kind **shangalo** there bet e no enter.
   (Giroud attempts a *bicycle kick* there but it is not accurate).

6. Fellaini dey scratch him face because him tall pass the guy, how this short man come take jump up nod ball for where **ogologo** like me dey.
   (Fellani is wondering how this short man nods the ball beside a tall player like him).

7. That man Harry Kane, Harry kane na the youngest **Skipo** wey England don carry come world cup before, the youngest **capito**.
   (Harry Kane is the younger *skipper* and *captain* that England has taken to the world Cup).

Considering examples 1 to 7, the items in bold font are some of the identified nouns that are used in the NP commentary analysed. In example 1, the noun *ginger* means *motivation* as used in that context. However, the word can also be deployed as a verb in some contexts to mean *protest* or *complain* as evident in the data as in (Them dey *ginger* make referee blow sey him hand touch ball: They are protesting/complaining that the referee should blow for a hand ball). This shows that, semantically, the term *ginger* in NP has extension of meaning. As hinted by Osoba (2004: 244), 'extension is a process whereby words are used to cover more situations than they do in their original languages'. Morphologically, *ginger* can be said to undergo the process of conversion which involves the functional changing or converting of a word from a word class to another without the involvement of any process of affixation. In example 2, *collabo* is used to designate *collaboration* based on the contextual usage. Just like *ginger*, *collobo* can also be used as a verb in another scenario as drawn from the data as in (John Jones and Kyle Walker, na them don dey *collabo* to lock up that England defence: John Jones and Kyle Walker are the ones collaborating to tighten the England defence.).

In addition, in example 3, *sabiness* means *performance* while in example 4, it designates *experience*. What this also suggests is that the word *sabiness* constitutes an instance of polysemy. According to Palmer (1976: 102), we have polysemy when there is 'one word with different meanings'. It is crucial to note that *sabi* which is the base of the word *sabiness* usually means *to know* in English (see Faraclas, 2004: 829) as in (He sabi where him dey waka go: He knows where he is going). However, the morphological anglicisation of the word with the suffix *-ness* has impacted its meaning. In example 5, *shagalo is* used in NP to refer to *bicycle kick*. While *bicycle kick* is usually a noun phrase in English and rarely used as a verb, it is common to use *shagalo* as a verb in NP as in (He shagalo am: *He bicycle kick the ball). In example 6, the term *ogologo* means *a tall player* while in example 7, there are two prominent NP nouns – *skipo* and *capito* which designate *skipper* and *captain* respectively in English.

Table 2: Lexical Metalanguage of Football Commentary in NP (verbs).

S/N	Verbs	Meaning
1	chop (goal/foul)	concede/commit
2	Nak	Beat/defeat or kick/play
3	Reason	check/argue/penalize
4	sama (shot)	take (a shot)
5	kakaraka (their defence)	tighten (their defence)
6	kolobi (the job/cup)	take/win
7	hammer (the shot)	Take (a shot) or beat/defeat
8	Continuate	Continue
9	Jollificate	Celebrate
10	Flex	to party
11	sabi (score goal)	Knows/understands
12	Kwanta	battle/quarrel

Table 2 (continued)

S/N	Verbs	Meaning
13	Yan	Discuss
14	Pepper	Hurt
15	troway (ball)	lose (the ball)

As evident in Table 2, 15 lexical verbs are identified as verbal metalanguage in the NP commentary data. The verbs *chop, nak, sama, kakaraka, kolobi, sabi, kwanta, yan, and troway* are typical NP words while *reason, hammer, continuate, jollificate, flex and pepper* are English words borrowed into NP with new semantic orientations and some morphological remodification. Morphologically, the typical NP words do not exhibit any process except for *troway* which is derived through the process of blending similar to the noun *domot* identified and described under the noun-metalanguage category. From the English borrowed words, continuate and jollificate are instances of clipping in that their last syllables have been cut-off from their original words (i.e. *continuation and jollification*) in their source language to form NP verbs. It is imperative to note that since English constitutes the superstrate of NP, many words in the language are of English origin. Thus, superstrate borrowing is one of the major sources of lexicalization for NP (Mensah, 2011: 216). Below are some of the contextual usages of some of the verbs listed in Table 2:

8. Five goals na him this Belgium defense don **chop** for this world cup, them **chop** two against Tunisia, them **chop** two again ehmn against Japan then them come **chop** one against Brazil for quarter final.
(England has conceded five goals in this World Cup, they conceded two against Tunisia, two against Japan, and one against Brazil in the quarter final).

9. De Bruyne don **chop** another foul, na another yellow card again for Belgium be that.
(De Bruyne has committed another foul, that is another yellow card again for Belgium).

10. The last time wey Belgium them lose any match na September 1st 2016 when Spain been **nak** them 2-0 for one friendly match that year.

(The last time Belgium lost a match was on September 1st 2016 when they were beaten by Spain in a friendly match that year).

11. Hazard no **nak** the shot well for that place.
    (Hazard does not kick the well over there).

12. Mandzukic cross the ball, Perisic come balance, he look well, he **hammer** the shot
    (Mandzuki crosses the ball, Perisic looks for stability and takes the shot).

13. If you use yepere eye take look France, my brother think am again o because once you start to play kekeyebu football them go punish you, them go seriously **hammer** you.
    (If you look down on France, kindly think twice because once you are not playing good football, they will punish you, they will beat/defeat you hands down).

14. President Emmanuel Macron he don dey follow **jolificate** goal as france them don carry one leg now dey match inside final.
    (President Emmanuel Macron has joined in the celebration as France is almost in the final).

15. Nobody don win each other anytime wey these two teams dem **kwanta** for inside world cup.
    (The two teams have not lost to each other in the World Cup whenever they battle each other).

16. Na him and him team mate dey **kwanta** for there.
    (Two team mates are arguing over there).

17. Witsel dey follow the referee **reason** say that one no suppose be foul bet the referee see am well and say na foul.
    (Witsel is arguing with the referee that that is not supposed to be a foul but the referee has a clear picture of the incident and says it is a foul).

18. Referee suppose blow there o but he go **reason** VAR (Video Assistant referee) first
(The referee is supposed to blow there but he goes to check VAR first).

19. Referee don dey take the match soft since morning, but now he don **reason** Ngolo Kante, come give am yellow card.
(The referee has been taking the match lightly but he has just issued Ngolo Kante a yellow card).

The four instances of *chop* in example 8 designate *concede (a goal(s))* as deployed in the contexts while in example 9, chop means *commit* especially when it occurs with the word *foul*. Curiously, in NP, the verb *chop* typically denotes *eat* in English (Deuber, 2005: 88), and usually co-occurs with *food* as in (My pikin chop rice yesterday: My child ate rice yesterday). *Chop* can also be used intransitively as in (my pikin don chop: My child has eaten). This manifestation is line with Elugbe and Omamor (1991: 98)'s observation that many NP verbs have the capacity to function transitively and intransitively depending on the context of use. Apart from this, *chop* can also mean *enjoy* when it precedes the word *life* in NP as in (Them dey chop life: They are enjoying (life)). The inference drawn from this is that the circumstances, the linguistic environment and the company that words keep usually influence their semantic orientation. As a result, the use of *chop* in NP is therefore polysemic as it has a set of different meanings based on its syntactic collocation and contextual deployment. Other verbal polysemies are *nak* in examples 10 and 11, *hammer* in examples 12 and 13, *kwanta* in examples 15 and 16, and *reason* in examples 17, 18, and 19. In sentence 10, for instance, *nak* means *beat/defeat* whereas in sentence 11 *nak* means *kick/play*. *Hammer* in examples 12 means *to play* (a shot) while it means *to defeat or beat* (a team) in example 13. The verb *kwanta* in example 15 means *to battle* but in example 16, it implies *to argue or quarrel*. The verbal item *reason* in example 17, 18 and 19 means *to argue, to consult* and *to penalise* respectively. It is clear that *nak* as used in example 10 and *hammer* as used in example 13 are synonyms in that both contextually denote *defeat/beat*. As observed by Palmer (1976: 88), synonymy is used to mean relatedness or sameness of meaning. However, the semantic force of defeat embedded in *hammer* is greater than that of *nak*. This is because *nak* simply means *to defeat/to beat*, perhaps with one or two goals, while *hammer* denotes *beating with a wide margin*. This reality therefore confirms the assertion of Palmer (1976: 89) that 'there are no real synonyms, [and] no two words have exactly the same meaning'. *Kwanta* and *reason* as utilised in examples 16 and 17 are also synonymous based on their semantic relatedness. *Jolificate* is the only verb out of the sentential examples that does not project

Table 3: Lexical Metalanguage of Football Commentary (Adjectives).

S/N	Adjectives	Meaning
1	Ogbonge	prestigious/international/quality/great
2	Otawarawara	Fantastic
3	Oshaprapra	Fantastic
4	Bestest	Best
5	Red	Difficult
6	Soft/soft soft	Easy
7	Big big	Giant
8	Plenty plenty (goals)	Many
9	Important important (goal)	Crucial (goal)
10	small small	Little
11	Better	Great

dual meaning as it only designates *to celebrate*. A general look at the verbal semantics analysed so far indicates that NP verbs are vastly rich not only in polysemy but also in synonymy and these are part of the essentialities of lexical semantics in any independent language.

Table 3 indicates that there are 11 linguistic items that are considered as the adjectival metalanguage identified in the NP commentary data. Of these, 8 items (bestest, red, soft/soft soft, big-big, plenty plenty, important important and small small) constitute superstrate borrowing. Of these 8 adjectives, 5 of them are instances of reduplication (i.e. soft soft, big big, plenty plenty, important important and small small). What this suggests morphologically is that reduplication is a rich source of adjectives in NP. This deducibility is in accordance with Mensah (2011: 219) and Osoba (2004: 244) findings that reduplication helps bigly in creating adjectives and other major word classes in NP. The lexical item *bestest* is another interesting adjective that has undergone new form of affixation in NP. The superstrate root of the word is *good* while the comparative and the superlative forms are *better* and *best* with the suffix *–er* and *–est* respectively. However, the word *best* has also been remodified morphologically with the addition of the *–est* suffix to form a new NP adjective *bestest*. What can be inferred from this is that it is possible for NP words to accommodate double superlative morphemes. Some contextual examples of adjectives in the data are:

20. See pickford again with another **ogbonge** punch.
    (That is Pickford with another save).

21. Na the first time since 2006 wey England them go enter semi-final for **ogbonge** competition.
    (This is the first time since 2006 that England is getting into Semi-final of this prestigious competition).

22. Ribstelle miss one **ogbonge** chance.
    (Ribstella misses a great chance).

23. **Ogbonge** star boy na him Eden Hazard be so if you no know.
    (Eden Hazard is a great player if you don't know).

24. The man wey score that **Ogbonge** goal against England . . .
    (The player who scored that great goal against England . . .).

25. Raphael Varane the Real Madrid **Ogbonge** defender nod that one comot.
    (Raphael Varane, the Real Madrid great defender cleared the ball with nodding).

26. Na one of the **bestest** mid-fielder for the whole wide world.
    (He is one of the best mid-fielders in the World Cup).

27. All the French team, them be **better** player
    (The French team comprise great players).

As seen in examples 20 to 25, ogbonge is one of the versatile adjectives used in the data. In examples 20, 21, 22, 23, 24 and 25, ogbonge means *great, prestigious/international, great, great, fantastic and quality* respectively. The versatility of ogbonge is projected in its ability to modify different nominal items. For instance, in example 20, *ogbonge* modifies *punch, competition* in 21, *chance* in 22, *star boy* in 23, *goal* in 24 and *defender* in 25. It is interesting to note that some of the meanings projected by the adjective are pragmatically similar. In example 26, *bestest* is used to replace *best* in NP without any semantic change. The use of *better* in example 27 is worthy of discussion in that it is used in that context to mean *good/great* without any sense of comparison. It is part of the peculiarity of NP to use *better* differently from its common usage in English as in (Him be better person: He is a great guy). Pragmatically, a popular synonym of *better* is *correct* as in (Him be correct guy: He is a great guy).

Table 4: Lexical Metalanguage of Football Commentary (Adverbs).

S/N	Adverbs	Meaning
1	Like play like play	Easily/gradually
2	Jejely	Quietly or easily
3	small small	Gradually
4	Well well	Excellently/very well
5	Sharperly	Quickly
6	las las	Lastly/at the end

As shown in Table 4, there are 6 popular adverbs identified in the data. Out of these, 4 are instances of reduplication which are *like play like play, small small, well well, and las las*. The morphological composition of the word *jejely* is also intriguing in that the base *jeje* (meaning gently) is an instance of substrate borrowing precisely from Yoruba language but the word has been anglicised morphologically with the *–ly suffix* to form a pidgin word *jelely*. Also, the root *sharp* as well as the stem *sharper* is borrowed from English but the word has undergone *–ly* anglicisation to form *sharperly* in NP, making the word non-existent in English. It is therefore clear that the users of NP especially commentators adopt morphological innovation and creativity to expand the linguistic resources of the language. While Mensah (2011: 221) foregrounds only *–y suffix* and *mis-prefix* as common affixes in NP, it is evident from these examples that *–ly suffix* is another viable one. Some contextual examples include:

28. **Like play like play**, we don dey enter the final 5 minutes for this game.
    (Gradually, we are the final five minutes of this game).

29. E go go down **jejely** go cover the ball dere.
    (He will quietly go and cover the ball there).

30. Even sef people think say Zlatan fit come back come play for this world cup but **last last**, e no come.
    (People thought that Zlantan would return to this Worlf Cup, but at the end, he did not).

In example 28, the phrasal reduplicative adverb *like play like play* which could mean easily/graudally is fronted for thematic prominence in the sentence. It is also possible for the same adverb to appear at the end-position of the sentence.

Table 5: Phrasal Metalanguage of Football Commentary.

S/N	Phrases	Meaning
1	block industry	Defence
2	star boy	a quality player
3	double exhaust	a tireless player
4	better play	a good play
5	genge things	some exciting moments
6	better work	a great job
7	oga at the top	a superior team
8	gbere pass	a poor pass
9	Sengenmenge things	some interesting moments
10	their domot/house	at home
11	better ball	a good pass
12	Sure boy	a reliable player
13	Soko things	Some moments of skill displays
14	oga presido	Mr president
15	oga patapata	Senior/retired players
16	Made-in-china shot	A powerful shot
17	The main the main actor	An outstanding player
18	Kampe pass	A through pass
19	Yepere eye	Disdain
20	Kekeyebu football	Poor football
21	Small pepper	A young talented player
22	Jara time	Added time

Jelely in example 29 is used to designate *quietly* while *las las* implies *at the end* as used in example 30. Like in English, adverbs in NP are capable of enjoying great intra-sentence mobility. As a result, the identified adverbs could change positions within the sentences in which they occur.

It evident that each of the items in Table 5 is made up of a modifier and a headword except for *oga at the top* which is post-modified by a prepositional phrase without any form of pre-modification. A critical look at the table also indicates that some headwords are pre-modified by nouns as in *block industry, star boy, oga presido, oga patapata, and jara time*; some by adjectives as in *double exhaust, better play, genge things, better work, gbere pass, sengemenge things, better ball, sure boy, soko things, kampe pass, yepere eye, kekeyebu football, their domot/house, and small pepper*; one is premodified by a reduplicative compound as in *the main the main actor* and another by a hyphenated compound as in *made-in-china shot*. These nominal compositions confirm Osakwe and Mowarin (2010: 1) that 'NP obligatorily contains a noun and it may be preceded by either a determiner or an adjective or both and it can be followed by a quantifier functioning as a plural marker and dependent clause(s)'. In addition, Faraclas (2004: 845) observes that noun phrases in NP can occur as 'bare nouns', pre-modified with an indefinite article 'one' or 'some' and a definite article 'the'. Apart from this, as manifested in some of the identified examples, NP also allows using nouns to modify other nouns to form noun phrases similar to the substrate and the superstrate structure. In addition, some of the noun phrases in Table 5 are fixed expressions in which their compositions cannot be altered. Such phrases include: *block industry, star boy, double exhaust, oga at the top, small pepper, and jara time*. For instance, it is usually not possible to replace *block, star, double, oga, small, and jara* respectively with some other items and still retain the same meanings in these contexts. Contextual examples of some the phrases include:

31. See as Hazard take dey find Alderweireld there but ehn **double exhaust** stand for him front there.
    (Look at how Hazard is looking for Alderweireld there but the tireless defender stood in front of him).

32. Courtois dey try arange (him) **block industry** here wey go cover am.
    (Courtoise is setting up his defence for good).

33. this man Antoine Griezmann na **star boy** for this France team he sabi all this kind free kick matter.
    (Antoine Griezmann is a young talented player in the French team, he is good at taking free kicks).

34. E be like say **jara time** na one minute make this first half finish
    (It is like there one minute of added time to the end of the first half).

Chapter 9 Metalanguage of football commentary in Nigerian Pidgin — 267

35. Any time wey the ball enter Mbappe leg you go dey expect **soko things** from am
 (Whenever the ball gets to Mbappe, one would expect great moments from him).

36. Mbappe na **small pepper**, him fit score if you give am shikini chance, na **sure boy** him be.
 (Mbappe is a young talented player, he can score with a half chance, he is a reliable player).

In example 31, 32 and 36, the use of *double exhaust, block industry* and *small pepper* contextually denotes *a tireless/energetic player*, *defence* and *a young talented player* respectively. The three phrases constitute good instances of metaphors in NP. For instance, the expression *double exhaust* is used to modify cars in English. There is a general belief that dual exhaust cars exhibit 'better performance' and 'more aggressive style' than the single exhaust cars. As a result, *double exhaust* metaphorically depicts a strong/tireless player within the context of football. Also, *block industry* as the term suggests, is a name given to an industry that specializes in producing blocks that are used to build houses in Nigeria. Generally, blocks are combinations of sand, cement and water which are usually moulded into size 6" or 9". After the production stage, the blocks are arranged on the floor in a cohesive manner to prevent people from walking through them so that they can be fully dried under the sun for adequate use. This cohesive arrangement of blocks is directly likened to a team's defence in football games. Thus, a *defence* is metaphorically a *block industry* in NP in that defence in football is usually arranged in a way that makes it difficult for opposition strikers to penetrate. More so, the noun phrase *small pepper* is another good metaphor. The power of *pepper* in relation to human eyes is metaphorically linked to a player who has the prowess of scoring goals to make the

Table 6: Clausal Metalanguage of Football Commentary.

S/N	Clauses	Meaning
1	fall (him) hand	To disappoint/embarrass
2	E no dey sweet the belle of their fans	It doesn't make their fans happy
3	Nothing dey happen	All is well
4	No shaking	All is well

Table 6 (continued)

S/N	Clauses	Meaning
5	E get as e be	It is somehow/It is boring
6	E no pure for eyes	It was not interesting
7	We go die for the matter	We will be resilient
8	Nothing spoil	It is not too late for a remedy
9	The match dey draw like ogbono	The match is boring
10	Their face dia o	They look fearless
11	25minuites don waka pass	25minutes has been spent
12	Nearly no fit kill bird	Accuracy is key
13	Them don soji themselves	They are more tactical
14	Road don clear	There is an open space
15	That na Pass wey no enter	That is a poor pass.
16	Make the defender shine their eyes	The defenders should be more conscious or careful
17	Nak the ball troway	Clear the ball
18	Time dey run comot	Time is running out
19	He no dey look Uche Face	He is very fearless
20	Hazard don comot Pogba for road	Hazard has dribbled pass Pogba.
21	Referee dey take everything soft	The referee is taking everything easy
22	No be who first call police dey win case	There is no guarantee that a team with the first goal will win the match
23	He comot for him body	He dribbled pass
24	Na referee na him hold knife, na him hold yam	It is the referee that has the final say or makes the final decision
25	The game dey red (for Crotia)	The game is becoming difficult for crotia.
26	Water don pass garri	The game is beyond redemption

opposition team suffer defeat and consequently weep if need be. In a nut shell, metaphoric creativities are essential components of NP commentary as evident from the data analysed. In examples 33, 34 and 35, *star boy, jara time* and *soko things* are used to denote *a quality player, added time and great moments* respectively.

Table 6 shows clausal metalanguage identified in the NP commentary data. Some of the expressions are idiomatic or proverbial in nature as in *nearly to fit kill bird* (Accuracy is key), *no be who first call police dey win case* (There is no guarantee that a team with the first goal will win the match), *na referee na him hold knife, na him hold yam* (The referee usually makes the final decision), *water don pass garri* (The game is beyond redemption), *He no dey look Uche face* (He is very fearless) and *The game dey red* (The game is getting tougher). Some of these expressions are fixed in terms of their syntactic compositions. For instance, it is not possible to replace *water* and *garri* in *water don pass garri* and *Uche* in *He no dey look Uche face*. Semantically, each of these aphorisms requires some clarifications. *Nearly no fit kill bird*, for instance, is a metaphoric expression that relates to a situation in which somebody attempts to kill a bird by whatever means but lacks accuracy in their targets. This scenario is likened to players having shots on goals without accuracy. Thus, that a player almost scores does not indicate that they actually score especially when accuracy is lacking. As a result, scoring goals requires adequate accuracy and focus.

Water don pass garri according to Mensah (2011: 222) depicts a 'bad situation' or 'a hopeless and helpless situation'. In football games, there could be a bad situation for a team that is losing to another especially when all hope is lost, hence the use of the expression in NP commentary. Garri is a popular food in Nigeria known as "cassava flour" which requires moderate potion of water to be edible. However, if too much water is carelessly poured on the flour, it becomes a bad situation and consequently inedible. The expression *na referee na him hold knife, na him hold yam* relates to a situation in which somebody has a knife and a tuber of yam. In such a case, the individual has all authority to do whatever they deem fit with the tuber of yam and the knife. This situation is likened to that of the referee who has a whistle and power to oversee and control the game fairly. In *he no dey look Uche face*, for example, Uche is an Igbo name. The Igbo traders in Nigeria are known to be very enterprising commercially. They are believed to have the business acumen to persuade one to buy what one does not really need especially if one gives them the chance or look them in the face. To buy whatever you want without going beyond your budget requires a lot of confidence, guts and without looking at them in the face. Thus, *he no dey look Uche face* literally means *he is not looking at Uche in the face* but figuratively means *to be fearless* or *confident* in NP. Another figurative expression is *the match dey draw like ogbono*. This is a clear instance of simile in that a football match is indirectly compared with a variety of soup in Nigeria with the use of the word *like*. Ogbono is a variety of soup that is made from 'docanut' and falls under the umbrella of draw soup within the Nigerian socio-cultural context. Draw soup is a phrase that is used to cover soups made from okra, docanut (ogbono) and jute (ewedu) that are popularly eaten by the Yoruba and the Igbo people in Southern Nigeria. Based on the 'elastic' nature of the soup, they are, to some, usually considered unattractive physically. Therefore, a football match with a slow tempo, lacking great moments and boring in actions can be likened to a "draw soup" symbolically. Other clausal metalanguage as shown in Table 6 could be considered as instances of free collocations. Let us look at some of the actual usages of these clauses:

37. Mbappe, the bross too good the youngest player for France 19 years na him he dey **he no dey look Uche face oh**! he no want know your age oh.
(Mbappe is a fantastic player, the youngest in the French team, he is just 19 years old, he is fearless).

38. France them dey always believe say any time wey them come world cup if them no do well **e no dey sweet the belle of their fans.**
(France believes that each time they at the World Cup, they have to perform well, if not, their fans won't be happy).

39. Because **na refree na him hold knife na referee na him hold yam**, person wey hold knife and hold yam na him go cut the yam how him take want am.
(The referee has the final say on the pitch, he has the authority).

In example 37, *he no dey look Uche face* is used by the commentator to refer to the high level of Mbappe's confidence. The commentator describes him as the youngest player in the French team who is only 19 years of age and who can take on opposition players with no iota of fear irrespective of their age. As a teenager, the commentator marvels at his talent, dexterity and self-reliance on the field of play. In example 38, the commentator uses the clause *e no dey sweet the belle of their fans* to mean *it does not make their fans happy*. The term *sweet (my) belle* can be used in different ways. For instance, one, it can be used without a preceding auxiliary verb *(E sweet my belle: It makes me happy)*. Two. it can be used with an auxiliary verb *(E dey sweet my belle: It is making me happy/It makes me happy)*. In example 39, the expression *na referee na him hold knife, na referee na him hold yam* is used to refer to the referee's final authority on the pitch.

4 Conclusion

This chapter has focused on the metalanguage of NP commentary. As NP ventures into different relevant domains, the language continues to adopt innovatively various morphological processes to expand its linguistic resources and accommodate new sociolinguistic realities and new areas of meanings. Adopting Systemic functional linguistics as the theoretical framework for data analysis, we have been able to show that the metalanguage of NP commentary thrives on certain lexical, phrasal and clausal features that are deployed to describe sports actions in NP. Majority of these linguistic features have undergone semantic and morphological reformulation and innovation to project their linguistic independence from the superstrate and substrate in order to establish more clearly the linguistic sovereignty of NP from these hegemonic languages. This study is in agreement with Mensah (2011) that NP responds to societal communicative demand through the development of its internal linguistic resources from various morphological practices. The study concludes that the metalanguage of NP commentary is projected through some unique nominal, verbal, adjectival, adverbial, metaphorical, phrasal and clausal expressions to characterize and depict sports activities. This indicates that that NP has grown beyond a language of limited lexicon to a productive linguistic system capable of expressing every social reality of life. Its productivity is foregrounded in the metalanguage of football commentary in which a creative use of language is required to account for the free flow of actions in a systematic manner. Considering the current realities in the country, we also conclude that NP will continue to exert its influence positively in every social stratum in multilingual Nigeria. As a result, NP should be encouraged with official recognition so as to optimally explore its potentiality for national development.

References

Abdullahi-Idiagbon, Mohammed S. 2010. The sociolinguistics of Nigerian Pidgin English in selected university campuses. *Ife Studies in English Language* 8(1), 50–60.

Adegbija, Efurosibina. 2004. *Multilingualism: A Nigerian case study*. Asmara: Africa World Press.

Adegbite, Wale. 2010. English language usage, uses and misuse(s) in a non-host second language context, Nigeria. *Inaugural lecture series 231*. Ile-Ife: Obafemi Awolowo university press.

Akande, Akinmade T. 2008. *The verb in standard Nigerian English and Nigerian Pidgin English: A sociolinguistic approach*. Leeds: University of Leeds PhD dissertation.

Akande, Akinmade T. 2012. *Globalization and English in Africa: Evidence from Nigerian hip-hop*. New York: Nova Science Publishers.

Akande, Akinmade. T. 2016. Multilingual practices in Nigeria army barracks. *African Identities* 14(1), 38–58.

Akande, Akinmade T. & Oladipo L. Salami. 2010. Use and attitudes towards Nigerian Pidgin English among Nigerian University students. In Robert M. Millar (ed.), *Marginal dialects: Scotland, Ireland and beyond*, 70–89. Aberdeen: Forum for Research on the Languages of Scotland and Ireland.

Amao, Temitope. 2012. The use of Pidgin English as a medium of social discourse among Osun State University students. *African Nebula* 5, 43–51.

Babalola, Adesoji. 2017. On the nature of syntactic complexity in Nigerian Pidgin: The example of the clause. *Madonna Journal of English and Literary Studies* 2(10), 76–89.

Babalola, Adesoji. 2018. *Tense and aspect in Standard Nigerian English, Waffi and Lagos Pidgin English*. Ile-Ife: Obafemi Awolowo University PhD dissertation.

Babalola, Adesoji. 2019. Twitter and language globalisation: The case of Nigerian Pidgin. In Innocent Chiluwa & Gwen Bouvier (eds.), *Twitter: Global perspective, uses and research technique*, 243–265. USA: Nova Science Publishers.

Balogun, Temitope A. 2013. In defense of Nigerian Pidgin. *Journal of Languages and Culture* 4 (5), 90–98.

Bamgbose, Ayo. 1982. Standard Nigerian English: Issues of identification. In Braj Kachru (ed.), *The other tongue: English across cultures*, 99–111. Urbana: University of Illinois Press.

Bergh, Gunnar. 2011. Football is war: A case study of minute-by-minute football commentary. *Veredas Tematical Linguistics* 2(5), 83–93.

Bokamba, Eyamba G. 1991. West Africa. In Jenny Cheshire (ed.), *English around the world: sociolinguistics perspectives*, 493–508. Cambridge: Cambridge University Press.

Bruce, Toni. 2013. Reflections on communication and sport: On women and femininities. *Communication and Sport* 1(1–2): 125–137.

Chapanga, Evans. 2004. An analysis of the war metaphors used in spoken commentaries of the 2004 edition of the Premier Soccer League (PSL) matches in Zimbabwe. *Zambezia* 31, 62–79.

Carrington, Ben & Ian McDonald. 2001. Introduction: Race, sport and British society. In Ben Carrington & Ian McDonald (eds.), *Race, sport, and British society*, 1–26. London: Routledge.

Deuber, Dagmar. 2005. *Nigerian Pidgin in Lagos: Language contact, variation and change in an African urban setting*. London: Battlebridge.

Durodola, Olufunke T. 2013. *The Rising Popularity of Pidgin English Radio Stations in Nigeria: An audience study of Wazobia FM, Lagos*. Grahamstown: Rhodes University MA dissertation.

Egbokhare, Francis. 2003. The story of a language: Nigerian Pidgin in spatiotemporal, social and linguistic context. In Peter Lucko, Lothar Peter & Hans-Georg Wolf (eds.), *Studies in African varieties of English*, 21–40. Frankfurt am Main: Peter Lang.

Elugbe, Ben & Augusta P. Omamor. 1991. *Nigerian Pidgins: Background and prospects*. Ibadan: Heinemann.

Faraclas, Nicholas. 1991. The pronoun system in Nigerian Pidgin: A preliminary study. In J. Cheshire (ed.), *English around the world: Sociolinguistics perspective*, 509–518. Cambridge: Cambridge University Press.

Faraclas, Nicholas. 1996. *Nigerian Pidgin*. London: Routledge.

Faraclas, Nicholas. 2004. Nigerian Pidgin English: Morphology and syntax. In Bernd Kortman, Kate Burridge, Rajend Mesthrie, Edgar W. Schneider & Clive Upton (eds.), *A handbook of varieties of English 2*, 828–853. New York: De Gruyter Mouton.
Ferguson, Charles A. 1983. Sports announcer talk: Syntactic aspects of register variation. *Language in Society* 12(2), 153–172.
France, M. N. 1976. Metalanguage and category acquisition. *Philosophy and Phenomenological Research* 37(2), 165–180.
Halliday, Michael Alexander K. 1985. *An introduction to functional grammar*. London: Edward Arnold Ltd.
Igboanusi, Herbert. 2008. Empowering Nigerian Pidgin: A challenge for status planning. *World Englishes* 27(1), 68–82.
Ihemere, Kelechukwu U. 2006. A basic description and analytical treatment of noun clauses in Nigerian Pidgin. *Nordic Journal of African Studies* 15(3), 296–313.
Jakobson, Roman. 1985. Metalanguage as a linguistic problem. In Stephen Rudy (ed.), *Selected writing*, 113–121. New York: Mouton.
Mair, Christian. 2016. Beyond and between "Three circles": World Englishes research in the age of globalization. In Elena Seoane & Cristina Suarez-Gomez (eds.), *World Englishes: New theoretical and methodological considerations*, 17–36. Amsterdam/Philadelphia: John Benjamins.
Mazzoli, Marco. 2017. Language nativisation and ideologies in Ajegunle (Lagos). *Language and Communication* 52, 88–101.
Mensah, Eyo. 2011. Lexicalization in Nigerian Pidgin. *Concentric: Studies in Linguistics* 37(2), 209–240.
Mensah, Eyo. 2012. Grammaticalization in Nigerian Pidgin. *Ikala, revista de lenguaje y cultura* 17(2), 167–179.
Moore, Jason & Mary Schleppegrell. 2014. Using a functional linguistics metalanguage to support academic language development in the English language Arts. *Linguistics and Education*, 26, 72–105.
Mowarin, Macaulay. 2007. A contrastive analysis of mood and aspect in English and Nigerian Pidgin. *A Journal of the Faculty of Arts, Delta State University Abraka* 2(1), 44–57.
Mowarin, Macauley. 2012. Question-word interrogatives in Nigerian Pidgin. *The Journal of the Linguistic Association of Nigeria* 15(1&2), 95–104.
Müller, Torsten 2007. Football, language and linguistics: Time-critical utterances in unplanned spoken language, their structures and their relation to non-linguistic situations and events *Language in performance* 36. Tübingen: Gunter Narr.
Levin, Magnus. 2008 Hitting the back of the net just before the final whistle: High- frequency phrases in football reporting. In Eva Lavric, Gerhard Pisek, Andrew Skinner & Wolfgang Stadler (eds.) *The linguistics of football*, 143–156. Tübingen: Gunter Narr.
Ofulue, Christine I. 2004. Creolization in Nigerian Pidgin: A sociocultural perspective. In Segun Awonusi & E. Babalola (eds.), *The domestication of English in Nigeria*, 265–279. Lagos: University of Lagos Press.
Osakwe, Mabel & Macaulay Mowarin. 2010. The internal structure of the noun phrase in Naija. *Conference proceeding on Nigerian Pidgin*, University of Ibadan, Nigeria.
Osisanwo, Ayo. 2012. A morphological analysis of Nigerian Pidgin: The example of selected advertisement jingles. *The Journal of the Linguistic Association of Nigeria* 15(1&2), 41–54.

Osoba, Sola. 2004. Word-formation processes in English and Nigerian Pidgin. In Segun Awonusi & E. Babalola (eds.), *The domestication of English in Nigeria*, 231–247. Lagos: University of Lagos Press.

Palmer, Frank R. 1976. *Semantics*. Cambridge: Cambridge University Press.

Peeters, Rens. & Jacco Sterkenburg V. 2017. Making sense of race/ethnicity and gender in televised football: Reception research among British students. *Sport in Society* 20(5&6), 701–715.

Schleppegrell, Mary. 2013. The role of metalanguage in supporting academic language development. *Language Learning* 63(1), 153–170.

Whannel, Garry. 1992. *Fields in vision: Television sport and cultural transformation*. London: Routledge.

Wilson, Shomir. 2013. Toward automatic processing of English metalanguage. *International Joint Conference on Natural Language processing, Nagoya, Japan, 2013*, 760–766.

Winthrop, Henry. 1945. Metalypsis and paradox in the concept of metalanguage. *The Philosophical Review* 54(6), 607–610.

Oluwabunmi O. Oyebode
Chapter 10
A social semiotic investigation of Nigerian Pidgin in select Nigerian church posters

Introduction

Nigerian Pidgin (henceforth NP) as opined by Osoba (2014a: 26) is "the fastest growing common language in Nigeria today". The extensive neutral role it plays in Nigeria (Akande, 2010) has enabled it to enjoy the attention of many Nigerians over the years. Its ability to aptly encode different interpretations of experience and forms of social interaction many Nigerian citizens can relate to despite their ethnic differences (Adegbija, 2004; Balogun, 2013) has also enhanced its acceptability among Nigerians. NP is noted to have the widest currency among Nigerians from diverse ethnic and linguistic backgrounds and this currency has been shown in all walks of life in Nigeria such as the language of media advertising (Mensah and Ndimele, 2013; Dalamu, 2017); and political campaigns (Opeibi, 2007; Osoba, 2014b). Religion is also an important aspect of Nigeria life whereby the currency of NP has been reflected (see Osoba, 2014a). In Christianity for instance, though English is the major medium used for church service in most urban centres (Bamgbose, 1995; Adegbija, 2004), the Nigerian church space is not a protected one reserved for English language alone as it is in Ghana (Frimpong, 2012). Unlike Ghana where Ghanaian Pidgin is heavily stigmatized (Huber, 1999; Dako, 2002), NP is a welcome language across Nigerian states even in Christian worship service.

In Nigeria, NP is used in conjunction with other indigenous languages, depending on the geographical location of the church, to include, solidarise and show cordiality with members of the congregation (see Frimpong, 2012; Balogun, 2013). Since language carries a functional load in religion, NP plays a vital role in church activities in Nigeria. It is a means of communicating and disseminating religious values, doctrines and teachings in the Church (Reinecke, 1964). As a marker of identity and solidarity (see Akande, 2008), NP enables Christians from different ethnic backgrounds to congregate together, interact and communicate easily without any language barrier. Hence, NP as used within the Christian circle can be described as an "intervening variable" (Awonusi, 2007: 86). It is deliberately deployed by church leaders to accommodate the different ethnical composition of their congregation members, persuade them as well as enhance functional/effective communication (see Balogun, 2013; Dalamu, 2017) in the church. As such, the choice of NP within the church setting is unique and purposeful. It is used in a specific way by religious leaders to give the congregation members a sense of belonging.

Christianity is one of the major religions in Nigeria. There are over 80 million Nigerians who are Christians (see Adegbija, 2004). It thrives on the footstool of language and all its various aspects use language deliberately and specifically to achieve a particular goal. Studies have identified that each of the genres of Christian worship such as prayers, sermons, Bible studies, church programme posters/bulletins, invocations and other ritual forms has highly distinctive discourse features (Taiwo, 2007). This means religious communications differ linguistically and may be characterised by variations along lexico-semantic dimensions (see Samarin, 1976). In sermons for instance, some statements are made to re-assure, challenge, judge, or inspire while others simply demand humility and submission from believers (Oshitelu, 1995). In other religious texts, like posters used to advertise church programmes, religious text producers also deploy language and other communicative resources deliberately for a purpose (Odoemenam, Ordu, and Omoghie, 2017). Through different discursive strategies such as anecdotes, gradation, rhetorical devices, (Ikupa, 2002) as well as the use of media multilingualism such as NP, indigenous languages, images, colours, gestures among others Christian leaders persuade and control the minds of their followers. They achieve this by deploying language and other communicative resources in a specific way to foreground certain religious and ideological worldviews Nigerian masses can relate with.

The use of linguistic facilities by Christian leaders in modern Nigeria is on the rise recently because Nigerian masses are perpetually in search of relief from their sordid existential realities (Magbadelo, 2004). To most Nigerians, religion is a means of inviting the intervention of the divine and celestial in the affairs of human beings (Magbadelo, 2004); as a result, religion occupies a central domain in their consciousness. Since the current socio-economic realities in Nigeria are not favourable to average Nigerians, many Christian leaders leverage on these socio-economic problems to creatively use language as a persuasive weapon to win followers/members to attend their programmes/crusades. They are usually intentional in their choice of codes and words to reflect and convey messages that resonate with the masses in the design of their various programmes (see Adetuyi and Patrick, 2019). Like sign-makers, according to "Kress and van Leeuwen (2006: 13), they choose forms for the expression of what they have in mind, forms which they see as most apt and plausible in the given context". Thus the meanings they convey with their words are identified by their immediate social, political and historical conditions (McGregor, 2003).

Although the heterogeneity of the Nigerian state has necessitated the adoption of the English language as the language of worship in Christian religion, the reality is that the language has been nativised and pidginised (Bamgbose, 1995; Adegbija, 2004) by religious practitioners to project their belief systems, values and relate with one another. Nigerian Pidgin is however favoured in Christianity because of its ability to meet the linguistic needs of many members of the church congregation. Therefore factors such as, linguistic diversity, different levels of educational background of the members of the congregation and the need to reach a wider audience serve as the reason why many Christian leaders choose NP to deliver their sermons. Thus, the ethnic-neutrality of NP has given it the capacity to carry everyone along.

Many Sociolinguistic studies (Bamgbose, 1995; Deuber, 2005; Chiluwa, 2007) have touched on the role of NP as one of the favoured languages in Christian activities in Nigeria, adequate attention has not been paid to its social semiotic significance as a semiotic mode used to interrogate religious and ideological issues that resonate with Nigerian masses in church programme posters.

1 Church programme posters as publicity media

Christianity is a religion that propagates and disseminates information conventionally referred to as 'the gospel.' In a bid to fulfil Christ's command "Go ye into all the world and preach the gospel to every creature" (Mark 16: vs. 15KJV), the church engages in various activities in their interpretations of this instruction. They come up with different initiatives such as going out for evangelism to preach the gospel, organising revivals and crusades among other programmes, to set people free from demonic attacks and bondage as well as to ensure spiritual liberation from the hold of satanic forces (Magbadelo, 2004: 19). As such, different media of communication are utilised by the church to publicise their programmes and invite people to these programmes. The church in Nigeria has perfected the art of public communication by using various media platforms to popularise their programmes and miracle claims (Magbadelo, 2004).

Posters are one of these media platforms the church utilises in the propagation of her programmes. As Ajayi (2005) opines, posters are a form of outdoor advertising done in the open air to display and expose a product to the public with a view to drawing attention to them and creating potential consumers. They are one of the preferred media of communication used for publicity because of their ability to enhance the cognitive mobilization of the public. This particular attribute has made it possible for the church to propagate the 'gospel' and other related programmes. Their pervasive nature to fill the public space disabling any escape from it (Molina, 2006) is also an important feature that has made them a welcome media outlet to publicise church activities.

Certain socio-economic factors have greatly influenced the uniqueness of posters as outdoor advertising in Nigeria. Among those factors are epileptic power supply, poverty, ethnicity and illiteracy. This aligns with Seidman's (2008: 2) submission that "today, illiteracy remains high in many countries, making it particularly appropriate to employ posters with prominent visuals in them". This has made it remain a vital communicative channel for publicity in Nigeria. Also, unlike other media mix like the television, radio, print, social media and cinema where exposure is contingent upon ownership or subscription fee, posters as a form of outdoor advertising give an involuntary opportunity to the public to see and this makes them the most accessible and simplest form of advertising as people do not have to pay to see them. Similarly, their longevity in the public space as well as the semiotic and visual representations deployed on them has qualified them to be one of the preferred media the church uses for the publicity of their programmes.

Posters are usually in the form of handbills, placards, banners, and sign boards etc., printed with large symbols, pictures, images and texts to communicate specific information to the public. They are non-verbal communication used by many institutions to meet the needs of various categories of people (Faleke, Abaya, and Ahamed, 2016). Thus, the church finds them apt for the propagation of the gospel. Church posters are unique in their design as all the semiotic resources such as images, colour-mix, language, symbols, signs among others, deployed on them are specifically for representation to reflect the sociocultural context of the church in question as well as address certain themes of appeal that can cognitively engage the Nigerian public. This is in tandem with "Kress and van Leeuwen's (2006: 13) submission that sign-makers choose forms for the expression of what they have in mind, forms which they see as most apt and most plausible in the given context".

Church posters can, therefore, be described as a form of religious discourse that deploys language and other semiotic resources strategically to pass across specific messages to the general public. One of such semiotic resources that is uniquely utilised for a specific purpose is 'Nigerian Pidgin.' However, in spite of plethora literature that exists on religious discourse, much attention has not been paid to the semiotic significance of this language (NP) in Pentecostal Church posters. Many of the studies have focused on the English language as the medium of communication (Keane, 1997; Osakwe, 1991; Daramola, 2006; Chiluwa, 2007; Odebunmi, 2007; Ugot and Offiong, 2013; Taiwo, 2015; Anyawu, Njemanze and Ononiwu, 2016) using sermons, prayers, speeches, songs, etc., as their data corpus.

The closest works to this study are Olowu's (2013) multimodal study of Christian magazines, Babatunde and Aremu's (2016) pragmatic study of conceptual metaphor in Nigerian Christian tracts, Odoemenam, Ordu and Omoghie's (2017) lexico-semantic interpretation of Pentecostal Church posters and Adetuyi and Patrick's (2019) stylistic analysis of selected Christian religion print advertisement in Ibadan metropolis. Olowu (2013) examines the Christians' perception of death and judgement as projected in selected editions of Christian Women Mirror Magazines of the Deeper Christian Life Ministry using multimodal discourse analysis framework. The study reveals that death is not the end of man as some semiotic indices (verbal and visual) depict through the discourse that there is an aftermath 'judgement' when any human exits this world. Through the semiotic resources deployed in the magazines, the author unraveled certain underlying meanings that depict the belief system upheld about death in Christianity. This is related to the present study as it deploys a social semiotic framework to examine certain belief systems germane to Christians. Babatunde and Aremu examined the use of conceptual metaphors in Christian tracts as a genre of Christian religious discourse used to propagate the gospel with a view to facilitating the understanding of their implicit meanings. The study is related to the present study as it used tracts, a print media as its data. Odoemenam, Ordu and Omoghie examined the lexico-semantic choices in the Pentecostal church posters with a view to revealing that the construction of church posters is a linguistically conscious activity which has impact on the readers/audience. The study is related to this study as it used handbills and posters as its data. Lastly, Adetuyi and Patrick investigated some religious advertisements with a view to determining how meaning is stylistically indexed in religious discourse. All these studies, though used different forms of advertising media as their database like the present study, they differ significantly from this study because they focused mainly on the role of English language in Christian faith to elicit patronage.

This study, therefore, examines the use of Nigerian Pidgin (NP) as a motivated semiotic resource in church special programme posters. Church special programmes are church activities that do not feature as part of the regular church services but which are planned and targeted towards meeting specific needs of the church members (and people from the society) at intervals. They are, therefore, considered semiotic medium in which semiotic resources such as NP, images, colour, etc., are appropriated to foster information dissemination, public engagement and persuasion.

1.1 Nigerian Pidgin as a semiotic resource in church programme posters

NP is a common alternative where there is no shared indigenous language and its usefulness has been recognised by many Nigerians (Deuber, 2005) across different social contexts. The import of NP in Christian worship cannot be overemphasized as the Nigerian church congregation is usually a mixed multitude in terms of culture, gender, ethnic groups and education. Church leaders therefore, always strive to choose a variety that is common to all members of their congregation to deliver their sermons in an inclusive manner. This reiterates "Deuber's (2005: 49) submission that Christian religious practice is one of the formal domains where indigenous languages and Pidgin (NP) have been able to make significant inroads".

Today, especially in urban centres, NP seems to be a preferred variety in church activities and programmes. As Osoba (2014a: 26) posits, "Pidgin is the common language of the city people who come from diverse socio-cultural and linguistic backgrounds". Since people of different ethnic backgrounds congregate in the church, NP is used to preclude the church and its leadership from being elitist, promote Christianity as a religion of inclusiveness, show endearment and friendliness and identify with the people (see Adegbija, 2004). NP therefore, plays a significant role in the Nigerian church as many Church leaders deploy it to communicate specific meanings that resonate with Nigerians.

As such, beyond solving the problem of multilingualism, NP, within the context of Christianity in Nigeria, has a social semiotic significance as its choice is contingent on the specific meaning the poster producers intend to convey to the public. Following the words of van Leeuwen (2005), NP as used in the context of church programme posters which is the fulcrum of this study, can be described as a social semiotic resource deployed as signifiers to communicate specific meanings. According to van Leeuwen (2005: 4)

> . . . social semiotic resources are signifiers, observable actions and objects that have been drawn into the domain of social communication and that have a theoretical semiotic potential constituted by all and their past uses and all their potential uses and an actual semiotic potential constituted by those past uses that are known and considered relevant by the users of the resource, and by such potential uses as might be uncovered by the users on the basis of their specific needs and interests.

This paper extends the existing studies on NP (Frimpong, 2012; Balogun, 2013; Osoba, 2014a, 2014b; Umera-Okeke and Okitikpi, 2017) to religious context to explore different affordances of meaning the language (NP) is used for in church posters.

2 Theoretical orientation

Van Leeuwen's (2005) approach to Social Semiotics serves as the theoretical underpinning for this study. It is characterised by two main terms which are 'semiotic potential' and 'affordance'. The approach takes 'anything' humans do or make as a semiotic resource capable of being deployed to project articulation of different social and cultural meanings. For instance, the art of walking which is seen as non-semiotic behaviour, basic locomotion common to every human and some other lower animals could be used as a semiotic resource depending on the social context of usage. Across different social institutions such as army, church, bridal train, and the fashion industry, people have developed their own special, ceremonial ways of walking. This is because, we express who we are, what we do and how we want others to relate to us through the way we way. Hence walking can function as a semiotic resource due to different affordances of meaning it possesses (see van Leeuwen, 2005). According to him, a given type of physical activity or that of material artefact constitutes a semiotic resource and as such it is possible to describe its semiotic potential for meaning–making. The term 'affordance' which is closely related to semiotic potential is concerned with the potential uses of a given object. It is about meanings that have not yet been recognized, that lie, as it were, latent in the object, waiting to be discovered.

Such meanings, however, could be made at different levels which are: representational, interactive and compositional levels respectively. Thus, the approach proposes that studying the semiotic potential of a given resource is studying how that resource has been, is, and can be used for purposes of communication. It is drawing up an inventory of past and present and maybe also future resources and their uses. Usually, such inventories are never complete, because they tend to be made for specific purposes. This reiterates Kress' (1993: 174) position that "all signs are [. . .] equally subject to critical reading', given the fact that 'no sign is innocent." Each sign used for meaning-making has a critical dimension whereby it has been specifically deployed to convey a particular message within the context of use. This is what this study proposes as regards the use of NP in the church posters. The study explores different semiotic potential and affordances of meaning NP has been specifically utilised for in church special programme posters. It investigates the new uses of NP as a social semiotic construct in the context of religious discourse in Nigeria.

3 Data for the study

The data for the study, made up of both verbal and non-verbal semiotic resources, were purposively sampled from a pool of forty church posters uploaded and circulated online by Nigerian netizens. Of these forty data samples, eight posters in which NP is overtly deployed as the anchor code to construe religious meaning and persuade people to attend the advertised church programmes were analysed. Although these posters were initially hung in the public space across the nation, their electronic forms were uploaded online by Nigerian netizens as a result of the peculiarities in their designs. Therefore, the data were shared on social media platforms such as Facebook, Twitter, and Nairaland to project and criticise how Nigerian church leaders/owners utilise semiotic resources in their posters to woo the masses to attend their church programmes. These data samples are labelled in Arabic figure: Figures 1–8. The study adopts van Leeuwen's (2005) Social Semiotic approach as the theoretical orientation for the analysis of the data. The theoretical orientation is deemed appropriate for this study because it provides a descriptive framework for investigating different semiotic potential and affordances of meaning NP has been utilised for in church programme posters.

4 Analysis and discussions

This section analyses the selected church posters in which NP has been deployed to communicate religious meanings that resonate with the public. The analysis indicates that NP serves as discourse construct deployed to foreground three dominant issues that permeate the Christian worldviews which are: (a) engagement of the African worldview; (b) invitation of the divine intervention in the affairs of human beings; and (c) framing problem-solving and promotion of a message of hope and deliverance from satanic oppressions. The data analysis of this study is therefore carried out along these three main categories.

4.1 Nigerian Pidgin as a semiotic resource for engaging the ideology of spiritual oppression

Designers of church special programme posters usually deploy semiotic resources to interrogate certain belief systems within the African context as an emotive appeal to persuade and invite people to their programmes. One of the semiotic resources deployed in such instances to give a Nigerian flavour to the discourse and identify with the predicament of the people is the use of NP. It is commonplace in the African worldview to attribute ill luck to some forces of evil that usually pose threats to people preventing them from making it in life. This is an ideological stance that most African cultures believe in. Thus we can label it the ideology of 'using spiritual powers against another/ spiritual oppression' (**emphasis mine**). Randy (2012: 217) submits that "spiritual powers threaten the supreme value of well-being and subvert it." Thus, the ideology of 'being oppressed by a higher power' is prevalent in the Nigerian culture and the church leverages on this to design their special programme posters in a persuasive manner to woo people to attend such programmes in order to secure their liberation.

There is a conjecture of this ideological worldview in Figure 1 below as the text producer deploys NP as a semiotic resource to strategically conceptualise the masses' ordeals in the hand of a 'super force' that is more powerful than they are and making their lives miserable.

Figure 1: Na You Dey Do Me? (Projection of Spiritual Oppression in Pidgin).

The text: "WETIN I DO YOU, NA YOU DEY DO ME? YOU GO DIE O . . . ABI YOU WON CRAYS", is a combination of both interrogative and declarative statements respectively used to challenge the prevailing situation. The text producer uses the dialogue style of writing as a reactional process (see Kress and Leeuwen, 2006) to depict a sense of revolt and rebellion against the status quo. Two major social actors (van Leeuwen, 1996) are projected in the text: the oppressed and the oppressor. While the first person singular pronoun 'I' is used to represent the oppressed, the second person singular pronoun 'You' is used to represent the oppressor. Thus, there is a depiction of power relations in the text to project the ideological stance of oppression. This is a subtle emotive appeal to the psychology of the masses to instigate them to seek liberation and deliverance from their oppressor by deciding to attend the programme tagged 'One Month Morning Breakthrough', which is suggestive of a solution centre to the problem(s) facing them.

The use of pronouns 'I' and 'You' in the text is to personalise the social actors and construct the socio-cultural reality of the represented participants. This is further reiterated by the use of NP as a social semiotic construct in the text to depict reality and identify with the target audience's predicament. The choice of NP as a code in the context of the text, despite the fact that other information is in the English language, is apt and plausible in the given context as it suggests that meaning is motivated. The code suggests the location of the poster which may be somewhere in the South-south region of the country as well as the probable set of people living in the environment who may be a mixture of literate and non-literate people.

Suggesting a sense of identification with the ordeal of the persona, the text producer aggressively projects the frustration of the represented participant through a rhetorical question, "WETIN I DO YOU, NA YOU DEY DO ME?" (What did I do to you, are you the one responsible for my problem?). This is to connote a sense of urgency and keep the masses on their toes. Thus the represented participant is presented in the text as sounding a note of warning that he/she has had enough from the oppressor and that he/she is ready for his/her liberation and deliverance. The desire for liberation is instantiated in the declarative and interrogative statements, 'YOU GO DIE O . . . ABI YOU WON CRAYS.' (You will die . . . or you want to run crazy). These statements indicate the height of intolerance the represented participant now has for the 'evil force' that has hitherto repressed, exploited and subjected him/her to sordid existential realities. This is suggestive of the kind of response the text producer wants her audience to have against the oppressor by deciding to attend the programme so as to be liberated. The lexical choices, 'die' and 'crays' are discursive strategies used as negative connotations to portray violence and declare war on the oppressed.

Therefore, beyond being used as a code for communication, the choice of NP in Figure 1 has an affordance of meaning. It is a social semiotic strategy cryptic with meaning as it is used to construct socio-cultural realities – an African ideology of being tormented by 'superior powers' – of the target audience in the context of the text and identify with their ordeals so as to persuade them to attend the special programme. A similar situation is projected in Figure 2 below.

Figure 2: Uncle Wetin I Do You? (Constructing a Socio-cultural milieu in Pidgin).

The interrogative statement in Figure 2 above is also a subtle way of engaging the African worldview, the ideological stance of being oppressed by a 'higher power.' This is a pervasive ideology in the consciousness of an average Nigerian. Thus an average Nigerian is usually on the quest to proffer solution to this societal problem.

In the Christian world, especially Pentecostalism, this 'higher power' that poses a threat to the general well-being of the people is usually clothed in human body and can manifest through anybody; be it one's mother/father, uncle, aunt, daughter/son, mother-in-law/father-in-law or even one's friend. Therefore, it is possible for both men and women to manipulate forces of darkness in the celestial realm to perpetrate evil in the physical world. Figure 3 below corroborates this submission.

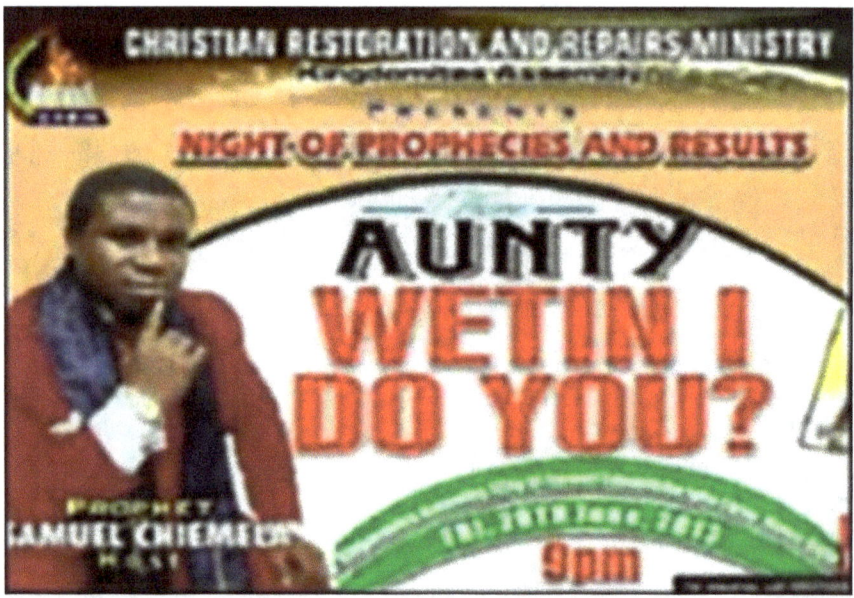

Figure 3: Aunty Wetin I Do You? (Constructing a Socio-cultural milieu in Pidgin).

The statement, "AUNTY WETIN I DO YOU?", in Figure 3 is an interrogative used as a reactional process to query the status quo. This is similar to the message conveyed in Figure 2.

However, while Figure 2 portrays uncle as the oppressor in the context of the text, Figure 3 portrays aunty as the oppressor. Arguably, spiritual oppression in the Nigerian context is not sex bound. The most important thing is that, whosoever harbours this kind of evil power is one's enemy and such person must be fought with every weapon at one's disposal.

The supernatural that manifests in human flesh is analogous to what van Dijk (1998: 256) refers to as "'delegitimated Other' in his concept of ideological square.'" The operation of this 'delegitimated Other' who is represented as the represented participant's uncle in the text is negative, therefore, it must be vehemently resisted so that the represented participant can live the desired good life. The graphological representation of the word 'Uncle' in Figure 2 carries a meaning potential of a dominant power who as a matter of fact is oppressing the persona as the first person singular pronoun 'I' used to represent the oppressed could hardly be seen in the text. This reiterates the notion of power dominance which projects the ideological stance of oppression. Hence, the layout of the text confirms the ideology of spiritual oppression in the text.

The use of 'uncle' in NP does not necessarily imply a blood relation as used in Nigerian English. Usually, the word 'uncle' is used to refer to any male adult that is older than someone. Hence, the way the word is used in the text may not imply that the 'uncle' is a close relation; he may just be someone in a position of authority or an elderly neighbour of the persona 'I' in the text. NP, therefore, is a strategy deployed to portray the socio-cultural orientation of the target audience as well as construct the ideological stance of oppression as an African order which may not be a shared belief system in other climes especially in the West. Hence through the presentation of this belief in a more general variety that is common to all ethnic groups in Nigeria, there seems to be a tone of shared belief system as far as the ideology of ' using spiritual powers against another/ spiritual oppression' is concerned. Arguably, the semantic significance of using NP as a variety in the text goes beyond making the message accessible to the general populace but also serves as a discourse construct to project a socio-cultural reality. It is used to project a world view or outlook collectively shared by a social group. The same submission holds for the notion of 'aunty' in Figure 3.

4.2 Nigerian Pidgin as a semiotic resource for inviting divine intervention

Most Nigerians believe in the reality of demonic oppressions, therefore, they see religion as a means of inviting the intervention of the divine and celestial in their affairs (Magbadelo, 2004). No matter how powerful a demon or deity is, the general belief in the Christian faith is that the God Almighty (the God of the Bible) is superior and has the ultimate power to disarm such a god/deity. It is believed that God is the creator of everything, including man and deities. Therefore, there is a perceived belief that he intervenes in their affairs when called upon. This supernatural intervention is one of the pillars of Christian faith and it has produced a strong attraction for the Nigerian masses that are under one bondage or the other seeking to be liberated or get their conditions improved. Figure 4 below reveals this worldview as the represented participants beckon on God for his intervention in their present predicament.

Figure 4: Na Like This We Go Dey? (Seeking divine intervention through Pidgin).

Figure 4 is an overt call. The interrogative statement, 'OH GOD NA LIKE THIS WE GO DEY?,' presupposes a dismal situation and a cry that shows helplessness from the represented social actor – the oppressed. Though the oppressor is not definite nor mentioned in the text like what we have in Figures 1, 2 & 3 above, the tone of the discourse instantiates a negative and unpleasant situation under a supposed 'task master' higher and mightier than the represented participants. The perceived oppressor is no match for the represented participants, therefore they have to reach out to the superior God who has the unsurpassable power to take charge of difficult situation, liberate and deliver them.

The use of NP to beckon on God in the text is a social semiotic resource used for interactive meaning. Through the choice of NP to express frustration and seek help, the text producer conveys an interactive meaning of a "personal message" (Kress and van Leeuwen, 2001: 121) to the supreme God. "Just as handwriting is used as a semiotic resource in advertising to address members of an audience as unique individuals . . . (Kress and van Leeuwen, 2001: 121)", the text producer presents the represented social actor, the oppressed, as unique individuals who can freely reach out to God for divine intervention in their predicament. Hence, the choice of NP conveys an affective tone which religious language is known for (see Donovan, 1976).

Language use by people in religion is pivotal to the expression of their emotion. People usually go emotional when they are in a state of desperation in the religious circle, as a result, they prefer to commune with God in the language that is natural and indigenous to them rather than using a foreign language, e.g. the English language, in which they have limited vocabulary. NP is wittily used as a code in the text in conjunction with the choice of rhetorical question, 'OH GOD NA LIKE THIS WE GO DEY?' to identify with certain sociological problems working against human beings, especially Africans. Through these semiotic resources, the text producer is able to create an ideological stance of being aware of the problems the masses are battling with and in a way challenging them to rise up to the task and get their deliverance. This is conveyed through the imperative statement, 'Pray Until Something Happen.' To an average Nigerian, prayer means presenting a catalogue of problems for God to solve (see Mbefo, 2001). Therefore Nigerians seek divine intervention of God through prayers in order to positively improve their fortune.

Given the above, it can be inferred from the text that the church is trying to address those issues of life that have hitherto plagued the masses; subjecting them to demonic oppression and making their lives miserable. By using a tone of 'personal message' technique, which is captured in the first person plural pronoun 'WE,' they are able to give the target audience a sense of belonging and identification which could be classified as 'inclusion' (see van Leeuwen, 1996). The use of declarative statement 'Festival of Fire' with the visual representation of fire and the representation of a man whose facial expression is that of "offer" (Kress and van Leeuwen, 2006: 121) further reiterates the social semiotic significance of a 'call to wake up from slumber' and seek divine help as a way of escape from helplessness. This could only be achieved however (as suggested in the text) by attending the advertised special programme.

A similar situation is depicted in Figure 5 below. Although the tone depicted here does not make an outright call to God, the represented participant also expresses a critical state of affairs (frustration) which could only be resolved by divine intervention.

Figure 5: I Don Taya (Venting anger through Pidgin).

The deployment of NP as a resource in the text makes the message conveyed more forceful and personal. The declarative statement, 'I Don Taya for this NONSENSE', is more of an exclamation which the represented social actor, the oppressed, specially utilises to vent his anger and show exasperation. The statement means 'I'm fed up with the present situation' in the English language but to identify with the predicament of the target audience and suggest how to respond to their problems, the text producer employs a more culturally flavoured code, NP which is an ethnic-neutral language that has the capacity to carry everybody along than the English language.

The use of first person singular pronoun 'I' gives a tone of inclusion as we have in Figure 4 and depicts a search for a way of escape which could only come to reality through divine intervention. Thus, Figures 4 and 5 depict the affordance of meaning of NP as it is used in the church posters to instantiate that the kind of relationship that exists between humans and God could be personal; that God is approachable and accommodating; and that through the choice of a particular language the church can create a sense of inclusion and identification with the masses' predicaments so as to help them find solutions to them.

4.3 Nigerian Pidgin as a semiotic resource for framing problem-solution appeal

Generally, the search for solution to different socio-economic problems and survival has enticed many people to Christianity in Nigeria. Since the church is aware of these myriad of socio-economic problems, different frames are creatively deployed on special programme posters in Nigeria as persuasive strategies to convey messages of hope, deliverance and solutions to those challenges of life the masses are confronted with. Although frame is a media/advertising technique that is commonplace in political communication (Scheufele and Iyengar 2012), it also plays a significant role in religious posters to create emotive appeals. In the data, we observe that poster producers use NP as frames to construct the ideology of problem-solving and promotion of message of hope and deliverance from satanic oppressions.

In Figure 6 the declarative statement (in Nigerian Pidgin), MY GARI DON – DONE!, is one of the problem-solving frames deployed across the data to construct an ideology of solution and hope to the masses. Randy (2012: 234) submits that "the promise of solutions to life problems is one of the major appeals of Pentecostalism" Therefore, Africans, most importantly, are in perpetual search for solutions to their problems. This is evident in Figure 6 as the frame 'MY GARI DON – DONE!' is used strategically to invoke a sense of solution to compelling socio-economic problems which are germane to many Nigerian masses.

The statement 'MY GARI DON – DONE!' is a positive declaration of absolute state of rest as far as the basic needs of life, food, shelter and clothing are concerned for an average human being to survive. This is a message of assurance projected in the text to the people about what the year 2013 holds for the people. Through this frame of solutions to life burdens, the represented participant subtly persuades the masses to identify with the church so that year 2013 can be smooth, free of life challenges. This view is further reiterated in the other linguistic resources used in the text. Through the phrase 'SETTLEMENT @ MOUNTAIN OF SOLUTION FIRE MINISTRY SOLUTION ASSEMBLY' and the imperative statement 'JOIN THE SOLUTION FAMILY', the represented participants confirms a frame of problem-solving at the advertised church which is initiated by the declarative statement in Pidgin, MY GARI DON – DONE!'

Figure 6: My Gari Don-Done! (Framing Problem-solution appeal in Pidgin).

The choice of Nigerian Pidgin to construct a problem-solving frame in the text is strategic to contextualise the issues that are germane to Nigerian masses, identify with them and construct a frame of better solution to those problems within the ambit of the church if the people identify with the church. Thus, the direct call 'Join the solution family.' Through the choice of NP as the code to open up the text, the represented participant is able to place a 'demand' on the masses to come for solutions to their socio-economic problems.

A similar situation is projected in Figure 7 below. However, while the problem-solving frame constructed in Figure 6 is that of solution to socio-economic problems, a frame of dominion and victory over Satan/Devil the perceived arch enemy of Christians is constructed in Figure 7.

The shared knowledge in Christianity, irrespective of the denomination is that Satan is in perpetual struggle as recorded in John (10:10) "to steal, kill and destroy" the children of God known as Christians. However, Christians usually operate in the perceived consciousness of the victory their Christ (Saviour) promised them in

Figure 7: Satan Your Own Don Finish (Framing Problem-solution appeal in Pidgin).

John (16: 33) " . . . be of good cheer for I have overcome . . . ." Therefore, the declarative statement, 'Satan your own don finish . . . ' is a problem-solving frame used to conjure a sense of victory and dominion. To assert what the Evangelical Ministry represents and offers the target audience, NP is used as a social semiotic resource in the text as an interactive meaning that portends viewers' power (Kress and van Leeuwen, 2006) over Satan. Viewer power is a sub-category of the attitudinal response of participants in examining interactive meaning in the social semiotic interrogation of texts. Therefore NP is used to give viewers an information value of the victory already at their disposal which is total destruction of their enemy – Satan. This is reinforced by using colour yellow to give salience to the message.

Figure 8 presents a problem-solving frame of 'favour'. The art of betting/gambling has been on the increase in the contemporary Nigeria. Many Nigerians engage in this art as a way to escape from abject poverty. The problems of mass unemployment, poor leadership, poor salaries and conditions of service, and mass poverty, could have caused many Nigerians to engage in this culture. Therefore some Nigerians see betting as a "quick fix" to come out of poverty. Betnaija is a Nigerian sport betting premier (web.betnaija.com) that many Nigerian sport fans, especially youth, engage in to win a huge sum of money. It is a form of gambling particularly focused on sporting activities in Nigeria. Since one episode of betting can change one's fortune overnight, some Nigerians who are desperate to win usually seek spiritual help in order to achieve their desired goal. This is premised on the fact that many Nigerians believe that everything is spiritual and as such they seek spiritual help and favour to summon their mountains.

Having understood this common ideology among the Nigerian betters, the church in Figure 8 below, cashes in on this need and uses it as a frame construct to invite the masses to their special programmes.

Figure 8: bet9ja (Pidgin and sport betting).

Through this frame the represented participant in the poster (the pastor) suggests that he could help betters get the right number that will make them win the game. This ideology is reiterated in some of the responses gotten online from the netizens which are:

a. *pastor abeg send me booking code, will pay after win.*
b. *nice one pastor bet9ja . . . Pls profesize and give us booking No's.*
c. *attract a dog with what he like, the dog will submit to your command, the pastor might have something vital for the people, and uses bet9ja as a centre of attraction.*
d. *listen. he said u should bet as in believe that Nigeria will favour you.* <https://www.gqbuzz.com/photo-of-the-day-what-is-wrong-with-this-church-poster-bet9ja-edition/>

The above submissions by netizens depict the perception of Nigerian betters about the vital role the celestial plays in winning the bet.

Although the word 'bet9ja' is the name of a sport betting premier in Nigeria, the word '9ja' is an acronym for 'naija', the NP variant of the word Nigeria. In the youth culture, the NP variant 'naija' is a preferred term used to discuss pressing issues facing common man in Nigeria. Thus, the NP '9ija' deployed by the pastor, the represented participant in the text, is used as a social semiotic resource for interactive meaning to portray 'intimate relationship' with Nigerian betters and depict some level of 'involvement' in their world. Therefore, the declarative statement 'bet9ja shall favour you' is a semiotic artefact used to depict what the pastor can offer his target audience. With the NP '9ija', the text producer is able to frame a problem-solution appeal to the target audience and create a message that resonates with Nigerian betters.

5 Conclusion

This study has interrogated the deployment of Nigerian Pidgin as semiotic strategies in Christian special programme posters in Nigeria to engage the African worldview of spiritual oppression, invite divine intervention in the affairs of human beings, and frame a problem-solution appeal to the target audience. NP is appropriated by Church poster producers to foster information dissemination, persuade the masses and interrogate religious issues that resonate with average Nigerians. The analysis shows the strategic appropriation of Nigerian Pidgin as a code for negotiating different layers of meaning as espoused by van Leeuwen's (2005) social semiotic approach to meaning-making in different sociocultural contexts. The text producers utilise different narrative processes to give salience to different ideological stances they attempt to engage and project in the texts. Through the investigation of Nigerian Pidgin as a semiotic resource in the context of religious discourse, we are able to unravel specific social structures and practices common in African cosmology. These socio-religious practices reflect the belief system of the posters' designers about Christianity in Nigeria.

The study reveals that the choice of a code as a semiotic resource in the realization of a text is purposive, political and ideological. Through the theoretical framework adopted for the study, we are able to discover that no semiotic resource should be taken ostensibly as ordinary in texts; they are couched to achieve specific social goals. Thus, this study has shown how NP has been utilised as a semiotic resource in Church special programme posters to depict different affordances of meaning within the socio-cultural contexts of use.

References

Adegbija, Efurosibina E. 2004. The domestication of English in Nigeria. In Segun Awonusi & E. A. Babalola (eds.), *The domestication of English in Nigeria: A festschrift in honour of Abiodun Adetigbo*, 20–39. Lagos: University Press.

Adetuyi, C. Ajibade & Patrick C. Alex. 2019. A stylistic analysis of selected Christian religion print advertisement in Ibadan metropolis, Oyo State. *International Journal of English Literature and Culture* 7(3), 40–48.

Ajayi, Olufemi B. 2005. *Understanding outdoor advertising*. Lagos, Nigeria: Fem Publicity Ltd.

Akande, Akinmade T. 2008. *The verb in Standard Nigerian English and Nigerian Pidgin English: A sociolinguistic approach*. Leeds: University of Leeds PhD dissertation.

Akande, Akinmade T. 2010. Is *Nigerian Pidgin English* English? *Dialectologia et Geolinguistica* 18(1), 3–22.

Anyanwu, Esther Chikaodi, Queen Njemanze Ugochi & Mark Chitulu Ononiwu. 2016. English usage pattern in Nigerian religious settings perspectives from selected worship centers in Imo State. *Journal of Humanities & Social Science* 21(6), 1–6.

Aremu, Moses Adebayo. 2013. Pragmatic presuppositions in tracts of Deeper Christian Life Ministry. *Papers in English and Linguistics* 14, 60–82.

Awonusi, Victor Olusegun. 2007. Invitation as style and discourse in Nigerian English Literature and Language. In Adeyemi Daramola & Olubukola Olugasa (eds.), *Literature and language: A drama of life: A festschrift in honor of Z. A. Adejumo*, 86–97. Lagos: BPrint.

Babatunde, Sola Timothy & Moses Aremu. 2016. A pragmatic study of conceptual metaphors in Nigerian Christian tracts. In Akin Odebunmi & Kehinde Ayoola (eds.), *Language, context and society: A festschrift for Wale Adegbite*, 129–148. Ile- Ife: Obafemi Awolowo University Press.

Balogun, Temitope Abiodun. 2013. In defense of Nigerian Pidgin. *Journal of Language and Culture* 4(5), 90–98.

Bamgbose, Ayo. 1995. English in the English environment. In Ayo Bamgbose, Ayo Banjo, Andrew Thomas & L. Ayo Banjo (eds.), *New Englishes*, 9–26. Ibadan: Mosuro Publishers.

Bruce, Ralph T. 1993. *An analysis of certain features of discourse in the New Testament book of 1Corinthians*. Arlington: University of Texas PhD dissertation.

Chiluwa, Innocent. 2007. English and the Church in Nigeria. *Kiabara: Journal of Humanities* 13(1), 51–63.

Dalamu, Taofeek. 2017. A functional approach to advertisement campaigns in Anglo-Nigerian Pidgin. *Studies in Linguistics* 44, 155–185.

Dako, Kari. 2002. Student Pidgin (SP): The language of the educated male elite. *Research Review* 18(2), 53–62.

Daramola, Adeyemi. 2006. Directions in creativity: A discourse analysis of church choruses in Nigeria. *UNAD Studies in Language and Literature* 2(1), 39–60.

Deuber, Dagmar. 2005. *Nigerian Pidgin in Lagos: Language contact, variation and change in an African urban setting*. London: Battlebridge.

Donovan, Peter. 1976. *Religious language*. London: Sheldon Press.

Faleke, Victoria O., Sheila A. Abaya, & A. Ahmed. 2016. The language of medical posters in Nigeria. In Akinola Odebunmi & Kehinde Ayoola (eds.), *Language, context and society: A festschrift for Wale Adegbite*, 309–332. Ile- Ife: Obafemi Awolowo University Press.

Frimpong, George Kodie. 2012. Pidgin English in Ghanaian churches. *Legon Journal of the Humanities*, 177–201.
Huber, Magnus. 1999. *Ghanaian Pidgin in its West African context. A socio-historical and structural analysis*. Amsterdam: John Benjamin.
Keane, Webb. 1997. Religious language. *Annual Review of Anthropology* 26, 47–71.
Kress, Gunther. 1993. Against arbitrariness: The social production of the sign as a functional issue in critical discourse analysis. *Discourse & Society* 4(2), 169–191.
Ikupa, Olusegun J. 2002. Strategies of discourse in religious texts. A paper presented at the English Language Teaching Today, Federal University of Technology, Akure, Nigeria, 2–5 October, 2002.
Kress, Gunther & Theo van Leeuwen. 2001. *Multimodal discourse: The modes and media contemporary communication*. London: Arnold.
Kress, Gunther & Theo van Leeuwen. 2006. *Reading images: The grammar of visual design*. 2nd ed. New York: Routledge.
Magbadelo, John O. 2004. Pentecostalism in Nigeria: Exploiting or edifying the masses. *African Sociological Review* 8(2), 15–29.
Mensa, Eyo & Roseline Ndimele. 2013. Linguistic creativity in Nigerian Pidgin advertising. *Sociolinguistic Studies* 7(3), 321–344.
Mbefo, Nnamdi L. 2001. *The true African: Impulses for self-affirmation*. Onitsha: SpiritanPublications.
McGregor, Sue L. T. 2003. Critical discourse analysis – A Primer. *Kappa Omicron Nu FORUM*. 15(1), 15–31.
Molina, Rose R. 2006. *Public spaces or private places? Outdoor advertising and the commercialisation of public space in Christ church. New Zealand*. UK: University of Canterbury dissertation http://digitallibrary.canterbury.ac.nz/data/collection3/etd/adtNZCU20070215.152400/02whole.pdf
Odebunmi, Akin. 2007. The stylistic analysis of religious media advertisement in Nigeria. In Akin Odebunmi & Adeyemi O. Babajide (eds.), *Styles in religious communication in Nigeria*, 1–26. Muenchen, Europa.
Olowu, Ayodeji. 2013. Christians' perception of the concepts of death and judgment: A multimodal discourse analytical study of selected editions of *Christian Women Mirror* Magazine. *International Journal of English and Literature* 4(10), 508–515.
Opeibi, Babatunde. 2007. One message, many tongues: An exploration of media multilingualsm in Nigerian political discourse. *Journal of Language and Politics* 6(2), 225–250.
Odoemenam, Chibueze Temple, Ordu Rosemary Chinyere & Omoghie Ikphemhosimhe Aslem. 2017. Lexico-semantic interpretation of Pentecostal Church posters. *English Linguistics Research* 6(4), 69–78.
Osoba, Joseph Babasola. 2014a. The use of Nigerian Pidgin in media adverts. *International Journal of English Linguistics* 4(2), 26–37.
Osoba, Joseph Babasola. 2014b. The use of Nigerian Pidgin in political jingles. *Journal of Universal Language* 15(1), 105–127.
Oshitelu, Gideon A. 1995. *Problems of philosophy of religion: Study course material, external studies programme*. Ibadan: University of Ibadan Press.
Osakwe, Mabel. 1991. The tenor in the style of public speech: A stylistic analysis of a radio sermon. *Language and Style* 25(3), 1–13.

Randy, Arnett R. 2012. *Pentecostalization: The changing face of Baptists in West Africa*. The Southern Baptist Theological Seminary dissertation.

Reinecke, John E. 1964. Trade jargons and Creole dialects as marginal languages. In Dell Hymes (ed.), *Language in culture and society*, 534–546. New York: Harper and Row.

Samarin, William J. 1976. The language of religion. In William J. Samarin (ed.), *Language in Religious practice*, 3–14. Rowley: Mass Newbury House Publishers.

Seidman, Steven A. 2008. *Posters, propaganda, and persuasion in election campaigns around the world and through history*. New York: Peter Lang.

Scheufele, Dietram A. & Iyengar Shanto. 2012. The state of framing research: A call for new directions. In Kate Kenski & Kathleen Hall Jamieson (eds.), *The Oxford handbook of political communication theories*, 1–26. New York: Oxford University Press.

Taiwo, Rotimi. 2007. Tenor in Electronic Media Christian Discourse in South-western Nigeria. *Nordic Journal of African Studies* 16(1), 75–89.

Taiwo, Rotimi. 2015. Pentecostal Discourse Communities of SMS Users in Southwestern Nigeria. In Rosalind I. J. Hackett & Benjamin Soares (eds.), *New media and religious transformations in Africa*, 190–204. Bloomington: Indiana University Press.

Ugot, Mercy, I. & Offiong Ani Offiong. 2013. Language and communication in the Pentecostal church of Nigeria: The Calabar axis. *Theory and practice in language studies* 3(1), 148–154.

Umera-Okeke, Nneka & Mercy Okitikpi. 2017. Age variation in the use of Nigerian Pidgin (NP): A case of Sapele, Delta State, Nigeria. *International Journal of English and Literature* 8(2), 16–25.

van Dijk, A. Teun. 1998. Opinions and ideologies in the press. In Allan Bell & P. Garrett (eds.), *Approaches to media discourse*, 21–63. Oxford: Blackwell.

van Leeuwen, Theo. 1996. The representation of social actors. In Carmen R. Caldas-Coulthard & Malcolm Coulthard (eds.), *Texts and practices: Readings in critical discourse analysis*, 32–70. London: Routledge.

van Leeuwen, Theo. 2005. *Introducing social semiotics*. London and New York: Routledge.

Joseph Babasola Osoba
Chapter 11
Nigerian Pidgin as national language: Prospects and challenges

Introduction

Nigerian Pidgin (NP) (or *Naija*, a name given to the Pidgin spoken in Nigeria in 2010 by *Naija Languej Akedemi*) appears to be among the few eligible candidates as national lingual franca or official national language in Nigeria. Owing to its inherent features as an ethnically and politically neutral as well as being the most widely spoken indigenous language in the country (as it is now claimed, it has over 5 million first language speakers and over 110 million second language speakers), plus its recognition as a full-fledged language by the so-called *Naija Languej Akedemi* in 2009, NP has been proposed as the best candidate for the lofty status of Nigeria's national language. Thus many linguists and anthropologists such as Rebecca Aigheyisi, Ben Elugbe and Omamor, F. Niyi Akinnaso, ABK Dadzie, David Esizimetor and Francis Egbokhare, Akinmade Akande and Joseph Osoba have directly or indirectly through their works recommended its adoption as an official lingua franca in Nigeria since it has been considered to meet the most crucial criteria requirements of an official national language. Awobuluyi's (2010: 4) restatement of Aristotle's 2500 year old conclusion that language and state or nation as a political entity are inseparable is instructive here. This is simply because of its three basic and indispensable functions, being symbolic, unifying and instrumental, which every human language performs. But adopting NP as an official language or that of national identity in Nigeria, which Awobuluyi has rightly described as a delicate matter, may not be as easy as the call by the language experts. Without adequate and proper language planning and policies as well as wise counsels and consultation, adopting a language among several competitors may spell an unforeseen doom for the nation as the case of Mauritania reported in the *University Word News* Issue: 0052 of late April 2010 (http://www.universityworldnews.com/article.php?story=20100424181813316). In this case, the Mauritanian President's unilaterally announcement of Arabic as the nation's new and only official national language, in place of French, was greeted with riotous and violent demonstrations with several students of the University of Nouakchott, seriously wounded.

Based on the meta-analytical approach adopted in this paper and based on most statistical surveys as well as quasi-quantitative and qualitative investigations conducted in last decade about the use and prospect of NP becoming an official national language, it appears that Nigerians are not yet ready to accept NP as their official national language. Many reasons can be adduced to this. First, most Nigerians, especially the elite, the educated and the professionals, consider it as a substandard variety of English which, at best, is only useful or acceptable in a strictly informal situation. Second, it still lacks a standard orthographic form and so it cannot be accepted as a literary language in spite of the volumes of literary works already done fully or partly in it. Third, because it is mostly associated with the masses which constitute the lowest rung of the Nigerian social ladder, it lacks the prestige of a standard language (Akande, 2010). Fourth, those who have it as their first language are negligible in size and population and lacks political power that could precipitate its consideration through favourable language and educational policies as well as an ideological proposition as a language for everyone but of no one! Fifth and finally, unless and until, it is perceived as some sort of linguistic justice and / or efforts at being even-handed in the matter of language policy (Wright, 2004: 206), NP will likely continue to be denied its rightful position in the scheme of things as far as national language question is concerned.

Based on the foregoing and considering the contrasting and contradicting perspectives with which the use and prospects of the NP as an official language have been viewed in Nigeria, I adopt a meta-analytical based socio-ethnographic study to provide illuminating and rewarding insights into the national language question, language planning and policies, as well as the ideology of language and development in Nigeria. Thus, this paper is organized in nine sections as follows: 11.0 Introduction; 11.1 Methodology, Theoretical and Conceptual Framework; 11.2 Emergence; 11.3 Development; 11.4 Impact; 11.5 Language Planning and Policy and Nigerian Pidgin: 11.6 National Language Question; 11.7 Challenges of NP as a National Language; 11.8 Conclusions.

1 Methodology, theoretical and conceptual framework

In this paper, I evaluate relevant previous statistical and descriptive investigations and studies in the areas of language planning and policy, language and national development, ideology as well as the national language question in relation to the use and prospects of adopting NP as an official national language in Nigeria.

Ethnolinguistic Identity theory (ELIT), as proposed by Giles and Johnson (1987: 70–72), is more or less a socio-psychological approach which takes into account socio-structural influences on ethnic groups in contact and how they are perceived by group members. According to them, we categorise the social world and, hence, perceive ourselves as members of various social groups. Such knowledge of ourselves as group members is defined as our social identity. This may be positive or negative according to how our in-groups fare in social comparison with relevant outgroups.

ELIT based on Giles and Johnson's proposal, seems appropriate and useful when we consider how NP speakers perceive themselves in relation to the educated elite and political class. Speakers of Ajegunle-based NP, as well as Wafi (Warri-based NP) speakers who are first language speakers of the NP, do not have a low opinion of themselves or the language as outsiders do. In fact, they are proud to be NP speakers and believe they are smarter than the elite and the ruling class as Akande (2010), Balogun (2013) and Osoba (2018) demonstrate. Thus even though they are negatively perceived by the educated, the elite or the ruling class as social miscreants and irresponsible, they have a different and positive perception of themselves and their language. Thus, in their case, the claim by Giles and Johnson (1987: 71) that "language comes into the picture when a group regards its own language or speech variety as a dimension of comparison with the outgroups" such that members adopt various strategies of 'psychological distinctiveness' like switching to in-group language, accentuating ethnic language and slang, etc. in their attempt to assume a positive identity, is valid. Moreover, among the NP speakers in Ajegunle, there is sometimes the accentuation of in-group speech markers to distinguish speakers as Wafi and non-Wafi. This may be considered an intergroup strategy in conversational discourse in an attempt to dominate and control the tread of their arguments. Thus NP speakers further identify themselves as being superior to other speakers based on the variety of the language they speak. Thus, since Wafi speakers have the NP as their first language, they tend to enjoy the prestige that is associated with the first language speakers and consider speakers of the other varieties as inferior. The fluency and confidence with which Wafi speakers express themselves seem to be incomparable with and stronger than those of the speakers of other indigenous languages in Nigeria. This variety also sounds raw, undiluted and emotive! Thus it seems to be full of expressions such as "shuo! Dem fit? Dem no bon dem! Hau dem go fit? Wafi! Lifa (liva)!" as exclamations, expletives etc. which demonstrate the boldness and sincerity not found in most unctuous indigenous language varieties (see Faraclas, 1996; Douglas, 2012; Mann, 2000; Osoba, 2018).

In addition, they no longer regard or perceive themselves as hoodlums, impoverished, unlearned and inarticulate but rather as professional artistes, comedians and musicians. Truly, the Nigeria's artistic and music landscape has been dominated by NP speakers and their works in the last four decades. The late Ras Kimono, a popular Reggae artiste; Majek Fashek, another Reggae musician, Daddy Shokey and, recently, several other contemporary ones like P Squire, Simi and Tiwa have been able to put the Nigeria's music pop culture on the global map. Thus the identity conflict is part of the social indices between the Nigerian masses who mostly speak and use NP and the educated and political class who only use it in their informal capacity and situation with relish. This interesting scenario can aptly be considered or regarded as language politics or language power.

Akinnaso (2015: 337) provides an insightful socio-/ethno-historical perspective. To him, in Nigeria, as in other ex-colonial nations, language politics has come to represent two major types of struggle, one against the vestiges of colonialism and the other against the domination of ethnic and minority languages by the larger ethnic groups. The first struggle has led to the rejection of colonial languages in certain domains, the ultimate goal being to reallocate the official status accorded to colonial languages to indigenous languages, and the second to ambivalent policies which call for linguistic unification under one or a few indigenous 'national' languages, while simultaneously promoting linguistic pluralism and cultural diversity.

Looking further at the situation, especially from the perspective of ideology of language planning and policy in Nigeria, Akinnaso (1989: 133) examines Nigeria's language policies in terms of their conflicting objectives, ideological motivations and orientations. He explains them in terms of the sociological development of the nation; its complex ethnographic landscape; the conflicting demands of "nationalism" and "nationism"; and the attempt to maintain linguistic and cultural pluralism, while advocating linguistic unification and national integration. His insights and observations are germane to this study because they serve as the ideological basis for the adoption of an official national language in a multicultural and multilingual country such as Nigeria. The issue here is that Nigeria must select one or more national languages from its over five hundred ethnic languages as its official language(s) now or in the future, as the situation dictates. This actually gave rise to the conflicting objectives, ideological motivations and orientations observed in its language policies. The aim of the Nigerian government seems to be to preserve, revitalize and standardize its major indigenous languages and thereby maintain some kind of linguistic and cultural pluralism. But the need for linguistic unification and national integration has led to the adoption of the English language as its official language at all the levels of governance. Hausa, Igbo and Yoruba are accorded the status of official regional languages but none of them can be adopted as an official national language or language of governance because of their ethnic affiliation, biases and prejudices which are resented by other ethnic groups in Nigeria. As a result, the only language devoid of the acrimony is NP which can be described as the "language for everyone but of no one!" Hence, its potential for achieving nationism (see Akinnaso, 1989). Yet Wafi speakers, who are the first language speakers of NP, tend to claim it as their own demonstrating its nationalism! A number of recent works and research (see Osoba, 2018) on NP simply demonstrate that those who use the language as their primary form of speech show a strong emotional identity or bond with it, such that linguistic prejudice associated with all the natural languages can be identified in their use of the language to distinguish them from other speakers of NP and other languages. Thus features of nationalism can be found to be inherent in NP and among its primary speakers.

Relevant to language potential in the politics of power is Fairclough's (2001: 27) exegesis which attempts to relate ideological power to economic and State power by considering the relationship between social classes which starts in economic production but extends to all the parts of a society. The state is assumed to be the key element in maintaining the dominance of the capitalist class, and controlling the working class. Ideology is considered as institutional or naturalized practices, which originated in dominant class, but which people draw upon without thinking embodying assumptions which directly or indirectly legitimatize existing power relations. Thus ideological power is described as the power to project one's practices as universal and 'common sense', a significant complement to economic and political power.

This directly relates to the users of NP who have unequal political and economic power with the elite and the ruling class and their use of the English language in Nigeria. Since those who control the State also control its economy, the politics of power tends to favour them. Thus their dominance and control of the lower class is seen to be in the interest of the State and all its citizenry. Here lies the power struggle between NP speakers, mainly of the lower class, and the elite class, which exercises authority over them. Little wonder then that NP speakers, especially Ajegunle residents, are regarded as the scum of the earth, hoodlums, and ragamuffins despite their achievements in and contribution to the national and global art, music and pop-culture. Because their achievements are considered to be of little significance by fellow Nigerians, NP speakers are looked down upon as poor and impoverish not just as a reflection but also a result of their use of a non-standard language.

Interestingly, Fairclough (2001: 28–29) provides an illuminating perspective on power relations, class relations and social struggle which clearly interrogates the scenario between the NP speakers and non-NP speakers in Nigeria. To him, power relations exist not only in social groupings in institutions but also between men and women, between ethnic groupings and between young and old which may not be specific to particular institutions. Furthermore, there seems to be a clear connection between power relations and class relations which defines the nature of the society with a fundamental and pervasive influence on all aspects of the society. In this regard, power relations are perceived as relations of struggle, the process whereby social groupings with different interests engage with one another. He also observes that class struggle is the most fundamental form of struggle just as class relations are the most fundamental relations in class society. In essence, class struggle is considered a necessary and inherent property of a social system in which the maximization of the profits and power of one class depends upon the maximization of its exploitation and domination of another. Moreover, language is seen as both a site and a stake in class struggle since those who exercise power through language must constantly be involved in struggle with others to defend (or lose) their position. This situation reflects the exploitation and domination of the masses of Nigerians who speak NP, especially for those whose first language is NP.

But the exercise and distribution of power can be observed to be embedded in the prevailing sociolinguistic conventions which not only incorporate differences of power but also arise out of – and give rise to – particular relations of power. Thus existing conventions can be explained as the outcome of power relations and power struggle (Fairclough, 2001: 1–2). Thus in Nigeria, speakers of the Standard English variety are distinguished from the speakers of non-standard varieties of English and from the speakers of indigenous languages and NP, which groups them into elite class on the one hand and lower social class on the other, based on the existing conventions.

Consequently, for NP to develop in Nigeria, community-based individuals with clear sympathy for the language must be identified and located, as Awobuluyi (2010: 24) suggested in the case of other indigenous languages in Nigeria. These must be individuals who hold not only economic power (the rich and the wealthy) but also socio-political power. Nigerian politicians who employ NP in their radio and television jingles and campaigns to come to power usually neglect the language after their electoral victories. Neither do artistes who came into limelight through their use of NP associate with those in power as they try to demonstrate their critical orientation towards the so-called oppressors of the masses – the ruling class. Thus natural empathy for the development of the language's status, corpus and acquisition, which would have ensured as a result of close interaction between the speakers or users of NP and policy makers, is lacking. This attitude of 'we versus them', separating NP speakers from the policy makers or the ruling class, would continue to undermine the process of standardization of the language in terms of acceptance. The point is NP will not be accepted as an official language among those who hold political influence and policy makers until it is perceived as a true language of sustainable economic opportunities and valued by them (see Donwa-Ifode, 1984; Igboanusi, 2008 and Kioko *et al,* 2014). They would then be able to accede to the rights of the NP to equity and justice in their enactment of language related policies, acts and laws. The rights of NP to socio-political advancement and empowerment would naturally foster its economic opportunities for its users. This may partly or fully transform their social status or class from low to high. Unfortunately, to the detriment of socio-political empowerment of NP, unequal distribution of resources and power relations between the ruling class and NP users would persist until a level of cooperation is established between them (see Kioko *et al.,* 2014 and Osoba, 2018).

Disturbingly, the scenario clearly demonstrates a power struggle that suggests that the so-called mental or psychological superiority claimed by NP users over the ruling class appears to be a mere illusion since those, among them, who tend to achieve their wealth and artistic fame could often lose them as quickly as they acquire them or simply remain apolitical. So, this could prevent a long lasting legacy from being bequeathed to the next generation of its speakers in terms of economic and political influence.

Moreover, the awareness created by their artistry in NP does not seem to translate into socio-political weaponry of sustainable success and advancement. It seems that most of the successful NP speakers decry mainstream politics which is the only means of further promoting and empowering their language. Without a serious effort on their part to join mainstream Nigerian politics, a global acceptance of and support for NP to be used as an official medium of instruction in places where it has creolized and become the first language of a new generation of speakers, would remain in jeopardy. Thus it would seem that linguistic identity and affinity attached to a language as well as its usefulness might not be enough to promote its acceptance and advancement. Rather, the importance of a language at a global level seems to be determined by the importance of its speakers who are in the position to push for its global acceptance. This is perhaps what informs Awobuluyi's (2010: 37) suggestion that "Given the situation as it is now, it would seem to me that the time has come for people who are both culturally and linguistically enlightened to go on the political offensive for those languages".

Introspectively, it appears, from the foregoing, that the usefulness and relevance of NP as a language of huge potential for economic and political success might not be sufficient enough to accord it its rightful position among Nigerian indigenous languages until its speakers such as Bisi Olatilo (the ace Nigerian broadcaster), Frank Aig-Imoukhuede (the author of *Pidgin Stew and Sufferhead* who introduced NP into the broadcasting media in Nigeria), and Prof. Sam Oyovbaire (erstwhile Minister of Information during Gen. Ibrahim Babangida's regime as Head of State), who hold political influence and power, aggressively advocates for its official recognition as medium of instruction, especially in places like Ajegunle, Calabar, Port Harcourt, Warri, Sapele, Sabo ngaris and military and police barracks. As noted by Kioko *et al.* (2014) in their abstract, it is important to focus on the success stories from Africa and the economic benefits in the use of the mother tongue in creative media or economies because there are returns on such investment.

2 Emergence

Pidgins can naturally be observed to encapsulate the process of language origin, emergence and evolution. To this extent, one can safely claim that every human language, just like every pidgin, must have evolved to meet the need for social interaction. This is simply because wherever and whenever two or more people of different languages come in contact, a language evolves to facilitate their communication or cooperation. If this fails, their interaction breaks down which could lead to separation, conflict or war.

Dadzie (1987: 3) provides an interesting etymology of "The word "pidgin", first used for Chinese pidgin English, which evolved because of the need to do business. The word itself originally is said to mean "business". He also notes that a creole was originally used to refer to a white colonist born in the tropics. Later, its meaning widened to include African slaves and others residents in the colonies. In Nigeria, in Victoria times, up to the late thirties, it was used to describe Sierra Leoneans and the free slaves who found themselves in Lagos, particularly those who came back from Brazil. It is interesting to know that there was an attempt to give the word a Yoruba etymology by pronouncing it 'Kiriyo', in conformity with the Yoruba phonology, that is, a wanderer who gets sated in the end. He however observes that this usage could be an example of linguistic lexical transfer. Today, this word (Krio) is used in reference to Sierra Leoneans who now call their language by this name and differentiate it from the general linguistic concept by spelling it differently. He also notes that this is " . . . indeed a creole and . . . Professor Eldred Jones and his colleagues in Fourah Bay have complied a dictionary of this language. (Dadzie, 1987: 3)"

A background perspective provided by Dadzie (1987: 4) suggests that "Not much is known of pidgin/ creole before the 19th Century. But the general belief is that the home of pidgin/ creole is the Caribbean to which slaves brought some kind of pidgin or other from the West African countries on the Guinea Coast." To him, the view by some other scholars that pidgin evolved after the arrival of slaves from their respective countries is also plausible. The latter view seems to have more to recommend it considering that several West African – Twi and Yoruba particularly – lexical items, and of course, cultural manifestations, mix freely with the English base that goes to make our pidgin. In other words, the heterogeneous crowd became homogenized as a result of contact and the need to identify with one another in their plight resulted in the growth of pidgin English there. It was a "result of syncretism between West African and European patterns" as noted by Rickford (1974).

The emergence of an incipient pidgin in the Nigerian coaster areas can be traced to the 15th Century AD when the Portuguese traders and explorers visited the areas. This contact between the Portuguese and peoples of the Niger Delta during that period became so extensive that it precipitated the emergence of an incipient Portuguese-based NP due to the absence of a common lingua franca among the linguistic/ethnic communities comprising Annang, Edo, Efik, Ibibio, Igbo, Ijaw, Isoko and Itsekiri. Words such as 'sabi' meaning 'to know' and 'pikin' meaning 'a child' are considered as evidence of the Portuguese-based pidgin. This pidgin later became widespread as a common language. After the exit of the Portuguese, the arrival and exit of the Dutch and French were followed by the arrival of the British missionaries and traders who established a strong base in the region.

By the early 19th Century, the strong British influence in the missionary work, education, trade and colonialism came with the introduction of their language, English, which was later to replace Portuguese as the major lexifier of pidgin, the common language of the peoples of the areas. The incipient pidgin gradually became a more useful language of trade and social interaction. By Nigeria's independence in 1960, the English-based NP had spread beyond the Niger Delta areas to major cities such as Lagos, Kano and Port Harcourt and featured in literary works, print and electronics media adverts and political jingles. These are areas and fields of creative economies that could lead to more sustainable economic opportunities for speakers of NP if the language is empowered today.

3 Development

The development of NP may be traced to its widespread use as a lingua franca by Nigerians of diverse cultural, ethnic and linguistic affiliations; its use in the print and electronic media adverts, comedies and jingles as well as its political and ethnic neutrality. Its use in standard literature by Nigerian poets, playwrights and novelists such as Mamma Vatsa, Ken Saro Wiwa, Chinua Achebe, Wole Soyinka and the publications of standard textbooks on the grammar and other aspects of the language generally are an eloquent testimony of its development today. Moreover, since its adoption as the language of his music by the Late Fela Anikulapo Kuti in the early 1970s to its use as the language of modern Nigerian pop music by Ras Kimono, Fajek Masek in the 80s to 90s as well as continued use today by most popular pop musicians, comedians and artistes in Nigeria, NP has rapidly developed into a language of economic opportunities and values. This sudden and quick transformation of NP from its incipient stage and status of trade language to that of the language of socio-economic success and status of an unofficial lingual franca and creole appears to favour its future candidacy as one of Nigeria's official languages in education, trade and commerce and politics. This fact is attested to by Eriata Oribohabor an article published in June 8, 2016 entitled "Lingua Franca: From Nigerian Pidgin to Naija Languej" when he suggests that

> ... the overwhelming need for standardisation was addressed at the first Conference on Nigerian Pidgin by IFRA-Nigeria, an organization which promotes research in the social sciences and the humanities in Nigeria, from the 8th to 9th July, 2009 at the University of Ibadan, Nigeria where a Naija Languej Akedemi (NLA) was formed to work towards realizing the complete repositioning of the language in the scheme of things ... The biggest challenge facing promoters of Naija Languej is the provision of reference material s/guides, scholarly exploits and the like. With standardized Naija languej, the Federal Government would have no reason holding back an official seal for the language; the soul and spirit of an irrepressible people, uniting them on all front.

To buttress the fact that NP is developing more rapidly through the expanding population of its speakers, Esizimetor and Egbokhare (2012) claim that over 5 million people speak Naijá as first language while over 75 million people use it as a second language in Nigeria and in Nigerian Diaspora communities in Europe, America and other parts of the world as at 2010. But the current estimate is said to be over 110 million speakers.

Akinnaso's (1989: 136) observation of the rivalry between English and NP as lingua francas is instructive. This is because while English continues to perform "High" functions, NP is noted to have almost taken over the role of lingua franca in nonformal domains. This development seems to have transformed the language into the most popular medium of intergroup communication in various heterogeneous communities throughout the country. Moreover, he also notes that, apart from developing into a mother tongue, NP has spread both horizontally across the entire country and vertically across various categories of speakers, literate and illiterate, male and female, old and young, and so forth.

In the same vein, Osoba and Alebiosu (2016: 23) appear to buttress Akinnaso's observation in their claim that

> More so, its profile in Ajegunle Town, advertises it as adorable lingua francafor residents from diverse ethnic and linguistic backgrounds. In terms of function, form, structure, and status, it is a prestigious creole for the vast majority of those who now speak it as a primary or first language. The precipitation of this unusual development of the NP, noted by Donwa-Ifode (1984), in the use of Nigerian Pidgin (NP) in Port-Harcourt has graciously led to its unofficial adoption as lingua franca of the Nigerian masses.

Furthermore, they also consider the development of NP as a language of political jingles and campaigns by politicians and political jobbers in their attempt to woo the masses and win their votes. In fact, according to Osoba (2014: 26–27) the presumed or actual winners of the past presidential elections in Nigeria could attribute their successes partly to the use of NP in their campaigns and jingles. Among them are (1) the late Chief MKO Abiola (1993 Presidential Elections), (2) the ex-President Goodluck Jonathan (2011 Presidential Elections), and (3) President Mohammed Buhari (2015 Presidential Elections) (see Osoba and Alebiosu, 2016).

In some tertiary institutions in Nigeria, NP seems to have begun to replace other indigenous languages as the language of social interaction and fraternity. Douglas's (2012) work shows clearly the inevitability of NP completely displacing the ethnic languages in the parts of the Bayelsa State which constituted her sample population. Nonetheless, the attitude to NP appears to undermine its further development and standardisation. Akande and Salami (2010: 70) report their analysis of attitudes to, and use of the language among students in two Nigerian universities in the two cosmopolitan cities of Benin and Lagos. Their findings, which reveal consistent transformation of the NP in form and function, include the fact (see Akande and Salami, 2010: p. 83) that, though widely used by the Nigerian undergraduates, it is largely marginalized as a result of its neither being completely codified nor standardised. Little wonder, more than 75% of students from each of the two institutions were found not disposed to the teaching of the language in the Nigerian schools.

From the above analysis, claims and observations, it may not be implausible to assume that while NP is expanding and developing rapidly in usage and function, its standardizing processes appear to drag in terms of general acceptance of its official use, uniform orthography, standard variety and its status as either a variety of English or an autonomous or natural language.

4 Impact

Since language has been noted to impact on its speakers in all ramifications: social, economic, political, religious, psychological, we may not be too surprised when it affects their lives positively or negatively in those areas (see Bailey and Robinson, 1973; Giles and Johnson, 1987; Fairclough, 2001 and Wright, 2014). The impact of NP can be seen and felt in the lives of its speakers locally and globally.

Socio-culturally, speakers of NP are seen by outsiders as low classed people and regarded as poor and depraved of civility and acceptable standard of behaviour. They are therefore often relegated to the background in the scheme of things and neglected by the political class. Thus their use of NP can be seen as a factor responsible for their low social status and poverty. This comes as a result of lack of economic value and opportunities associated with their language. It becomes almost impossible for them to aspire to higher social rung or political office. In fact, to them, that kind of aspiration is unimaginable. It may not be far from the truth to assume that their language is responsible, directly or indirectly, for their impoverishment. Moreover, up till the late 1990s, evidence in major cities in Nigeria, where NP speakers reside, clearly shows slum-like residency and seems unthinkable to hope to find an NP speaker who lives or desires to live in a high-brow area such as Ikoyi, Lagos Island or Banana Island in Lagos State where some of them now live. Worst still, government officials often embark on slum demolition exercise to flush out so-called miscreants from designated areas. In Lagos State, in the recent past, such exercise affected places such as Ajegunle, Maroko, Makoko, Mushin and Agege areas. Aside from being considered an eye-sore, the slum dwellers are seen as a threat to civilized culture since their way of life is judged as anti- culture. Little wonder, they are often tagged as criminals and hoodlums and hence the need to sanitise them and their slums. However, the current sociolinguistic reality in the domain of stand-up comedy evidently shows highly educated professionals such as judges, lawyers, lecturers and bankers also get involved in the use of NP.

Interestingly, NP speakers, especially speakers of Wafi variety, seem to have a positive opinion about themselves and their language. Contrary to the widely held belief among outsiders, NP speakers attempt to demonstrate their irrepressible mindset for displaying intelligence, superiority, candour and artistic mastery in music, pop culture, comedy and verbal eloquence as well as propagandist vituperations. So it appears that what they lack in political and economic power is compensated for in an assumed psychological superiority. This can be observed in their seemly bold attitudes even in the face of adversities such as a threat to or actual demolition of their slums or eviction from their residence. The legacy left behind by Ras Kimono, Majek Fasek and younger artistes who rose from the ashes of slum areas like Ajegunle and whose main music was and is still rendered in NP is huge testimony to their daunting spirit, courage and resilience. They do not usually see themselves as a minus in the scheme of things in relation to the economy of Nigeria rather they are contributors to the growth of Nigeria's economy through the music industry and other artistic forms.

Paradoxically, it may not be so far-fetched to state that the impact of NP is both negative and positive. From a critical perspective, it is easy to observe that the positive impact of NP outweighs its negative impact. This is because as long as the language continues to function as an economic language for its speakers as they generate living incomes through its use for their artistic endeavours, their lifestyle is bound to become more sophisticated and would eventually lead the transformations of their slums into high-brow areas. Some may decide to rebuild their environment or relocate to better places when economically empowered to do so.

Opportunities that are open in the area of creative economies have been exploited by NP speakers to their advantage and that of Nigeria's development as a result of their contributions to national income in terms of the local taxes and foreign exchange earnings from their output. Nigerian pop music has both local and global impact. As noted earlier, the most formidable actors in the Nigerian pop music industry today are more or less NP speakers. Their works are embraced by all and sundry. Daddy Showkey, Naira Marley, Ruggedman, Basketmouth and a couple of others are brilliant examples of successful NP speakers in Nigeria. Owing to the global achievement of NP speakers, Nigeria now has a high stake in the pop culture as it keeps her youths out of unemployment and crimes.

Quite unexpectedly, the global impact of NP speakers' creative economies can be described as a big step forward in the march toward giving the country a positive face in the comity of nations. Nigeria can now be seen as a nation full of talented youths who are potentially able to transform the economy of their country from its sorry state into an enviable position and status. It seems that if the Nigerian government could harness the potentials of her youths in creative economies, impoverishment and underdevelopment would become history soon. The lost glory of the 70s and early 80s would then be recovered.

In spite of the achievements and potentials of the NP speakers as highlighted, from a close observation, one may see the weakness in their apparent political apathy or apolitical attitude. This attitude may be described as the root cause of the marginalization of NP and its speakers. The political class and the elite enjoy their creative works but subtly dissociate from their language. During campaigns for elective offices, NP becomes relevant for adverts and jingles. But as soon as elections are won and lost in Nigeria, the glory of the language departs. Thus politicians appreciate the usefulness of NP as the language of the masses in order to win their votes. But the realization that NP is a potential tool for political advancement and success has neither partly nor fully translated into a tangible opportunity or result for the language or its speakers. One can only hope that "as the Nigerian society is developing socially and politically, the influence of NP and its acceptance rate may also grow among the educated and the political elite (Osoba, 2014: 25–126)."

5 Language planning and policy

The role of language planning and policy (LPP) in the development of a strong united nation can be said to be fundamental to its overall national development, especially in a multilingual country such as Nigeria. The main reason for this is that both the communicative and identity functions of language may not be naturally performed by one or the same language as in most multilingual nations. The point really is that people in such countries may need to communicate or access information outside their primary language group (see Sue Wright, 1914: 7). Thus it is usually the case that the official lingua franca is not coterminous with the individuals' mother tongues in a multilingual nation. In Nigeria today, as in many African and Asian countries, most people, especially the literates, are bilinguals speaking English, as their official language, in addition to their mother tongues. As noted also by Wright (2014: 42), since language takes on some essential roles in the nation building processes, the need for a national language becomes inevitable to develop a shared culture, to unite the various segments and to allow it to function efficiently in its political and economic life.

Choosing an official or a national language that would bring about the desired unity, loyalty and patriotism as a convergence of community of communication certainly requires careful ideological decisions on the part of the ruling class. Thus the decisions on LPP must be predicated on time-tested and acceptable approaches to have the desired outcomes for the overall good of the citizenry of a multilingual nation. Tollefson (1996: 22) explains the relevance of neoclassical and historical-structural approach to the ideological basis of LPP, particularly in a multilingual nation such as Nigeria. To him, the neoclassical approach emphasizes individual linguistic decisions while the historical-structural approach emphasizes constraints on individual decision making. Furthermore, he suggests that, even though the neoclassical approach appears to be common with most researchers, "the historical-structural approach offers greater opportunity for explaining language behavior and for resolving language problems facing individuals (Tollefson, 1996: 22)." Realistically, both approaches have been employed in this study for a broad explication of relevant treads of our arguments. The point really is that both are useful for language planning in a multilingual country and the formulation of appropriate policies and enactment of adequate laws that would promote the national development based on the recognition of the potential and contributions of all languages used in country. The orientation is usually towards the preservation of self-interest of the individual based on language convergence or shift. Thus the individual's interest is subsumed and embedded in the collective interest of the group or community of communication. In this regard, the spirit of brotherhood thrives toward nation cohesion which also accommodates individuals as valuable contributors to nationalism or nationism as applicable. These approaches and ideology must have informed the provisions of the relevant language sections of the Nigerian Constitution and the National Policy on Education (NPE).

With the Nigerian Constitution and NPE clearly stipulating the use of language in Nigeria in terms of function and status, the enviable role as well as status of the English language as official language, the language of administration, education, media, judiciary, commerce and diplomacy has led many Nigerians to become bilingual in English and their mother tongues. The prestige associated with its knowledge and use makes it imperative for Nigerians from diverse ethnicities to put their hope in their competence in the language for social advancement and employment in the mainstream. Within the same Constitution and NPE are embedded the provisions which recognize the use of three regional Nigerian languages, Hausa, Igbo and Yoruba, as official national languages. Thus within their regions, these language can be used for formal and official purposes at the State and local government levels in addition to English. Moreover, based on the provisions of NPE, they could be used as languages of education from the kindergarten up unto primary three. From primary four, pupils are then supposed to be introduced to the use of English as language of education. Section 2 No 14 (d. i & ii) of NPE (1987, revised) stipulates the role of government as to ensure that the medium of instruction is principally the mother tongue or the language of the immediate community with the aim of developing the orthography of many more Nigerian languages as well as producing textbooks in Nigerian languages. The significance of the policy is aptly captured by Oyeleye (2016: 31) in his opinion that

> A meaningful and functional bilingual/multilingual policy in education will definitely ensure that those with minimal education can absorb and transmit information either in their (MTs) or in a combination of English and their MTs. When allowance is made for the

> growth and development of our indigenous languages, then the majority of our compatriots will be able to participate and contribute fully to the holistic development of the nation.

His viewpoint is instructive in the sense that our indigenous languages can contribute to Nigeria's national development if and when benevolent policies are formulated to ensure and maintain their growth and development. It may also be proper to consider these languages as invaluable contributors as compendiums of knowledge and civilization with great potentials for productive and creative economies necessary to transform the nation into an enviable position in the comity of nations.

As far back as 1988, the World Bank had identified the following ten principal languages in Nigeria: Hausa, Yoruba, Igbo, Fulfulde, Pidgin, Kanuri, Edo, Ijo, Efik, Idoma. These are the few documented ones among about five hundred as at that time. Since then and up till now, several more have been documented and are in the process of being standardized (see Adegbija, 1997 & 2001; Igboanusi, 2008; Oyetade, 2003). The fact that NP has been recognized as a principal Nigerian language simply attests to its growth, developments, functions, status and spread among its users. As it is the case with Ghanaian Pidgin, NP seems through careful and pragmatic language planning and engineering to have the potential for emerging as not only an official national language but also transnational language. This is well noted in Dadzie's (1987: 11) comment about the use of Ghanaian Pidgin below:

> However, it is possible through language planning and engineering to determine its course and push it on its way. It is to be noted that the language is current among the educated, which gives it some prestige, and in addition, there is a strong motivation for even the less educated to want to speak it since it comes handy when they move out of Ghana into the neighbouring English-speaking countries where language difficulties compel many to express themselves in pidgin . . . . Without any pretentions yet to be used as language of development (overall) it should be allowed to chart its own course, maybe with a little help from language planners and engineers.

The role of language planners and engineers cannot be overemphasized in an attempt to develop a language for empowerment in all its ramifications. They assist in ensuring that appropriate policies evolved, proposed and advanced or formulated for the standardization through documentation involving proper codification of its corpus, determination of status and motivation of process of its acquisition. Since NP is already being unofficially codified, all it needs is an official recognition by the Nigerian government through a revision of its extant language policies and laws to reflect its new position thereby granting the language its well-deserved status and prestige among its teeming speakers, users and outsiders.

6 National language question

The national language question is almost an utmost issue particularly in a multilingual democratic nation such as Nigeria. One of Nigeria's renowned educationists and a Professor of African Linguistics, Awobuluyi (2010: 10) provides an insightful overview. To him,

> Choosing a language, whether for official use or for national identity, is a very delicate matter that ideally should be based on wide consultation as well as on many considerations, including political ones. If a country or nation happens to have a multiplicity of languages, only one of which is truly eligible for consideration, such a country or nation may jolly well decide on that single eligible language with little or no fear of opposition or adverse reactions.

He gives an example of one such country in the contemporary world as Tanzania in East Africa. That country is said to have over a hundred indigenous but rather localized languages with Swahili as the only exception because it is very widely spoken as first or second language in the country. Thus at the country's independence, Swahili was declared the national language, a role it has peacefully been playing ever since. He then notes, by contrast, the unsuccessful attempt to make the same widely spoken language the national language of Kenya and Uganda because those two countries have many eligible indigenous languages that are in competition with Swahili. The difficulty is well-highlighted by Milton Obote, a former Uganda President, in his opening address to a Seminar on Mass Media and Linguistic Communication in East Afinca in 1967 (see Obote, 1967: 3–6).

From Awobuluyi's submission, it may not be out of place to presuppose that the expediency of the choice of a national language imposes the obligation on the citizenry to accept and support one or few languages, which are designated national languages, from several numerous and available potential candidates. This obligation on the part of the populace is subtly or intrinsically embedded in ideology of common sense belief that acceding or acquiescing to the proposition of one language one nation is for the good of all particularly in our multilingual community. But the background problem that must be addressed squarely is the reality of linguistic pluralism that confronts convergence of community of communication in the Nigerian situation. Language experts, teachers, anthropologists, linguists and those with interest in language use in Nigeria have expressed their reservations as well as optimism about the current linguistic milieu and its possible implications and prospects. However, similar to Awobuluyi's (2010) view, Akinnaso (1989: 133) had earlier remarked as follows:

> Since colonial times, Nigeria has been faced with the problem of forging National unity out of diversity and since that time it has been generally recognized that language factors are at the heart of this diversity. For example, in his 1945 proposal for the development of a Nigerian constitution, Sir Author Richards, their colonial governor, identified language diversity as one of the major difficulties in promoting Nigerian unity, Similarly, the late Chief Obafemi Awolowo, Nigeria's foremost nationalist and revered statesman, repeatedly drew attention to language diversity, having indeed once advocated the creation of "linguistic states." Thus, since 1947, no constitution has been written, and indeed no major government policy has been formulated, which does not recognize the problem of language diversity and its effect on national development.

The English language brought to Nigeria by the British missionaries, traders and colonialists has remained as Nigeria's official language since the colonial era, after the independence and till date. But, not minding its official status, as a language of colonial heritage, it can never become our national language. Frankly speaking, and perhaps compassionately, Dadzie (1987: 5) has wisely suggested a way out. To him the solution to Nigeria's search for an official national language lies in the choice of NP. In his words,

> The search for a national language for Nigeria, and for other countries in West Africa, has-sled to a consideration of several options all of which have proved unacceptable for one reason or another. So, pidgin, which is not tied specifically to any of the problems posed above could be adopted as a national language – one which is nobody's language and yet everybody's language.

From all indications, it appears appropriate for the ruling class to heed Dadzie's words of wisdom as regards our national language question.

7 Challenges of NP as a national language

Having examined the emergence, the development as well as the impact of NP, in the previous subsections, it becomes needless to over-flog the facts of its prospects as a suitable candidate for the prestigious position and status of an official national lingua franca. Rather our focus should be the challenges that its choice would most likely confront. Herbert Igboanusi (2008: 1), in his stimulating paper, entitled "Empowering Nigerian Pidgin: A Challenge for Status Planning?" provides us with findings that shed light on the basic challenges confronting NP in relation to its status planning. The abstract to his paper presents a clear picture of his main goal, objectives and conclusion as follows:

> This paper explores the possibility of empowering NP (and its speakers) by raising the value of the language through status planning, especially in the education system. On the

way to realising this goal, it analyses the attitudes of 200 educated Nigerians towards its use as well as towards steps aimed at empowering it. The results show that, although there is no consensus as to whether NP should be granted official status, a large majority of respondents did not favour its use in education. The study highlights three major problems associated with the promotion of NP: (1) lack of economic value, (2) perceived effects on the local languages, and (3) the effect of the use of NP on English language proficiency. The study discovers that empowering[1] NP is a challenge, which will be very difficult to overcome in the near future . . .

The above findings seem to be related to Akinnaso's (1989: 136) earlier observations which expressed the concern educators today have about "the gradual adoption of pidgin English as lingua franca in many educational institutions, especially federal government colleges, which, as a rule, admit children from different ethnolinguistic backgrounds . . . ." The main reason for their fear is that NP is still largely "associated with illiterate or 'uneducated' users, partly because it is viewed as a corrupt form of language, and partly because it poses a threat to standard Nigerian English, which is taught in schools and used in formal, official settings." Thus, to Akinnaso, because of the stigma, "it has had no place in the nation's language policies, despite its increasing role as a lingua franca" (Akinnaso, 1989: 136). Moreover, NP tended to have been placed down on a very low scale of preference. The language is one that is believed to be below an accepted standard. It may then seem that most Nigerians, particularly the educated class, would consider the idea of adopting the Nigerian Pidgin as a national language would impact negatively on the society, especially looking at her from the global perspective.

8 Conclusion

From the foregoing treatise, my submission is that, since the positive impact of the NP in the socio-political and economic life is seen and felt by all Nigerians today, and weighs more than its negativity, it should be officially recognized as Nigeria's second and national (official) language. Thus there is an urgent need to codify NP and standardise its orthography so as to ensure a rich literature in the language. It is hoped that when NP is accorded this recognition, the solution to our socio-political problems of developing and sustaining a fledgling democratic structure, forging unity amongst diverse ethnic groups and resolving our national language question may be seen to have been proffered.

References

Adegbija, Efurosibina. 1997. The identity, survival, and promotion of minority languages in Nigeria. In *International Journal of the Sociology of Language*, 125(1), 5–28.

Adegbija, Efurosibina. 2001. *Multilingualism: A case study of Nigeria*. New York: Africa World Press.

Afolayan, Adebisi. 1980. Towards a new approach to teachers education for effective implementation of the language medium provisions of the *National policy on education*. An unpublished paper prepared for the consideration of the old Oyo State Ministry of Education, Molete, Ibadan.

Agheyisi, Rebecca. 1984. Linguistic implications of the changing role of Nigerian Pidgin. *English World-wide*, 5, 211–233.

Akande, Akinmade. 2010. Is Nigerian Pidgin English English? *Dialectologia et Geolinguistica* 18(1), 3–22.

Akande, Akinmade & Oladipo Salami. 2010. Use and attitudes towards Nigerian Pidgin English among Nigerian university students. In Robert M. Millar (ed.), *Marginal dialects: Scotland, Ireland and beyond*. 70–89. Aberdeen: Forum for Research on the Languages of Scotland and Ireland.

Akinnaso, F. Niyi. 1987. Language planning and political development in Nigeria. Paper presented at the university roundtable, University of Wisconsin-Parkside, 5 October 1987.

Akinnaso, F. Niyi. 1989. One nation, four hundred languages: Unity and diversity in Nigeria's language policy. *Language Problems and Planning* 13(2), 133–146.

Akinnaso, F. Niyi. 2015. The politics of language planning in education in Nigeria. *WORD* 41(3), 337–367.

Awobuluyi, Oladele. 2010. *Linguistics and nation building: The Prof. Emeritus Ayo Bamgbose personality lecture*. Ibadan: DB Martoy Books.

Bailey, Richard W. & James L. Robinson. 1973. *Varieties of present-day English*. London: Collier Macmillan Publishers.

Balogun, Temitope A. 2013. In defense of Nigerian Pidgin. *Journal of Language and Culture* 4(5), 90–98.

Bamgbose, Ayo, Ayo Banjo & Andrew Thomas (eds). 1995. *New Englishes: A West African perspective*. Ibadan: Mosuro.

Cargile, Aaron C., Howard Giles & Richard Clément. 1995. Language, conflict, and ethnolinguistic identity theory. *Human Social Conflict* 1, 189–208.

Giles, Howard & Patricia Johnson. 1987. Ethnolinguistic identity theory: A social psychological approach to language maintenance. *International Journal of Sociology of Language* 68, 69–100.

Dadzie, Anthony B. K. 1987. Pidgin in Ghana: A theoretical consideration of its origin and development. Unpublished paper delivered at the Department of English, University of Lagos, Akoka, Lagos.

Donwa-Ifode, Shirley. 1984. Is Nigerian Pidgin creolising? *Journal of Linguistic Association of Nigeria* (2), 99–203.

Douglas, Blessing. 2012. The status of Nigerian Pidgin and other indigenous languages in Bayelsa State tertiary institutions. Unpublished M.A. dissertation. Ile-Ife: Department of English, Obafemi Awolowo University.

Egbokhare, Francis. 2001. The Nigerian linguistic ecology and the changing profiles of Nigerian Pidgin. In Herbert Igboanusi (ed.), *Language attitude and language conflicts in West*. Ibadan: Enicrownfit Publishers.

Elugbe, Ben Ohiomamhe & Augusta P. Omamor. 1991. *Nigerian Pidgin: Background and prospects*. Ibadan: Heinemann Educational Books Nigeria PLC.

Esizimetor, David Oshorenoya. 2010. Histocal development of Naija in *NAIJA*. Proceedings of the 'conference on Nigerian Pidgin' held at the University of Ibadan, 8–9 July, 2009.

Esizimetor, David Oshorenoya. 2011. A Study of the history and structure of Naijá words. A paper presented at the meeting of the society for pidgin and creole linguistics (SPCL), Accra, Ghana, 2–6. August, 2011.

Esizimetor, David & Francis Egbokhare. 2012. Naija (Nigerian Pidgin) in *Language varieties langnet in Pidgins and creoles in education (PACE)* http://www.hawaii.edu (updated September 9, 2014)

Igboanusi, Herbert. 2008. Empowering Nigerian Pidgin: A challenge for status planning? *World Englishes* 27(1), 68–72.

Ihemere, Kelechuckwu U. 2006. A basic description and analytic treatment of noun clauses in Nigerian Pidgin. *Nordic Journal of African Studies* 15(3), 296–313.

Fairclough, Norman. 2001. *Language and power*. London: Longman.

Faraclas, Nicholas. 1996. *Nigerian Pidgin*. London: Routledge.

Fawehinmi, Patrick. 1987. Communication in Pidgin in Nigeria: Origin, problems, and prospects. In Solomon Unoh (ed.), *Topical issues in communication arts*, 71–87. Uyo: Modern Business Press.

Jibril, Munzali. 1995. The elaboration of the functions of Nigerian Pidgin. In Ayo Bamgbose, Ayo Banjo & Andrew Thomas (eds.), *New Englishes: A West African perspective*, 232–247. Ibadan: Mosuro.

Jowitt, David. 1995. Nigeria's national language problem: Choices and constraints. In Ayo Bamgbose, Ayo Banjo & Andrew Thomas (eds.), *New Englishes: A West African perspective*, 34–56. Ibadan: Mosuro.

Kioko, Nduku, Angelina, Ruth Ndung'u, Martin C. Njoroge & Jayne Mutiga. 2014. Mother tongue and education in Africa: Publicising the reality. *Multilingual Education* 4(1), 1–18.

Mann, Charles C. 2000. Reviewing ethnolinguistic vitality: The case of Anglo-Nigerian Pidgin *Journal of Sociolinguistics* 4, 458–474.

Obote, Milton. 1967. Language and national identification. *East African Journal*, 4(1), 3–6.

Oribohabor, Eriata. 2016. Lingua franca: From Nigerian Pidgin to Naija languej. In *Jalada Africa. Jalada 04: The language issue*. Bonus edition. https://jalada.africa.org> lingua (accessed 30 May 2016)

Osoba, Joseph. 2014. The use of Nigerian Pidgin in political jingles. *Journal of Universal Language* 15(1), 105–127.

Osoba, Joseph. 2014a. The use of Nigerian Pidgin in media adverts. *International Journal of English Linguistics* 4(20), 126–307.

Osoba, Joseph. 2015. Analysis of discourse in Nigerian Pidgin. *Journal of Universal Language* 16(1), 131–159.

Osoba, Joseph. 2018. Power in Nigerian Pidgin (NP) discourse. *Journal of Universal Language* 19(1), 1–32.

Osoba, Joseph & Tajudeen Alebiosu. 2016. Language preference as a precursor to displacement and extinction in Nigeria: The roles of English Language and Nigerian Pidgin. *Journal of Universal Language* 17(2), 111–143.

Oyeleye, Lekan A. 2016. *In my father's house: Globalisation, linguistic pluralism and the English language in Nigeria*. Inaugural lecture delivered at the University of Ibadan. Ibadan: University of Ibadan Press.

Oyetade, Solomon O. 2003. Language planning in a multi-ethnic state: The majority/minority dichotomy in Nigeria. *Nordic Journal of African Studies* 12(1), 105–117.

Rickford, John R. 1974. The insights of the mesolect. In David Decamp & Ian Hancock (eds.), *Pidgins and creoles: Current trends and perspectives*, 92–117. Washinton, D.C.: Georgetown University Press.

Searle, John. 1969. *Speech acts*. Cambridge: Cambridge University Press.

Tollefson, James. 1996. *Planning language, planning inequality*. London: Longman.

Ugoagwu, Peter. 2006. *Vernacular, plain, and simple*. http://yeyeolade.wordpress.com/author/yeyeolade/

Wright, Sue. 2014. *Language policy and language planning*. London: Palgrave Macmillan.

Oladipo Salami and Akinmade T. Akande
Chapter 12
Non-state actors, language practices, language policy and Nigerian Pidgin promotion

Introduction

In this study, we try to explore the place and contribution of non-state actors to the vitality and promotion of Nigerian Pidgin through their language use practices and policies. de Bres (2015: 309), citing Spolsky (2009), observes that studies in language planning and policy (henceforth LPP) have progressed, in recent years, from a focus on the language policies of governments to policies within language use domains such as the workplace, the family, the public space and the media. Traditional or mainstream LPP has assumed, until relatively recently, that its work is the domain of the government or state and its agencies only. The studies by de Bres (ibid.) as well as Spolsky (ibid.) have, however, taken the perspective of the expanded view of LPP to include any language practice that we engage in which can be seen as an instance of language policy activities. Such activities may include each word we speak or write aligning with, modifying or resisting the language norms operating, explicitly or implicitly, in a given setting or polity (de Bres, 2015: 310). Thus, the official, governmental or state policy of a given setting, for example, may not be in tandem with the actual linguistic norms or practices of language users within that state or setting. This is why de Bres is, therefore, of the view that language policies are connected to the context of the language practices of their target audience and their associated language ideologies or beliefs and that these practices are also constituted by a dynamic composite of elements constantly under construction and always subject to change.

According to Kayam and Hirsch (2012: 623), language policies "are present and stem not only from the 'top-down' national policies but also from institutional policies of the school, the workplace, and from the 'bottom-up' sources such as the individuals and the families." In looking at the emerging emphasis in LPP, Hornberger (2006: 34) notes that calls have been made for greater attention, among others, to the role of the human agency, and in particular bottom-up agency in LPP. In line with de Bres' (2015:310) view, language policy "can be defined as any activity in which a social actor attempts to modify the language practices, language ideologies, or, indeed, language policies of others." In Nigeria, the existing language norms acknowledged in the country's National Language Policy do not give official recognition to Nigerian Pidgin (henceforth NP) as a language even though it is widely used in the country as a means of communication between and among educated and not-so-educated Nigerians, in commercial interactions, for radio and television announcements or jingles; for comedy and so on (Akande and Salami, 2010). Nigerian Pidgin has no formal status while it is not formally allocated any function in the polity. It is not recognized for use in formal situations or by officials of government at government functions. However, everyday language practices of Nigerians show that it is a language that cannot be ignored as a result of its roles in a number of domains, even though some of these roles may seem to be at the margins of the state or government-driven language policies.

1 Language policy and non-state actors

Language planning and policy can be understood as charting or formulating the directions regarding the structure and functions or uses of a language. It may be done for the purposes of influencing or exerting influences on either the structures or status and use of the given language. Embedded in this effort is the goal of promoting the language for efficiency or use. In promotion, policy directions may be invisible, especially when they involve social or non-state actors. This may take place in contexts where there are challenges as to the structure, status and functional allocation of specific languages in a given polity. As observed by Fasold (1984: 246), LPP results from the evaluation of alternatives where the best choice is made. In situations where languages in contention are considered as resources that can be used in improving social lives, language planning would attempt to determine which of the available linguistic alternatives is most likely to improve a problematic situation (Fasold, 1984: 250).

As noted by Candlin (1996: vi), LPP can impact social issues such as education and political participation while it can in itself be influenced by history, politics and the identities of the institutions or forces in which the planning is taking place. In other words, LLP is historically and socially-driven. This cannot but be true also of policies under-guarding language planning. Candlin (1996) argues further that the governing forces of the state as well as the individual, power, hegemony and discrimination must be considered as they have critical roles to play in LPP. The view is that LLP is connected to a number of historical and social issues, including decolonization, national, group and personal identities. This is why we need to begin to interrogate the agencies of the individuals and social actions in LPP as there is a dynamic relationship between LPP and the constructs of power, state, social structure, dominance and exploitation (Candlin, 1996: viii).

2 Nigerian national language policy and Nigerian Pidgin

In Nigeria's national language policy on education, NP is neither legitimized nor delegitimized. In other words, there is no law expressly directing or restricting its use while there are no documented policies allocating functions to it. However, the language is used in ways that we can claim, in this work, that there are contextual bottom-up policies in the language practices of its speakers and users. For example, even though the courts are formal institutions in the country that will call for the use of English, it is not impossible to find situations where 'accused' persons can use NP during interrogation, especially if they are not competent or proficient in spoken English. In this context, what the court may do is to seek the interpretation of the accused person's NP responses. What the accused persons would have done is to, unconsciously, disrupt the language-license of the Nigerian court by using NP. They do this because for them what seems to matter is that NP meets their communicative need(s). In other words, the speaker of NP is focused on the 'socio-linguistic' value of the language as observed by Fasold (1984: 250) that language is seen "as a resource that can be used in improving social life. This way of practicing language planning would attempt to determine which of the available linguistic alternatives is most likely to improve a problematic situation."

Fasold (ibid.) notes further that to solve language-related problematic situations involves decision taking almost by anybody, including governments and its agencies, language academies, the Church, private citizens and so on. Citing Ray (1968: 764), Fasold (1984: 251) quotes:

> . . . any formal organized action by an acknowledged authority, such as a State or a Church or a learned society or author, can be successful in its intention to encourage or discourage linguistic habits only if it correlates maximally to informal unorganized action on the part of numerous locally more accessible authorities.

What we note, so far, is that while, in the main, there are LPP decisions about languages taken by the government and its agencies (top-down), there are also possibilities of such related LPP decisions from ordinary citizens and non-state actors (bottom-up). These decisions taken can be about the language as a tool of communication (to make it more efficient for use) or just to work on it as a social resource to be made available for some social ends.

3 Approach to the study

The approach to this study is based on the conceptualization that even though non-state actors are not overtly making laws or formulating policies concerning their own language practices, they are bottom-up sources for practices for managing language use and functions that become eventually theirs. We agree with Spolsky (2004, cited in Kayam and Hirsch, 2012: 623) that LPP is a field which works on beliefs and ideologies about language practices and efforts in order to influence language practices through various management techniques. Thus, in this study, we will examine the roles of non-state actors which include individuals and groups in the management of NP. In doing this, we will describe language activities involving NP in the contexts of the workplace, the social media, entertainment (music) and the electronic medium (the radio). We explore the language practices of these non-state actors in order to uncover the underlying goal(s) they seek to achieve as well as their contribution to the promotion of NP.

As noted earlier, LPP motivations may include making a language more efficient and expanding its functions or roles. Besides, decisions taken or policies about a language could also be driven by ideology or beliefs concerning the language or its users. For example, LPP could target the need to achieve solidarity among the speakers of a particular language or to promote their social, cultural or linguistic identity. Language practices may even be motivated by the desire to challenge the hegemony of state-imposed or mainstream language norms. Ndhlovu (2008: 138, citing Mazrui and Mazrui, 1998: 14) notes that every language in a multilingual society has the right to exist and to be given equal opportunity to flourish. Among the forces that may contribute to this possibility are entertainment, the social media, the electronic media (radio and television) and the workplace.

4 The role of entertainment: Hip-hop music and Nigerian Pidgin

Like in all human performances or acts, linguistic practices occur in entertainments such as cultural festivals, stage plays and music. These practices may embed acts of language management, especially if the sociolinguistic space presents multilingualism or code diversity. States or their agencies do promote cultures and languages through festivals and entertainments. For example, in Nigeria, the federal as well as the state governments often organize national cultural festivals where different ethnic and socio-cultural groups participate to showcase the cultures of their various groups, including indigenous theaters, dances, music and so on. These festivals help in one way or the other to promote both majority and minority cultures, including keeping the languages in use at the festivals alive.

Although one is not aware of any efforts to promote NP in any national cultural festivals, the language seems to be assuming a very prominent place in the entertainment industry in the country, especially in stand-up comedies and music. It has been the most popular code used in the genre of music called Afrobeat and, today, it is the toast of the hip-hop genre of music. The lyrics of many of the hip-hop artistes are not only often multilingual but they usually also include NP (Akande, 2014; Babalola and Taiwo, 2009). According to Akande (2014: 272), the artistes, in most cases, use Nigerian Pidgin to ensure that fans outside their ethnic groups understand their lyrics. Furthermore, they do multilingual code-switching in order to reflect the multiethnic and multilingual nature of the country. For Akande (2013), lyrics written in NP seem more appreciated than those composed in other Nigerian languages.

From the foregoing, we can observe that NP has some status and functions attaching to it in Nigerian hip-hop music. There are, today, a large number of Nigerian musicians in the hip-hop genre whose language practices can be seen to be underlined by some policies to use NP. Many of these musicians are relatively young (under 40) and their audience is largely the educated youth (between the age of 18 and 35). They seem not only to be utilizing their language policy options but are, ostensibly, also promoting NP via intra-generational diffusion of a code that is considered to be that of the non-literate and the uneducated.

5 The social media and social network sites and LPP

des Bres (2015: 310) notes that the new media is one of the possible and compelling domains of language policy activities. He observes further that sociolinguistic research has been carried out in this domain in relation to language use in messaging, discussion forums, blogs and so on. Some of the research works have focused on language practices such as code-switching, style-shifting and identity construction. However, des Bres (2015) opines that not much has been done to uncover the language policies guiding the language practices on social network sites because as also noted by Androutsopoulos (2009: 285, cited in des Bres, 2015: 310), the social media, in general, is not a key concept in language policy research. Nevertheless, he notes that if we explore social network sites (henceforth SNSs) as domains of language policy activities, we may have new and interesting things to bring to the fore both on language use in the new media and language policy.

It is important to note that the social media has assumed a powerful position in the 21st century in shaping and reshaping cultural, social and political behaviours and norms. As observed by Yerima (2019), the social media has the power to excite, inspire and empower the user. It is thought to spread what seems to be the compulsive feeling to speak to the world (p. 36). Aniga and Jeje (2019: 239) are of the view that the social media have become very veritable tools for quick communication and dissemination of information using the internet. Talking about the use of the social media, Aniga and Jeje (2019: 240) note, for example, as follows:

> Nigerians participate on Facebook actively. A good number of them engage in positive portrayal of the country towards projecting the cultural heritage of the country. Postings and images on Nigeria's delicacies, wears, idioms, proverbs, and even jokes and songs are normally engaged in.

It is observed that though many of the global and local social media platforms in Nigeria are driven by English, users can communicate to their world in the languages or codes that they or their communities have chosen or legitimated whether or not they are state-approved official languages. Today, Tweeter, WhatsApp, Telegram etc are used by many people, including state officials, as platforms of communication in Nigeria. The state officials do not only engage in the use of these social media platforms to communicate with citizens but do so often using the country's official language – the English language. However, at the levels of individuals who are non-state actors, the languages in use in communicating on these platforms tend to vary. The variation may result from factors such as the topic of interaction and persons involved in interactions on a given social media platform.

In the language practices that individuals and non-state actors engage in, it is not unlikely that norms or policies of interaction are often negotiated within their specific communities of practice. Such policies are, probably, informally formulated, promoted and made to gradually diffuse into the larger polity. In fact, it can be observed that quite a number of language practices have emerged from social media platforms that have become very influential in the language behaviour of users. According to Taiwo (2019), one of the prominent features of social media is the creativity in language use; its capacity to allow users to generate and express themselves in new ways from time to time (p. 48). The SNSs have become some ubiquitous arena for promoting many products, including, indirectly, languages and language use in Nigeria.

6 The electronic media and LPP

The place of the electronic media such as the radio and television as tools for education, entertainment and dissemination of information is also considered an important instrument in driving language policies, including the promotion of the status, use and functional allocation of languages. In Nigeria, national news broadcast was in the three majority languages of Hausa, Igbo and Yoruba up till 1967. This was before the creation of the twelve states from the three regions along which the country was administered at independence. The creation of those twelve states soon gave visibility and vitality to more languages that hitherto had no national recognition. They included, among others, Edo, Efik, Fulfude, Kanuri, Idoma, Tiv and Izon. In this process of status promotion and functional allocation, NP was never given a place as a language of news delivery, even though it has been observed to be a language that has always been very widely used in the Niger-Delta region (Elugbe and Omamor, 1991). Part of the reason for this non-recognition, perhaps, could be that the electronic media was controlled mainly by the state or government. In the last twenty years or so, especially with increased democratization of the polity, there had been established a substantial number of radio and television stations by private concerns for the purposes of information, education and entertainment. These private stations are observed to broadcast in English, Nigerian mother tongues and their local varieties and NP. This is not to say that NP was never used on governments' radio or television but it had functioned more in adverts and jingles for mobilization and sensitization than in news broadcast. In other words, NP could not be said to have the equality of status as 'a language for news broadcast' as the English language, Hausa, Igbo or Yoruba. However, since the beginning of Nigeria's 4th republic, especially with the establishment of private radios and televisions in the different parts of the country, the monopoly of government over the electronic media for the dissemination of information, entertainment and educational programs has been seemingly broken.

The de-monopolization of the electronic media seems also to have led to a development where the government has little or no control on the language to be used. In other words, the private electronic media stations seem now to have the freedom to manage their language practices. This is why it can be observed that a number of them have expanded the functional allocation of NP on radio and television beyond jingles and adverts. Also, today, with growing urbanization, it has become increasingly important to use NP to reach urban agglomerations to achieve successful communicative goals. Thus, many newly established electronic media houses across the country are not only using NP in advertisements and entertainment but in news programming. For example, Raheem (2013) investigates language choice in news delivery in Rivers State because of its linguistic diversity with a population of five million people speaking close to twenty indigenous languages. The study shows that while government radio stations in the state promoted mother tongues and NP usage policy, the private radio stations used English only. This, he observes, was because the proprietors of the private radios were driven by the commercial value of English in their enterprises. That is they had more positive attitude to English than to NP because it fetched their businesses more money to use English than NP.

7 The workplace: The individual agency and LPP

The users of a given language are its best transmitters and, perhaps, also its best promoters and protectors. Individuals as members of a family or groups or communities of practice can and do 'formulate' their personal and group language policies in the guise of their language practices. They may be, in their language practices, agents of conservation, resistance, promotion, progress or change. Thus, their personal and group values may become implicated in the choice they make in their language behaviour or practices. Such values may be underlined by a number of factors, including, for example, the promotion or sustenance of family or a groups' social or cultural identity. In other words, the individual, the family or a group's language use options come into play in language polices at the level of the non-state actor.

Individuals commune and interact in workplaces. Therefore, the role of the workplace is important in understanding the LPP practices of individuals or workers where they work. Language is very critical for the smooth working of any organization or institution, especially in multilingual contexts such as Nigeria. Apart from enhancing efficiency at work, shared language can promote team-work and mutual understanding. Our language behaviour can influence and as well be influenced by our workplaces.

In terms of workplace language policies, we have not found any expressly stated laws and regulations guiding the use of language in workplaces in Nigeria. What exists in the country's constitution is the recognition of the English language as the country's official language. It can be observed, however, from the linguistic landscapes of such institutions as schools, hospitals, state or government houses and many other administrative offices of governments that the English language predominates. This seems to reflect the place of the English language in the country.

As noted earlier, the official language of business in Nigeria is English. It will be interesting, however, to find out what the language practices of Nigerian workers look alike in relation to the use of NP in their workplaces. In this study, we have focused mainly on professional individuals in their workplaces. The choice of this group was based on the assumption that their positive attitude to NP would serve more to enhance the status of the language and promote it than what less-educated artisans, traders and farmers would. This is simply to say that their education and professional status would provide authenticity for NP to grow.

This study set out to answer three important research questions. It is believed that answers to these questions will elucidate our knowledge on LPP in relation to NP. The questions are: (1) Do the non-state actors in this study have policies relating to the use of NP?, (2) What functions do they allocate to NP?, and finally (3) What impact(s) have their language practices and policies have on NP?

8 Methods

In carrying out the data gathering for this study, we used a mixed design involving quantitative and qualitative data gathering methods. We used semi-structured questionnaire with both close and open-ended questions. We also used documents sourced from the social media and the internet (WhatsApp and blogs). The data were gathered from the four domains as described below:

(i) Music: We sampled and downloaded thirty (30) lyrics of thirty hip-hop musicians for this study. They were purposively selected as the songs released early in 2020 and were popular on radio and entertainment outlets (Trace/Naija, Afro and Urban on Digital Satellite TV). We audited language use or code selection in the lyrics by counting or identifying the occurrence of a particular code or codes in a given lyric.

(ii) Social Network Sites (SNSs): Four social media platforms were purposively sampled: Nairaland, Nigerian Village Square, Linda Ikeji Blog and WhatsApp Language Group. These sites cover group and individual interactions and exchanges occurring in discussion forums, news, events, politics and the development in Nigeria. They also cover such banal issues as the dating stories of local artistes and celebrities. The WhatsApp platform, however, belonged to a group which we created for our undergraduate students in sociolinguistics course. We purposively downloaded three sets of comments or exchanges from each SNS. These exchanges cover politics, Covid-19 pandemic and entertainment. We proceeded to audit code or language selections in each of these categories of comments to have a broad perception of the language practices of the participants on the sampled platforms.

(iii) Electronic media (radio): data on LPP on radio was collected through a semi-structured survey questionnaire prepared on Google Forms. The survey focused on use of NP in 18 purposively selected radio stations in six states of Southwestern Nigeria. It was done to cover the Yoruba-speaking region of Nigeria. Three radio stations were sampled from each state, two private and one government. These radio stations are in Lagos, Ogun, Oyo, Osun, Ondo and Ekiti States. The questions asked are: (i) does your station have a policy on language to use on radio? (ii) can you give reason(s) for your answer? (iii) Do you have any programme in NP? (iv) can you give reason(s) for your answer? (v) If answer to (iii) is yes, what is the reaction of the people/public to your pidgin programme? (vi) whose initiative is the pidgin programme? (vii) what purpose is the programme for? (viii) what does your proprietor think about the use of pidgin on your radio?

(iv) The workplace: The survey of language practices and policies in the workplace was done with the use of Google Forms (https://docs.google.com/forms). The questionnaire was forwarded via an e-mail to 52 professionals in our social networks. They included teachers, academics, civil servants, corporate employees etc. Only 48 of the 52 (92.3%) professionals returned the questionnaire filled in. It contained the following questions: (i) Do you speak Nigerian Pidgin? (ii) Do you speak Nigerian Pidgin at work? (iii) Do you think it is OK to speak pidgin in your place of work? (iv) Give reason(s) for your answer in (iii) above

Besides, the foregoing, we will like to mention that when necessary we had to follow up our questionnaire for data gathering with phone interviews and discussion.

9 Data analysis and discussion

9.1 The music industry and Nigerian Pidgin

In this section, we will attempt to examine the language practices among hip-hop musicians in the lyrics of the songs they play and air to their audience across the country and internationally. Table 1 below shows the musicians and the languages in use.

Table 1: Musicians and the Choice of Language in Lyrics.

S/N	Musician	Song title	English	Nigerian Pidgin	Mother Tongue
1	Tiwa ft. Joeboy	Let them Know	Yes	Yes	Yes
2	Dremo	STFU	Yes	Yes	Yes
3	Crayon	Kpano	Yes	Yes	Yes
4	Simi	Duduke	Yes	Yes	Yes
5	Buju	Lenu Remix	Yes	Yes	Yes
6	Mayorkun	Of Lagos	Yes	No	Yes
7	Teni	Isolate	Yes	Yes	Yes
8	Joeboy	Call	Yes	Yes	Yes
9	Peruzzi ft. Not3s	Reason	Yes	Yes	No
10	Skales	Kowope	Yes	Yes	Yes
11	Teckno	Kata	Yes	Yes	No
12	Sound Sultan	Area	Yes	Yes	Yes
13	Iyanya	Fever	Yes	Yes	No
14	Obesere ft. Zlatan	Egungun Be Careful	Yes	Yes	Yes
15	Blaqbonez	Haba	No	Yes	No
16	Wande Cole	Again	Yes	Yes	No
17	9ice	Sekuseye	Yes	Yes	Yes
18	Falz ft. Ms Banks	Bop Daddy	Yes	Yes	Yes
19	Burna Boy	Odogwu	Yes	Yes	Yes

Table 1 (continued)

S/N	Musician	Song title	English	Nigerian Pidgin	Mother Tongue
20	Rema	Beamer	Yes	Yes	No
21	Zinoleesky ft. Naira Marley	Caro	No	Yes	Yes
22	Olamide	Rich and Famous	Yes	Yes	No
23	Patoranking	I'm in Love	Yes	Yes	Yes
24	Oluwadamilola	Dey my head	Yes	Yes	Yes
25	Mr. Eazi	Kpalanga	Yes	Yes	Yes
26	Lil Kesh	Kowope	Yes	No	Yes
27	Davido	2020 Letter to you	Yes	Yes	Yes
28	Ycee	Vacancy	Yes	Yes	Yes
29	Fireboy	Vibration	Yes	Yes	Yes
30	Kizz Daniel	Jaho	Yes	Yes	Yes

From the table above, we can observe that in the thirty (30) lyrics of the songs of the different artists, three codes are in use: English, NP and Mother Tongue (mostly Yoruba). This is interesting but not unusual. As reported by Babalola and Taiwo (2009) and Akande (2013 and 2014), the genre of hip-hop music in Nigeria exhibits a lot of multilingual code-switching. It is important to note that a large number of the musicians are young (under 40) and educated, with at least secondary school education. They live in cities and urban areas of the country, especially in Lagos, Port Harcourt and Enugu. Although the artistes whose lyrics form the data used in the present study speak English, Yoruba or other Nigerian languages, they chose, regularly, also to use NP in their lyrics. According to Akande (2013), NP has a high prevalence in hip-hop lyrics as the songs are easier to understand by non-Nigerians in pidgin than in the mother tongues. Also, Omoniyi (2006, cited in Akande, 2013: 45) holds that rap songs in NP are more appreciated locally and internationally than those composed in mother tongues. Furthermore, these songs are also highly valued because a wider audience can identify with the language used in them across the country. Babalola and Taiwo add that the code-switching behaviour involving NP in Nigerian hip-hop music reflects stylistic innovation and done to achieve commercial success. They also hold that NP is seen by the artistes as the language of the

Nigerian youth community irrespective of their origin or educational background (2009: 10–11).

9.2 The social network sites and Nigerian Pidgin

We explored language practices in interactions among participants in social network sites with particular focus on the use of NP. Table 2 below shows data on code use behaviour in the SNSs investigated.

Table 2: Showing Code Use Behaviour of Interactants on Social Network Sites.

	English Only	MT Only	NP Only	English + MT	English + NP	NP + MT	Total No of Comments
Nairaland	61 (91%)	–	01 (1.5%)	–	04 (6%)	01 (1.5%)	67
Linda Ikeji Blog	104 (83%)	–	–	–	17 (13.5%)	05 (4%)	126
Nigerian Village Square	34 (92%)	–	–	01 (3%)	02 (5%)	–	37
WhatsApp Language Group	86 (50.3%)	18 (10.5%)	15 (9%)	27 (16%)	08 (4.5%)	07 (4.1%)	171

From the table, we will observe that the use of NP only occurs at 1.5% and 9% in the interactional exchanges on two of the SNSs, that is, Nairaland and WhatsApp Language Group. These do not point to any significant use of NP. When we look at the combined usages in code-switches, we will note that NP is used at 9%; 17.5%; 8% and 17.6% of exchanges in Nairaland, Linda Ikeji Blog, Nigerian Village Square and WhatsApp Language Group respectively. Although the data shows that NP is used in these SNSs, the percentage usage is insignificant compared to the use of the English language. There could be a number of reasons for this outcome. First, these SNSs could have been seen by users as formal writing platforms and therefore required the use of the official/formal language, the English language. The second reason could be that very few interactants on the platforms were sufficiently good at expressing themselves in writing NP whose orthography is rather variable. The third possible reason could be that many of the interactants whose exchanges we used were, probably, not positively disposed to writing NP. In any case, NP is still largely an oral medium among its users as it has no standard orthography yet.

9.3 The radio and Nigerian Pidgin

In this section, we examine the data on language practices in radio stations as a case study on the influence of the electronic media on NP. Table 3 below shows the data on the use of NP in eighteen (18) purposively selected government and private radio stations across the six states of Southwestern Nigeria.

Table 3: Showing Radio Stations and the use of NP in Southwestern States.

Radio Station	Location	Ownership	Is NP Used?	Programmes
Radio Lagos	Ikeja	Government	No	95% Yoruba 5% English
Wazobia	Lagos Island	Private	Yes	Almost all programmes are in Nig. Pidgin
Traffic Radio	Ikeja	Government	Yes	Has two-hour belt for use of NP daily; traffic advisories
Smash FM	Abeokuta	Private	Yes	No specific programme but OAPs can use NP
Ogun State Radio		Government	No	The Radio languages are English and Yoruba
Sweet FM	Abeokuta	Private	Yes	As e dey go
Oluyole FM	Ibadan	Government	Yes	Talk your own
Fresh FM	Ibadan	Private	Yes	Weekend jollof, Talk your own, Pidgin news,
Space FM	Ibadan	Private	Yes	Tori tori, Lovalova,
Orisun FM	Osogbo	Government	No	No Programme
Crown FM	Ile-Ife	Private	Yes	News delivery daily
Adaba FM	Akure	Private	Yes	News delivery, newspaper reviews, call-in programmes, weekend groove
Orange FM	Akure	Private	Yes	Breakfast show every Friday morning
Alalaye FM	Akure	Private	No	Programmes are broadcast in Yoruba and its dialects in Ondo
Ekiti FM 91.5	Ado-Ekiti	Government	Yes	E get as e be, How una dey, una gudu morning

Table 3 (continued)

Radio Station	Location	Ownership	Is NP Used?	Programmes
Voice FM	Ado-Ekiti	Private	Yes	Pidgin News, Pidgin lounge, Waffi junction
Our Peoples FM	Ado-Ekiti	Private	Yes	Shikini tori (news in brief), berekete tori (newspaper reviews), how una dey, aproko junction (discussion), request programme, sports

From the table above, we can observe that 15 out of the 18 radio stations, that is 83% of those sampled, claimed to use NP for programming. Most of these radios are non-governmental outfits. We can observe, from the table, that NP is now used for a wide range of programmes, including entertainment, discussions, calls-in, traffic advisory; news delivery and newspaper review. In other words, it seems that NP is getting increasing recognition in the prestigious domain of electronic media. The allocation of functions to it by the private radios cover, today, several programme areas beyond its erstwhile roles as a language of jingles and adverts. The result here contrasts, however, with the absence of the use of NP on private radios in Rivers State, as reported by Raheem (2013), where the language is considered commercially unviable, even though it is used on government radios.

We tried to seek further, from practitioners in the stations, to know the underlying motivations for the use of NP in their radio stations. The responses obtained can be summarized as follows:
i) It is the station's policy to use Nigerian Pidgin
ii) We are a Pidgin radio station
iii) It is the Head of programmes' initiative to use Pidgin
iv) The Proprietor is positive towards its use (NP)

What these responses implicate is that these stations, as non-state institutions, have expressed policies for the use of NP, even when the initiatives come from their staff. In other words, the agency of the individual staff can play a critical role in the use of NP on radio.

Of the six government-owned radio stations, four use NP for programming. This is high. However, unlike the private radio stations, NP is not used in a 'high function' like news delivery on these government radios. There are two possible reasons for this outcome. The first reason is that the government's language is English, its language of official business which does not allow the use of NP in news delivery. The second is that the government radio stations seem to be continuing with the unexpressed policy of NP as a 'limited language' to areas such as jingles, adverts and entertainment but not for a high function as news delivery.

Although the BBC is not a Nigerian radio, its presence (World Service Pidgin) in Nigeria's social space as a non-state actor and its role in promoting and enhancing the vitality of Nigerian pidgin cannot but be mentioned. Since the establishment of BBC Pidgin in 2017, it has continued to broadcast news in pidgin and has also continued to carry out interviews, stories and documentaries in pidgin. The perception of BBC as an English language organ that loves and validates pidgin is a plus for NP among the people. As Dr, Christine I. Ofulue says *"[T]oday, it (pidgin) represents African pride, seen in the flourishing number of radio stations and television programs that use Pidgin"*. Dr. Ofulue commends the BBC's decision to offer Pidgin service saying also that "it helped remove the stigma attached to Pidgin, often derided as a corruption of standard English". (https://www.nytimes.com2017/12/30/world/africa/bbc-pidgin.html)

9.4 Nigerian Pidgin in the workplace

Here, we will examine the data on responses to questions on the use of NP in the workplace. Table 4 below shows the responses of individuals to questions relating to NP usage in workplace that we sought.

Table 4: Showing the Use of Nigerian Pidgin in the Workplace.

Comments	Yes	No	Total
I am able to speak Nigerian Pidgin	40 (83.3%)	08 (16.7%)	48 (100%)
I speak Nigerian Pidgin at work	31 (65%)	17 (35%)	48 (100%)
It is appropriate to speak Nigerian Pidgin at work	28 (58.3%)	20 (41.7%)	48 (100%)

The statements about the ability to speak Nigerian Pidgin are important because not every Nigerian can speak NP. The table shows that 40 out of 48 (83.3%) of the respondents claimed to be able to speak NP. This is quite high. The result may point to some positive attitude towards pidgin usage among the professionals sampled for this study. We can observe that 31 out of the 48 (65%) of the professionals claimed they speak pidgin in their workplaces. This relatively high percentage of respondents seems also to point to a reality that even though NP is not the language of official business in the country, that is, the recognized language of workplace, it is still used in workplaces. When we tried to find out from the respondents if this language practice was appropriate, the result showed that 28 out of 48 (58.3%) claimed that it was. In other words, a greater number of the respondents had positive attitude towards the code's usage in the workplace. This confirms Akande and Salami's (2010) study which reveals that university students generally have positive attitude towards the use of NP. We can observe, however, that there is a percentage difference between those who claimed to speak pidgin at work and those who claimed it was appropriate to use it (65% and 58.3%) respectively. Although the difference is not so large, one would have expected that all those who claimed to use NP in the workplace would also have claimed that it was appropriate to use it in that context too. There are, possibly, two related reasons for this discrepancy. First, it could mean that they themselves use NP in the workplace because there is no policy that restricts its usage. They are exercising their human agency to formulate a language policy for themselves. Secondly, the seeming contradiction between their claim of usage of the code in the workplace and the claim of its inappropriateness might, perhaps, be underlined by the value they place on pidgin. This value could be that they see NP as not a language of formal work.

It is interesting when we tried further to inquire about the reasons the respondents claimed to use NP in the workplace as the summary below shows:
(i) pidgin helps you to be less formal and express yourself better
(ii) because we some time deal with tax payers who are not educated
(iii) pidgin is a language spoken across social classes
(iv) because my work has to do with relating with people and not everyone can speak correct English
(v) because at place of work, there are also unlearned personnel ... one needs to speak in pidgin in order to pass across the message to them

These reasons given relate to persons, formality, level of education, class etc. In other words, the professionals seem to be saying that NP serves many important interpersonal and contextual functions which make its use critical.

10 Findings and conclusion

A number of findings result from this exploratory study. From the language practices of the non-state actors that we investigated, we can observe that, generally, the actors in the various domains seem to have and operate some bottom-up language policies where NP functions. In the music domain, NP functions prominently in lyrics where they are used for aesthetic, cultural, solidarity and communicative purposes. What we see is in that domain is, on the one hand, NP promoting hip-hop music while, on the other hand, hip-hop music is also promoting NP among the consumers of hip-hop locally and internationally. The study has also shown that independent private radio stations, through staff initiatives and the support of proprietors, have scaled up the use of NP by allocating more functions to it in their programming. In addition, the availability of social media platforms and social network sites (SNSs) have placed at the disposal of the individual language users the opportunity to demonstrate and practice their language use options. In the study, however, we observe that NP is still, largely, at the margins because it is minimally used in comments and interactions in the four SNSs that we explored. Furthermore, the study shows that the human agency plays critical roles in LPP as we can see in the language practices in the workplace by the professionals studied in relation to NP usage.

From the foregoing, it can be inferred that just like governments and their agencies, non-state actors have, in their language management efforts, motivations for the options they take in their language practices. For a government, the management of a language could be for the purpose of educational use or for the promotion of national integration. In this study, we can conclude that the motivations for the language policy options taken by the non-state actors we studied are also varied. However, what seems to be playing out is that, generally, there is a covert behaviour involving some minimal disruption of the social space occupied by the English language or the indigenous mother tongue by NP. This disruption is underlined by the speakers' fundamental rights (individual and collective) to choosing the language they wish to use in specific domains in the social space. NP, which is largely at the social margins, is thus seemingly being promoted, in spite of the Nigerian state.

References

Akande, Akinmade T. & Oladipo Salami. 2010. Use and attitudes towards Nigerian Pidgin English among Nigerian university students. In Robert M. Millar (ed.), *Marginal dialects: Scotland, Ireland and beyond*, 70–89. Aberdeen: Forum for Research on the Languages of Scotland and Ireland.

Akande, Akinmade T. 2013. Code-switching in Nigerian hip-hop lyrics. *Language Matters* 44 (1), 39–57.

Akande, Akinmade T. 2014. Hybridity as authenticity in Nigerian hip-hop lyrics. In Veronique Lacoste, Jacob Leimgruber & Thiemo Breyer (eds.), *Indexing authenticity: Sociolinguistic perspectives*, 269–286. Berlin/Boston: De Gruyter.
Androutsopoulos, Jannis. 2009. Policing practices in heteroglossic mediascapes: A commentary on interfaces. *Language Policy* 8: 285–290.
Aniga, Uga & Toyin Esther Jeje. 2019. The role of marriage in security management: A case study of language and style of Nigerian Facebook Users. In Gbemisola Adeoti, Femi Abiodun, Ibrahim Olaosun & Olusegun Oladosu (eds.), *Humanities, security and social Media*, 232–243. Ibadan: Bookminds Publishers.
Babalola, Emmanual T. & Rotimi Taiwo. 2009. Code-switching in Contemporary Nigerian hip-hop music. *Itupale online Journal of African studies* 1(1), 1–26.
Candlin, Christopher N. 1996. General Editor's Preface. In James W. Tollefson (ed.), *Planning language, planning equality*, vii–ix. Lodon/New York: Longman.
de Bres, Julia. 2015. Introduction: Language policies on social network sites. *Language Policy* 14: 309–314.
Elugbe, Ben O. & Augusta P. Omamor. 1991. *Nigerian Pidgin: Background and prospects*. Ibadan: Heinemann Educational Books (Nigeria) PLC.
Fasold, Ralph. 1984. *The sociolinguistics of society*. Oxford: Basil Blackwell.
Hornberger, Nancy H. 2006. Frameworks and models in language policy and planning. In Thomas Ricento (ed.), *An introduction to language policy*, 24–41. Malden, MA: Blackwell Publishing.
Kayam, Orly & Tijana Hirsch. 2012. Family language policy of the English-speaking immigrant community in Israel: Families with young children and their FLP planning, management, and outcomes. *International Journal of Linguistics* 4(4), 622–635.
Ndlovu, Finex. 2008. Language and African development: Theoretical reflections on the place of languages in African studies. *Nordic Journal of African Studies* 17(2), 137–151.
Mazrui, Ali A. & Alamin M. Mazrui. 1998. *The power of babel: Language and governance in the African experience*. London: James Currey Ltd.
Omoniyi, Tope. 2006. Hip hop through the world Englishes lens: A response to globalization. *World Englishes* 25(2), 195–208.
Raheem, O. Saheed. 2013. Multilingualism and language choice for news delivery: The case of Radio stations in Rivers State of Nigeria. In Chijioke Uwasomba, A. Mosobalaje & Oluwole Coker (eds.), *Existentialism, literature and the humanities in Africa*, 389–400. Gottingen, Germany: Cuvillier Verlag.
Ray, Punya Sloka. 1968. Language standardization. In Joshua Fishman (ed.), *Readings in the sociology of language*, 754–765. The Hague: Mouton.
Ricento, Thomas. 2006. *An introduction to language policy*. Malden, MA: Blackwell Publishing.
Spolsky, Bernard. 2004. *Language policy*. Cambridge: Cambridge University Press.
Spolsky, Bernard. 2009. *Language management*. Cambridge: Cambridge University Press.
Taiwo, Rotimi. 2019. Social media and security: A discursive and humanistic perspective. In Gbemisola Adeoti, Femi Abiodun, Ibrahim Olaosun & Olusegun Oladosu (eds.), *Humanities, security and social media*, 41–52. Ibadan: Bookminds Publishers.
Tollefson, James W. 1996. *Planning language, planning inequality*. London and New York: Longman.
Yerima, Ahmed. 2019. Humanities, security and social media in Nigeria. In Gbemisola Adeoti, Femi Abiodun, Ibrahim Olaosun & Olusegun Oladosu (eds.), *Humanities, security and social media*, 34–40. Ibadan: Bookminds Publishers.

Index

aboutness topic 222
acronymy 208
adjective 223
adjunct 237, 243
affixation 209
African immigrants 41–42, 56, 60–61
Afro-Portuguese varieties 21
ancestral languages 22, 34
anglophone 2, 4, 40–42, 60–63
anglophone immigrants 62–63
Atlantic coast 20, 22, 180
audience 87–88
authentic users 41
authenticity 148

British colony 21

church programme posters 277
citizenship 68, 77, 80, 102, 111
clauses 268
clefting 231
clipping 207
code-switching 46–47, 56, 335
community vernacular 44
complementizer 217
completive 213–214
contrastive topic 222
covert prestige 2, 57, 250
creole 9–12, 20–22, 30–31, 34, 36, 148, 177, 189, 192, 213
cultural capital 68
cultural colonial era 20

demographic growth 12
dialects 30, 33, 40, 179, 182, 334
diaspora 28, 31, 42, 308
digital revolution 39, 110
discourse Marker 218

ekporoko 124, 126
electronic media 340
English as a Lingua Franca 39

English Language 40
English lexifier creole 11
ethnicity 95

familiar topic 222
focus construction 221, 244
football Commentary 254, 258, 262, 264–265, 267
formal education system 11, 13, 23
francophone 4, 42, 60–62

German English as a Lingua Franca 41
globalization 106, 110

Hausa, Yoruba, Igbo 22, 75, 314

identity 109, 111, 139, 301
illegal immigrants 42
immigrants 4, 40–42, 58, 60–62, 78, 119, 148, 150, 159
intelligible varieties 9

language development 33–34, 71
language planning 329
language planning and policy 329
languagescape 39–40
left dislocation 223
linguistic adaptation 39
linguistic heritage 39, 119
Lusophone 42

massive emigration 35
Mc Reo 205
metalanguage 254, 258, 262, 264–265, 267
migration 147
mono-identification 32
mother tongue 74
multilingual ecologies 43
multilingual repertoires 4, 43–44, 57, 61
multilingual spaces 39
multilingualism 40, 47, 98, 156, 178, 251, 276, 280, 333

Index

Naija 1, 4–5, 9–13, 18, 20–25, 28–36, 54, 111, 115–117, 121–123, 125–127, 129, 132–136, 138–140, 142, 158, 160, 175, 181, 191, 201, 203, 239, 251, 299, 308, 340
Nairaland 4–5, 41, 43–45, 47–48, 50–51, 53, 149–151, 154, 159, 161, 282, 333, 340
national Assembly 73
national identity 77
national Language 300, 315–316, 328, 330
national Policy on Education 72, 185, 313
national population 11–13, 28, 35
National Population Commission of Nigeria 12–13
negation 108, 216
negative attitudes 2, 33, 68, 81, 156–157, 163
Negritude 68, 108
neo-colonial order 22
Nigerian diaspora 28, 154, 159
Nigerian English 4, 40, 44, 50, 53, 57, 63, 70, 178, 287, 317
Nigerian hip-hop music 251, 335
Nigerian languages 11, 32, 74–75, 88, 98, 100, 102, 106, 111, 151, 179, 186–187, 192–193, 313, 335
Nigerian Pidgin 1, 3, 9, 40, 44, 68–70, 77, 80–81, 92, 95, 98–99, 102, 109, 115–116, 118, 123, 127, 129, 134–136, 138, 140–142, 147, 150, 159, 163, 175, 177, 191, 201–203, 205, 221, 239, 249–251, 275, 277–280, 282, 287, 291–292, 295, 299–300, 308–309, 316–317, 328, 330, 332–333, 335–336, 340
Nigerianised spelling 186–187
Njakiri 123, 126, 139
Nko 226, 245
noun 223

official census 9
official pronouncements 74, 98

orthography 5, 34, 70, 150, 177–179, 183–186, 188, 190–195, 309, 313, 317

Pentecostalism 129, 285, 291
phrase 223
policy makers 11, 185, 195, 304
politics 103, 134, 225, 245
Portuguese mercenaries 21
postcolonial African context 40
prepositional phrase 238
problem-solution appeal 292–293
pronouns 211

reduplication 206
relative Clause 217

Sabongari phenomenon 78
serial verbs 215
social-media communication 40, 51
socio-cultural milieu 285–286
sociolinguistics of globalisation 39–40
spoken languages 4, 9, 29, 31
stigma 110, 119, 317
structural Adjustment Programme 138
structural simplification 51
syntactic 210

TMA markers 213, 216, 218
translanguaging 11

unmarked Nouns 210
urbanization 9, 12–13, 18, 20, 23–25, 35, 96, 98, 108, 338

verb Phrase 213, 223

wazobia FM 84

youth 106

www.ingramcontent.com/pod-product-compliance
Lightning Source LLC
Chambersburg PA
CBHW071734150426
43191CB00010B/1574